Forensic Evidence in Court

Forensic Evidence in Court

Evaluation and Scientific Opinion

CRAIG ADAM

WILEY

This edition first published 2016
© 2016 John Wiley & Sons, Ltd

Registered Office

John Wiley & Sons, Ltd, The Atrium, Southern Gate, Chichester, West Sussex, PO19 8SQ, United Kingdom

For details of our global editorial offices, for customer services and for information about how to apply for permission to reuse the copyright material in this book please see our website at www.wiley.com.

Library of Congress Cataloging-in-Publication Data

Names: Adam, Craig.
Title: Forensic evidence in court: evaluation and scientific opinion / Craig Adam.
Description: United Kingdom : John Wiley & Sons, 2016. | Includes bibliographical references and index.
Identifiers: LCCN 2016012014 (print) | LCCN 2016012473 (ebook) | ISBN 9781119054412 (cloth) |
    ISBN 9781119054429 (pdf) | ISBN 9781119054436 (epub)
Subjects: LCSH: Evidence, Expert–Methodology. | Forensic sciences. | Evidence, Expert–History.
Classification: LCC K2283 .A935 2016 (print) | LCC K2283 (ebook) | DDC 347.73/67–dc23
LC record available at https://lccn.loc.gov/2016012014

A catalogue record for this book is available from the British Library.

Set in 10/12pt Times by SPi Global, Pondicherry, India
Printed and bound in Malaysia by Vivar Printing Sdn Bhd

1   2016

Contents

Preface   xvi

Part 1   1

1   An Introduction to the Admissibility of Expert Scientific Opinion   3
   1.1   Admissibility, Reliability and Scientific Evidence   3
   1.2   The Impact of the DNA Revolution   5
   1.3   The Miscarriage of Justice   6
      1.3.1   The United Kingdom   7
      1.3.2   The United States   8
      1.3.3   Canada   8
      1.3.4   Australia   9
   1.4   DNA Reveals Wrongful Convictions   9
   1.5   The Causes of Wrongful Conviction   10
   1.6   Unreliable Scientific Evidence   11
      1.6.1   The Status and Expertise of the Expert Witness   11
      1.6.2   The Expert is not Impartial   12
      1.6.3   The Evidence was Wrong   13
      1.6.4   Exaggerated Evaluation by the Expert   13
      1.6.5   Unethical Behaviour   14
      1.6.6   Human Error   14
      1.6.7   Non-validated Methodology   15
      1.6.8   Overconfidence in New Techniques   15
   1.7   The Scientist and the Laboratory   16
   1.8   Conclusions   17
   References   17
   Further Reading   18

2   Admissibility from the Legal Perspective   20
   2.1   Admissibility, Relevance and Reliability of Evidence   20
   2.2   Admissibility in the United States   22
      2.2.1   Reliability and the Frye Test   22
      2.2.2   Meeting the Frye Criterion: US v Stifel 1970   23
      2.2.3   Admissibility and the Gatekeeper Role: The Daubert Test   23
      2.2.4   The Daubert Trilogy   25
      2.2.5   General Electric v Joiner 1997   25
      2.2.6   Kumo Tire Company v Patrick Carmichael 1999   26
      2.2.7   Post-Daubert Hearings: US v Dennis Mooney 2002   26

2.3   Admissibility in Canada   27
      2.3.1   R v Mohan 1994   27
      2.3.2   R v Abbey 2009   29
      2.3.3   R v Trochym 2007   29
2.4   Admissibility in Australia   30
      2.4.1   R v Bonython 1984   30
      2.4.2   Makita v Sprowles 2001   31
      2.4.3   Dasreef Pty Limited v Hawchar 2011   31
2.5   Admissibility in England and Wales   32
      2.5.1   R v Turner 1975   33
      2.5.2   R v Gilfoyle 2001   33
      2.5.3   R v Luttrell 2004   34
2.6   Conclusions on Admissibility   35
      2.6.1   Relevance and Expertise   35
      2.6.2   The Scientific Basis of the Opinion   35
      2.6.3   Weight of Evidence   37
References   37
Further Reading   38

3   **Forensic Science and the Law: The Path Forward**   **39**
3.1   National and Legal Developments in the United States   39
      3.1.1   Federal Rules of Evidence   40
      3.1.2   Strengthening Forensic Science in the United States 2009   41
      3.1.3   US Reference Manual on Scientific Evidence   43
3.2   National and Legal Developments in Canada   44
      3.2.1   Legal Enquiries into Miscarriages of Justice   44
      3.2.2   The Science Manual for Canadian Judges   45
3.3   National and Legal Developments in Australia   46
      3.3.1   The Uniform Rules of Evidence   47
3.4   National and Legal Developments in England and Wales   48
      3.4.1   Forensic Science on Trial 2005   49
      3.4.2   The Law Commission Report 2011   49
      3.4.3   The Royal Statistical Society Guides   51
      3.4.4   HCSTSC Report Forensic Science 2013   52
      3.4.5   UK Government Response (2013) to the Law
              Commission Report   52
3.5   Conclusions   53
References   53
Further Reading   54

4   **Scientific Opinion and the Law in Practice**   **56**
4.1   Scientific Opinion and the Judicial System   56
      4.1.1   Adversarial and Inquisitorial Systems of Justice   56
      4.1.2   Scientific Evidence Within the Inquisitorial System   57
      4.1.3   Inquisitorial Versus Adversarial   57
4.2   The Scientist in Court   58

4.3 The Role and Duties of the Scientific Expert Witness   59
    4.3.1 Definitions of the Role   59
    4.3.2 Duties and Responsibilities of the Expert Witness   60
4.4 Quality Control of Analysis and Opinion   61
    4.4.1 An Australian Standard for Forensic Analysis   61
    4.4.2 Regulation of Forensic Science in the United Kingdom   62
    4.4.3 Codes of Conduct and Practice   62
    4.4.4 Accreditation of the Expert   63
4.5 Conclusion   63
References   64
Further Reading   64

Part 2   **65**

5 Fundamentals of the Interpretation and Evaluation of Scientific Evidence   **67**
5.1 Analysis, Interpretation and Evaluation   67
5.2 The Role and Outcomes of Forensic Investigation   68
    5.2.1 Investigative Forensic Science   68
    5.2.2 Evaluative Forensic Science   69
5.3 Fact and Opinion   69
    5.3.1 Categorisation of Opinions   70
    5.3.2 Factual Opinion   70
    5.3.3 Investigative Opinion   70
5.4 Expert Opinion and the Forensic Science Paradigm   70
    5.4.1 Categorical Opinion   71
    5.4.2 Posterior Probabilities   72
    5.4.3 Explanations   73
    5.4.4 Where Does this Take Us?   74
5.5 What are Propositions?   74
    5.5.1 The Hierarchy of Propositions   74
    5.5.2 The Importance of Activity Level   75
5.6 Competing Propositions in the Court   76
References   77
Further Reading   77

6 Case Studies in Expert Opinion   **78**
6.1 Case Study 1: Facial Comparison Evidence   78
    6.1.1 The Crime and Conviction   78
    6.1.2 Expert Evidence and Opinion   79
    6.1.3 Opinion in Atkins   80
6.2 Case Study 2: Ear-mark Identification   81
    6.2.1 The Crime and the Evidence   81
    6.2.2 Interpreting the Evidence and Challenges to the Opinion   81
    6.2.3 The Conclusion of the Appeal   83
    6.2.4 Opinion in Dallagher   83

6.3	Case Study 3: Glass and Gunshot Residue	84
	6.3.1 The Crime and Trial	84
	6.3.2 Analysis and Interpretation of the Scientific Evidence	84
	6.3.3 Propositions for Evaluation	85
	6.3.4 Evaluative Opinion: Glass	86
	6.3.5 Evaluative Opinion: GSR	86
	6.3.6 Opinion in Bowden	88
6.4	Conclusions	88
	References	88
	Further Reading	89

7	**Formal Methods for Logical Evaluation**	**90**
7.1	Frequentist and Bayesian Approaches to Evaluation	90
	7.1.1 The Frequentist Approach to Formulating Opinion	90
	7.1.2 The Logical Evaluation of Evidence	91
	7.1.3 The Debate on Formulating Opinion	92
7.2	The Likelihood Ratio Method	92
7.3	Expressing Opinion Through Likelihood Ratio	93
	7.3.1 Statements of Evaluative Opinion	93
	7.3.2 Likelihood Ratio and Verbal Equivalent Statements	94
7.4	Evaluation and Bayes' Theorem	94
	7.4.1 Bayes' Theorem: Prior and Posterior Odds	95
	7.4.2 Combining Likelihood Ratios	97
7.5	Prior Odds	97
7.6	Posterior Probabilities	99
	7.6.1 Opinion and Posterior Probabilities	99
	7.6.2 The Prosecutor's Fallacy	99
7.7	Working Out Conditional Probabilities and Likelihood Ratio	100
	7.7.1 Likelihood Ratio at Source Level	100
	7.7.2 Likelihood Ratio at Activity Level	101
7.8	Conclusions	102
	References	102
	Further Reading	103

8	**Case Studies in Probabilistic Opinion**	**104**
8.1	People v Collins 1968	104
8.2	R v Michael Shirley 2003	105
	8.2.1 A Logical Evaluation of Scientific Evidence	106
	8.2.2 The Outcome of the Appeal	108
8.3	R v D J Adams 1996, 1998	108
	8.3.1 The Crime and the Evidence	109
	8.3.2 A Probabilistic Analysis of the Evidence: Prior Odds	109
	8.3.3 The Non-Scientific Evidence	110
	8.3.4 The Scientific Evidence	111
	8.3.5 Total Likelihood Ratio and Posterior Odds	112
	8.3.6 The Appeals	113
	8.3.7 Review of the Issues in R v D J Adams	114

8.4   The Defendant's Fallacy: R v J 2009   115
8.5   Conclusion   116
References   116
Further Reading   116

9   Cognitive Bias and Expert Opinion   117
9.1   Cognitive Bias   117
9.2   Contextual Bias   118
         9.2.1   Confirmation Bias   119
         9.2.2   Expectation Bias   119
         9.2.3   Motivational Bias   119
         9.2.4   Anchoring   120
9.3   Other Sources of Bias   120
9.4   Fingerprint Examination: A Case Study in Bias   120
         9.4.1   The Review of the Brandon Mayfield Case 2004   120
         9.4.2   The Fingerprint Inquiry Scotland 2009   121
         9.4.3   Bias Within Fingerprint Examination   121
9.5   Mitigating Bias   122
9.6   Mitigating Bias Versus Research on Traces   123
9.7   Conclusions   124
References   124
Further Reading   125

Part 3   127

10   The Evaluation of DNA Profile Evidence   129
10.1   DNA Profiling Techniques – A Brief History   130
10.2   Databases in DNA Profiling   131
         10.2.1   Allele Frequency Databases   131
         10.2.2   Identification Databases   131
10.3   Interpretation and Evaluation of Conventional DNA Profiles   131
         10.3.1   Combined Probability of Inclusion (CPI) or Exclusion (CPE)   132
         10.3.2   Random Match Probability (RMP)   132
         10.3.3   Likelihood Ratio   133
10.4   Suspect Identification from a DNA Database   133
         10.4.1   The Frequentist Interpretation   133
         10.4.2   The Likelihood Ratio Approach   134
         10.4.3   Database Search Evidence in Court   134
10.5   Case Studies of DNA in the Court   135
         10.5.1   R v Andrew Philip Deen 1994   135
         10.5.2   Issues Raised by Expert Opinion in R v Deen   136
         10.5.3   R v Alan Doheny 1996   138
         10.5.4   The Doheny Trial   138
         10.5.5   The Doheny Appeal   139
         10.5.6   R v Gary Adams 1996   140
         10.5.7   Challenges to the Interpretation of DNA Profiles:
                  US v Shea 1997   141

10.6   Current Practice for Evaluating DNA Profile Evidence   142
    10.6.1   The Impact of Doheny and Adams in the United Kingdom   142
    10.6.2   Current Practice in the United Kingdom   144
    10.6.3   Current Practice in Australia   145
10.7   DNA – The Only Evidence   146
10.8   Errors and Mistakes in Forensic DNA Analysis   147
    10.8.1   Adam Scott 2012   147
    10.8.2   R v S 2013   148
    10.8.3   Laboratory Error Rates Versus the RMP   148
10.9   Conclusions   149
References   149
Further Reading   150

11   Low Template DNA   **151**
11.1   Technical Issues   151
    11.1.1   Terminology   151
    11.1.2   Samples   152
    11.1.3   Technical Issues in Interpretation   152
    11.1.4   Quantitative Evaluation in LTDNA Profiles   153
11.2   Importance of the Chain of Custody: Queen v Sean Hoey 2007   154
11.3   The Caddy Report 2008   155
11.4   Case Studies in LTDNA opinion in the UK Courts   156
    11.4.1   Partial Profiles   156
    11.4.2   Quantities of DNA; Interpretive Issues on Transfer   157
    11.4.3   Very Low Quantities of DNA   159
    11.4.4   Opinion Without Statistics   160
    11.4.5   Experts Differ in Opinion   162
11.5   LTDNA in Jurisdictions Outside the United Kingdom   163
    11.5.1   United States   164
    11.5.2   Australia   165
11.6   Conclusions   167
References   167
Further Reading   168

12   Footwear Marks in Court   **169**
12.1   The Analysis and Interpretation of Footwear Marks   169
12.2   Match Opinion: R v D S Hall 2004   170
    12.2.1   The Crime and the Evidence   170
    12.2.2   Footwear Mark Evidence and Opinion   171
    12.2.3   Review of Expert Opinion in R v Hall   172
12.3   The Likelihood Ratio Approach to Evaluation of Footwear Marks   172
12.4   Standardising Scales for Expert Opinion   173
    12.4.1   SWGTREAD Scales of Opinion   173
    12.4.2   ENFSI Scales of Opinion   175
12.5   Challenges to Opinion on Footwear Evidence: R v T 2010   175
    12.5.1   Outline of the Footwear Mark Evidence in R v T   176

	12.5.2	The Expert Witness' Notes	177
	12.5.3	Evaluation Using an Alternative Database	179
	12.5.4	The Summary by the Appeal Court Judge	179
12.6	Discussion of R v T		180
	12.6.1	Terminology, Probabilities and Statistical Methodology	180
	12.6.2	Footwear Databases	181
	12.6.3	Was the Jury Told the Basis of the Expert Opinion?	182
	12.6.4	The Appeal Court Ruling: Bayes, Mathematics and Formulae	183
12.7	Footwear Mark Evidence After R v T: R v South 2011		184
	12.7.1	The Crime and Evidence	184
	12.7.2	Evaluation of the Footwear Evidence	184
	12.7.3	Review of the Expert Opinion	185
12.8	ENFSI Recommendations on Logical Evaluation 2015		186
12.9	Conclusions		187
	References		187
	Further Reading		188

13 Fingerprints and Finger-Marks – Identifying Individuals?   **189**

13.1	Fingerprint Identification on Trial		189
13.2	ACE-V: A Scientific Method?		190
13.3	Evaluation Criteria		191
	13.3.1	Thresholds for Categorical Evaluation	191
	13.3.2	The Balthazard Model	192
	13.3.3	Identification Thresholds and the Points Standard in the United Kingdom	192
	13.3.4	The Basis of the Non-Numeric (Holistic) Approach	193
	13.3.5	Identification Thresholds in Other Jurisdictions	194
	13.3.6	R v Buckley 1999	194
13.4	Evolution of the Basis of Fingerprint Opinion in the Court		196
13.5	A Critical Summary of Fingerprint Identification		198
13.6	Challenges to Fingerprint Testimony		198
	13.6.1	R v P K Smith 2011	198
	13.6.2	Shirley McKie and the Scottish Fingerprint Inquiry 1997–2011	200
13.7	Identifying a Mark from a Database		202
	13.7.1	AFIS Versus Manual Systems	202
	13.7.2	The Madrid Bombing Case (Brandon Mayfield) 2004	203
13.8	Admissibility of Fingerprint Evidence		204
	13.8.1	US v Byron Mitchell 2004	204
	13.8.2	US v Llera Plaza 2002	205
13.9	Towards a Probabilistic Evaluation of Fingerprint Evidence		206
13.10	Conclusions		208
	References		208
	Further Reading		209

14   Trace Evidence, Databases and Evaluation   **210**
   14.1   Analytical Methodologies for Glass, Fibres and GSR   210
          14.1.1   Glass Analysis   211
          14.1.2   Fibre Analysis   211
          14.1.3   GSR Analysis   211
   14.2   Databases for Source and Activity Levels   212
          14.2.1   Source Level   212
          14.2.2   Activity Level   212
          14.2.3   Glass   213
          14.2.4   Fibres   213
          14.2.5   GSR   213
          14.2.6   Statistical Models and Case Pre-Assessment   214
   14.3   Glass Evidence in Court   214
          14.3.1   R v Abadom 1983   214
          14.3.2   R v Lewis-Barnes 2014   215
          14.3.3   R v L and Others 2010   216
          14.3.4   People v Smith 2012   216
          14.3.5   Review of the Evaluation of Trace Glass Evidence   217
   14.4   Fibre Evidence in Court: R v Dobson 2011, R v Norris 2013   218
          14.4.1   Fibre Evidence: Dobson   219
          14.4.2   Fibre Evidence: Norris   220
          14.4.3   Review of the Evaluation of the Fibre Evidence   221
   14.5   Gunshot Residue (GSR) Evidence in Court   222
          14.5.1   R v Wooton and Others 2012   222
          14.5.2   R v Gjikokaj 2014   224
          14.5.3   Review of the Evaluation of GSR Evidence   225
          14.5.4   R v George 2007   226
   14.6   Conclusions   227
   References   227
   Further Reading   227

15   Firearm and Tool-Mark Evidence   **229**
   15.1   Pattern Matching of Mechanical Damage   229
   15.2   The Interpretation and Evaluation of Tool-Mark Evidence   230
          15.2.1   US Opinion   230
          15.2.2   UK Opinion   232
   15.3   Critical Review of Tool-Mark Evaluation   232
   15.4   Consecutive Matching Striations   234
   15.5   Databases   234
   15.6   Tool-Marks and Evaluation by Likelihood Ratio   235
   15.7   Firearms Evidence in the US Courts   236
          15.7.1   United States v Hicks 2004   236
          15.7.2   United States v Darryl Green *et al.* 2005   237
          15.7.3   US v Glynn 2008   240

15.8   Concluding Comments on Firearms Cases   241
References   241
Further Reading   242

16   Expert Opinion and Evidence of Human Identity   243
16.1   Introduction to Ear-Marks   243
16.2   R v Kempster 2003, 2008   244
       16.2.1   The First Appeal 2003   245
       16.2.2   The Second Appeal 2008   245
       16.2.3   Conclusions From R v Kempster   246
16.3   State v Kunze 1999   247
       16.3.1   The Frye Hearing   247
       16.3.2   The Trial   248
       16.3.3   The Appeal   249
16.4   Review of Ear-Mark Cases   249
16.5   Introduction to Bite-Mark Evidence   250
16.6   The ABFO Guidelines and Expert Opinion   250
16.7   Bite-Mark Cases in the United States   251
       16.7.1   People v Marx 1975   252
       16.7.2   The Appeal   252
       16.7.3   State v Garrison 1978   253
       16.7.4   State v Stinson 1986   254
       16.7.5   Bite-Mark Testimony in the Courts   255
16.8   Body Biometrics: Facial Mapping and Gait   255
       16.8.1   R v Hookway 1999   255
       16.8.2   R v Otway 2011   256
16.9   Conclusion   257
References   257
Further Reading   258

17   Questioned Documents   259
17.1   Handwriting and Signature Comparison – A Scientific Methodology? 260
17.2   Scales of Expert Opinion   261
17.3   Jarrold v Isajul and Others 2013   263
       17.3.1   Dr Strach's Testimony   264
       17.3.2   Mr Holland's Testimony   264
       17.3.3   Mr Lacroix's Testimony   265
       17.3.4   The Appeal Court Judge's Conclusion   265
17.4   Gale v Gale 2010   266
       17.4.1   ESDA Analysis   267
       17.4.2   Signature Analysis   267
17.5   The Bridgewater Four (R v Hickey and Others) 1997   268
       17.5.1   Molloy's 'Confession'   269
17.6   R v Previte 2005   270

17.7   Admissibility and Other Issues in Handwriting and
        Signature Evidence   271
17.8   Admissibility and Evaluation in the US Courts   272
        17.8.1   US v Starzecpyzel 1995   272
        17.8.2   US v Velasquez 1995   274
17.9   Conclusions   275
References   275
Further Reading   276

18   Bloodstain Pattern Analysis   277
18.1   The Nature of Bloodstain Pattern Evidence   277
18.2   Issues for BPA Expert Opinion in the Courts   278
        18.2.1   The Scientific Basis of BPA   278
        18.2.2   Who is the Expert?   279
        18.2.3   The Courts' and Lawyers' Knowledge of BPA   280
        18.2.4   The Evaluation and Significance of BPA Evidence   280
18.3   The Scientific Basis of Bloodstain Pattern Analysis: The Murder
        of Marilyn Sheppard   281
18.4   Three Approaches to the Presentation of Blood Evidence   282
        18.4.1   Activity and Propositions: R v Thompson 2013   283
        18.4.2   No Expert Testimony: R v White 1998   283
        18.4.3   Reconstructing Activity as a Narrative: R v Hall 2010   284
18.5   The Problem of Expirated Blood   285
        18.5.1   R v O'Grady 1995, 1999   286
        18.5.2   R v Jenkins: The Trial and First Appeal 1999   287
        18.5.3   R v Jenkins: The Second Appeal (2004) and
                 Two More Retrials   289
18.6   Experts in Disagreement: R v Perlett 2006   289
18.7   Conclusions   291
References   291
Further Reading   292

19   Conflicting Expert Opinion: SIDS and the Medical Expert Witness   293
19.1   Eminent Experts: Issues and Conflicts   293
19.2   R v Clark 2000, 2003   294
        19.2.1   The Testimony of Meadow   295
        19.2.2   The Second Appeal 2003   297
19.3   A Bayesian Analysis: Murder or SIDS?   298
        19.3.1 $Pr(H_2)$ – The Probability of Two SIDS Deaths in
                 the Same Family   298
        19.3.2 $Pr(H_1)$ – The Probability of Two Murdered Infants in the
                 Same Family   299
        19.3.3   The Posterior Odds   299
19.4   R v Cannings 2004   300

19.5   Trupti Patel 2003   302
     19.5.1   The Rib Fracture Evidence   302
     19.5.2   The Judge's Summing Up   303
19.6   Conclusions   304
References   304
Further Reading   305

Appendix: Some Legal Terminology   **306**

Index of Cases, Individuals and Inquiry Reports   **307**

General Index   **309**

Preface

This book is about how science and scientific opinion impinge upon and influence legal debate. It is written by a scientist, principally for an audience of scientists, more specifically for those in the later stages of an undergraduate degree in forensic science, studying at postgraduate level or working as practitioners. As such, a basic understanding of the discipline and of technical matters relating to evidence examination and analysis is assumed, although relevant science is recapped and expanded upon where appropriate. The context throughout is the court of law. Legal cases from across jurisdictions, including principally those based on the Anglo-American legal system, are used to demonstrate the evolution of expert opinion, to illustrate the difficulties faced by the scientists and the legal professionals and to provide a real world backdrop to material intended for exposition and discussion in the lecture room.

Although this book is an educational text and not a research monograph, this field of study is subject to developments and advances from both the professional and academic spheres. It is relevant therefore to include some discussion of the scholarship that underpins professional practice and, more specifically, I have incorporated recent research that seeks to resolve current difficulties and may impact directly on expert testimony in the future.

To meet the aims of this text the material is organised within three sections. The first serves the dual purpose of setting the scene, by reviewing the impact of forensic science in the courts over the past thirty years, as well as providing the overall context within which methods for interpretation and evaluation of scientific evidence have been and continue to be developed. This is followed by five chapters in which the focus centres on the forensic scientist as expert witness and ways in which scientific opinion may be formulated from the interpretation of experimental findings, particularly through logical evaluation by likelihood ratio; this includes discussion of many of the issues around the delivery of such opinion.

The final section presents scientific opinion in the context of evidence types. Starting from full DNA profiles where quantitative approaches are informed by rigorously derived databases, the discussion moves to other types of evidence such as footwear marks, glass and fibres where the interpretation may be more qualitative and the associated databases more open to challenge. Later chapters deal with evidence such as handwriting and bloodstain pattern analysis where opinion is formulated much more in accordance with the experience of the individual expert and indeed where the members of the court may believe they can achieve their own evaluation by reviewing the evidence for themselves.

I am very grateful to Dr Ian Evett CBE and Mr Mike Allen for reading and commenting on draft sections of this text. I trust that I have been able to use their feedback to improve the accuracy and clarity of the discussion but the final responsibility for that, of course, must rest with me. I also wish to thank my wife, Alison, for her invaluable advice, patience and support throughout the development and writing of this book.

Craig Adam,
January 2016

Part 1

Part I

1

An Introduction to the Admissibility of Expert Scientific Opinion

1.1 Admissibility, Reliability and Scientific Evidence

The investigative and legal processes, from the discovery of a crime to the verdict of the court, should ultimately ensure that the guilty person is correctly identified and that the innocent are exonerated. However, in many cases, the complexity, both of these processes and of the contributions to the debate, may lead to difficulties and challenges that act to impede and divert both scientific and legal arguments and which may lead to an unsatisfactory outcome. This book is concerned principally with the contribution of scientific evidence to legal debate. Central to this is an understanding of how the scientist's findings can be properly interpreted, evaluated and communicated to the court and how the court draws appropriate inferences from the expert opinion in reaching its decision on the ultimate issue. In doing so, the court must necessarily be satisfied that the science is valid and the evidence relevant to its deliberations.

Although the concept of relevance has been enshrined in law across most jurisdictions for many years, in more recent times a debate has emerged across wider aspects of the presentation of scientific evidence to the court and the role of the scientist as an expert witness. There are many reasons for this, which include significant advances in scientific techniques, the need for investigators to deal with more complex and high-profile crimes, increasing attention to these concerns and the ongoing responses of the legal profession and lawmakers to those events. The chapters in the first part of this book are intended to describe and discuss these aspects in detail across several jurisdictions.

As a precursor to this, it will be helpful to outline some of the key issues that mark out the path of this later discussion.

The law provides for an expert witness to contribute both factual and opinion evidence to the court. Within the legal system, the judge is empowered to decide on whether any evidence is relevant to the case being debated. However, there is some diversification of rules and practice, which, in many jurisdictions, is largely driven by case law where so-called landmark judgments by courts of appeal clarify points of law, which then apply to subsequent cases. In this way, across Anglo-American and related jurisdictions in particular, the law governing the handling of scientific evidence by the courts has evolved, and continues to evolve, punctuated by changes to the law at a national level and other relevant activities by governments and agencies.

Over the past thirty years or so, concerns around scientific evidence in the court have focused on three main issues:

1. Is the evidence admissible to the court?

    Admissibility includes whether the evidence is relevant to and therefore has value for the legal debate (probative value), as well as a variety of other factors such as the status of the expert witness, the quality of the methodology and the underpinning science. Admissibility is determined by the judge and is categorical, since the expert witness will either be permitted or not permitted to give their testimony. The judge is said, by some legal authorities, to act as a 'gatekeeper' for expert evidence. The judge's decision on admissibility and the grounds for that conclusion is crucial to the legal process.

2. Is the evidence reliable?

    Reliability may contribute to admissibility but is itself a complex concept which is subject to considerable variation in how it is dealt with across courts and jurisdictions. At a basic level, the court has to assess the validity of the scientific methodology and whether the evaluation delivered by the expert is soundly based on the results of their work. However, the extent to which this contributes to admissibility or whether reliability may instead be a factor in deciding the legal weight of the evidence is open to debate. Therefore, it is the degree of reliability and not necessarily whether evidence is reliable or unreliable that matters. The significance of these two factors has been summarised by Susan Haack in the phrase:

    'Admissibility is categorical, reliability is continuous'

    [Haack, quoted in Cole, 2007]

3. Has the significance of the evidence been properly assessed, then communicated to and understood by, the court?

    It is the responsibility of the scientist to design and carry out experimental measurements, to analyse results and then to interpret what they mean in the context and circumstances of the case. However, as an expert witness, the interpretation of this work must be presented to the court so that the judge, the jury and the legal professionals may fully understand its significance to their debate. The extent to which this may be achieved and the manner in which it is done varies hugely across the subdisciplines of forensic science, between individual scientists and across courts and jurisdictions. The process of the evaluation and presentation of scientific evidence forms the discussion in the main section of this book.

Given that expert evidence, as we understand it, has been delivered to the courts for around two hundred years, why has the debate over admissibility, reliability and the quality of scientific opinion come to the fore with such an intensity in more recent times? In the mid-Victorian period, scientific expert witnesses were often pitted against each other in the courtroom. Such public displays of warring experts tended to dent the reputations both of science for objectivity and of the scientists themselves as impartial seekers of truth. The situation was somewhat mitigated in the first part of the twentieth century with the professionalisation of forensic science and the consolidation of much expertise into regional and national laboratories. The situation began to change from the 1970s onwards, with increasing criticisms of 'junk science', particularly in the United States, where scientists were held to be influenced by the interests of the big corporations that had hired them and by the continuing stream of miscarriages of justice where forensic science and forensic scientists were seen as significant contributors to the problem.

It is convenient and informative to begin this discussion with cases where the legal process has clearly broken down and miscarriages of justice have taken place. Though such events cannot be laid at the door of any single cause, the impact of DNA profiling has probably had a greater significance than any other factor in bringing these to light and so that shall be our starting point.

1.2   The Impact of the DNA Revolution

The conviction of Colin Pitchfork in 1988 for the rape and murder of Lynda Mann and Dawn Ashworth can rightly claim to be the first case where DNA profile evidence was key to a successful prosecution. However, this should not overshadow a second milestone achieved through this investigation. The reason the police initially approached Alec Jeffreys at Leicester University, with a view to trying out his new DNA identification technique, was that they had obtained a confession to one of these murders from a different man, Richard Buckland, and were looking for scientific proof of his involvement in the second case, which Buckland denied. When the analysis revealed that Buckland was not the source of the semen sample from either crime, this revolutionary technique prevented a potential miscarriage of justice. The impact of DNA profile evidence when it contradicted and quashed, not only other forensic evidence, but also witness testimony and suspect confessions, was to provide an impetus for challenges to wrongful convictions that would endure for the next thirty years.

However, DNA was to initiate a deeper and more subtle revolution, both in the paradigm of forensic identification sciences and, more particularly, in the evaluation of forensic evidence and its contribution to legal debate (Saks and Koehler, 2005). For just over a hundred years, fingerprint evidence had been the gold standard against which other forensic techniques were measured and, as an identifier of individuals, the fingerprint was unchallenged by the courts. Not only was it accepted that fingerprints were unique, but both legal professionals and lay people working in the courts had a general appreciation of the process of identification and trusted the word of the fingerprint examiner as an expert witness who stated that a crime scene mark matched a fingerprint taken from a suspect. By providing such categorical testimony, the fingerprint ranked above all other forensic evidence in the court.

Once the DNA profile arrived on the scene, as rival to the fingerprint, it is easy to see why the term 'DNA fingerprint' became fashionable, as the new technique sought to promote its apparent infallibility. However, DNA testimony did more than just state a match between two profiles, it was supported by an additional statement on the rarity of the profile within the relevant population and, unlike the uniqueness claim from the finger-print expert, this was underpinned by rigorous scientific research in the field of population genetics. Thus, DNA was perceived as objective and scientific while the interpretation of fingerprints, for the most part, depended on subjective criteria, implemented according to the judgement and experience of the individual examiner. Over the following ten years or so, the DNA profile, with its strong scientific basis, became established as the new stand-ard while fingerprinting, and indeed many other techniques within forensic science came under increasing scrutiny as their scientific foundation, validity and reliability became questioned by the legal profession, by many scientists and indeed by governments and their agencies. Consequently, the concept of a 'DNA fingerprint' fell into disuse and the 'DNA profile' became the accepted term. In addition, the onus fell on other forensic methods to provide statistical support to strengthen their statements of scientific opinion, thereby enhancing their quality in order to attempt to meet that of the new biometric. As this is easier for some types of evidence, for example, glass or footwear marks, than others, such as bite-marks, challenges to the validity and reliability of various types of evidence became increasingly common.

The arrival of the DNA profile in the courts has also led to a more critical appraisal of the wording of expert testimony and the use of terms such as 'match', in particular. This, and similar expressions, had been used extensively for many forms of evidence, often without much thought as how that could be explained or justified in an objective manner. With the acceptance of the scientific basis underpinning the comparison of DNA profiles, it was apparent that, for many other forms of forensic evidence, the expert's declaration of a match attached an exaggerated weight to its significance in the legal debate. This was particularly true in conveying the results of serological (blood grouping) tests and microscopic hair examinations which, although potentially providing useful class characteristics, had often been regarded by juries, and indeed by many forensic scientists, as strongly individualising and so the evidential value was frequently grossly overestimated by the court.

In summary, the implementation of DNA profiling within the forensic arena has contributed to the questioning of the value and legal significance of many other forms of scientific evidence and highlighted many instances of faulty interpretation or exaggerated opinion. Thus, there have been two revolutions in the discipline: first, the legal review of past convictions has led to the identification of miscarriages of justice – this will be examined in the following sections; and second, the scientific basis of much of forensic science has been questioned by the legal and scientific communities, as well as by governments. This will be the subject of the subsequent chapters.

1.3 The Miscarriage of Justice

Where the trial of an accused person leads to conviction, this may be overturned by a successful appeal to a higher court on a limited range of grounds, including procedural irregularities. On some occasions, other facts or evidence may come to light that lead to the sentence being quashed and, in some cases, this may not happen for many years and may be initiated by legal and political mechanisms, as well as by the individuals themselves. In these cases, the original conviction may be termed a miscarriage of justice or wrongful conviction. In 2011, the England and Wales Supreme Court considered such events and declared that:

> '... a miscarriage of justice occurs "when a new or newly discovered fact shows conclusively that the evidence against a defendant has been so undermined that no conviction could possibly be based upon it".'
>
> [R (Adams) v Secretary of State for Justice, 2011]

The Supreme Court also identified the circumstances whereby a conviction may be quashed. The first is where fresh evidence clearly shows the innocence of the defendant. Had this evidence been available at the trial, a 'reasonable jury' would either have not convicted the defendant or a conviction would have been in doubt. The second circumstance arises when the conduct of either the investigation or the trial was subject to serious error, thereby leading to an improper verdict.

Although miscarriages of justice from across the world have been recognised and studied over the past century, the reasons and circumstances under which they occur have been examined more intensively over the past thirty years or so. Although, as we shall see, faulty forensic science was sometimes responsible for such events, good forensic science, including the new methods for identifying individuals based on DNA profiles, has contributed immensely to the discovery and quashing of wrongful convictions. Particular circumstances in different countries have initiated and sustained surveys, studies and reports by academic researchers, legal professionals and government agencies on miscarriages of justice and these have provided not only an indication of the scale of these events, but also a converging picture of the range of causes that have given rise to their occurrence.

1.3.1 The United Kingdom

A series of serious bombing incidents on the British mainland, linked to the 'Troubles' in Northern Ireland, occurred from the 1970s onwards. The deaths of British soldiers and civilians which resulted from these terrorist incidents meant that the police were under significant public and political pressure to bring the perpetrators to justice. However, many of the subsequent convictions that followed were later overturned, either on appeal or after campaigns highlighting a miscarriage of justice, but not until those convicted had spent many years in prison. These include the cases of the Guildford Four (1974, freed 1989), the Birmingham Six (1975, freed 1991), the Maguire Seven (1976, freed 1991) and Judith Ward (1974, freed 1993). Following these exonerations, the Criminal Cases Review Commission (CCRC) was formed in 1995 as a body tasked with reviewing potential miscarriages of justice with a view to presenting them to the Court of Appeal. Nevertheless, in recent years, further examples of wrongful convictions, not linked to the Northern Ireland situation, have emerged, such as the cases of Sean Hodgson (1982, freed 2009) and Michael Shirley (1987, freed 2003), both of whom were exonerated by fresh DNA profile evidence, Stephen Downing (1974, freed 2002) whose second appeal was upheld on the grounds of an unreliable confession and a reappraisal of blood-spatter evidence and Barry George (2001, freed 2008) who was released after a reevaluation of trace gunshot residue evidence.

1.3.2   The United States

In the United States, the existence of the death penalty in many states gave an added importance to the prevention of wrongful convictions and raised public awareness of the scale of, and the reasons behind, miscarriages of justice, particularly for those on 'death-row'. Some states set up innocence commissions to review cases, such as that of Governor Ryan in Illinois in 2000. In 1992, the Innocence Project was set up as a not-for-profit, legal organisation, initially as part of the Cardoza Law School, campaigning for the exoneration of those believed to have been wrongly convicted. It has accumulated a substantial amount of information on such cases that forms an invaluable resource for academic studies. Much later, in 2012, the University of Michigan Law School set up the National Registry of Exonerations that provides a database of all wrongful convictions in the United States since 1989. The statistics accumulated by these projects have enabled the full impact of DNA profile analysis to be appreciated as a means of identifying instances of wrongful conviction. These data have also contributed to highlighting a wide range of other major factors that have contributed to miscarriages of justice, ranging from the incompetence of police or forensic scientists, through to misidentification by witnesses.

1.3.3   Canada

In Canada, the unprecedented case of Steven Truscott was an early example of wrongful conviction. He was found guilty and originally sentenced to death in 1959, aged only 14, for sexual assault and murder, though this sentence was commuted to life imprisonment on appeal in 1960. He was freed in 1969 but only declared innocent of the crime when he was pardoned in 2007. Over the same period there were several other significant miscarriages of justice, most notably in cases involving the murder of a young girl: Donald Marshall (1971, inquiry report 1989), Thomas Sophonow (1981, inquiry report 2001), Guy Morin (1992, freed 1995, inquiry report 1998) and James Driskell (1991, freed 2005). These were each subject to a full public provincial inquiry, often many years later and, in all cases the report was not only highly critical of the investigative and legal process but also of the forensic examination of evidence and subsequent court testimony. These Canadian inquiries are highly regarded across the world for their thoroughness in looking beyond the facts of the case in question in order to identify systemic issues and failures in the justice system as a whole. Indeed, the Morin inquiry report has been described by Macfarlane as:

> '... arguably the most comprehensive judicial review that has ever been undertaken into the causes of wrongful conviction, and how to avoid them.'
>
> [Macfarlane, 2006]

The Canadian approach to the investigation of miscarriages of justice has, more recently, gone beyond individual murder convictions. At least five individuals were wrongfully convicted of murder, based on the paediatric forensic pathology evidence provided by Dr Charles Smith. This was the subject of the Goudge Inquiry (2008) and will be discussed later in section 1.6.1.

1.3.4   Australia

The most publicised miscarriage of justice among Australian cases in recent decades is undoubtedly that of Alice Chamberlain (1982, exonerated 1987) who was convicted of the murder of her young daughter Azaria while the family were camping in the outback near Ayres Rock. As the mother claimed that her baby was carried away by a wild animal, this achieved notoriety as the 'dingo baby' case. Chamberlain was exonerated following a Royal Commission of inquiry (Morling Report, 1987) and an appeal hearing. However, it was not until 2012, following more recent cases where it was proved that a baby had been abducted by a dingo, that a coroner's court ruled that this was, in fact, the legal cause of death of Azaria Chamberlain.

Over the next thirty years, further convictions in Australia became the subject of Royal Commissions and appeal hearings that frequently found faulty forensic science testimony had contributed to the subsequent miscarriage of justice. Most notable was the case of Edward Splatt whose conviction in 1978 for murder was based on a range of circumstantial trace evidence associating him with the murder scene. Two subsequent inquiries (Moran, 1981 and Shannon, 1984) were strongly critical of the forensic services within South Australia and Splatt was finally released in 1984. Recently, laboratory contamination was responsible for an erroneous result from DNA profile analysis that led to the conviction of Farah Jama for rape, solely on the basis of this evidence, in 2008. This contributed to ongoing reviews into the quality of DNA testing services within Victoria and New South Wales.

The Australian experience with miscarriages of justice led to a focus amongst stakeholders on the quality of forensic science and testimony both within individual states and at federal level, particularly after the Chamberlain and Splatt cases. Consequently, the National Institute of Forensic Science was established:

> '… to be an integral part of and a support base for the forensic science community, by working in partnership with all the elements of that community for the advancement of forensic science.'
>
> [ANZPAA-NIFS, 2015]

1.4   DNA Reveals Wrongful Convictions

The high evidential value of a DNA profile, together with the ability to obtain, retrospectively, high-quality profiles from evidential materials many years after a crime had been committed, has led to a significant increase in the identification of wrongful convictions over the past twenty-five years. The first such case was that of Gary Dotson, convicted for rape in Illinois, United States in 1979, following misleading forensic testimony at the trial. As Dotson, the semen donor and the victim all belonged to the relatively unusual blood group B, serological analysis of a vaginal swab from the victim was, in fact, of no evidential value, despite the court being told of a blood group match with Dotson. In 1988, a DNA profile from the swab was found, not only to exclude Dotson, but further, to include the victim's boyfriend as a potential source of the semen. Thus, the use of the new DNA technology provided evidence resulting in the exoneration of Dotson and his release from prison in 1989.

More recent exonerations have resulted in the release from prison of others who have been wrongly incarcerated for much longer periods of time. In December 1979, Teresa de Simone was raped and murdered in Southampton, United Kingdom. Sean Hodgson was tried and convicted of these offences in 1982 on the basis of a confession that he later retracted, on blood group evidence of limited evidential weight and on minor circumstantial evidence. At the trial, Hodgson admitted to being a 'pathological liar'. In 1998, an attempt was made to re-open the case based on DNA analysis but the authorities claimed that the necessary exhibits had not been kept. Nevertheless, in 2009 the case was referred to the Appeal Court on the basis of fresh DNA profile evidence that revealed that Hodgson was not the donor of the semen samples taken from the body of the victim, and he was released after 27 years in prison.

DNA profile evidence continues to be a major contributor to the identification and exoneration of victims of miscarriage of justice across the globe. In the United States, in particular, such cases are monitored by the Innocence Project and other organisations. The statistics they provide are indicative, not only of the impact of such evidence on the legal process, but also of the ongoing scale of wrongful convictions by the courts and the consequent reduction in the public's confidence with the legal system. For example, in the United States, of the 873 exonerations identified by the National Registry of Exonerations between 1989 to 2012, 325 were cleared at least in part by DNA evidence (Gross and Shaffer, 2012). The causes of these miscarriages of justice include not only faulty forensic science and testimony, but also a variety of other factors that will be reviewed next.

1.5 The Causes of Wrongful Conviction

The plethora of studies, inquiries and reports into cases of miscarriage of justice over the past thirty years or so from across the world have produced a remarkably consistent picture of the factors responsible. Although there is some variation in the significance of each factor across jurisdictions, the spectrum of failure, both within the criminal justice system and in the provision of forensic investigation and expert testimony, is evident throughout the world. Although the focus here must be on those factors rooted in the science, it is beneficial to summarise all areas at issue. Macfarlane (2006) has identified a set of 'predisposing circumstances' that provide a context for potential miscarriages of justice. These include cases that have a high profile with the public, leading to pressure to convict; cases where the defendant is unpopular, for whatever reason; a legal environment where the ethos is to 'win the game' whatever the evidence might imply; and cases where there is an over-riding belief in the guilt of the defendant and where a conviction must be obtained, even through improper practices. Within these contexts, there may be other, more specific factors within the criminal justice system that may lead directly to a wrongful conviction. Based on Macfarlane (2006) and others, these 'immediate causes' may be defined as:

1. Eyewitness misidentification; such evidence is generally unreliable since it relies on human perception skills and memory.
2. Police mishandling of the investigation; this includes a range of factors from incompetence and ineffectiveness through to professional misconduct, including police brutality, fabrication of evidence and nondisclosure. A significant factor here is the concept of

'tunnel vision' where police preconceptions about a crime act as the driver, so that the investigators attempt to use forensic science to confirm their suspicions, rather than to provide genuine leads to the investigation.

3. Poor communication between the forensic scientists and police or prosecutors is a systems failure that not only impedes the investigation, but may cause misinterpretation of the scientific evidence and misunderstanding of its implications and significance.

4. Inadequate training of criminal justice professionals may impact across many stages of the investigative and legal process.

5. Lack of forensic awareness by the police may lead to scientific evidence not being used effectively in the investigation, being misunderstood or being ignored. This often occurs due to insufficient or ineffective training and the absence of professional development.

6. There may be misconduct by the prosecution or relevant evidence may not be disclosed to the defence team.

7. If the prosecution case depends on informants who are in custody, have a criminal record or are incentivised in some way in order to provide testimony, such evidence is often unreliable.

8. Defence lawyers may be incompetent, represent their clients inadequately or indeed behave unprofessionally.

9. The prosecution case may rely on a false confession either through police tactics, mental health or other personality issues with the defendant or other circumstances.

10. Circumstantial evidence may have been misleading or misinterpreted.

In addition, there are other factors that relate specifically to unreliable scientific evidence and require more detailed discussion.

1.6   Unreliable Scientific Evidence

The causes of unreliable scientific evidence may either arise from a number of generic circumstances or, more specifically, from issues relating to a particular type of evidence.

1.6.1   The Status and Expertise of the Expert Witness

The expert witness may not be an expert or at least may not have expertise in the area of testimony. The status of the expert may have led the jury to accept the testimony uncritically. Within the field of forensic pathology, expert evidence is frequently given by experienced and, often renowned, medical practitioners and consultants who, however, may stray outside their area of expertise or indeed be unaware of, or be unwilling to admit to, the limitations of their knowledge. The often flawed testimony of Dr Charles Smith across many cases involving the deaths of children in Ontario from 1981 to 2001 led to up to twenty verdicts being reviewed in cases where parents had been convicted of murdering their young children, identified by Smith as shaken baby syndrome, but which were revealed as miscarriages of justice. The subsequent Goudge Inquiry (2008) into these cases stated:

> 'Dr Smith is a pediatric pathologist, not a forensic pathologist. He has neither formal forensic pathology training nor board certification in that field'
>
> [Goudge Inquiry, 2008, exec summary p. 11]

Indeed, Smith told the inquiry that he did not regard forensic pathology as a separate discipline, though he had lectured and acquired an increasing reputation within that field throughout this period. Goudge concluded that not only did Smith not have a basic understanding of forensic pathology but that he was unaware of the damaging impact that could have on the validity of his expert testimony.

> 'The expert must be aware of the limits of his or her expertise, stay within them, and not exaggerate them to the court. Dr Smith did not observe this fundamental rule.'
>
> [Goudge Inquiry, 2008, exec summary p. 14]

In the United Kingdom, Professor Sir Roy Meadow, an experienced paediatrician, provided testimony in the trial of Sally Clark in 1999 for the murder of her two young sons where the defence case was that both had died of Sudden Infant Death Syndrome (SIDS). However, he went significantly beyond his area of expertise when he quoted and then misused statistical data on the occurrence of this condition within the population at large. Indeed, his error was significant enough for the Royal Statistical Society to publish a statement highlighting it and warning of the danger of courts being misinformed on statistical matters by eminent experts who were nevertheless not qualified to do so. Clark was eventually freed, following a second appeal in 2003, mainly based on fresh medical evidence. The Clark case will be discussed in Chapter 19.2.

1.6.2   The Expert is not Impartial

In most cases where the expert is not impartial this means favouring the prosecution by highlighting those aspects of the testimony that support their arguments at the expense of alternative explanations. During the IRA bombing campaign on the British mainland in the 1970s, Judith Ward was convicted in 1974 on twelve counts of murder as a result of causing three separate explosions across the country. The evidence against her comprised alleged confessions, supported by forensic evidence that she had had personal contact with nitroglycerine and that traces of this explosive had also been found in a caravan in which she had been living. Ward denied having any involvement in handling explosives but she did not appeal at the time and it was only after her case had been referred to the Court of Appeal by the UK Home Secretary that she was exonerated of these crimes and freed in 1993. Crucially, the validity, reliability and interpretation of the results of chemical analysis on the residues from swabs, that were claimed to reveal nitroglycerine, were thoroughly investigated and criticised at this appeal. In particular, it was found that the scientists had suppressed experimental data which weakened the prosecution's case by establishing that a dye in boot polish could provide a positive outcome to a test for this explosive. Other work into contamination by secondary transfer of these explosive traces which proved not to support the prosecution was also not revealed at the original trial. The appeal court judge found that the scientists had misled the court over contamination, not disclosed relevant scientific information and had abandoned neutrality in an attempt to support the police and the prosecution. This led to a serious miscarriage of justice.

> 'It is the clear duty of government forensic scientists to assist in a neutral and impartial way in criminal investigations. They must act in the cause of justice…'
>
> [R v Ward, 1993]

1.6.3 The Evidence was Wrong

The police investigation into the murder of Marion Ross in Kilmarnock, Scotland, in 1997 effectively led to two miscarriages of justice, both based on the erroneous identification of finger-marks. David Asbury was convicted of the crime based on the presence of a finger-mark which was identified as from the victim, found on a tin containing money at his house. At his appeal, fresh evidence from fingerprint experts from outside Scotland revealed that this identification was incorrect and Ross was not in fact the source of the mark. Asbury was then exonerated and freed in 2000. What gave this case particular prominence, however, was that another finger-mark, found on the bathroom doorframe in the victim's house, was identified as that of Shirley McKie, a police officer who had attended this murder scene. McKie, who consistently denied that she had ever entered the house or was the source of the mark, was tried for perjury in 1999. Once again, testimony external to the Scottish Criminal Records Office, this time from two American experts, succeeded in convincing the court of McKie's innocence and that the original identification of the doorframe mark as her fingerprint, was wrong. The McKie case will be discussed in Chapter 13.6.

1.6.4 Exaggerated Evaluation by the Expert

The expert witness may have provided an exaggerated evaluation of the significance of the evidence. The physical comparison of hairs is amongst the most qualitative of the more established areas in forensic analysis and one where the interpretation and evaluation of the evidence depends almost entirely on the judgement and experience of the expert. The basis of hair examination is a process of comparison and classification, but rarely is there any data on the size of the class to which evidential hairs might belong, and no scientific under-pinning of the resulting opinion. There have been examples of the expert claiming indi-viduality and unique characteristics attributable to particular hair exhibits or quoting supposed statistical data in support of testimony. Indeed, more recently, the FBI reviewed past expert testimony on microscopic hair comparisons and found 90% of the reports con-tained erroneous statements.

Jimmy Ray Bromgard was wrongfully convicted in 1987 for the rape of a child in Montana, United States, finally being freed in 2002 when DNA profiling of stains on the victim's underwear proved that he was not the source of the semen. The only evidence for the prosecution was a tentative eyewitness identification by the child and forensic examina-tion of head and pubic hairs recovered from the victim's bedding. The expert witness at the trial testified that these evidential hairs had:

> '… the same microscopic characteristics as the head and pubic hairs collected from Bromgard …'
> [Jimmy Ray Bromgard v State of Montana, 2004, paragraph 19]

He also claimed, without any statistical foundation whatsoever, that:

> '… there was a one in ten thousand chance that the hairs belonged to anyone other than Bromgard.'
> [Jimmy Ray Bromgard v State of Montana, 2004, paragraph 23]

In fact, it was later proved that the head hair came from the victim and that Bromgard could be excluded as the source of the pubic hair. The State crime laboratory was criticised for failing to adequately train and supervise the hair examiner and Bromgard was paid substantial damages following his exoneration.

Guy Paul Morin was charged with the rape and murder of his next-door neighbour's child, Christine Jessop, in 1984 in Ontario, Canada and initially acquitted. However he was re-tried and convicted, only being released in 1995 after more than ten years in prison, following the submission of fresh DNA profile evidence. The crucial evidence that was claimed to prove physical contact between Morin and the victim, was transferred hairs and fibres. The hairs were found to be microscopically similar to those from Morin and the interpretation of this was that the hairs 'could have originated from him' (Report of the Kaufman Commission, 1998). Amongst the many thousands of fibres found following tape-lifts were several that 'could have' come from the same source as reference fibres from Morin. The Royal Commission that investigated this miscarriage of justice criticised the scientist for exaggerating the evaluation of the hair evidence when initially communicating her findings to the police; this had initiated Morin's arrest. The Commission's report was critical of the use of phrases such as 'consistent with' and 'match' in the experts' evaluation as they could potentially lead the court to misunderstand the forensic findings.

1.6.5 Unethical Behaviour

The testimony may have resulted from unethical behaviour or even have been fabricated by the expert witness. In 2004, Jacqueline Blake pleaded guilty to charges of misconduct in her professional duties as a forensic biologist with the FBI, as she had made false statements in her laboratory book in relation to many DNA profile analyses that she had carried out during 2001 and 2002. Specifically, she knowingly had not followed the FBI DNA Analysis Unit protocols by failing to process the negative controls and reagent blanks necessary to ensure the process was free from contamination when using capillary electrophoresis. Consequently, this resulted in virtually all her work being invalid. Although it was believed that no miscarriage of justice had resulted from her misconduct, the inability of the FBI quality assurance procedures to detect her behaviour significantly dented the credibility of the work of that laboratory.

The wrongful conviction of Glen Dale Woodall for double rape in 1987 was largely due to the testimony of Fred Zain who provided misleading and exaggerated serology evidence on the blood group of the donor of semen retrieved from the victims. Woodall was exonerated in 1992, after it was found that his conviction was only one of many that had relied on the evidence of Zain. Consequently, Zain was investigated for misconduct and incompetence and the report presented to the appeal court of West Virginia in 1993. This concluded that not only had Zain altered laboratory records, provided fraudulent reports and committed perjury on an extensive scale, but he had also gained a reputation for being unusually proactive in his support for the prosecution case in the courts over many years. He was indicted on multiple charges in 1994 but the jury could not reach a verdict and he died before a retrial could take place.

1.6.6 Human Error

The forensic analysis may have been subject to human error or have been carried out by inadequately trained personnel or without attention to accepted procedures and quality safeguards. The use of presumptive tests for explosives' residues on the hands of suspects, featured strongly in cases arising from the IRA bombing campaign in the United Kingdom in the 1970s. In particular, the results of the Griess test for nitroglycerine proved to be crucial in the arrest and conviction of the Birmingham Six in 1975. These tests, which were carried out in a makeshift fashion at Morecambe police station, claimed to prove that two of the six men who were travelling to Ireland from Birmingham had had contact with this explosive. Together with alleged confessions made while in police custody, this was the principal evidence presented by the prosecution. It was eventually revealed that the scientist who performed the tests had not followed standard analytical procedures or run control samples to check for contamination. Indeed, one of the arguments presented at the appeal in 1991 was that, as the Griess test is not specific to nitroglycerine, the positive results obtained may have been due to other chemical traces, including soap contamination of the glassware, residues arising from smoking cigarettes or indeed from the suspects handling playing cards over a period of several hours prior to the tests being performed. By neglecting to implement proper quality assurance procedures, or to include appropriate control tests, the scientist's testimony contributed to a major miscarriage of justice, leading to sixteen years' imprisonment before all six men were exonerated of this crime.

1.6.7   Non-validated Methodology

The method itself or the science underpinning it may not have been validated by peers and so have unknown probative value. Kim Ancona, a bartender, was found stabbed to death in her place of work in Phoenix, Arizona, United States in December 1991. Although saliva stains on her clothing were tested for blood group, no DNA profile was attempted at the time, and the only forensic evidence was bite marks on her body. As it was believed that Ray Krone had been helping the victim to lock up the nightclub that evening, he was arrested when imprints of his irregular teeth revealed an apparent similarity to the marks on the body. At his trial, two forensic odontologists both claimed, in their testimony, that Krone had made the bite marks and, together with the fact that he shared a common blood group with the source of the saliva stains, this comprised the totality of the evidence against Krone. He was found guilty of murder and sentenced to death. However, after an appeal and a second trial this sentence was commuted to life imprisonment. Eventually, after ten years in prison, Krone was exonerated in 2002 when a DNA profile taken from the saliva stain excluded him as a donor and, in fact, identified Kenneth Phillips, a convicted attacker, as the source.

In a review of forensic odontology that predated Krone's release (Pretty and Sweet, 2001), the absence of any rigorous scientific foundation to the analytical process or indeed evidence of uniqueness in human dentition were identified as fundamental reasons for the inaccuracy and unreliability of forensic bite-mark analysis. A few years later the NRC report – Strengthening Forensic Science in the United States (2009) – re-iterated these weaknesses when it identified bite-mark comparison as the most contentious topic in forensic odontology.

1.6.8   Overconfidence in New Techniques

The confidence of the courts in DNA profile evidence became established through proven techniques applied to cellular material of recognisable origin such as blood, semen or body tissue. Once the amplification technology had succeeded in obtaining profiles from samples invisible to the eye and containing very few cells, it did not follow that the outcomes would sustain this confidence. The difficulties in the interpretation and evaluation of such new Low Copy Number (LCN) DNA evidence came to the fore in the trial of Sean Hoey for the murder of twenty-nine people, following a car bomb explosion in Omagh, Northern Ireland in August 1998. The key forensic evidence were LCN DNA profiles obtained from swabs taken from some of the bomb mechanism parts retrieved after the explosion. It was evident at the trial that the police, the forensic investigators and indeed the forensic laboratory staff were unaware of the enhanced precautions necessary to deal with control of the crime scene, to prevent contamination and to ensure continuity of evidence when working with potential LCN DNA materials. In his conclusion the trial judge declared that he was:

> '... not in the least satisfied in relation to any one of the items upon which reliance is sought to be placed for the results of their LCN DNA examinations that the integrity of any of those items prior to its examination for that purpose has been established by the evidence.'
>
> [Queen v Hoey, 2007, paragraph 61]

Further, the defence and prosecution expert witnesses gave conflicting testimony on whether the core methodology underpinning the use of LCN DNA profiles as forensic evidence was, in fact, reliable, validated and indeed accepted by the scientific community beyond the United Kingdom, the Netherlands and New Zealand. Consequently, Hoey was acquitted on all charges against him. The Hoey case will be discussed further in Chapter 11.2.

1.7   The Scientist and the Laboratory

In addition to shortcomings in expert testimony, in techniques and in the competence of individual scientists, the operation and management of forensic laboratories overall has also contributed to miscarriages of justice. For example, the quality control procedures may have failed to prevent errors by the individual or to ensure their professional competency and, in some cases, such fundamental failures have brought into doubt forensic analyses carried out by a particular laboratory over an extended period of time. Where such systemic failures are suspected or identified, major reviews have often been carried out, such as those at the FBI laboratories on explosives-related cases in 1997, DNA analysis in 2004 and in the failure of fingerprint examination in the case of Brandon Mayfield in 2004. Other reviews have been related to doubts as to the fundamental validity of testimony based on specific techniques, previously promoted by a laboratory, such as the compositional analysis of bullet lead, which was discontinued by the FBI in 2005 following an extensive review and the use of the microscopic examination of hair evidence in 2015.

Failures by the forensic organisation itself are not restricted to the United States, however. In Canada, the Centre of Forensic Sciences (CFS) in Ontario was subjected to an investigation, following the successful appeal by Guy Morin in 1995, against his conviction for the murder of Christine Jessop. The Kaufman Inquiry established that the CFS had mishandled vital hair and fibre evidence that at the trial had played a crucial role in allegedly proving close contact between Morin and the victim. The report concluded that:

> 'The contribution of the CFS to Mr. Morin's wrongful arrest, prosecution and conviction was, indeed, substantial.'
>
> [Kaufman Report, 1998, Ch 2, p. 250]

Following allegations from a whistleblower, the storage and handling of drugs exhibits at the Victoria Police Forensic Services Centre in Australia was investigated in 2009. The report blamed the laboratory management for failing to ensure that staff followed appropriate policies and procedures, which in turn could impinge on the laboratory's role within the criminal justice system. Elsewhere, the procedures for the examination of fingerprints across Scotland were scrutinised in 2011, following the miscarriage of justice in the case of Shirley McKie.

Nevertheless, ongoing difficulties persist in the United States right up to the present time, at both state and county laboratory level, where instances of malpractice and failure to ensure the competence, and indeed the integrity, of scientists have been reported. These have fuelled the calls for all forensic science laboratories to be regulated and subjected to appropriate accreditation, including decoupling them from the investigative authorities. This issue will be discussed further in Chapter 4.4.

1.8   Conclusions

This discussion has demonstrated that both the quality of the science and the quality assurance of the entire forensic process, from the crime scene to the court, underpin the admissibility, validity and effectiveness of expert opinion. Unfortunately, it has taken many instances of wrongful conviction to alert the criminal justice system to weaknesses and failures within the legal and forensic procedures, a process facilitated largely by the introduction of DNA profile analysis, some thirty years ago. To understand further the issues facing the scientist and the courts when considering expert testimony, we need to discuss, in detail, the admissibility of scientific evidence which is the subject of the following chapter.

References

Australia New Zealand Policing Advisory Agency (ANZPAA) National Institute of Forensic Science [Online]. (2015). Available at https://www.anzpaa.org.au/forensic-science/10636 [Accessed 30 November 2015].

Bromgard v State of Montana; Civil rights complaint CV-04-192-M-LBE, 2004.

Cole S.A. (2007). Where the rubber meets the road: thinking about expert evidence as expert testimony, *Villanova Law Review* 52(4), 803–842.

Goudge S.T. (2008). Inquiry into pediatric forensic pathology in Ontario. [Online]. Available at http://www.attorneygeneral.jus.gov.on.ca/inquiries/goudge/report/v1_en_pdf/vol_1_eng.pdf [Accessed 12 October 2015].

Gross S.R. and Shaffer M. (2012). Exonerations in the United States, 1989–2012, Report by the National Registry of Exonerations, [Online]. Available at http://www.law.umich.edu/special/exoneration/Pages/about.aspx [Accessed 12 October 2015].

Macfarlane B.A. (2006). Convicting the innocent: a triple failure of the justice system, *Manitoba Law Journal*, 31(3), 403–484.

Morling Report (1987). Summarised by Coroner Lowndes. Available at http://law2.umkc.edu/faculty/projects/ftrials/chamberlain/moorlingreport.html [Accessed 12 October 2015].

National Research Council: Strengthening Forensic Science in the United States: A Path Forward, Document 228091. [Online]. (2009). Available at http://www.nap.edu/catalog/12589.html [Accessed 10 October 2015].

Pretty I.A. and Sweet D.J. (2001). The scientific basis for human bitemark analyses – a critical review, *Science and Justice*, 41, 85–92.

Queen v Hoey [2007] NICC 49

R (Adams) v Secretary of State for Justice [2011] UKSC 18, 11 May 2011

R v Ward [1993] 2 All ER 577

Report of the Kaufman Commission on proceedings involving Guy Paul Morin. [Online]. (1998). Available at http://www.attorneygeneral.jus.gov.on.ca/english/about/pubs/morin/ [Accessed 12 October 2015].

Saks M.J. and Koehler J.J. (2005). The coming paradigm shift in forensic identification science. *Science*, 309, 892–895.

Further Reading

Adam A. (2016). *A History of Forensic Science: British beginnings in the twentieth century.* Routledge.

Cole S.A. (2006). The prevalence and potential cause of wrongful conviction by fingerprint evidence, *Golden Gate University Law Review*, 37, 39–105.

Edmond G. (2014). The science of miscarriages of justice. *University of New South Wales Law Journal*, 37(1), 376–406.

Etter B. (2013). The contribution of forensic science to miscarriage of justice cases, *Australian Journal of Forensic Sciences*, 45(4), 368–380.

The Fingerprint Inquiry Report – Scotland. [Online]. (2011). Available at http://www.webarchive. org.uk/wayback/archive/20150428160022/http://www.thefingerprintinquiryscotland.org.uk/ inquiry/3127-2.html [Accessed 12 December 2015].

FBI laboratory announces discontinuation of bullet lead examinations [Online]. (2005). Available at https://www.fbi.gov/news/pressrel/press-releases/fbi-laboratory-announces-discontinuation-of-bullet-lead-examinations [Accessed 12 October 2015].

FBI/DOJ (2015). Microscopic hair comparison analysis review [Online]. Available at https://www. fbi.gov/about-us/lab/scientific-analysis/fbi-doj-microscopic-hair-comparison-analysis-review [Accessed 12 October 2015].

Garrett B.L. and Neufeld P.J. (2009). Invalid forensic testimony and wrongful convictions, *Virginia Law Review*, 95(1), 1–97.

Giannelli P.C. (2007). Wrongful convictions and forensic science: the need to regulate crime labs, *North Carolina Law Review*, 86, 163–235.

Giannelli P.C. (2011). Daubert and forensic science: The pitfalls of law enforcement control of scientific research, *University of Illinois Law Review*, 53, 54–90.

Gould J.B., Carrano J., Leo R. and Young J. (2013). Predicting erroneous convictions: a social science approach to miscarriages of justice, NIJ report from award 2009-IJ-CX-4110.

Gould J.B. and Leo R.A. (2010). One hundred years later: wrongful convictions after a century of research, *Journal of Criminal Law and Criminology*, 100(3), 825–868.

Gross S.R., Jacoby K., Matheson D.J., Montgomery N. and Patil S. (2005). Exonerations in the United States 1989 through 2003, *Journal of Criminal Law and Criminology*, 95(2), 523–560.

Innocence project. [Online]. Available at http://www.innocenceproject.org/ [Accessed 12 October 2015].

Lynch M. (2003). God's signature: DNA profiling, the new gold standard in forensic science, *Endeavour*, 27(2), 93–97.

Path to Justice: Preventing wrongful convictions: Department of Justice, Canada [Online]. (2011). Available at http://www.ppsc-sppc.gc.ca/eng/pub/ptj-spj/ptj-spj-eng.pdf [Accessed 12 October 2015].

R v Clark [2003] EWCA Crim 1020

R v R G (Sean) Hodgson [2009] EWCA Crim 490

Report on the prevention of miscarriage of justice: Department of Justice, Canada [Online]. (2005). Available at http://www.justice.gc.ca/eng/rp-pr/cj-jp/ccr-rc/pmj-pej/pmj-pej.pdf [Accessed 12 October 2015].

Review of the FBI's handling of the Brandon Mayfield case: Office of the Inspector General, US Dept of Justice [Online]. (2006). Available at http://www.justice.gov/oig/special/s0601/exec.pdf [Accessed 12 October 2015].

Royal Commission of Inquiry into Chamberlain Convictions, Report, Commonwealth Parliamentary Papers [Online]. (1987). volume 15, paper 192. Available at http://www.nt.gov.au/justice/courtsupp/coroner/findings/other/appendix_a_chamberlain_findings.pdf [Accessed 14 December 2015].

Thompson W.C. (2009). Beyond bad apples: analysing the role of forensic science in wrongful convictions, *South-Western Law Review*, 37, 1027–1050.

Trager R. (2014). Hard questions after litany of forensic failures at US labs, *Chemistry World*. Available at http://www.rsc.org/chemistryworld/2014/12/hard-questions-after-litany-forensic-failures-malpractice-labs-us [Accessed 12 October 2015].

USDOJ/OIG Special Report. (1997). The FBI Laboratory: An investigation into laboratory practices and alleged misconduct in explosives-related and other cases [Online]. Available at https://oig.justice.gov/special/9704a/ [Accessed 12 October 2015].

US Department of Justice. (2004). The FBI DNA laboratory: a review of protocol and practice vulnerabilities [Online]. Available at https://oig.justice.gov/special/0405/final.pdf [Accessed 12 October 2015].

Victorian Ombudsman. (2009). Investigation into the handling of drug exhibits at the Victoria Police Forensic Services Centre [Online]. Available at https://www.ombudsman.vic.gov.au/getattachment/64fbc7f6-c51b-439d-aac8-e451381572b8//publications/parliamentary-reports/investigation-into-the-handling-of-drug-exhibits-a.aspx [Accessed 12 October 2015].

2

Admissibility from the Legal Perspective

This chapter will focus on the issues raised and standards discussed in the courts, across the world, which have shaped the admissibility of expert evidence, and which have focused attention at national level on the need to develop rules and guidelines. The criteria that may determine admissibility will be explored through landmark cases and the question of whether admissibility should be considered separately, or along with the reliability of the evidence, will be explored. The impact of such issues on the presentation of expert opinion will be highlighted.

2.1 Admissibility, Relevance and Reliability of Evidence

In English-speaking jurisdictions and in some parts of the British Commonwealth, the legal system is founded on common law, though there are examples where the alternative, civil law, coexists with aspects of common law, for example, in Scotland. Civil law forms the basis of the legal systems in mainland Europe and most of the rest of the world. Expert opinion will be discussed, in the context of these legal systems in Chapter 4.1. Common law endeavours to ensure that cases are dealt with equitably within a legal system that is subject to change through the development of case law. Under this system, points of law are established and may evolve through decisions by courts, which set a judicial precedent that must be recognised in future legal debate. This does not mean that there is no statutory legal framework set by parliament; it means simply that the interpretation of those laws is subject to scrutiny when they are examined in the courts and this

Forensic Evidence in Court: Evaluation and Scientific Opinion, First Edition. Craig Adam.
© 2016 John Wiley & Sons, Ltd. Published 2016 by John Wiley & Sons, Ltd.

may establish precedents that are as much law as the original statutes. So the law is made through its interpretation.

The laws specifically relating to evidence are subject to this same process. For the current discussion, the fundamental issue is the distinction between expert testimony (opinion evidence) and other forms of witness evidence. Under common law, witnesses may only state factual information when giving statements in court; they may not express any opinion, for example, on what they saw or heard. On the other hand, testimony from an expert witness may include both factual and opinion evidence, but this must be relevant to the matters under discussion. What defines an expert?

'Expert witnesses stand in the very privileged position of being able to provide the jury with opinion evidence on matters within their area of expertise and outside most jurors' knowledge and experience.'
[Law Commission: Expert Evidence in Criminal Proceedings in England and Wales, 2011]

This, then, becomes the starting point for the court's decision to admit such evidence. However, the nature, extent and relevance of the expertise of a witness may become an issue for the court to establish and challenges at various levels may be made to such expert testimony that raise fresh difficulties that the court has to resolve. Here, the role of the judge may ultimately be to act as 'gatekeeper' on the admissibility of the expert opinion.

In coming to a decision on the admissibility of expert evidence, the judge may need to consider many interlinking and often complex factors. However, these may be focused ultimately down to two: relevance and reliability. Relevance relates to the probative value of the evidence in enabling the jury, as the trier of fact, to come to an ultimate decision on the outcome of the case. However, relevant evidence may be excluded if its benefit to the court may be outweighed by the danger that it proves unfairly prejudicial, leads to confusion or significantly delays the proceedings of the court.

Since expert opinion is outside the common knowledge of the court, assuring its reliability is essential, otherwise the judge, jury and counsel would be unable to decide whether the testimony is valid and correct. Determining the basis of reliability, and deciding whether this is indeed a necessary prerequisite to admissibility, or whether it should contribute to the determination of the weight of the evidence, is one of the principal issues that has been debated within the courts.

For scientific expert evidence in particular, despite an expectation of inherent reliability in a general sense, there have been a significant number of cases where the testimony has been questioned, for example when the science is novel or not yet established. Consequently, precedents have been set that have influenced subsequent debates.

In the recent past, there has been increased discussion of admissibility, leading to some significant rulings in courts across many jurisdictions. Interestingly, many of the landmark cases which have led to the development of legal criteria for admissibility have been civil cases, for example, those dealing with health and safety or medical issues. There are fewer examples where experts gave testimony in the mainstream subdisciplines that form the core of forensic science, though there are several associated with fringe areas of the subject. Nevertheless, the consequences of these rulings have, in the end, come to apply to all forensic expert evidence, as much as to expert evidence in general.

We will start with the United States, as it has a longer history of awareness of and activity in discussing and setting admissibility standards within common law, then move to those countries that have adhered more strongly to a common law foundation, which has less rigid and clear criteria for admissibility, and indeed where the concept of admissibility has been intertwined with the weight of evidence perceived by the court. The US experience will also act as a reference point for the discussions on other jurisdictions. The cases discussed are not intended to provide a comprehensive survey, though those acknowledged as the most significant will be included. Rather, the intention is to illustrate how such cases contribute to the evolution of admissibility criteria, in general.

2.2   Admissibility in the United States

In addition to courts at district, state and federal level, the United States has a two-tier system of appeal courts, at state as well as at federal level, with a supreme court in each state and the US Federal Supreme Court as the ultimate arbiter. Some cases may move between these courts and discussion of admissibility has taken place throughout this system.

2.2.1   Reliability and the Frye Test

Legal criteria and processes to deal with issues around the admissibility of expert scientific evidence in the courts have been to the fore in the United States for almost a century, ever since the Frye ruling in 1923. Prior to that date the US courts followed a practice similar to that in the United Kingdom, by basing admissibility on the perceived expertise of the witness. At the trial of James Frye for the murder of Dr Robert Brown, an expert witness was called who had used the measurement of systolic blood pressure as an alleged lie detector on the defendant. The issue here was not the expertise of this witness but whether the detection of abrupt changes in blood pressure correlated with the individual telling a lie and whether this technique was accepted as such by the broader scientific community. The defence claimed that no instances of the success of this technique were recorded and this point was accepted by the court. In response, the judgment of the court was summarised as:

> 'Just when a scientific principle or discovery crosses the line between the experimental and demonstrable stages is difficult to define. Somewhere in this twilight zone the evidential force of the principle must be recognized, and while courts will go a long way in admitting expert testimony deduced from a well- recognized scientific principle or discovery, the thing from which the deduction is made must be sufficiently established to have gained general acceptance in the particular field in which it belongs.'
>
> [Frye v United States, 1923]

This established the so-called Frye criterion that the scientific basis of expert evidence must have gained acceptance within its field to be admissible in a court of law. This admissibility criterion of general acceptability essentially underpins the reliability of expert evidence, in that the court as a whole should have confidence, that the scientific opinion being given will not mislead it in its deliberations or prejudice its decisions. This arguably conservative criterion was often applied quite rigorously during the 1970s when many new analytical techniques were being developed, though it was not adopted by all states. This led to forensic evidence being excluded on the grounds of the novelty and hence on the inadmissibility of the science behind the testimony.

2.2.2 Meeting the Frye Criterion: US v Stifel 1970

In October 1970, the US Appeal Court considered the appeal of Orville Stifel against his conviction for the murder of Dan Ronec, by sending him a bomb through the post. Amongst the evidence presented by the prosecution were the results of neutron activation analysis (NAA) on fragments of the exploded bomb and on reference materials obtained from the defendant's place of work. At the time, NAA was a new technique with the potential to strongly characterise materials according to their trace element composition. The expert witness, James Scott:

> '... testified that in his opinion the mailing label and the cardboard tube fragments were of the same 'elemental composition' as their Proctor & Gamble counterparts and that 'within reasonable scientific certainty' they were 'of the same type and same manufacture.'
> [US v Stifel, 1970, paragraph 58]

This opinion agreed with findings from the other, more established techniques of microscopy and atomic absorption analysis. Stifel's appeal was based on the novelty of the NAA technique and he argued that this expert evidence was inadmissible, according to the Frye criterion, as:

> '... the test is too new and unreliable and has not yet been generally accepted by scientists in its particular field.'
> [US v Stifel, 1970, paragraph 60]

Both sides produced further expert witnesses to debate whether NAA was a technique accepted by the scientific community, with some alluding to the extensive range of research publications underpinning the method and that NAA-based evidence had been accepted by other courts in recent years. The appeal court judge commented:

> '... neither newness nor lack of absolute certainty in a test suffices to render it inadmissible in court. Every useful new development must have its first day in court ...'
> [US v Stifel, 1970, paragraph 81]

The court therefore rejected the appeal and ruled that the trial court was right in admitting the results of neutron activation analysis in this case.

2.2.3 Admissibility and the Gatekeeper Role: The Daubert Test

The next development in defining the admissibility of scientific evidence came about, not through a criminal trial, but as a result of civil litigation against a large company. At the time the issue was becoming more prominent, through the belief that there was a tendency for some experts in corporate litigation cases to act in a biased fashion, in support of those for whom they were acting, and through large corporations using junk science arguments to counter litigation by individuals. Further, the contradictions between the Frye test and the more recent and liberal criteria of Federal Rule 702, which will be discussed further in Chapter 3.1.1, were becoming more apparent. At that time, Rule 702 stated that:

> 'If scientific, technical, or other specialized knowledge will assist the trier of fact to understand the evidence or to determine a fact in issue, a witness qualified as an expert by knowledge, skill, experience, training, or education, may testify thereto in the form of an opinion or otherwise.'
> [Federal Rules of Evidence, 1975, Rule 702]

The judgment, in the case of Daubert v Merrell Dow by the US Appeal Court in 1993, was intended to reconcile and clarify the position on the admissibility of scientific expert testimony.

The pharmaceutical company, Merrell Dow Incorporated, manufactured an anti-nausea drug for pregnant women called Bendectin, which was alleged to have caused birth defects in children whose mothers took the drug during their pregnancies. Two of those children, Jason Daubert and Eric Schuller, jointly sued the company for damages. The position taken by the company in court was that no scientific study had proved that this drug was responsible for birth defects, whereas counsel for the children claimed that such evidence was, in fact, available and based on animal cell and live animal studies, pharmacological research and a re-interpretation of previously published epidemiological studies. The federal court judgment rejected the case presented by the plaintiffs, thereby supporting the position taken by Merrell Dow. The court's view was that the petitioners' evidence was inadmissible as it failed to meet the Frye criterion. The ruling stated that the animal studies and molecular-based pharmacological studies did not and could not show direct causation while the re-analysis of previously published data had not of itself been subject to peer review. As such, its reliability was not confirmed. Peer review refers to the standard practice of scientists and other experts reading, understanding and accepting the work of others in a field and endorsing it as genuine and reliable new knowledge.

Ironically, in justifying this ruling which starts by quoting part of the Frye criterion, the judges declared that the Frye test had been effectively superseded by the more relaxed barriers to admissibility of Rule 702 in particular. They re-iterated that, on behalf of the court, the judge:

> '... must ensure that any and all scientific testimony or evidence admitted is not only relevant, but reliable'

> [Daubert v Merrell Dow, 1993]

The judgment expanded on this by adding that:

> '... scientists typically distinguish between "validity" (does the principle support what it purports to show?) and "reliability" (does application of the principle produce consistent results?). ...Although "the difference between accuracy, validity, and reliability maybe [sic] such that each is distinct from the other by no more than a hen's kick."'

> [Daubert v Merrell Dow, 1993]

Although most scientists would dispute this last throwaway line, these points have become crucial following the adoption of this judgment by many states. In summary, the ruling states the importance of both relevancy and reliability in the consideration of scientific expert opinion, by emphasising the importance of the validity of the scientific methodology and designating the trial judge the gatekeeper for admissibility.

> '"General acceptance" is not a necessary precondition to the admissibility of scientific evidence under the Federal Rules of Evidence, but the Rules of Evidence – especially Rule 702 – do assign to the trial judge the task of ensuring that an expert's testimony both rests on a reliable foundation and is relevant to the task at hand. Pertinent evidence based on scientifically valid principles will satisfy those demands.'

> [Daubert v Merrell Dow, 1993]

The Daubert ruling has, at federal level, and in just over half the states of the United States, replaced the general acceptability rule of Frye with one based on relevance and reliability, in which the latter is assessed through specific questions relating to validity, accuracy and the acceptability of the methodology and the underpinning science by the scientific community. More specifically the judgment itemises the following points (paragraphs 24–30 and paraphrased here), which should be addressed specifically by the court:

1. Is the testimony based on methods and techniques that are scientific knowledge which have been tested, for example by generating appropriate hypotheses and subjecting them to experimental examination?
2. Has the methodology been subjected to peer review to examine its validity and has this been demonstrated, for example by publications?
3. Is the error rate known for the specific technique used to examine this evidence and are there standard procedures for carrying out these measurements that were adhered to in this work?
4. Is the methodology and underpinning science accepted generally by the relevant scientific community?

The application of these criteria to specific cases in the years since the Daubert ruling have raised many difficulties and been the subject of much debate and discussion in the legal and scientific literature and elsewhere.

2.2.4 The Daubert Trilogy

In the years immediately following Daubert v Merrell Dow, two other rulings, both in the litigation context, contributed minor but significant amendments to the guidelines on admissibility of expert evidence in the United States. Together these three rulings have gained the title of the 'Daubert Trilogy'.

2.2.5 General Electric v Joiner 1997

Robert Joiner was an electrician at the General Electric Company who later developed lung cancer. He alleged that his work there had exposed him to a variety of chemicals, particularly PCBs, furans and dioxins that had consequently promoted the development of this disease. His petition was supported by expert evidence that the likely cause of his cancer was exposure to these materials. The issue for the appeal court was whether the district court judge had not used appropriate legal decision-making skills – 'abused his discretion' – in not admitting this expert evidence. It was argued that the combination of animal-related and four epidemiological studies on the carcinogenic nature of PBCs was not a sufficient basis for the expert testimony, citing a direct causal link between exposure and disease. Thus, the ruling questioned not only the relevance of the data, but whether it did indeed support the conclusions of the expert witness.

> 'But conclusions and methodology are not entirely distinct from one another … A court may conclude that there is simply too great an analytical gap between the data and the opinion proffered.'
>
> [General Electric v Joiner, 1997]

This ruling focused on the role of the judge as gatekeeper and the need for the judge to be able to call on highly qualified and objective experts at the pretrial stage, to advise on such technical matters where decisions on admissibility may rely on deep understanding and subtle arguments.

2.2.6 Kumo Tire Company v Patrick Carmichael 1999

Although Federal Rule 702 is clear in that it applies to scientific, technical or other specialist expert evidence, the Daubert case dealt only with scientific testimony. In the case of the Kumo Tire Company Ltd v Patrick Carmichael, the expert witness acting for Carmichael was a specialist in tyre failure analysis who supported the claim that the fatal blowout in one of Carmichael's tyres was due to a manufacturing defect. The Kumo Tire Company sought to have his evidence declared inadmissible on the grounds that his methodology was not reliable under Rule 702. The court considered that distinction could not be made across the spectrum of expertise, from cutting-edge scientific knowledge through to engineering and other specialist technical areas, which were underpinned by scientific principles. Thus, the Daubert criteria should be applied to this case of tyre safety examination and the judge should act as gatekeeper to its admissibility. Since the court concluded that the testimony given here was not supported by peer review, had no known error rate and that there was no evidence that the methodology had general acceptance, the evidence was declared inadmissible. The significance of this ruling is that it extends the Daubert criteria across all specialist technical evidence, including those from an experience-based expertise, whether perceived as directly scientific or not.

Despite these developments, at the present time, many states within the United States have chosen not to implement either or both of these post-Daubert rulings.

2.2.7 Post-Daubert Hearings: US v Dennis Mooney 2002

After Daubert, challenges to forensic testimony were frequently made by the defence, on the grounds that it did not meet these criteria. In many cases, the judge ordered a separate, pre-trial hearing at which the admissibility of the relevant expert testimony would be decided. These became known as 'Daubert hearings' and they have played a significant role in attempting to identify those types of evidence and those areas of forensic science that appear to be founded on a less robust scientific base.

Dennis Mooney was found guilty of robbery, conspiracy and using or carrying a firearm in the commission of a violent crime, following an incident at Waterville, Maine in November 2000. Part of the evidence against him were letters to his girlfriend in which he admitted taking part in the crime, though at the trial he denied these were in his handwriting. Prior to his trial, Mooney filed a motion to exclude expert testimony from the prosecution in document and fingerprint examination, on the grounds that they did not meet the standard of the Daubert test, recently also implemented in Rule 702. Consequently, this was considered at a separate Daubert hearing.

The fingerprint evidence was deemed admissible on the basis of its past success and scrutiny in the courts. It was agreed that handwriting analysis was a recognised and reliable field of expertise and that the skills demonstrated through the comparison of handwriting evidence had also been accepted in the US courts over many years as a reliable methodology. The hearing ruled that:

> 'While not completely scientific, handwriting analysis is clearly an area of technical expertise governed by Rule 702'
>
> [US v Dennis Mooney, 2002]

The motion did not challenge the expert's expertise in this area, but it did propose that:

> '… there is no data upon which handwriting analysis can determine one "author" of a particular writing'
>
> [US v Dennis Mooney, 2002]

However, this was seen as irrelevant at the hearing, since the Rules of Evidence only require that:

> '… expert testimony assist juries in making disputed facts either more or less likely than not.'
>
> [US v Dennis Mooney, 2002]

Several cases cited in the motion were examined, including examples where the court had allowed the expert to point out similar and dissimilar features, yet was denied the right to express an opinion as to the source of the handwriting. The hearing dismissed this 'bifurcation' of testimony, citing Rule 702 as evidence that the expert witness may testify 'in the form of opinion or otherwise'.

On this basis, the hearing rejected the motion, thereby allowing the expert witnesses to testify. In justifying this decision, the judge recognised that it was not the intention of Daubert to exclude testimony, for example based on established techniques such as handwriting analysis, which may have hitherto been admitted under Frye. Where Rule 702 had been satisfied, any challenges to the reliability of expert opinion should be resolved through cross-examination, rather than through the exclusion of testimony.

2.3 Admissibility in Canada

As in the United States, Canadian jurisdiction is split between the federal courts and those of the ten provinces and three territories. However, unlike the United States, Canada has developed its admissibility conditions for expert testimony only over more recent years, coinciding to a large extent with, but independently from, the Daubert ruling and its aftermath. Previously, Canadian law applied the more liberal common law principles, similar to those in English law, and there was no equivalent to the Frye standard in Canada.

2.3.1 R v Mohan 1994

This landmark case was an appeal in the Court of Ontario, in 1994, against an earlier decision of an appeal court to quash the conviction of a practising paediatrician, Chikmaglur Mohan, on four counts of sexual assault of girls. The expert evidence was that from a psychiatrist, Dr Hill, who claimed he had identified that the psychological profile of the perpetrator of the assaults revealed an unusual combination of paedophile and sexual psychopath, which would define a very small group of people. He testified that:

> 'Doctor Mohan does not have the characteristics attributable to any of three groups in which most sex offenders fall.'

> [R v Mohan, 1994]

On this basis, the original prosecution of Mohan had failed. The issue for the appeal court was the admissibility of Dr Hill's testimony. This was considered under the principles governing the admission of expert evidence, which the judges listed as:

The relevance of the testimony to the case

This should be considered on a cost-benefit basis, in that the reliability of the opinion will impact on its relevance to the court's deliberations. This implies that new techniques or areas of scientific knowledge should face a threshold test for their reliability.

> 'Evidence that is otherwise logically relevant may be excluded on this basis, if its probative value is overborne by its prejudicial effect, if it involves an inordinate amount of time which is not commensurate with its value or if it is misleading in the sense that its effect on the trier of fact, particularly a jury, is out of proportion to its reliability.'

> [R v Mohan, 1994, page 21]

The necessity of the testimony in assisting the trier of fact

The substance of the testimony should be outside the common knowledge of the court, for example, concerning scientific or technical matters. It should not however distort the fact-finding process or overwhelm the jury. If the evidence is not reliable, it cannot be necessary or advisable for the court to consider it.

The absence of any exclusionary rule

The expert evidence should properly relate to appropriate matters under the rules of evidence.

A properly qualified expert

The witness should prove that they possess specific knowledge, that it has been acquired through study or experience and that it is directly related to the substance of their testimony.

Although not specifically stated within these criteria, the court was careful to emphasise that the reliability of the testimony, particularly when relating to novel techniques and areas of knowledge, was implicit when considering admissibility.

> '... it appears from the foregoing that expert evidence which advances a novel scientific theory or technique is subjected to special scrutiny to determine whether it meets a basic threshold of reliability and whether it is essential in the sense that the trier of fact will be unable to come to a satisfactory conclusion without the assistance of the expert. The closer the evidence approaches an opinion on an ultimate issue, the stricter the application of this principle.'

> [R v Mohan, 1994, page 25]

In this particular case, the appeal court judges decided that there was no data to show that Dr Hill's methodology was generally accepted, or that the matching of psychological profiles of this nature was a reliable process, or even that such distinct classes of profile could be defined in any reliable way. On this basis Dr Hill's evidence was declared inadmissible.

2.3.2   R v Abbey 2009

Following from Mohan, a later case reinforced and clarified the process whereby expert evidence may be admitted to the Canadian courts. In R v Abbey the expert witness, a sociologist, testified as to the links between styles of body tattoos and the culture of Canadian street gangs. In particular, the testimony was to the effect that the accused in a murder trial had a tear-drop tattoo on his face that the expert interpreted as a badge meaning that the wearer had killed a fellow gang member. The trial judge had excluded this evidence on the grounds of reliability, based on the alleged novelty of the area of study, the lack of relevant publications, unproven error rate and small sample size. The appeal court, however, ruled that this testimony was expert knowledge from the social sciences and should be subjected to a more flexible approach to admissibility. Daubert-style criteria were inappropriate here. In particular, the ruling emphasised that:

> '... the judge must perform a gate-keeping function by weighing whether, even if the proposed evidence meets the criteria for admission, its benefits to the trial process outweigh the risks of admitting it including the consumption of time, prejudice and whether the evidence is so complex that may confuse a jury.'
>
> [R v Abbey, 2009]

This case clarifies the role of the judge as a gatekeeper based on the Mohan rules, albeit that these are less rigorous than those defined by Daubert. Further, established forensic techniques have remained largely outside such scrutiny, which has been reserved for testimony based on novel areas of work.

2.3.3   R v Trochym 2007

More recently, there has been a move, through some Supreme Court rulings, to modify the Canadian position closer to the Daubert criteria, a tendency fuelled, to some extent, by the miscarriages of justice revealed over the past twenty years (see Chapter 1.3.3) and through a number of notable cases, for example that of R v Trochym. Stephen Trochym was found guilty of second-degree murder in 1995, following the killing of his girlfriend, Donna Hunter. Crucial identification evidence from a neighbour who testified that she saw Trochym entering the victim's apartment on the night of the murder was admitted at the original trial, despite only being obtained from the witness under hypnosis; a fact of which the jury were unaware. This evidence was later challenged in the court of appeal in Ontario on the grounds of inadmissibility.

On a majority verdict, the appeal court ruled that evidence obtained post-hypnosis was not admissible, as it was based on novel science and, as such, did not meet the necessary requirements. These shortcomings included an unknown error rate, the absence of any evidence on its accuracy or, indeed, of its acceptance as a valid area of study:

> 'When the factors for evaluating the reliability of novel scientific evidence are applied, it becomes evident that the technique of hypnosis and its impact on human memory are not understood well enough for post-hypnosis testimony to be sufficiently reliable in a court of law.'
>
> [R v Trochym, 2007]

The appeal court judges, to some extent, endorsed the Daubert criteria, by stating that they could provide a 'reliable foundation' for establishing the admissibility of novel scientific evidence, such as this witness statement obtained under hypnosis. Despite this, there has been no consistent referral to Daubert in the Canadian courts and, indeed, expert scientific evidence is rarely excluded on reliability grounds, particularly where routine or recognised methods are concerned.

2.4 Admissibility in Australia

Unsurprisingly, Australian laws of evidence are founded largely on the common law originating from England and Wales. In more recent times, however, they have developed independently and have also been less influenced by practices in the United States than has their fellow Commonwealth country of Canada. Like Canada, Australia has a federal system with the courts of the six states and two territories responsible for the majority of prosecutions, with the Federal Supreme Court being the ultimate arbiter. The Commonwealth Evidence Act (1995) was an attempt to bring some uniformity across the Federation (the Uniform Evidence Law or UEL) but, to date, only federal courts and some states have legislated to comply with this standard.

2.4.1 R v Bonython 1984

In recent decades, one of the more prominent issues has been whether the court should be able to cross-examine an expert witness on detailed matters of technical methodology when determining admissibility. This was the subject of an appeal to the Supreme Court of South Australia in R v Bonython.

In this case, the appellant, Bonython, was convicted of obtaining money by forging a signature but later appealed on the grounds that the testimony of the expert witness, Sergeant Daly, should not have been admitted. At the original trial, the judge had allowed an admissibility hearing of Daly's evidence, unusually in the presence of the jury, to establish his status as an expert in handwriting and signature analysis. Daly was asked by counsel about how he would arrive at an opinion based on his examination of signatures; in particular, what number of reference signatures would be required in order to reach a view as to whether a questioned signature had come from the same source.

> 'At that point the Judge ruled that that question related to the weight of the evidence and not to its admissibility. In the course of discussion with counsel, the learned Judge indicated his view that questions designed to establish that the materials upon which the witness formed his opinion were inadequate, related to weight and not to admissibility.'
>
> [Queen v Bonython, 1984]

The appeal court agreed with the trial judge on this point. They ruled that admissibility was based on two questions:

1. Does the subject matter of the opinion fall within the class of subjects upon which expert testimony is permissible and is it sufficiently organized or recognised to be accepted as a reliable body of knowledge?
2. Has the witness acquired by study or experience sufficient knowledge of the subject to render his opinion of value in resolving the issues before the court?

If these are both satisfied, as they were in this instance, then any discussion of the methodology relates to the weight of opinion. In other words, cross-examination aimed at disputing the testimony on matters of the techniques employed should ultimately influence the weight attached by the court to this evidence. Indeed, the expert may, in fact, refer to the reliability of aspects of the methodology in the testimony, in this case on the minimum number of reference signatures required.

2.4.2 Makita v Sprowles 2001

However, the courts' interest in the methods employed by the expert witness, and how these relate to the opinion itself, came to the fore at the New South Wales Court of Appeal in Makita v Sprowles. Ms Sprowles was employed by Makita Pty and was suing the company for injuries she received following a fall at work. At the original hearing, the expert witness, Professor Morton, gave testimony on whether the surface quality of a set of concrete stairs was sufficient to have contributed to the accident. The essence of his, highly technical, investigation was that the minimum safety threshold for slipping was represented by a friction coefficient of at least 0.4–0.5, whereas that for the stairs was 0.34. On this basis, the court accepted that the stairs were unsafe, assigned liability to the company and awarded a large sum of money in damages to Ms Sprowles.

Makita appealed against this verdict and the outcome overturned the original decision. The numerical values for the friction coefficients were challenged by the appeal court on the basis that, crucially, the precision of the numbers was not justified by Morton and there was no history of any previous slipping incidents on that particular set of stairs. On this basis, the appeal court preferred to draw their conclusion from this last point rather than from the expert's testimony:

> '… and so far as the opinion is based on assumed or accepted facts, they must be identified and proved in some other way; it must be established that the facts on which the opinion is based form a proper foundation for it … If all these matters are not made explicit, it is not possible to be sure whether the opinion is based wholly or substantially on the expert's specialised knowledge. If the court cannot be sure of that, the evidence is strictly speaking not admissible, and, so far as it is admissible, of diminished weight.'
>
> [Makita v Sprowles, 2001, paragraph 85]

This ruling linked admissibility directly to the reasoning processes by which the expert interpreted the factual data and reached an evaluation, and which would enable the court to determine the validity and reliability of that opinion. This is often called the 'basal principle'; that the opinion is rigorously based on the admissible facts, as determined by the expert.

2.4.3 Dasreef Pty Limited v Hawchar 2011

Nawaf Hawchar who worked as a stonemason for Dasreef, claimed that the silicosis disease, from which he suffered, was caused by unsafe levels of exposure to silica dust in the workplace. His counsel called Dr Basden, as an expert witness, in support of his claim for compensation at a Dust Diseases Tribunal in 2009. His claim was upheld but Dasreef appealed to the NSW Court of Appeal, which confirmed the decision in 2010. However, in a final appeal in 2011, the Australian Supreme Court ruled that the expert witness testimony was, at least in part, inadmissible, though the decision against Dasreef was upheld.

The crucial part of Dr Basden's testimony related to quantitative measures of the concentration of silica dust particles, arising from the typical work activities undertaken by Hawchar, and the comparison of these to the legal limits. He stated that these silica dust levels would be 'of the order of a thousand or more times' the prescribed maximum. In his report and under cross-examination, he gave various numerical values for silica dust concentrations and used expressions such as 'considerable proportion of' without defining what he meant. Further, he did not offer any calculations directly about the dust concentrations that Mr Hawchar may have experienced nor had he, in fact, measured these himself. The court was concerned that the expert's training and experience did not extend to detailed quantitative calculations and estimates of exposure under specific conditions, points initially agreed by Basden.

The appeal court summarised the position as:

'He gave no evidence of ever having measured respirable silica dust. He gave no evidence of having measured dust concentrations, or the respirable fractions of those concentrations, arising from the type of work the respondent was doing. He did not explain how he had reasoned from his specialised knowledge … accordingly the evidence was inadmissible'

[Dasreef v Hawchar, 2011, paragraph 137]

In ruling that this important aspect of the expert testimony was not admissible, the court was arguing that the numerical statements were not 'wholly or substantially based' on the knowledge of this particular expert witness. This was reinforced by adding:

'A failure to demonstrate that an opinion expressed by a witness is based on the witness's specialised knowledge based on training, study or experience is a matter that goes to the admissibility of the evidence, not its weight.'

[Dasreef v Hawchar, 2011, paragraph 42]

As in Makita, the admissibility of opinion was linked to the expertise of the witness and to the clarity of the arguments whereby the expert's opinion related to that expertise and was therefore reliable. It also implied that consideration of evidential weight should follow admissibility and they should not be seen as two sides of a single process. However, in practice, the Australian courts are reluctant to refer directly to reliability and, more usually, are liberal in admitting expert testimony, thus leaving:

'… questions about validity and reliability to the trial and the tribunal of fact.'

[Edmond, Cole, Cunliffe, and Roberts, 2013]

2.5   Admissibility in England and Wales

In England and Wales, the principles under which expert evidence is dealt, come from common law and the courts have taken a fairly relaxed and pragmatic approach, both to admissibility and to the criteria and qualifications that define an expert. Over the years, this approach has been amended and refined through occasional key cases at appeal, with no major changes or challenges arising from the courts. Indeed, the contradictions apparent in several rulings have done little to focus or clarify the admissibility criteria within this jurisdiction.

2.5.1 R v Turner 1975

Terence Turner was found guilty, in February 1974, of the murder of his girlfriend with a hammer, following her admission that he was not the father of the child she was carrying. Although he did not claim to have any mental illness, Turner appealed the guilty verdict, on the basis of psychiatric expert evidence that his was a crime of passion, reflecting the depth of his emotional attachment to her. However, the judge ruled that such evidence was inadmissible as, on such matters of 'common knowledge and experience', the court was in no need of expert advice. The appeal court ruling went on:

> 'An expert opinion is admissible to provide the court with scientific information which is likely to be outside of the experience of a judge or jury. If, on the proven facts, a judge or jury can form their own conclusions without help, then the opinion of an expert is unnecessary.'
>
> [R v Turner, 1975]

This provides a focus on the nature of expert testimony and a criterion for deciding when it may be declared inadmissible. If, in addition, the witness can convince the court as to the quality of their expertise, and of its relevance to the matters under consideration by the court, then their testimony will be admitted.

Interestingly, despite the activity elsewhere around the issue of reliability, the English courts appear to regard this as a matter for the court to address in the context of the weight of evidence, and hence no criteria have been discussed or proposed that might make this a condition underpinning the admissibility of expert testimony. On the other hand, there have been many relatively minor challenges to the qualifications and areas of expertise of witnesses, especially those for the defence, over recent years.

2.5.2 R v Gilfoyle 2001

Here, Gilfoyle was convicted of murdering his heavily pregnant wife by hanging, though the medical evidence alone was finely balanced between murder and suicide. Two appeals followed, the second in 2001 following referral from the CCRC, at which psychological profiling evidence, based on an apparent suicide note and other writings, was presented by the defence to show the deceased's state of mind at the time of her death. This testimony was declared inadmissible, not because of any doubts as to the expert's level of expertise, but because:

> '... his reports identify no criteria by reference to which the court could test the quality of his opinions: there is no data base comparing real and questionable suicides and there is no substantial body of academic writing approving his methodology.'
>
> [R v Gilfoyle, 2001, paragraph 25]

Similar testimony had been rejected elsewhere and this second appeal by Gilfoyle was unsuccessful.

This ruling provides criteria by which the substance of the area of expertise, and the reasoning by which the expert arrives at their opinion, may be tested when considering admissibility. Although reliability is not specifically mentioned, the matters listed in this ruling clearly relate to the foundations underpinning the testimony and the need for the court to understand how the opinion itself is justified by the factual basis identified by the expert witness. On the other hand, the appeal in the case of R v Luttrell moves the reliability issue away from admissibility towards the weight of opinion.

2.5.3 R v Luttrell 2004

In 2003, Gerrard Luttrell was found guilty at Reading Crown Court, along with six others, of handling stolen goods to a value of over six million pounds. He appealed against this conviction on the grounds that lip-reading evidence, taken from CCTV images, should not have been admitted as evidence, as it was novel and unreliable or, if admitted, the judge should have cautioned the jury as to its limitations. At the original trial, expert opinion was received from a qualified and experienced lip-reader on a conversation, involving Luttrell, about his criminal activities. However, when tested by another expert, the lip-reader was correct in only around half the words she interpreted and two other experts endorsed the inherent unreliability of such evidence, particularly from CCTV. Despite this, the trial judge ruled that the evidence was admissible and he rejected a submission that lip-reading did not comprise a reliable body of knowledge or experience.

The appeal court agreed with this view and, interestingly, referred to the criteria in the Australian Bonython case (1984) as providing the two conditions necessary for admissibility (see Chapter 2.4.1), though it was added that the weight of the opinion would be assessed by the jury. Counsel for Luttrell claimed that a further test should be applied, specifically to determine its reliability and validity, whereby the methodology should be explained to the court and subject to cross-examination. This was rejected on the grounds that lip-reading was an acquired expertise or skill, rather than a scientific discipline, and such testing would not be appropriate. This view is opposite to that taken in the United States in the Kumo Tire case, in 1999. Although it may be a necessary consideration when establishing admissibility, the expectation would be that reliability should contribute to the jury's deliberations on the significance of the evidence to the case. Unlike in Gilfoyle, this ruling clearly does not consider reliability as a primary factor when establishing admissibility.

Nevertheless, the appeal court did add that in this and similar cases, the judge should alert the jury to the limitations that may accompany lip-reading or similar evidence where the expert 'may not be completely accurate':

> '...a "special warning" is necessary if experience, research or common sense has indicated that there is a difficulty with a certain type of evidence that requires giving the jury a warning of its dangers and the need for caution, tailored to meet the needs of the case.'
>
> [R v Luttrell and others, 2004]

The view of the appeal court was that, at the original trial, the jury were properly informed of these limitations in the case of Luttrell and hence his appeal was rejected. This case demonstrates that a court may admit expert evidence that is known to be unreliable, as long as the jury is informed of the nature of this unreliability, which it then may take into account in its evaluation of the weight to be attached to the evidence.

It is pertinent to compare this court's view of lip-reading with that of the court in Gilfoyle when considering the rather more nebulous technique of psychological profiling. The area of expertise is certainly subject to scrutiny in determining admissibility but issues of reliability tend to be left to the jury to contend with as part of their deliberations on the weight of the evidence presented to them.

2.6   Conclusions on Admissibility

It is useful to summarise the range of issues relating to admissibility that have arisen across all these cases and others and how they impact on the core criteria of relevance and reliability. The diagram given in Figure 2.1 provides a flowchart indicating the main issues exposed in these cases and how they influence on the process of admitting and conveying expert opinion. This flow chart is generic with differences of emphasis, rather than in substance, across different jurisdictions.

2.6.1   Relevance and Expertise

Ensuring the evidence is outside the common knowledge of the court (1) and accepting that the witness is an expert (2) are relatively uncontroversial criteria and have been embedded into all these jurisdictions for some time. However, examples can arise where the judge may view the opinion, either in whole or in part, as something the jury is quite able to evaluate without expert assistance. A more serious issue involves determining how far the court needs to go to assess that the expertise being presented is wholly appropriate, and of sufficient depth, to prove reliable and accurate in each particular case.

2.6.2   The Scientific Basis of the Opinion

The heart of establishing reliability is enshrined in the following two points (3 and 4) and these are where most of the conflicting views and approaches have arisen within these landmark cases. In the United States, the Daubert criteria, in essence, cover these issues in a systematic way, though the wording is more detailed and specific than in this summary. Essentially the same areas of discussion have emerged in Canada, though not as explicitly as in Daubert and these have merged to some extent with relevancy and expertise. In contrast, in Australia and England, these criteria have been dealt with in a more flexible way by balancing doubts on admissibility, for example, on grounds of uncertain reliability, against the weight of evidence accorded to the opinion by the jury. On the other hand, the courts in these jurisdictions have been more cautious by highlighting the importance of the jury being fully informed as to the reasoning that led the expert from the factual basis to the opinion (5). This point was also picked up in the United States in Joiner. A common feature in the assessment of admissibility is the possible use of a separate hearing or *voir dire* process, for example, the Daubert hearing in the United States, at which the decision on admissibility may be made without the jury's involvement and before the trial commences (*in limine*). Despite the courts' awareness of reliability, and efforts such as Daubert to enshrine the assessment of reliability as key to admissibility, there is evidence that this is not reflected generally in the practice of courts across jurisdictions. As Edmond *et al.* put it:

'… too much incriminating opinion evidence, based on techniques of unknown value and expressed in terms whose influence on lay persons is simply unknown, is routinely admitted in criminal proceedings.'

[Edmond, Cole, Cunliffe, and Roberts, 2013]

1. Is the opinion evidence relevant?	*Is it outside the common knowledge of the court and will it assist the trier of fact?*
2. Is the witness qualified as an expert, through qualifications and experience?	*Is the expert qualified in the precise area of study needed to give opinion and in all aspects contributing to the opinion?*
3. Is the area of study an established field, a novel area of work or not scientific in nature?	*If there are any doubts on this aspect, should the evidence be exclude or admitted with a health warning to the jury?*
4. Is the methodology based on accepted scientific principles and valid as demonstrated through peer review and publications?	*Should the court require some measure of validity such as an error rate and how should this be interpreted by the jury? What measure of validity meets the admissibility standard?*
5. Has the reasoning by which the expert arrived at the opinion from the results of the method, been made clear to the court?	*If the reasoning is not clear or in doubt, should the evidence be excluded or the doubts considered by the jury when evaluating the weight of evidence?*
6. Should the expert provide a weight of evidence for the court as part of the opinion and how is that expressed?	*Is weight of evidence always required? Will the jury come to a view on this independently of the expert? Should unspecified unreliability contribute to weight of evidence?*

Figure 2.1   *Admissibility of Expert Opinion: A Summary of Issues From the Courts*

2.6.3 Weight of Evidence

Probably the most significant issue to emerge from this discussion has been how the weight of evidence is arrived at by the jury and how this relates to the content of any evaluation provided by the expert opinion (6). The main thrust of the Daubert approach was intended to ensure that only the results of scientific work arriving in court, which had been quality assured to be reliable and valid, could be put before the jury (the gatekeeper role). The issue of evaluation was not specifically addressed in these rules, as they aimed to deal directly with admissibility. Ideally, expert evidence either met the criteria and the jury determined the weight of evidence knowing that the science was valid and proven, or the expert opinion was excluded. However, the concept of evidence with unproven reliability being admitted, with its weight then in some way being evaluated by the jury, has been positively encouraged by some courts in England and Australia.

Over the past ten years or so, the whole debate around admissibility, and the increasing significance of establishing the reliability of evidence and how that might be achieved, has been a major contributor to the reviews of laws and guidelines related to expert evidence. While the status of forensic science itself has been more to the fore in the United States, in England, the inconsistent approaches taken by the courts with regard to reliability, has been the more prominent issue. As Redmayne declared:

'... the current [England and Wales] law is inadequate because no burden of proof is explicitly placed on the proponent of scientific evidence, and because current rules give little guidance to judges on the factors to take into account when reviewing scientific evidence.'

[Redmayne, 2001, p. 137]

This provides an appropriate lead into the discussions of the following chapter.

References

Dasreef Pty Limited v Hawchar (2011). HCA 21

Daubert v Merrell Dow Pharmaceuticals Inc, 509 US 579 113 S Ct 2786, 1993

Edmond G., Cole S., Cunliffe E. and Roberts R. (2013). Admissibility compared: the reception of incriminating expert evidence (i.e., forensic science) in four adversarial jurisdictions. *University of Denver Criminal Law Review*, 3, 31–109.

Federal Rules of Evidence (USA). [Online]. (1975). Available at http://www.gpo.gov/fdsys/pkg/STATUTE-88/pdf/STATUTE-88-Pg1926.pdf [Accessed 2 December 2015].

Frye v United States 293 F 1013 (DC Cir 1923)

General Electric Company v Joiner, 522 US 136 (1997).

Kumo Tire Company Ltd v Patrick Carmichael, 119 S Ct 1167 (1999).

Law Commission: Expert Evidence in Criminal Proceedings in England and Wales, Law Com No 235, The Stationary Office [Online]. (2011). Available at https://www.gov.uk/government/uploads/system/uploads/attachment_data/file/229043/0829.pdf [Accessed 2 December 2015].

Makita (Australia) Pty Ltd v Sprowles [2001] NSWCA 305

Queen v Bonython [1984] 38 S A S R 45

R v Abbey [2009] 97 O R (3d) 330

R v Gilfoyle [2001] 2 Cr App R

R v Luttrell and others R v Dawson and another [2004] EWCA Crim 1344

R v Mohan [1994] 2 S C R 9, [1994] S C J No 36

R v Trochym [2007] S C C 6

R v Turner [1975] 1 All ER 70

Redmayne M. (2001). *Expert Evidence and Criminal Justice*. Oxford: Oxford University Press.
United States v Dennis Mooney, 315 F 3d 54 2002
United States v Stifel, 433 F 2d 431 1970

Further Reading

Bernstein D.E. and Jackson J.D. (2004). The Daubert Trilogy in the States, *Jurimetrics Journal*, 44, 351–366.

Boylan-Kemp J. (2008). *English Legal System: the fundamentals*. Sweet and Maxwell.

Cromwell The Hon T.A. (2011). The challenges of scientific evidence, The Macfadyen Lecture [Online]. Available at http://www.scottishlawreports.org.uk/publications/macfadyen-2011.html [Accessed 2 December 2015].

Durston G. (2005). The admissibility of novel "fields" of expert evidence. *Justice of the Peace*, 169, 968–971.

Edmond G. (2012). Is reliability sufficient? The Law Commission and expert evidence in international and interdisciplinary perspective (Part 1). *International Journal of Evidence and Proof*, 16(1), 30–65.

Edmond G. and Roach K. (2011). A contextual approach to the admissibility of the state's forensic science and medical evidence. *University of Toronto Law Journal*, 61(3), 343–409.

Federal Rules of Evidence (USA) [Online]. (2015). Available at http://federalevidence.com/downloads/rules.of.evidence.pdf [Accessed 2 December 2015].

Giannelli P. (1994). Daubert: Interpreting the Federal Rules of Evidence, *Cardoza Law Review*, 15, 1999–2026.

Imwinkelried E.J. (1981). A new era in the evolution of scientific evidence – A primer on evaluating the weight of scientific evidence, *William and Mary Law Review*, 23(2), 261–290. Available at http://scholarship.law.wm.edu/wmlr/vol23/iss2/4 [Accessed 2 December 2015].

Kiely T.F. (2006). *Forensic Evidence: science and the criminal law,* 2nd Ed. CRC Press.

Kumar M. (2011). Admissibility of expert evidence: Proving the basis for an expert's opinion, *Sydney Law Review*, 33, 427–457.

Moriarty J.C. and Saks M.J. (2005). Forensic science: grand goals, tragic flaws, and judicial gatekeeping, *Judges' Journal*, 44(4), 16–33.

Page M., Taylor J. and Blenkin M. (2011). Forensic identification science evidence since Daubert: part II – judicial reasoning in decisions to exclude forensic identification evidence on grounds of reliability. *Journal of Forensic Sciences*, 56(4), 913–917.

3

Forensic Science and the Law:
The Path Forward

Following from concerns about the reliability of forensic evidence, both in the context of miscarriages of justice and from the appeal court rulings related to the admissibility of expert opinion, it became inevitable that there would be some reaction both from the legislature and from the judiciary. In some jurisdictions, bodies were set up to review, not only the laws and guidelines around expert evidence, but also the organisation and delivery of forensic science. In Canada, the focus was on high-profile inquiries into the miscarriages of justice themselves, whereas in several countries, national legal organisations attempted to enhance the understanding of scientific evidence by the courts through publishing authoritative documents on scientific method, terminology, data analysis and statistics, as well as detailed explanations of particular techniques and methods, intended for an audience of judges and lawyers.

This chapter reviews and critically assesses these developments across the United States, Canada, Australia and England. The intention is to determine the current approaches to admissibility across these jurisdictions, to identify pertinent similarities and differences and to discover whether any of the present systems for dealing with scientific expert testimony in the courts may be considered to have overcome the difficulties faced in the recent past.

3.1 National and Legal Developments in the United States

In the United States, post-Daubert, issues surrounding the admissibility of expert evidence formed only one part of a growing disquiet with forensic science that included not the scientific reliability of the evidence itself, but concerns over the resourcing and organisation

Forensic Evidence in Court: Evaluation and Scientific Opinion, First Edition. Craig Adam.
© 2016 John Wiley & Sons, Ltd. Published 2016 by John Wiley & Sons, Ltd.

of the discipline, standards of quality assurance and indeed notable examples of fraudulent testimony from expert witnesses. Consequently, the US Congress decided, in 2006, to initiate a comprehensive, national study of forensic science that led to the National Research Council (NRC) report, Strengthening Forensic Science in the United States: A Path Forward, published in 2009. In addition to this, the publication of the Reference Manual on Scientific Evidence by the National Judicial Center, and the National Research Council in 1994, and its later editions in 2000 and 2011, provided a forum for the scientific and legal communities to review and record current best practice in all aspects of working with and presenting scientific evidence in the court. In parallel, the Federal Rules of Evidence were updated in 2000, and again in 2011, to reflect the national legal position on admissibility and reliability, following from Daubert and related cases.

3.1.1 Federal Rules of Evidence

The Federal Rules of Evidence were introduced in 1975 and have been amended in various ways over the past forty years or so. Courts at state level admit evidence according to their own rules. Of particular interest to the current discussion are those federal rules that apply specifically to expert opinion. Relevance in the context of expert evidence is governed by rules 401, 402 and 403, the first originally drafted as:

> '"Relevant evidence" means evidence having any tendency to make the existence of any fact that is of consequence to the determination of the action more probable or less probable than it would be without the evidence.'
> [Federal Rules of Evidence, 1975, Rule 401; see Federal Evidence Review, 2015]

Rule 402 confirmed that relevance was a prerequisite to admissibility, whereas Rule 403 dealt with instances where relevant evidence may be excluded:

> '… if its probative value is substantially outweighed by the danger of unfair prejudice, confusion of the issues, or misleading the jury, or by considerations of undue delay, waste of time, or needless presentation of cumulative evidence.'
> [Federal Rules of Evidence, 1975, Rule 403; see Federal Evidence Review, 2015]

The admissibility of expert opinion is dealt with in Rule 702. This does not relate or refer to the Frye criterion, which was not universally adopted by all states. More specifically, Rule 702 appears to focus more on the expertise of the witness than on the scientific foundations of the testimony, though the detailed interpretation of this rule has been the subject of much debate since its inception. Rule 702 also appears to offer a more liberal threshold for admissibility than does Frye. Indeed, the relationship between the Frye criterion and Rule 702 was referred to as the 'most controversial and important unresolved question' by judges Becker and Orenstein, as late as 1992.

> 'If scientific, technical, or other specialized knowledge will assist the trier of fact to understand the evidence or to determine a fact in issue, a witness qualified as an expert by knowledge, skill, experience, training, or education, may testify thereto in the form of an opinion or otherwise.'
> [Federal Rules of Evidence, 1975, Rule 702; see Federal Evidence Review, 2015]

However, following the Daubert Trilogy, rulings and concurrent debate, Federal Rule 702 was radically amended in 2000 to include a significant addition reflecting the four points in the Daubert test. This was further rephrased in 2011 to the version now in current use (2015):

> 'A witness who is qualified as an expert by knowledge, skill, experience, training, or education may testify in the form of an opinion or otherwise if:
>
> a. the expert's scientific, technical, or other specialized knowledge will help the trier of fact to understand the evidence or to determine a fact in issue;
> b. the testimony is based on sufficient facts or data;
> c. the testimony is the product of reliable principles and methods; and
> d. the expert has reliably applied the principles and methods to the facts of the case.'
>
> [Federal Rules of Evidence, 2015, Rule 702; see Federal Evidence Review, 2015]

The importance of this rule is that it reveals that the impact of the Daubert Trilogy on US law was considerable and resulted in the essence of these rulings being enshrined in national legal guidelines. In particular, the importance of reliability, both of the underpinning science and methodology and of the manner in which the scientist has implemented these in the context of any particular case, are explicit in Rule 702.

3.1.2   Strengthening Forensic Science in the United States 2009

In seeking to strengthen forensic science, the NRC report explored an extensive range of factors contributing to the reliability and hence admissibility of scientific evidence, thereby recognising that the ultimate aim of the discipline is to serve the courts. In doing so, it acknowledged the example of DNA profiling technology that demonstrated how a strong scientific research base, underpinning a forensic technique, could not only enhance the quality and reliability of the evidence, but also the subsequent testimony. In contrast, many examples from established areas of forensic science, including the gold standard of finger-prints, were criticised for an absence of a scientific rigour, potentially leading to unreliable and faulty expert testimony.

> 'In a number of forensic science disciplines, forensic science professionals have yet to establish either the validity of their approach or the accuracy of their conclusions, and the courts have been utterly ineffective in addressing this problem'
>
> [NRC Report 2009, p. 53]

In attempting to implement the Daubert criteria, and unequivocally establish the scientific validity of evidence, the courts were acting to quality assure, not only the forensic process, but also the forensic practitioners, a role that clearly lay outside both their capability and their remit. The responsibility for this should lie with the forensic community itself. The solution recommended by the report was a systematic and thorough overhaul of both the discipline, and its delivery across the country, in an attempt to ensure that only reliable, valid and accurate scientific evidence, which was clearly admissible as testimony reached the courts. Consequently, the report established clear links to admissibility from every strand of the forensic process, and hence the rationale of its recommendations was that if the issues around each part of the process were resolved, then the path from crime scene to court would be quality assured and reliable expert testimony would follow.

The key points in its recommendations were:

A National Institute

A national body should be formed – The National Institute of Forensic Science – to promote 'the development of forensic science into a mature field of multidisciplinary research and practice'. This became a federal advisory committee – the National Commission on Forensic Science – on its foundation in 2014.

Best Practice

Best practice should be identified, disseminated and regulated across the sector. This included the use of standard terminology in reporting results and the implementation of model laboratory reports for particular types of evidence. All laboratories would operate under routine quality control processes that would identify errors, fraud and bias, thereby ensuring the validity and reliability of experimental results while also providing a means for the enhancement of quality.

Quality Standards

A standards framework would be established that provided for the accreditation of forensic laboratories and the certification of scientists and other expert practitioners. This framework should be referenced to international standards, such as ISO. Mandatory certification would be required to practise as a professional forensic scientist and hence to prepare and deliver expert testimony in the court. It was proposed that all laboratories should operate separately from, and independently of, law enforcement agencies such as police forces or public prosecutors.

A Robust Research Base

At the heart of the report was a call for a sound, peer-reviewed research base underpinning all casework in forensic science and medicine. This was seen to be an essential prerequisite in ensuring that forensic analyses and investigations were accurate, based on valid methods and provided reliable results. Moreover, fundamental studies were required to quantify and to determine the limits of accuracy and reliability for forensic techniques applied in realistic casework scenarios. Additional funded research was required into sources of human error and issues of bias in carrying out and interpreting experimental work, and to quantify these aspects.

Education and Training

To ensure good forensic science and to reinforce the credibility of the discipline, well-qualified and trained forensic scientists were regarded as essential. This could only be achieved through improvements to educational programmes, at both undergraduate and graduate level, and some oversight of the standards of these by accreditation processes. Legal professionals, from judges to law students, should receive some forensic science education, including the interpretation of experimental results. There should be a national code of ethics for all practising forensic scientists.

The net outcomes of these reforms was summed up in the following:

'With more and better educational programs, accredited laboratories, certification of forensic practitioners, sound operational principles and procedures, and serious research to establish the limits and measures of performance in each discipline, forensic science experts will be better able to analyze evidence and coherently report their findings in the courts.'

[NRC Report 2009, p. 53]

Progress on implementing these recommendations has been reported from the National Institute for Justice in February 2014.

3.1.3   US Reference Manual on Scientific Evidence

The Federal Judicial Center has published its reference manual on scientific evidence periodically, since the first edition in 1994, to assist judges in dealing with scientific evidence in the courts. The intention was to provide an authoritative reference source for consultation where complex scientific or statistical matters need to be resolved. The second edition emerged in 2000, post-Daubert and Joiner, and after it was known that Rule 702 was to be modified to reflect these rulings. The most recent (third) edition was produced in 2011 after the NRC report had been digested by the legal and scientific communities.

The majority of the manual is concerned with discussions around specific forms of scientific evidence. However, an early chapter on admissibility provides a detailed review of relevant issues, in particular the operation of the Daubert criteria across US courts in recent years. Reflecting on the origins of Daubert within commercial rather than criminal litigation, Margaret Berger remarks:

'To date, Daubert has rarely been raised in the forensic context, but this may be about to change. We do not know as yet what shifts may occur in response to the National Academies' highly critical report on the forensic sciences.'

[US Reference Manual on Scientific Evidence, 3rd Ed, 2011, p. 26]

There was little evidence in the recent past that the existence of the Daubert guidelines had any great impact on the admissibility of prosecution expert opinion, as there had been only occasional limitations imposed by the courts on their testimony. However, it was anticipated that courts may in future challenge such opinion in specific areas. These included the validity of the forensic techniques, evidence of error rates and proficiency testing of experts, laboratory quality controls and accreditation, an awareness of expert bias and the expectation of detailed challenges from the defence counsel. Amongst serious concerns were whether Daubert limited the judges' discretion in dealing with complex cases, whether the jury's influence had been reduced in favour of that of the judge in assessing the credibility of the expert and of the testimony and whether the courts have the capability to reach admissibility decisions that are embedded in science.

In conclusion, it is evident that, although the Daubert rulings and the consequent changes to the rules of evidence may appear to provide clear and rational guidelines to the courts on admissibility, in practice, there are fresh difficulties and these may in fact be exacerbated as the developments within forensic science, as laid down in the NRC report, have an impact on the scientific evidence entering the legal system in the years ahead.

3.2 National and Legal Developments in Canada

Current practice on admissibility and reliability of expert evidence in Canada has been informed principally through experience with a number of cases of miscarriage of justice over the past twenty years, as well as by the case law set, both through notable appeals such as Mohan and Abbey, and by the parallel experience within the United States, most significantly in Daubert. Although it is not the case that Canada has had more cases of miscarriage of justice than in comparable jurisdictions, the country has been consistent in its practice of carrying out high-profile, judge-led provincial or federal inquiries into such incidents. These have included the cases of Morin (1998), Sophonow (2001), Driskel (2007) and the Goudge Report (2008). These inquiries have contributed recommendations related, not only to expert opinion and the courts, but also to police and prosecution procedures, and technical and organ-isational matters for the forensic science provider. Indeed the impact of these inquiries has been so significant that the Canadian Department of Justice has produced two reports drawing together the work of these inquiries; the first Report on the Prevention of Miscarriage of Justice in 2005, followed by The Path to Justice: Preventing Wrongful Convictions in 2011.

Despite this wealth of largely consistent rulings and recommendations, there have been no statutory changes to the law governing expert opinion in Canada, and it has fallen to the National Judicial Institute (a not-for-profit, independent institution in Ottawa) to produce the NJI Science Manual for Canadian Judges (2013), which provides detailed guidance on many matters related to the interface between science and the law within the courtroom. A further consequence of these reports has been the review and limited reform of the delivery of forensic science in Canada, more specifically Ontario, quite independently of and prior to, the NRC report in the United States.

3.2.1 Legal Enquiries into Miscarriages of Justice

It was evident from the series of inquiries that the state had to review the role and duties of the expert witness and, in particular, to prevent the presentation of biased and unreliable scientific testimony. For example, in Goudge (2008) the pathologist Dr Charles Smith had never received any formal training or advice for the role and, as he was called by the prosecution, believed that he was acting for them and that it was his purpose to support their case as far as possible. However, ensuring expert witnesses were independent, and did not give partisan opinion, formed only part of the reforms coming from these inquiries. A key recommendation from the 2005 report, and re-iterated in 2011, was that:

'Prosecutors should not shy away from the use and reliance on novel scientific technique or theory in the appropriate situation providing there is a sufficient foundation to establish the reliability and necessity of these opinions and that the probative value does not exceed the potential prejudicial effects.'

[Report on the prevention of miscarriages of justice, 2005]

This report reviewed many of the recent landmark appeal cases and declared support, both for the four point admissibility test proposed in Mohan, and the gatekeeper role for the judge, as emphasised in Abbey. In reference to Mohan, the Goudge report declared that this approach:

'... is consistent with both the evolving nature of science and the responsibility of the trial judge as gatekeeper to exclude expert evidence that is insufficiently reliable. The justice system should place a premium on the reliability of expert evidence if it is to maximize the contribution of that evidence to the truth-seeking function and be faithful to the fundamental fairness required of the criminal process.'

[The Goudge Inquiry, 2008, p. 484]

It was suggested that judges had become lax in acting as gatekeeper, thereby falling back on reliance on the jury to assess reliability, as a contributing factor to the weight of evidence.

Again, in Goudge it was reported that expert opinion had been admitted repeatedly, based only on the reputation of the individual and the report defined ten pitfalls into which expert testimony too often fell. These included biased opinion, overstating the case, speculation, use of casual language and attacking colleagues.

To assist in establishing the reliability of evidence, it was proposed that judges set up pre-trial meetings ('hot-tubbing'), involving expert witnesses from both sides, in order to discuss any technical or other issues of dispute. Following this, they would convey to the court the points on which they were all agreed and those where dispute remained. Following from an amendment in 2010, this expert conference now forms part of the Federal Courts Rules (SOPR/98-106).

3.2.2   The Science Manual for Canadian Judges

The NJI Science Manual for Canadian Judges (2013) was primarily aimed at enhancing the judiciary's understanding of the scientific method, its application to the analysis and inter-pretation of forensic evidence and to provide a basic knowledge of how statistics, including Bayesian inference, can inform expert testimony. This was intended to strengthen the ability of the trial judge in deciding whether to admit scientific evidence and hence enhance the gatekeeper role. In the foreword to the third chapter, entitled 'Managing and Evaluating Expert Evidence in the Courtroom', the Honourable Ian Binnie states:

'The heart of the debate is reliability. The court's focus has to be on what is said, not just the credentials and demeanour of who says it. Moreover, a lot of court time may be wasted unless the trial judge properly exercises a 'gatekeeper' function to exclude expert evidence that is unreliable, or beyond the expertise of the witness, or is wholly unnecessary to the disposition of the case.'

[NJI Science Manual, 2013, p. 144]

The rulings of the appeal court in Mohan and Abbey are presented as providing the legal framework for admitting expert opinion. Thus, the four pre-conditions are re-iterated from Abbey:

1. 'The proposed opinion must relate to a subject matter that is properly the subject of expert opinion evidence;
2. The witness must be qualified to give the opinion;
3. The proposed opinion must not run afoul of any exclusionary rule apart entirely from the expert opinion rule; and
4. The proposed opinion must be logically relevant to a material issue. Logical relevance exists if the evidence has a tendency as a matter of human experience and logic to make the existence or non-existence of a fact in issue more or less likely than it would be without the evidence.'

[NJI Science Manual, 2013, p. 167]

If these are satisfied, the gatekeeper role acts to ensure that admitting the evidence will be of benefit to the court, taking into account any potential prejudicial effect it may have. The Guide systematically discusses the factors any trial judge needs to consider when evaluating the four criteria, such as whether the evidence is necessary to the case, whether the science is novel and ensuring the expert opinion is impartial and unbiased. Particular attention needs to be given to factors that directly impact on the threshold for admissibility. These include:

- Factors related to the expert's discipline:

  Such as whether it is an accepted field of study, whether the science is novel or controversial and whether the methodology is documented and peer-reviewed.

- Factors related to the expert's qualifications or experience:

  In particular, the credentials, including education, training and experience, underpinning the expertise, that verify the independence of the expert from those undertaking the investigation and the extent to which the opinion depends on data external to the case.

- Factors related directly to the actual opinion:

  Including whether the opinion lies within the boundaries of the expertise, is non- speculative, has a clear basis on proven facts, and whether the reasoning on which it is founded is made clear to the court.

- Factors relating to the methodology used in arriving at the opinion:

  These relate closely to the criteria set out in Daubert and include testing of the underlying theory and evidence of peer review and publication, the known error rate for the method and whether it is accepted by the scientific peer community.

Caution and flexibility in applying the last of these factors is advised, particularly when dealing with expert evidence that is on the fringes of science or where the full rigour of the scientific method is in doubt. Equally, where a clear scientific basis is established, the Guide provides further detail on how these Daubert-related criteria should be examined.

In conclusion, it is evident that, within the Canadian justice system, there is considerable support for testing the reliability of expert testimony as a precondition to admissibility and that this process embeds and enhances the Daubert criteria as demonstrated by this most recent published document. To what extent this is reflected in judicial practice or whether the jury bear the burden of incorporating doubtful reliability into their overall evaluation of the evidence remains to be seen.

3.3   National and Legal Developments in Australia

Under the Australian Evidence Act (1995), the Uniform Rules of Evidence were established to supersede those based on common law; these now govern the admissibility of expert evidence. At the time, the law commission was clear that the Frye test or related criteria were not to be included, and that these rules would be based on a statement about specialist knowledge, together with supplementary statements, which included the exclusion of evidence on prejudicial grounds and which provided considerable latitude on the judge's part in reaching a decision. Despite reviews, these rules have remain unchanged and are seemingly immune to influences from the evolution of, and experiences in admitting, expert opinion across other jurisdictions since they were first drawn up.

3.3.1   The Uniform Rules of Evidence

Rule 79 defines opinion evidence as 'specialised knowledge based on the person's training, study or experience'. It does not mention that this specialist knowledge should be an established field and have general acceptance by the scientific community, or include any reference to the validity of the methodology. This point has been highlighted by Justice McClellan:

> 'Under the Act an expert witness is not required to identify the particular field from which they draw their knowledge and demonstrate that that field is reliable by reference to considerations of peer review, legitimacy or testability.'
>
> [McClellan, 2009]

However, McClellan suggests that the possession of specialist knowledge, in itself, ensures some reliability of the opinion, though this relates to the reliability of the science underpinning the opinion, rather than of the opinion itself, which is what is understood in jurisdictions such as the United States.

Rules 135 and 137 offer the potential for significant debate where admissibility is challenged.

> '**Rule 135 General discretion to exclude evidence**
> The court may refuse to admit evidence if its probative value is substantially outweighed by the danger that the evidence might:
>
> a. be unfairly prejudicial to a party; or
> b. be misleading or confusing; or
> c. cause or result in undue waste of time.'
>
> [Australian Evidence Act, 1995]

Rule 135 may be used, for example, to exclude testimony based on new areas of expertise or methodologies that have not yet had their validity fully demonstrated.

> '**Rule 137 Exclusion of prejudicial evidence in criminal proceedings**
> In a criminal proceeding, the court must refuse to admit evidence adduced by the prosecutor if its probative value is outweighed by the danger of unfair prejudice to the defendant.'
>
> [Australian Evidence Act, 1995]

Rule 137 relates admissibility directly to the weight of the evidence and sets a threshold whereby testimony must be excluded if it is of low value to the debate and its inclusion may unfairly influence the jury against the defendant. Note that Rule 137 is mandatory ('must refuse'), whereas Rule 135 is simply advisory ('may refuse'). Neither of these rules includes an explicit reference to reliability or indeed any other factors deemed important by the Daubert ruling in the United States. In addition, these rules do not reflect the provision under common law for the disclosure of the factual basis of the opinion to be a requirement for admissibility. This point was reinforced in the appeal of Makita v Sprowles, but many judges regard this as a 'counsel of perfection', preferring to take a more lenient line and relying on the strategy of balancing doubts on reliability against the weight accorded to the evidence.

> 'It is plain that there has been considerable resistance to the stringent application of Makita to expert opinion evidence in circumstances where it may be impractical, or indeed impossible to prove the factual basis upon which an opinion has been formulated.'
>
> [McClellan, 2009]

Interestingly, a survey of Australian judges by Freckleton *et al.* (1999), a few years after these rules came into being, reveals that the reliability of expert opinion was very much in their minds when considering admissibility, but there were different schools of thought on the detail of how this should be dealt with. Around 70% of respondents admitted to not always understanding expert opinion and a large minority overall supported the use of pre-trial hearings, possibly including input from external referees or assessors as a means of testing reliability and ensuring that the opinion was fair and reasonable.

> 'Decision-makers need to look for touchstones of reliability, indicia including the expert being impartial, a disinclination by the expert to step beyond their limits of expertise, and a familiarity on the part of the expert with the relevant facts'
>
> [Freckleton *et al.*, 1999]

These criteria, though worthy, are a far cry from the apparent clarity and rigour of those set out in Daubert only a few years before. It is no great surprise then to find that the survey revealed that the majority of judges believed that reliability should not be a precondition to admissibility, though around a quarter indicated that it should.

Although it appears that the admissibility of expert opinion in the Australian courts is now enshrined within these established rules of evidence and that the judiciary largely believe that issues of reliability can be dealt with through these rules, there is much evidence that this is not always the case. In particular, where the reliability of evidence is unknown or in doubt, Rule 137 provides a means for excluding it. Judges are reluctant to exclude evidence on grounds of doubtful reliability, preferring to admit it and let the grounds of the opinion, its validity and its reliability be scrutinised through cross-examination. This favours the prosecution since the burden is then on the defence to demonstrate that the evidence is unreliable. The consequence of these actions is that the assessment both of reliability and of the weight of evidence, too often falls on the jury rather than the court playing its part in providing some reliability threshold for the admission of expert opinion.

3.4   National and Legal Developments in England and Wales

Over a period of almost ten years, a series of inquiries, consultations and reports on expert evidence and the law took place in England and Wales, which led, in the end, more or less to retention of the status quo. This process was initiated partly through pressure from both the scientific and legal professions and partly as a result of an inquiry by the House of Commons Science and Technology Select Committee, published in 2005, entitled 'Forensic Science on Trial'.

3.4.1   Forensic Science on Trial 2005

The principal aim of this inquiry was to investigate the consequences for criminal justice of government plans to continue to reduce the costs to the state of running the England and Wales national Forensic Science Service, through ongoing part-privatisations. However, the committee took a broader scope by also examining the delivery of forensic services to the courts through expert witness testimony. In doing so, they admitted that the committee was 'in danger of straying into areas beyond our remit in looking at the courts'. This included consideration of cases from the recent past that had proved to be miscarriages of justice, such as the convictions of Sally Clark and Angela Cannings, as well as those relating to the troubles in Northern Ireland, including that of the 'Birmingham Six'.

> 'Although we accept that flaws in expert evidence are unlikely to have led, in isolation, to a significant number of miscarriages of justice, it is impossible to determine the number of cases which have been adversely affected by the conduct of an expert, or the handling of expert evidence in court. We emphasise that where miscarriages of justice have arisen in association with problems in expert evidence, this reflects a systems failure.'
>
> [Forensic Science on Trial, Summary, 2005]

The response of the report was to recommend various measures that could be put in place to improve and monitor the trial process, including improvements to the scrutiny of scientific evidence and to communication between the legal and scientific professions, in addition to the registration of expert witnesses, pre-trial meetings and a review of the wording used in conveying evaluative statements.

It was proposed that a Forensic Science Advisory Council be set up to provide oversight of science within the criminal justice system. After taking evidence from several leading scientists and legal authorities on the issue of admissibility, the committee's view was clear:

> 'The absence of an agreed protocol for the validation of scientific techniques prior to their being admitted in court is entirely unsatisfactory. Judges are not well-placed to determine scientific validity without input from scientists. We recommend that one of the first tasks of the Forensic Science Advisory Council be to develop a "gate keeping" test for expert evidence. This should be done in partnership with judges, scientists and other key players in the criminal justice system, and should build on the US Daubert test.'
>
> [Forensic Science on Trial, 2005, paragraph 173]

Although this council was, in fact, set up under the office of the Forensic Science Regulator (see Chapter 4.4.2), this report, together with further calls from within the legal and scientific professions, also prompted the Law Commission of England and Wales to establish a consultation process to review the manner in which the admissibility and understanding of expert evidence was handled within the justice system and to propose changes to the law. The consultation paper was published in 2009 and, following a further review, the final report was published in 2011.

3.4.2   The Law Commission Report 2011

The Commission's starting point was that past cases of miscarriage of justice demonstrated that expert evidence was being admitted with insufficient scrutiny and that the common law approach, currently operating, was too *laissez-faire*, resulting in evidence being admitted without its reliability being questioned in sufficient detail. They were particularly concerned of instances, such as in the Sally Clark case, where the jury's view of complex scientific evidence amounted to accepting the expert opinion without question, rather than their engaging in their own evaluation of highly technical matters that were difficult to understand in sufficient depth. Their over-arching conclusion was that:

> '... special rules are required for assessing the reliability of expert evidence as a factor bearing on admissibility, and that opinion evidence with insufficient indicia of reliability (that is, pointers to reliability) ought not to be admitted in criminal proceedings.'
> [The Law Commission, Expert Evidence in Criminal Proceedings, 2011, paragraph 1.11]

Thus, the Law Commission, once again, supported a gatekeeping role for the judge based on a set of admissibility guidelines, similar to those provided by Daubert. The report reinforced reliability as a necessary requirement for admissibility, emphasised the need for the scientific or expertise base for the opinion to be sound and the strength of the opinion to be justified by the material on which it was based. Like Daubert, it rejected, as inadmissible, any opinion based on a flawed or unproven hypothesis.

However, the admissibility rules would not need to be applied in all cases; for example, for evidence based on established techniques. Expert evidence would be assumed reliable and hence admissible unless it was challenged on reasonable grounds and if so, there would be a hearing to resolve admissibility, in the absence of the jury and before the trial, with the provision for input from a panel of independent experts.

Where the gatekeeping test needed to be applied, the Law Commission Report (2011, paragraph 5.35) provided a list of factors that, where relevant, should guide the decision of the court:

> '(a) the extent and quality of the data on which the expert's opinion is based, and the validity of the methods by which they were obtained'

This reflects the Daubert criteria. By emphasising validity, it requires that the specific methodology should be accepted by the community, have been subject to testing and calibration and that accepted standard procedures have been adhered to.

> '(b) if the expert's opinion relies on an inference from any findings, whether the opinion properly explains how safe or unsafe the inference is (whether by reference to statistical significance or in other appropriate terms)'

This relates to the 'error rate' in the opinion, rather than in the experimental methodology that form the basis of that opinion. By doing so, it demonstrates an increasing awareness by the courts of the importance of statistical considerations in the interpretation of findings, and in the evaluative process, and how that aspect may be conveyed to the court as part of the testimony. This factor was not explicit in Daubert.

> '(c) if the expert's opinion relies on the results of the use of any method (for instance, a test, measurement or survey), whether the opinion takes proper account of matters, such as the degree of precision or margin of uncertainty, affecting the accuracy or reliability of those results;'

This factor directly reflects the error rate in the method which is a prominent feature within the Daubert criteria and which has troubled US courts and scientists over the past years.

However, here the factor is written in a more pragmatic, qualitative fashion without inclusion of the term 'error rate' itself.

'(d) the extent to which any material upon which the expert's opinion is based has been reviewed by others with relevant expertise (for instance, in peer-reviewed publications), and the views of those others on that material'

The inclusion of a criterion related to the acceptance of the basis of the opinion within its field of study, as demonstrated by peer review, publication or other evidence, is one of the core admissibility factors both within Daubert and across other jurisdictions.

'(e) the extent to which the expert's opinion is based on material falling outside the expert's own field of expertise'

Here, the purpose is to establish the limits of the expert's expertise and the relationship between that and the scope of the testimony being offered. This is not explicit in Daubert, but was the subject of the Australian ruling in Dasreef v Hawchar in 2011.

'(f) the completeness of the information which was available to the expert, and whether the expert took account of all relevant information in arriving at the opinion (including information as to the context of any facts to which the opinion relates)'

This factor introduces the importance of the context of the case to the formation of opinion, as well as relating to the process followed by the expert in reasoning from the results to arriving at the opinion and whether that is clear to the court. The first point is now recognised as an important factor for the scientist to engage with, as part of interpretation and evaluation, while the second relates, to some extent, to the US court ruling in Joiner (1997).

'(g) whether there is a range of expert opinion on the matter in question; and, if there is, where in the range the expert's opinion lies and whether the expert's preference for the opinion proffered has been properly explained'

This relates partly to (b) and (f) and partly to peer views and practice within the field of study. Its aim is to facilitate the court's understanding of potential uncertainties in the opinion itself, through assessing any variation amongst experts in the evaluation of the same set of findings. This fairly subtle point was not part of Daubert.

'(h) whether the expert's methods followed established practice in the field; and, if they did not, whether the reason for the divergence has been properly explained'

The final factor arises directly from the need to follow standard and acceptable procedures in carrying out the methodology that was an important part of the Daubert criteria. It is explicit that, if these were not fully implemented, then departures from standard practice should be explained to the court and any impact on reliability assessed. This report also made recommendations on the presentation and delivery of expert testimony to the courts (paragraph 7.21).

3.4.3 The Royal Statistical Society Guides

One positive contribution to enhancing the understanding of statistical aspects of the evaluation of evidence, came from a series of authoritative practitioner guides, produced under the auspices of the Royal Statistical Society, from 2010. These were intended, not only for forensic scientists acting as expert witnesses, but also for the lawyers and judges involved in debates over such testimony.

3.4.4   HCSTSC Report Forensic Science 2013

A second report into forensic science was produced by the House of Commons Science and Technology Select Committee in 2013 that aimed to assess the consequences to the criminal justice system of the closure of the England and Wales Forensic Science Service initiated by the government in 2010, including the ongoing development of future provision within the private sector. On this front the committee concluded that there was a risk that research was not being fully exploited and new technologies were not being effectively implemented within the criminal justice system. Moreover, that government policy:

> '... runs the risk of continuing the pattern of short-sighted decision-making that led to the demise of the FSS and the creation of an unstable market for the remaining commercial providers.'
>
> [House of Commons STSC report, Forensic Science, 2013, summary]

Once again, it included discussion of expert evidence within its agenda and received reports and interviewed leading professional figures as part of its investigation. The content of the Law Commission's report, published in the previous year and awaiting a formal government response, was known to all those involved. Although the chair of the Criminal Bar Association felt that the current system was fit for purpose, support for testing the reliability of expert evidence through a set of rules came both from the chair of the Law Society's Criminal Law Committee and from the Forensic Science Regulator. The latter complimented the Law Commission on the thoroughness of their work and the detail within the report. He agreed 'wholeheartedly' with the recommendation for an admissibility test within the courts and added that the report provided:

> '... solid recommendations about how we should manage expert witnesses in the future to give the courts the real powers to manage experts and lawyers the ability to assess them properly'
>
> [House of Commons STSC report, Forensic Science, 2013, Q251]

3.4.5   UK Government Response (2013) to the Law Commission Report

In order to become part of the legal statutes, the UK government has to approve and implement recommendations such as those from the Law Commission. In November 2013, the Ministry of Justice rejected the proposal for a formal set of admissibility criteria, on the grounds that the extent to which the current system led to miscarriages of justice was not quantified and that the cost of implementing the proposals was uncertain and may exceed any savings generated elsewhere. Instead, it proposed to modify the Criminal Procedure Rules to provide the judge with more information on any expert evidence being considered and to recommend that a list of independent experts be drawn up from which advice could be provided to the court on request.

Thus, the issues around the admissibility and reliability of expert evidence in England and Wales remain unresolved, despite the debate over a ten-year period and ultimately the support from the scientific and legal professions for reliability tests as described in the Law Commission's report.

3.5 Conclusions

Across all the jurisdictions discussed here, there have been many attempts, through the legal and political systems, to address those issues of concern relating to the admissibility of expert evidence. There are clearly some differences in emphasis, reflecting national and state practices and experiences, but there is also some convergence of views on what aspects relate directly to the reliability of scientific evidence and how this might be assured by the courts. Nevertheless, there remain many difficulties in formulating and implementing clear admissibility thresholds for expert testimony in practice. Despite this, all concerned have a much-increased awareness of the legal issues, than was the case in the recent past, most especially the scientists themselves. In parallel, the judiciary, barristers and lawyers can take advantage of the many resources now available, to enable them to better understand and debate the scientific and statistical basis of expert opinion presented to the court.

References

Australia

Australian Evidence Act (1995). Available at https://www.legislation.gov.au/Details/C2015C00553 [Accessed 31 March 2015].
Freckelton I., Reddy P. and Selby H. (1999). Australian judicial perspectives on expert evidence: an empirical study, Australian Institute of Judicial Administration Inc. Available at http://www.aija.org.au/online/Pub%20no54.pdf [Accessed 10 October 2015].
McClellan Justice Peter. (2009). Admissibility of expert evidence under the Uniform Evidence Act, Judicial College of Victoria, Emerging Issues in Expert Evidence Workshop, Melbourne, 2 October 2009. [Online]. Available at http://www.austlii.edu.au/au/journals/NSWJSchol/2009/13.pdf [Accessed 10 October 2015].

Canada

Government of Ontario: The Goudge Inquiry into Pediatric Forensic Pathology in Ontario [Online]. (2008). Available at http://www.attorneygeneral.jus.gov.on.ca/inquiries/goudge/index.html [Accessed 10 October 2015].
The National Judicial Institute: Science Manual for Canadian Judges [Online]. (2013). Available at https://www.nji-inm.ca/nji/inm/nouvelles-news/Manuel_scientifique_Science_Manual.cfm [Accessed 10 October 2015].
Report on the Prevention of Miscarriage of Justice [Online]. (2005). Available at http://www.justice.gc.ca/eng/rp-pr/cj-jp/ccr-rc/pmj-pej/pmj-pej.pdf [Accessed 10 October 2015].

England and Wales

House of Commons Science and Technology Select Committee: Forensic Science on Trial, Seventh Report of Session 2004–05, HC96/1 [Online]. (2005). Available at http://www.publications.parliament.uk/pa/cm200405/cmselect/cmsctech/96/96i.pdf [Accessed 10 October 2015].
House of Commons Science and Technology Select Committee: Forensic Science, Second Report of Session 2013–14, HC610 [Online]. (2013). Available at http://www.publications.parliament.uk/pa/cm201314/cmselect/cmsctech/610/610.pdf [Accessed 10 October 2015].

The Law Commission (LAW COM No 325), Expert Evidence in Criminal Proceedings in England and Wales, HC 829 London: The Stationery Office [Online]. (2011). Available at https://www.gov. uk/government/uploads/system/uploads/attachment_data/file/229043/0829.pdf [Accessed 10 October 2015].

United States

Federal Evidence Review: Federal Rules of Evidence [Online]. (2015). Available, with links to earlier versions, at http://federalevidence.com/downloads/rules.of.evidence.pdf [Accessed 10 October 2015].
Federal Judicial Centre. (2011). US Reference Manual on Scientific Evidence, 3rd Ed. Available at http://www.fjc.gov/public/pdf.nsf/lookup/SciMan3D01.pdf/$file/SciMan3D01.pdf [Accessed 13 October 2015].
National Research Council: Strengthening Forensic Science in the United States: A Path Forward, Document 228091 [Online]. (2009). Available at http://www.nap.edu/catalog/12589.html [Accessed 10 October 2015].

Further Reading

Australia

Edmond G. (2008). Specialised knowledge, the exclusionary discretions and reliability: reassessing incriminating expert opinion evidence. *University of New South Wales Law Journal*, 31, 1–55.
Edmond G. (2010). Impartiality, efficiency or reliability? A critical response to expert evidence law and procedure in Australia, *Australian Journal of Forensic Sciences*, 42(2), 83–99.

Canada

Canadian Federal Courts Rules (2015). Available at http://canlii.ca/t/52dm6 [Accessed 10 October 2015].
Department of Justice, Canada: The Path to Justice: Preventing Wrongful Convictions [Online]. (2011). Available at http://www.ppsc-sppc.gc.ca/eng/pub/ptj-spj/ptj-spj-eng.pdf [Accessed 10 October 2015].

England and Wales

Aitken C., Roberts P. and Jackson G. (2010). Royal Statistical Society Practitioner Guide No 1: Fundamentals of probability and statistical evidence in criminal proceedings [Online]. Available at http://www.rss.org.uk/Images/PDF/influencing-change/rss-fundamentals-probability-statistical-evidence.pdf [Accessed 10 October 2015].
The Law Commission Consultation Paper No 190: The Admissibility of Expert Evidence in Criminal Proceedings in England and Wales, A New Approach to the Determination of Evidentiary Reliability, A Consultation paper [Online]. (2009). Available at http://www.lawcom.gov.uk/wpcontent/uploads/2015/03/cp190_Expert_Evidence_Consultation.pdf [Accessed 10 October 2015].
UK Ministry of Justice: The Government's response to the Law Commission report: "Expert evidence in criminal proceedings in England and Wales" (Law Com No 325) [Online]. (2013). Available at https://www.gov.uk/government/uploads/system/uploads/attachment_data/file/260369/govt-resp-experts-evidence.pdf [Accessed 10 October 2015].

United States

Becker E.R. and Orenstein A. (1992). The Federal Rules of Evidence after sixteen years – the effect of "plain meaning" jurisprudence, the need for an advisory committee on the Rules of Evidence, and suggestions for selective revision of the Rules, *George Washington Law Review*, 60, 857–914.

Giannelli P.C. (1994). Daubert: Interpreting the federal rules of evidence. *Cardozo Law Review*, 15, 1999–2026.

Roach K. (2009). Forensic science and miscarriages of justice: some lessons from comparative experience. *Jurimetrics*, 50(1), 67–92.

National Institute for Justice: Strengthening Forensic Science: a progress report [Online]. (2014). Available at http://www.whitehouse.gov/sites/default/files/microsites/ostp/forensicscience_progressreport_feb-2014.pdf [Accessed 10 October 2015].

4

Scientific Opinion and the Law in Practice

The final chapter in the first section of this book compares the ways in which expert evidence is admitted, presented and contributes to the legal process in both the adversarial and inquisitorial judicial systems. This leads into a discussion of the role of the scientist as an expert witness and the expectations the court has of the expert. The chapter concludes with a brief discussion of issues in assuring the quality of scientific opinion, from the perspectives of the process, the laboratory and the scientists themselves.

4.1 Scientific Opinion and the Judicial System

Worldwide, democratic judicial systems fall either into one of two categories or, alternatively, into some hybrid of these. The implications for the role of scientific opinion within these systems offer interesting and relevant insights.

4.1.1 Adversarial and Inquisitorial Systems of Justice

Much of the discussion so far has been in the context of jurisdictions based on common law where the adversarial (sometimes termed accusatorial) judicial system operates; these countries include the United Kingdom, Ireland, United States, Canada, Australia and New Zealand. Here, the police investigation informs the prosecution case while the defence team prepare to counter this by separately assembling evidence in support of their arguments. These are then presented to the court for debate where both sides may state their case and cross-examine witnesses, including expert witnesses, called by the opposing side.

Forensic Evidence in Court: Evaluation and Scientific Opinion, First Edition. Craig Adam.
© 2016 John Wiley & Sons, Ltd. Published 2016 by John Wiley & Sons, Ltd.

Depending on the indictment, the role of fact-finder is taken by either a magistrate or judge or, for serious crimes, a jury of lay people supervised by a judge.

For those jurisdictions under civil law, which includes most of Europe, the system is based on an inquisitorial, or more correctly a mixed, process whereby the investigative stage is directed by an examining magistrate (judge) who subsequently presents the complete case to a trial process. Here, although both sides are represented, there is generally no debate on the substance of the evidence as that has been agreed prior to the trial. Rather, the prosecution and defence lawyers attempt to persuade the fact-finders to view the evidence from their particular perspective. In that sense, this stage of the process is adversarial. Depending on the jurisdiction, either a professional judge, either alone or more commonly in combination with lay assessors or a jury, will adjudicate at the court. In Scotland, the system is a hybrid where, for most serious crimes, the Procurator Fiscal directs the investigative stage, leading to an adversarial trial.

4.1.2   Scientific Evidence Within the Inquisitorial System

The role of scientific evidence, and that of the scientist as expert witness, differs within these two contexts. At the investigative stage, within the inquisitorial system, the role of the examining magistrate is to assemble all the evidence and, where forensic examination is required, to employ scientists to undertake the analyses and submit their reports. As long as they remain within their brief, the forensic experts may carry out their work independently and according to their professional judgement, so ensuring thoroughness and impartiality. Any comments, requests or challenges from the defence regarding the forensic evidence must be directed through the magistrate who has full control over what is examined, and how the results contribute to the case being assembled. In reaching the decision on whether to prosecute, and if so, what evidence should be admitted and presented to the court, the examining magistrate has the freedom to follow their own judgement, experience and even intuition. There are no formal criteria on admissibility, or on the assessment and evaluation of the evidence, both scientific and non-scientific, though all decisions must be justified by the magistrate. The intention is that, when the report from the investigating magistrate is complete, all concerned should have agreed to the factual content, including the outcomes from the examination of the forensic evidence. If this is not the case, challenges from the defence are still possible after the suspect has been charged, though these should be resolved before the papers are submitted to the court. In this way, the resolution of any issues around expert evidence, its analysis, interpretation and, hopefully also its evaluation, should be completed before the start of the trial.

4.1.3   Inquisitorial Versus Adversarial

Under the inquisitorial system, the courtroom is no longer the forum for debate on scientific opinion or the cross-examination of expert witnesses. Some would argue that by eliminating the ability of the scientist to impress the court through their authority as an expert, or to convey the strength of opinion by theatrical display, avoids distraction from the facts and their interpretation and so leads to better justice. On the other hand, by failing to engage with the detail of scientific debate, the legal professionals may be less aware of the scope and limitations of the science, thereby letting its quality, and that of the scientific opinion, go unchallenged. In any case, the majority of scientific evidence is now presented solely through written reports. However, by being presented with all evidence in the case before the trial starts, the judges themselves may be better educated and briefed about the scientific issues than would be the case in the adversarial system. Nevertheless, it could be argued that the inquisitorial system instills a culture of the perception of scientific opinion as infallible, despite being open to challenge by the magistrate, and, in the absence of any debate, in particular on interpretation and evaluation of evidence, justice is more poorly served.

A consequence of there being no admissibility thresholds is that there is a tendency in the inquisitorial system to deal with doubts as to the reliability of scientific evidence through the probative value assigned to it. By doing so, the distinctive issues of scientific reliability on the one hand and evaluation on the other can become confused, though this to some extent may also occur under the adversarial system, but not routinely so. Indeed, it is not always clear to those involved where the responsibility for ensuring the reliability of scientific evidence lies within an inquisitorial jurisdiction. A survey in Switzerland by Vuille (2013), in the context of DNA evidence, revealed that the courts believed this was the duty of the examining magistrate while the magistrates saw effective challenges by the defence prior to the trial and ultimately the trial judges themselves as guarantors of evidential reliability. This view of the magistrates is in fact correct in Swiss law.

Nevertheless, if the exchanges between the scientist, the defence and the examining magistrate operate effectively during the investigating stage, then 'equality of arms' is ensured by both sides having equivalent access to the forensic evidence, its analysis and interpretation. Although the pool of forensic scientists is more limited, with fewer individuals contributing to any case than under the adversarial system, accreditation or approved lists of experts should ensure the quality of the individual scientist, though excluding the incompetent is not ensured. Together with the neutrality of the examining magistrate, these factors are intended to minimise biased expert testimony.

The success of expert scientific testimony within the inquisitorial judicial process does depend very much on all these aspects functioning to full effect. Unlike in the adversarial system, there can be no final debate on the evidence through cross-examination, in front of the fact-finders themselves, to identify errors, misconceptions and exaggerated opinion, though some might feel this is not the best forum to discuss and resolve often highly technical matters.

In summary, neither system offers an ideal solution to the management of scientific evidence within the judicial process, specifically with respect to admissibility, reliability and the interpretation and evaluation of evidence, which are the cornerstones of expert testimony in the court.

4.2 The Scientist in Court

The nature of the professional duties of the forensic expert as a scientist aligns closely with that of scientists working in other fields. In the context of criminal justice and in a court of law, however, more is expected of the scientific expert. There is a significant gulf between the factual statements from the scientific work and the legal discussion of the case to which the forensic evidence relates. The court is eager to understand the implications of the scientific findings and, more particularly, both the prosecution and defence teams wish to evaluate its significance for the arguments put forward by each side. The judge needs to be sure that the court as a whole is giving the forensic testimony due weight and that it is being properly considered within the context of the case. In many courts, the lay jury who are focused on the balance between the prosecution and defence cases must attempt to decide the significance of the forensic evidence to each side, despite their inexperience in both legal and scientific matters.

In this overall context, how may the scientific expert witness assist the court, how should the testimony be presented and specifically, how should an opinion be formulated and conveyed to the court? These matters have been the subject of much debate and concern, particularly over the past thirty years or so, fuelled by verdicts overturned on appeal and some significant miscarriages of justice as discussed in the previous chapters. Ultimately, the aim of today's forensic scientist should be to provide a balanced and considered opinion on the evidence, thereby assisting the court in reaching a valid and sustainable verdict.

4.3   The Role and Duties of the Scientific Expert Witness

In recent decades, the role of the expert witness has become more closely examined and defined, with a view to ensuring that both the quality of the individual, as a scientist and an expert, and the quality of the science they expound, are appropriate to the work of the court. In this context, it is useful to review legal definitions of the expert witness.

4.3.1   Definitions of the Role

Most jurisdictions have set down definitions of the role of the expert witness and the duties and obligations associated with it. These generally form part of the legal guidelines governing the admissibility of expert evidence that were discussed in Chapter 2. For the most part, these are in harmony with the England and Wales definition, as set down in R v Cooper:

> '... to furnish the court with scientific information which is likely to be outside the experience and the knowledge of a judge or jury.'
>
> [R v Cooper, 1998]

Equivalent statements, for example, from the United States and Australia, emphasise that, to qualify as a expert, the witness will possess or have undergone:

> '... knowledge, skill, experience, training, or education ...'
> [Federal Rules of Evidence, Rule 702, 1975; see Federal Evidence Review, 2015]

For England and Wales, this definition is expanded by a further ruling on the expert witness role, interestingly taken from Scottish jurisdiction:

> 'Their duty is to furnish the Judge or jury with the necessary scientific criteria for testing the accuracy of their conclusions so as to enable the Judge or jury to form their own independent judgement by the application of these criteria to the facts proved in evidence.'
> [Davie v Edinburgh Magistrates, 1953]

This gets to the heart of the role, which is the nature of the expert opinion on the evidence provided by the scientist and how that is assimilated by the court. The expert is required to educate the fact-finders sufficiently, so that they, in turn, are able to understand and interrogate the expert evidence with a view, not only to testing its accuracy and hence its reliability, but also to reaching their own view as to its meaning and significance, independently of whatever opinion is proffered by the expert witness. There is no intention that the jury will simply defer to expert authority.

This requires the expert to present the testimony in language intelligible not only to the legal professionals, but to those lay people in the jury. This is often a considerable challenge. The first difficulty relates to technical matters underpinning the analysis of the evidence. The second lies in the formulation and expression of the final opinion itself, as, despite the last section in the quote from Davie, the fact-finders will expect to receive a view on the significance of the evidence from the expert. It will be evident in later chapters that, as we progress through a discussion of evaluation and scientific opinion and explore examples from past cases, this aspect may have a great impact on the deliberations of the court and frequently, on the ultimate issue itself.

4.3.2   Duties and Responsibilities of the Expert Witness

In England and Wales, the duties and responsibilities of an expert witness were re-iterated and expanded by Mr Justice Cresswell in the appeal in the case of the Ikarian Reefer (1993). This appeal concerned the grounding of, and subsequent fire on, the ship Ikarian Reefer and whether it had been started deliberately, with the knowledge of the owner and with the intention of claiming on the insurance policy. Expert evidence played an important role in the court's deliberations and, indeed, the judge suggested that the length of the original trial was caused, in part, through misunderstandings by the expert witnesses of their duties and responsibilities. The appeal by the insurance company was rejected and the cause of the grounding of the ship and subsequent fire was attributed to errors in navigation by the ship's master.

These definitions and duties have been expanded in subsequent cases and form the basis of the Criminal Procedure Rules for England and Wales (CPR), part 33 (2014) where not only the duties to the court, but also the content of the expert's report, are specified. In summary, these comprise:

- The expert's opinion must be objective, unbiased and within their own expertise area.
- The expert's overriding obligation is to the court and not to whoever has instructed them.
- There should be acceptable evidence of the credentials of the expert
- Experts should not stray outside their own area of knowledge, and if they do, that should be made clear to the court
- The expert must present the complete factual basis leading to the opinion and not omit anything which may detract from that opinion
- If the expert is aware of alternative approaches to the analysis, alternative views on the scientific basis to the work or other explanations that would explain the evidence then these should be described to the court

In addition, instructions and requirements for the expert witness' report are listed in the CPR, to ensure both consistency of reporting, and that the court is presented with exactly what it requires in order to be reassured as to the reliability and validity of the expert's work and conclusions. Adherence to these is particularly important should the scientist not be called to give oral testimony. If competing expert witness statements are to be presented, then provision is made for a pre-hearing discussion to establish those points where the experts are in agreement and those that are disputed.

Outside the formal legal requirements of the role, bodies with oversight of forensic scientists and their expert witness duties, such as the Forensic Science Regulator (FSR) in the United Kingdom, may publish guidelines for best practice in the profession. More specifically, these expand on the delivery of the core duties by the expert and the document published by the FSR, Legal Obligations (2013), provides useful background information and guidance, including those rulings from the courts that have contributed to current practice. Most significantly, recommendations are made on the key issues to be addressed in formulating opinion on the evidence.

Adherence to ethical behaviour and practice by the expert, to ensure that all reports and opinion are presented honestly and in good faith, that there are no conflicts of interest and that confidentiality is maintained, now feature more prominently in the expectations of the courts. Other jurisdictions have similar definitions of the role, though the level of detail may vary, for example, in the US Federal Rules of Evidence 702, 703.

4.4   Quality Control of Analysis and Opinion

It was clear from the discussions in the earlier chapters that the competency of the expert and the quality of both the methodology and the laboratory are key factors that may impinge on the reliability of the expert's testimony and, in some cases, may directly lead to errors, or at worst miscarriages of justice, in the court. With this in mind, organisations with responsibility for the quality of forensic services have developed accreditation standards and codes of practice as means of ensuring the reliability and validity of forensic examinations and measurements that are subsequently reported to the courts.

The International Standards Organisation (ISO) publishes the ISO 17025, General Requirements for the Competence of Testing and Calibration Laboratories, standard against which laboratories engaged in the testing and calibration of materials may be accredited. This forms the core international standard for laboratory analysis of forensic materials. However, quality assurance of the over-arching forensic process is much more than this and, to date, standards for other aspects are far less well-developed. Two examples of approaches to this will be described here.

4.4.1   An Australian Standard for Forensic Analysis

An Australian bespoke standard (AS5388) for the entire forensic process, from the examination of the crime scene to court presentation, has been developed and published in 2012 (see Robertson et al., 2013). This includes those parts of the process, unique to forensic science, that are not included in ISO 17025. It is structured in four linked sections:

1. Collection standard that includes activities at the crime scene through to the submission of evidence
2. Analysis standard that relates to the testing of materials, including record keeping and continuity of evidence
3. Interpretation standard includes the analysis of data, through to the formulation of expert opinion
4. Reporting standard defines the manner and format of the presentation of expert opinion, including matters such as the qualifications of the scientist and limitations on the conclusions

Individual laboratories and other agencies may apply to be accredited under those standards. In addition, further standards, specific to each of the subdisciplines within forensic science, may be developed to lie within these generic standards.

4.4.2   Regulation of Forensic Science in the United Kingdom

In England and Wales since 2008, the office of the Forensic Science Regulator, under the auspices of the UK Home Office, has had the task of ensuring that all providers of forensic science services to the police and to others in the criminal justice system, adhere to appropriate scientific quality standards in all the work they undertake. This is achieved through the development of codes of practice and conduct, in consultation with the professional forensic science community itself. These include, not only generic laboratory standards but also specific guidelines for dealing with evidence types from bloodstain pattern analysis and fingerprints through to toxicology. The Regulator is also responsible for investigating failure in those quality systems, such as occurred in the cases of Adam Scott (2012) and R v S (2013) (see Chapter 10.8 for a full discussion).

4.4.3   Codes of Conduct and Practice

The Codes of Practice and Conduct for forensic science providers and practitioners in the Criminal Justice System published in 2014 by the UK Forensic Science Regulator provides an illustrative example of a framework that supports and enhances the delivery of high-quality forensic science testimony to the courts, yet falls short of a full accreditation standard (Forensic Science Regulator, Codes of Practice, 2014).

The starting point is ensuring the quality of the scientists themselves. In addition to those specified in Chapter 4.3.2, there are further duties required of the scientist, in relation to professional and technical competence and practice, which together form a code of conduct; these additional duties may be paraphrased as:

- The scientist must ensure professional competence is maintained and enhanced through study and awareness of research and other developments within the field.
- Continuity of evidence is of foremost importance during any forensic examination or analysis and is the responsibility of all who deal with exhibits.
- The scientist should be proactive in accessing information about the circumstances of the case that may contribute to the interpretation and evaluation of the experimental findings.
- Only validated and approved experimental and interpretational methods should be used in casework.
- The scientist should review all findings and their interpretation in light of any new information or developments in the case.
- The scientist should always be prepared to act in any situation that is believed may lead to a miscarriage of justice.

The codes of practice apply over the complete forensic cycle from the crime scene to providing opinion in the court. It is convenient to split these into those that relate to the organisation and management of the laboratory, including the handling of exhibits, and those that apply to the methodology of the analysis and interpretation of the results.

Overall accreditation of the laboratory in provided by BS EN ISO/IEC 17025:2005 through an assessment by the United Kingdom Accreditation Service (UKAS). Within this are included the appropriate standards for the organisation of the laboratory itself; these include the provision of appropriate laboratory facilities, ensuring good working practices, agreed procedures for dealing with complaints and resolving issues, appropriate documentation and handling of exhibits, control of electronic data and technical records and the checking and reviewing of results. In addition, all forensic work should be agreed after establishing the requirements of the user, for example, through case pre-assessment (see Chapter 5.2.2). Finally, the laboratory has a responsibility to manage the training of all staff and, more specifically, to assess their technical competence on a periodic basis.

The second aspect relates to the analytical methods and procedures that are used for the examination of exhibits, together with standards for the interpretation and reporting of results. Accreditation standards apply to the selection and validation of appropriate test procedures, including methods of data analysis and interpretation. All analytical techniques should have a validation report that is capable of external verification. Databases and reference collections of materials held by the laboratory must be thoroughly documented so that users will be able to fully assess their applicability. In addition, inter-laboratory comparisons and proficiency test should be used to verify test procedures against those of other organisations. Finally, results should be reported in an appropriate format for the user and should demonstrate whether there is relevant published literature underpinning the work, include evidence in support of the validity of the methodology and provide an assessment of experimental and other uncertainties that might impact of the conclusions of the analysis.

4.4.4 Accreditation of the Expert

There are no objective threshold criteria that define or validate the individual as an expert, fully eligible to express scientific opinion to the court. The court essentially makes up its own mind on an individual basis, though within the inquisitorial system the examining magistrate may work from approved lists of experts. For those working within sizeable laboratories, operating under an organisational accreditation, this itself should provide evidence of their expertise and status. For those acting as lone consultants this option is not available. Past attempts, for example in the United Kingdom, to establish an accreditation scheme for those individuals aspiring to be recognised as experts, have failed, largely as the courts do not want to lose control of admissibility. More recently, the professional body, the Chartered Society of Forensic Sciences (CSFS) has set up a series of subdiscipline-specific competence tests that enable scientists to provide the court with some external assessment of their expert status – a certificate of professional competence – though this is not a requirement for expert witnesses in the UK courts.

4.5 Conclusion

Over recent years, there has been progress towards a greater consistency and understanding of the role of the expert witness, their duties and how they may work towards ensuring that all scientific opinion is admissible and reliable in the court whatever the jurisdiction in which they operate. However, despite over-arching quality standards, the formulation of opinion, both generically and within each subdiscipline, provides an even greater challenge to the scientist. How this may be achieved in a fair, logical and consistent fashion forms the basis of the next section of this book.

References

Davie v Edinburgh Magistrates [1953] SC 34, 1953 SLT 54

Criminal Procedure Rules (England and Wales) [Online]. (2014). Available at http://www.justice.gov.uk/courts/procedure-rules/criminal/rulesmenu [Accessed 12 December 2015].

Federal Evidence Review: Federal Rules of Evidence [Online]. (2015). Available, with links to earlier versions, at http://federalevidence.com/downloads/rules.of.evidence.pdf [Accessed 10 October 2015].

Forensic Science Regulator for England and Wales [Online]. (2015). Available at https://www.gov.uk/government/organisations/forensic-science-regulator [Accessed 12 December 15].

Forensic Science Regulator: Codes of practice and conduct for forensic science providers and practitioners in the criminal justice system, Version 2.0 (Online). (2014). Available at https://www.gov.uk/government/uploads/system/uploads/attachment_data/file/351197/The_FSR_Codes_of_Practice_and_Conduct_-_v2_August_2014.pdf [Accessed 12 December 2015].

Forensic Science Regulator: Legal obligations, FSR-I-400, Iss 2 (Online). (2013). Available at https://www.gov.uk/government/uploads/system/uploads/attachment_data/file/269812/LegalObligationsIssue2.pdf [Accessed 12 December 2015].

National Justice CiaNaviera SA v Prudential Assurance Co Ltd (Ikarian Reefer). (1993). 2 Lloyds Rep. 68 at 81; including the judgment [Online]. Available at http://www.uniset.ca/other/cs2/19932LLR68.html [Accessed 12 December 2015].

R v Cooper [1998] EWCA Crim 2258

Robertson J., Kent K. and Wilson-Wilde L. (2013). The development of a core forensic standards framework for Australia. *Forensic Science Policy and Management*, 4(3–4), 59–67.

Vuille J. (2013). Admissibility and appraisal of scientific evidence in continental European criminal justice systems: past, present and future. *Australian Journal of Forensic Sciences*, 45(4), 389–397.

Further Reading

Alldridge P. (1999). Scientific expertise and comparative criminal procedure. *International Journal of Evidence and Proof*, 3(3), 141–157.

Brandi J. and Wilson-Wilde L. (2015). Standard methods. In M. Houck (Ed.). *Professional Issues in Forensic Science*, Acad Press.

Champod C. and Vuille J. (2011). Scientific evidence in Europe – admissibility, evaluation and equality of arms. *International Commentary on Evidence*, 9(1), 1–68.

Hans V.P. (2008). Jury systems around the world [Online]. Cornell Law Faculty Publications, Paper 305. Available at http://scholarship.law.cornell.edu/facpub/305 [Accessed 12 December 2015].

Margot P. (1998). The role of the forensic scientist in an inquisitorial system of justice. *Science and Justice*, 38(2), 71–73.

Roberts P. (2009). The science of proof: forensic evidence in English criminal trials. In J. Fraser and R. Williams (Eds.). *Handbook of Forensic Science*, Willan.

Part 2

Part 2

5

Fundamentals of the Interpretation and Evaluation of Scientific Evidence

This chapter is concerned with the extension of the forensic science process into the court of law and how the scientist should present an opinion on the outcome of the examination of physical evidence. The discussion will centre on the forms of words that have been used, their meanings, implications, limitations and shortcomings. In contrast, the principles underpinning the logical evaluation of scientific evidence will be described in preparation for a much wider and deeper presentation in the following chapters. But first, the key stages in the work of the forensic scientist need to be defined and explained.

5.1 Analysis, Interpretation and Evaluation

Given that these words are used frequently, both within the forensic science discipline and within this book, it is essential to have a clear understanding of their meanings within the context of contemporary forensic science.

Analysis is the scientific method, measurement or set of observations that provides a result or finding. It is what the scientist does with the physical evidence in the laboratory and any follow-up work carried out as part of a standard method. It may be a straightforward procedure, such as obtaining a gas chromatogram from a drug sample, or a much more complex task, such as deconstructing a blood-spatter pattern. The results may require some interpretation that is part of the standard methodology such as calibration, calculations or using software tools or databases. Analysis, in this sense, is not unique to the forensic sciences.

Interpretation, in the forensic science context, is where the scientist attempts to understand the meaning of these results and an explanation for them in the context of the case itself.

Forensic Evidence in Court: Evaluation and Scientific Opinion, First Edition. Craig Adam.
© 2016 John Wiley & Sons, Ltd. Published 2016 by John Wiley & Sons, Ltd.

There is no single way of approaching this task, though basing interpretation on competing propositions, according to the principles of Bayesian inference, offers a balanced and logical way of achieving this and of taking into account explicitly the circumstances of the case.

> 'The crucial element that the scientist brings to any case is the *interpretation* of those observations. This is the heart of forensic science: it is where the scientist adds value to the process.'
>
> [Evett *et al.*, 2000]

The scientist, as an expert witness, may provide the court with an opinion on the significance or value of the findings, as part of the interpretation, thereby providing the court with an indication of the weight of evidence as a conclusion to the testimony. The term evaluative opinion tends to be used where competing propositions, Bayesian inference and the use of the likelihood ratio, coupled to a verbal equivalent scale, have been used in arriving at the opinion and this procedure provides a logical evaluation of the evidence. These terms will be discussed further in the following chapters.

There is a fourth part to the process, namely presentation. More precisely, this means the written witness statement, and any consequent oral presentation, to the legal professionals and lay people in the court. It includes, not only the reporting of the forensic work as expert testimony, but also the questioning and cross-examination that may follow and the impact of the responses of the scientist on the fact-finders, the consequent debate and their final judgement. As we shall see in the later chapters, this turns out to be a hugely important stage in the forensic–legal process.

Over the years and across different jurisdictions, there have been a wide variety of approaches taken by the scientist to interpretation and evaluation, with little consistency across, or sometimes even within, the different subdisciplines. Many of these have been unstructured or intuitive and the outcome justified on the basis of the expert's experience or status. Consequent inconsistencies were reflected in the written and oral testimony, specifically in the form of words used to express an opinion. In contrast, the framework to be discussed here is a logical and balanced approach that can be applied across all evidence types and case circumstances, thereby providing the criminal justice system with expert opinion that addresses the questions of importance to the court within a uniform framework, presented in a clear and direct way through the use of standard evaluative expressions.

5.2   The Role and Outcomes of Forensic Investigation

Before discussing the interpretation, evaluation and presentation of opinion, it is convenient to review two strategies for forensic science, within the investigative and legal process, in order to understand their contributions.

5.2.1   Investigative Forensic Science

The traditional, and one might say intuitive, use of forensic science in criminal investigation largely compartmentalises the work of the scientist from that of others, particularly the police investigators; the so-called black-box view. On receipt of physical evidence, the scientist selects a technique, carries out the measurements or observations and reports a result, perhaps with comments, to the originator of the evidence. The scientist is guided by what is in the exhibit package and what is found after the examination, rather than the specific case circumstances. In most instances, any discussion between the scientist and the investigator takes place after the work has been completed and this may lead to bias in the interpretation or attempts to rationalise the findings in light of police expectations (see Chapter 9).

Of course, this approach has advantages for some evidence types and in circumstances where a rapid forensic result may assist the police investigation or provide new leads. For this reason the term 'investigative forensic science' leading to 'investigative opinion' is appropriate. However, in the context of providing expert scientific testimony for the court, this is very often not the optimum strategy for forensic science or necessarily the most cost-effective way for the police to progress an investigation.

5.2.2   Evaluative Forensic Science

The difficulties encountered by the purely investigative approach, in terms of the impact of forensic science within the legal process, were realised around twenty years ago when the England and Wales Forensic Science Service (FSS) embarked on a project with the aim of completely reviewing the context of their work in order to focus on meeting the needs of, not only the police, but also the criminal justice system as a whole, and in a cost-effective manner. The outcome was a model for collaborative working that emphasised a partnership between the police and the scientists at the start of any investigation, to agree the questions needing answered and how forensic science could respond to these. This enabled the formulation of a forensic strategy for examination of the exhibits, driven by the circumstances of the case and where the interpretation and evaluation stages are part of that strategy. As the needs of the judicial system, and specifically those of the expert witness, are an integral part of this approach, it may be termed evaluative forensic science.

The model for delivery of evaluative forensic science is termed Case Assessment and Interpretation (CAI). Within this framework, a detailed methodology is proposed, based on Bayesian inference and called Case Pre-assessment, intended to guide and inform the development of the forensic science strategy for each case. CAI is the topic of the fourth of the RSS Practitioner's Guides where a summary of the methodology is provided:

> 'CAI provides a coherent intellectual framework and associated practical protocols that promote, within each individual case, intelligent decision-making about which items to examine and which techniques to employ. It guides the scientist in report writing and helps experts to formulate and communicate their findings, including any interpretational opinions, in a manner best calculated to support the proper administration of justice.'
>
> [Jackson *et al.*, RSS Practitioner Guide No 4, 2015, 1.5]

5.3   Fact and Opinion

The expert witness may provide both factual and opinion evidence from which the court may be able to infer material facts about the case. In this context, the expert's duty may be defined as:

> 'To provide information that helps reduce the uncertainty of a material fact in forensic (investigative or judicial) settings.'
>
> [Jackson *et al.*, RSS Practitioner Guide No 4, 2015, 2.3]

To better understand the scope of the testimony that a scientific expert may deliver, it is helpful to discuss and critically review the categories, types and examples of opinion statements available and how these relate to the nature of the scientific outcomes themselves.

5.3.1 Categorisation of Opinions

In order to be clear as to the nature of opinions that may be expressed by the expert witness, it is helpful to classify and organise these according to their format and purpose. For the present discussion, it is convenient to follow, to some extent, that organisation presented by Jackson, Aitken, and Roberts (2015). It should be noted that some of the distinctions within this scheme would not be recognised or regarded as providing difficulties by some scientists and practitioners.

5.3.2 Factual Opinion

This is where the scientist gives a purely factual account of an observation or the result of a test and there is no attempt to draw an explanation or inference from it. Such opinions are rarely controversial, and examples typically include:

- I found glass fragments embedded in the defendant's shoe
- Several red fibres were found on tape-lifts from the driver's car seat
- The sample is cocaine hydrochloride
- The blood sample contains $90\,\mathrm{mg\,dm^{-3}}$ of alcohol
- The transferred fibres on the jacket are acrylic

Clearly, where a test is involved, such as these last three examples, there may be challenges based on the specificity of the test method or the competency of its execution, but that would be unlikely. These are examples of categorical opinion on the identification of a material.

5.3.3 Investigative Opinion

Investigative opinion reflects the significance of the expert's findings to the case. Initially, we shall review some examples of the forms of investigative opinion that have been used in the courts across jurisdictions. Variation in the approaches to interpretation used by individual scientists may also lead to these statements being inconsistent with the outcome of the analysis and the circumstances of the case. In addition, differences in the form of words used by the expert may convey different evidential weights to the judge and to individual members of the jury, thereby leading to inconsistencies in understanding, or even to misunderstandings in the legal debate. Scientists may also work to different scales of significance, with different expert witnesses using different words to express the significance of the same piece of evidence. An extensive discussion of this topic is provided in Jackson (2009).

5.4 Expert Opinion and the Forensic Science Paradigm

Forensic science is a broad discipline so the analysis and interpretation of evidential materials takes many forms. According to the paradigm described by Inman and Rudin (2002), the forensic scientist works according to four modes of evidence examination, namely:

- Identification: – establishing, as a fact, the general nature or type of the evidence
- Comparison: – on the basis of observations and measurements, to determine whether the evidence is indistinguishable from some reference material and by implication that both may relate to some common source

- Classification: – characterisation based on the identification of a set of generic traits that place the evidence within a group defined by those traits
- Individualisation: – the observation of features that make this evidence stand out from its class, with a view to ultimately identifying the material as unique, within the limitations of the examination methods

We can understand better how the formation of opinion has come about, through discussion in the context of the forensic examination itself.

5.4.1   Categorical Opinion

There are two types of categorical opinion that may follow from this paradigm.

This first relates to the identification of materials and examples have already been given under the heading of factual opinion. Most identification measurements or observations will result in a categorical outcome that is without any doubt, and hence the expert is providing the court with an established fact, such as the chemical nature of a material based on an accepted test.

Among comparison tests, only fingerprint analysis is conventionally accepted as categorical, and, indeed, the fingerprint examiner will use the term 'identification' as an expression of a positive outcome of a comparison. In the United Kingdom, if three experts independently agree, by comparison methods, on the source of the finger-mark, then this is established as a fact by the court. All other forms of forensic identification evidence based on comparison of observable class and individual characteristics, and indeed other evidence types where the expert has often provided a categorical opinion, have, over recent years, proved problematic in the courts. The most common expression that carries the categorical implication on this basis, is the word 'match':

> The green transferred fibres on the defendant's jacket match those taken from the victim's dress

The implication is that two samples are identical in every respect, which of course cannot be true, and the assertion does not reveal how the scientist has dealt with any observed discrepancies. This opinion involves some subjective judgement yet conveys a categorical if not an actual factual outcome, which is inconsistent. Expressions such as 'match' or 'identical' may be used as shorthand to imply that many characteristics are common to both the questioned and reference samples but are inappropriate in the evaluative sense. No potential 'match' to a source, other than the victim's dress in this case, has been considered in the evaluation. Unfortunately, the subtleties in the meanings of many of these terms, and the scientific observations underpinning them, are frequently lost in court debate.

> The glass fragment originated from the window

This is a categorical statement about evidence based on scientific measurements on a continuous scale, here specifically refractive index, with an associated error. In addition, unless the specific chemical composition of the glass can be proved to have been manufactured for this window alone, then it is logically impossible to reach a categorical opinion on such evidence.

> I am sure that the ear-marks were made by the defendant

This is effectively categorical and has similar difficulties to the previous example, but more so, as the examination is based on measurements that are mainly qualitative, not quantitative as for glass, and indeed there is no agreed methodology for ear-mark examination and little peer-reviewed research literature on ear-marks to establish a body of scientific knowledge. The phrase 'I am sure' suggests that the court should take note of the implied authoritative basis of this opinion.

Statements of this kind, some based on unproven and often nebulous methods of individualisation, and others where the expert has simply exaggerated the outcome, are not justifiable and have been frequently criticised in the courts in the past but are fortunately less common nowadays.

The second form of categorical outcome is a negative assertion or exclusion. This may be based, for example, on differences in class features such as the size or shape of a suspect's shoe, which precludes it being the source of a crime scene mark or on the comparison of DNA profiles showing major differences that would justify a statement such as:

> The defendant cannot be the source of the bloodstain on the carpet

These provide fair statements of the outcome of the forensic examination.

5.4.2 Posterior Probabilities

Amongst the most common forms of opinion statement are those that include some reference to probabilistic language as a means of conveying the strength of the outcome or the expert's belief in the correctness of this outcome. These are not based on any rigorous statistical interpretation and the choice of words is purely subjective, though they may be linked to some reference scale of opinion; examples of these will be discussed in later chapters. Here, the interpretation and formulation of the opinion follows from the result of the analysis and is therefore conditional on that outcome. Such statements are therefore called 'posterior probabilities'. The opinion will be informed by some prior knowledge that may be based on an incomplete understanding of the circumstances of the case, may be biased through association with one side of the legal argument or simply based on speculation. Such a process is unreliable and opaque.

For example, the expert may conclude:

> It is likely that the blue fibres originated from the defendant's trousers

An opinion phrased in this way implies some probabilistic support to the stated view, without giving any detail on how this conclusion was reached with respect to the forensic examination. It could be based completely on the expert's subjective assessment or, in some way related to characteristics of the fibres, evaluated in the context of other information. It is unsatisfactory on either basis and indeed the use of the probabilistic term 'likely' may mislead the court as to the intended weight of evidence.

> The presence of GSR on the defendant's jacket means he very probably fired the weapon

Once again, some probabilistic weight appears to be attached to the statement, explicitly through the phrase 'very probably'. The implied significance of this may be viewed differently by each member of the jury. No alternative explanations for the presence of GSR, such as being close to some else while they fired the weapon, have been considered and the jury would be unaware of what weight might be attached to that or indeed to any other plausible explanation.

5.4.3   Explanations

An alternative, that is again conditional on the outcome of the examination, is to leave out any reference to probability, yet through the choice of words retain some link to the class features that underpin the interpretation and evaluation. However, there is an implied probabilistic nature to these statements that may lead to the weight of evidence being inferred by the recipient of the opinion that is not intended by its originator. In these cases the opinion is unbalanced, as the explanation would also apply to alternative sources of the evidence. For example:

> The hair could have come from the head of the defendant

This simply states some degree of similarity with the defendant's hair. It includes the defendant's hair as a possible source of the evidential hair without giving a view on alternative sources. It does not convey significance as it does not indicate how common the measured characteristics of the hair are or the degree of similarity that was established.

> 'In most situations "could have" is no more than a statement of the blindingly obvious …'
> [Berger *et al.*, 2011]

Another, well-used explanation is to refer to consistency between the questioned and reference materials:

> The shoe-mark is consistent with the defendant being present at the scene

This is similar to 'could have' but implies some specific knowledge of the detailed features on the mark, which, it may be believed, could lead to a categorical identification of the source but fall short of that outcome. What are the consistent features? Once again it attaches no level of significance to the conclusion, leaving the court to reach their own view without guidance from the expert. No view is expressed on alternative sources that may also be consistent with the mark.

A further example of an explanation is the exclusion statement, again based on such class and individual characteristics. Here the issue is more to do with the message contained within the opinion rather than the interpretation of these traits but the result is quite unsatisfactory from the jury's perspective.

> I cannot exclude the chisel found in the defendant's possession as the source of the mark on the window frame

This may be a perfectly correct statement given the outcomes of the forensic examination but what is the jury to make of it? It implies some common class characteristics and no significant dissimilarities between the questioned mark and reference marks from the chisel. This could amount to little more than the widths of the marks being in agreement or it could imply many common traits. In any case, the jury are likely to assign an exaggerated significance to such an opinion in the absence of detail on the relative quality of the mark and on alternative sources that might inform a view on evidential weight.

5.4.4 Where Does this Take Us?

The variety, inconsistency, and indeed incoherence, of these and many other forms of expert witness opinion suggest that a more consistent and uniform approach is needed, which is applicable across all evidence types and which provides an evaluation that is readily understood by the jury and the court. The basis of such an approach is the probabilistic interpretation of competing propositions or explanations for the evidence based on Bayesian inference and incorporating the circumstances of the case. Here, probabilities are defined in a logical fashion and provide a balanced view on the strength of the propositions thereby conveying the true weight of the expert's interpretation to the court. The formulation of clear and relevant propositions is a crucial first step in this process

5.5 What are Propositions?

The logical evaluation of scientific evidence is based on establishing competing propositions, sometimes also called hypotheses, and comparing the probabilities for the forensic findings on the basis of each in turn, thereby providing some indication of the significance or legal weight of a piece of evidence. It is essential, therefore, to understand the nature of a proposition and the importance of being quite precise about its nature and meaning.

A proposition is a statement that is capable of being tested in some way with a view of determining whether it is true or not. Although propositions normally relate to the positions held by the two sides in the adversarial court, in terms of the evidence and the role of the defendant, there are some to which the forensic scientist is readily able to respond while there are others that are clearly more often the provenance of the court. It is therefore convenient to organize propositions into a hierarchy, where those at the top are more closely related to the ultimate issue, whereas those at the bottom are more specifically about the scientific examination of the physical evidence. The hierarchy also takes into account the nature of the evidence under consideration. In the following list all propositions are put in the form appropriate to the prosecution case. By negating each it is possible to produce propositions from the defence point of view.

5.5.1 The Hierarchy of Propositions

Offence level relates to the ultimate issue being addressed by the court and, although the scientist should not pass a view directly on the guilt or innocence of the defendant, it may be appropriate to address propositions that include reference to actions and deeds by the accused, from which the court could conclude that they had or had not committed the offence. For example, on the basis of the range of evidence presented, the court will address propositions such as:

- Mr X is guilty of the rape of Miss Y
- Mr Z is guilty of the armed robbery at the post-office

However, in interpreting physical evidence, the scientist may consider other offence level propositions such as:

- Ms A shot Mr B with the revolver
- Mr C stabbed Mr D with a knife

Activity-level propositions are concerned with actions (or inactions) related to the crime but which are not necessarily criminal offences themselves; these may often be the concern of the forensic scientist:

* Mr X had intercourse with Miss Y
* Mr Z broke the glass screen on the post-office counter

Such activities at the crime scene are very important in helping the court form an accurate picture of what happened during the incident and scientific input based on relevant observations, measurements and material analyses will make an invaluable contribution to this. Of course, most activity-level evaluations will include any relevant results at source level; for example, in interpreting transferred glass evidence it is essential to know the outcome from any comparison at source level of the questioned glass with the reference glass, such as from the post-office screen.

Source-level propositions are mainly of interest to the forensic scientist; they concern the investigation or analysis of forensic materials:

* The semen on the vaginal swab came from Mr X
* The post office screen was the source of the glass fragments on Mr Z's balaclava

Occasionally, we may define **subsource-level** propositions that are related to the source material, but at a more fundamental level:

* The DNA from the swab came from Mr X

Here, the biological nature of the source material itself may be unknown, so the proposition must refer to the DNA profile it generated, which is termed subsource.

All source- and subsource-level propositions may be tested directly by specific measurements or analyses and a conclusion reached by the forensic scientist, which may be either categorical or probabilistic in nature.

The higher-level propositions contribute more strongly to the legal debate in the court, whereas those at lower levels are more amenable to being answered by forensic analysis, including provision of a weight of evidence in each case.

5.5.2   The Importance of Activity Level

The relevance and importance of activity-level evidence cannot be overestimated and it is probably the case that this is an area, which, if not overlooked, has not received the full attention it deserves from forensic scientists in the past. Some of that may be to do with the not insignificant difficulties involved in carrying out the interpretation and evaluation process for activity-level evidence. However, activity-level opinion may, in very many cases, provide additional forensic science input to add value to the legal debate and further, it lends itself well to logical evaluation, not least where the propositions have been carefully chosen and interpreted.

For example, a defendant A is accused of assault and of causing a serious head wound to B, but pleads self-defence on the basis of B having initiated an attack on him leading to a fight in which B sustained his injury. B claims that A attacked him without reason, resulting in his falling over and hitting his head.

Transferred fibres recovered from each individual are found to be indistinguishable from the clothes of the other. At source level, these fibres contribute evidence as to the close contact between the two during the incident. However, the number, locations and distribution of transferred fibres will reflect the nature and duration of this contact, and hence an evaluation at activity-level may enable the court to decide whether the two did indeed have a prolonged fight as alleged by A or whether the attack was sudden, unprovoked and brief, as stated by B.

The expert witness will be able therefore to incorporate both levels in the evaluation of relevant propositions regarding the transferred fibre evidence.

5.6   Competing Propositions in the Court

In providing evaluative opinion to the court, the level of the propositions should be established first, followed by the formulation of a statement on the evidence. Competing propositions may be proscribed in the initial request for forensic examination of the evidence or decided by the scientist in light of the circumstances of the case. To generate competing propositions, the first should reflect the prosecution's case. For example, at source level:

> The footwear mark on the kitchen floor originated from the presence of the defendant at the scene

Alternatively, at activity level, the prosecution proposition may be:

> The footwear marks on the kitchen work surface and on the floor beneath, originated from the defendant climbing through the window and jumping on to the floor

To evaluate the source level proposition, the class and any individual features of the crime scene mark would be compared with those in reference marks produced from the defendant's footwear. At activity level, the position, orientation and indications of variation in impact pressure in the marks would contribute to their interpretation. However, it is not sufficient under a balanced logical evaluation to consider the evidence under a single proposition. Unfortunately, this has occurred too often in the past and leads to statements of investigative opinion in the formats discussed earlier.

We also need to consider the evidence based on the truth of the defence case:

> The footwear mark on the kitchen floor originated from the presence at the scene of someone other than the accused

A similar statement may be formulated for the activity-level proposition. To evaluate these defence propositions we need to consider other sources of a shoe that provide the same classification features and any additional individual features that are indistinguishable from those on the scene mark. The quality of the comparison process itself should also be under scrutiny, particularly with respect to false positive outcomes.

The conclusions of the expert on the evidence of the crime scene footwear marks, based separately on each of these two propositions, then need to be compared, as if weighing them against each other on a two-pan balance, to arrive at a final view as to which explanation carries more evidential weight. If, for any reason, an alternative proposition cannot be formulated then evaluation is not possible and only investigative opinion may be given. In the words of Robertson and Vignaux (1993):

> 'In court as elsewhere, the data cannot 'speak for itself'. It has to be interpreted in the light of the competing hypotheses put forward and against a background of knowledge and experience about the world. Bayesian probability provides a mechanism for doing this.'
>
> [Robertson and Vignaux, 1993, p. 470]

We shall continue this discussion in the next chapter by reviewing some key cases that illustrate some of the difficulties faced by the expert witness in giving opinion in court, as well as some examples of the means by which the scientist may arrive at a balanced evaluation of evidence.

References

Berger C.E.H., Buckleton J., Champod C., Evett I.W. and Jackson G. (2011). Evidence evaluation: A response to the court of appeal judgment in R v T, *Science and Justice*, 51(2), 43–49.

Evett I., Jackson G., Lambert J.A. and McCrossan S. (2000). The impact of the principles of evidence interpretation on the structure and content of statements, *Science and Justice*, 40(4), 233–239.

Inman K. and Rudin N. (2002). The origin of evidence, *Forensic Science International*, 126(1), 11–16.

Jackson G., Aitken C. and Roberts P. (2015). Royal Statistical Society Practitioner Guide No 4; Case assessment and interpretation of expert evidence [Online]. Available at http://www.rss.org.uk/Images/PDF/influencing-change/rss-case-assessment-interpretation-expert-evidence.pdf [Accessed 20 December 2015].

Jackson G. (2009). Understanding forensic science opinions. In J. Fraser and R. Williams, (Eds.). *Handbook of Forensic Science*, 419–445, Willan Publishing, Cullompton, Devon, UK.

Robertson B. and Vignaux G.A. (1993). Probability – The logic of the law. *Oxford Journal of Legal Studies*, 13(4), 457–478.

Further Reading

Aitken C., Roberts P. and Jackson G. (2010). Royal Statistical Society Practitioner Guide No 1: Fundamentals of probability and statistical evidence in criminal proceedings [Online]. Available at http://www.rss.org.uk/Images/PDF/influencing-change/rss-fundamentals-probability-statistical-evidence.pdf [Accessed 14 October 2015].

Cook R., Evett I.W., Jackson G., Jones P.J. and Lambert J.A. (1998). A model for case assessment and interpretation. *Science and Justice*, 38(3), 151–156.

Jackson G., Jones S., Booth G., Champod C. and Evett I.W. (2006). The nature of forensic science opinion – a possible framework to guide thinking and practice in investigations and in court proceedings. *Science and Justice*, 46(1), 33–44.

6

Case Studies in Expert Opinion

In this chapter, three cases will be discussed that illustrate differing approaches to formulating and presenting expert scientific opinion to the court. In two of these, there is significant debate on the body of knowledge underpinning the forensic analysis, the scientific nature of that analysis and the information and data available to the expert in support of their interpretation. In the third case, such issues are not subject to debate in the court. Across all three, however, there are examples of investigative opinion and evaluative opinion expressed in a variety of ways and these form a focus for the discussion.

6.1 Case Study 1: Facial Comparison Evidence

This case concerns expert witness opinion on facial identification from CCTV images. It demonstrates that a subjective assessment by a recognized expert may yet lead to opinion expressed in a qualitative manner using a scale to convey the strength of support for the prosecution's proposition. The term facial identification was used in this case, despite the fact that the core forensic process is one of comparison with some control image, rather than identification alone, and for ease of continuity this terminology will be used here. It should, however, be more correctly termed facial comparison.

6.1.1 The Crime and Conviction

On the night of 5th November 2006 a gang of three men committed two armed robberies in west London. In the first, an elderly woman was beaten to death after the assailants failed to find a safe in her house. At the second house they were eventually repulsed by the

Forensic Evidence in Court: Evaluation and Scientific Opinion, First Edition. Craig Adam.
© 2016 John Wiley & Sons, Ltd. Published 2016 by John Wiley & Sons, Ltd.

occupants, even after terrorizing and wounding them. Two were alleged to be brothers called Michael and Dean Atkins. Dean had, in fact, escaped from prison with the help of others only the day before the incident. Both the Atkins brothers denied involvement in the crimes, citing alibis for these times.

At the second crime scene, CCTV cameras were installed and although all the criminals wore balaclava masks, at one point one of the gang was seen looking out of a doorway with his mask removed. This evidence of identification was examined by Mr Neave, an expert with twenty years' experience in facial comparison, recognition and reconstruction who gave opinion to the court on the prosecution's proposition that the face caught by the camera was that of Dean Atkins. Despite the relatively poor quality of the image, the view of the expert witness was supportive of this proposition, though he was clear that this was not a positive, implying categorical, identification of Dean. Following his subsequent conviction, Dean Atkins appealed on the grounds that the expert witness was not allowed to express his opinion on a scale implying some quantitative measure of likeness, where it was clear that no quantitative measures could be, or indeed were, made in the facial comparison process and that the opinion should be confined to points of similarity and dissimilarity, leaving the jury to reach a conclusion on identification.

6.1.2 Expert Evidence and Opinion

Neave compared the CCTV images with photographs of all three men suspected of involvement in the crime, as well as with twenty other known criminals operating in that area, though he accepted that this did not comprise a database of possible suspects. He worked with eight points of comparison to justify his conclusion and he also assessed nine risk factors that could impact on his final opinion. Two risk factors of particular interest are:

* The possibility that two different people may appear indistinguishable
* The fact that there exists no database of facial characteristics that would inform a view as to how many people share particular features

Neave expressed his outcome on a six-point scale running from 'lends no support' [point 0] to 'lends powerful support' [point 5] based on his experience and expertise in assessing the points of comparison and risk factors. His opinion was towards the top half of this scale and was summarised by the trial judge as follows:

> 'This comparison therefore offers a level of support for the allegation that Dean Atkins and the offender are one and the same person, between 'it lends support' [point 3] and 'lends strong support' [point 4] to that conclusion. But you should remember this, that, as Mr Neave conceded, there is no database which would enable him to give a statistical analysis and so his scale is based on his own experience and expertise …'
>
> [Atkins and another v R, 2009, paragraph 8]

The judge added that Neave had compared the images with those of others, specifically including Michael Atkins, Dean's brother, and this should be borne in mind when considering this opinion.

At the appeal, counsel for Atkins suggested that the expert witness had gone much further than was appropriate in reaching his conclusion, given the nature of the evidence. He submitted that:

> '..the use of the expressions of level of support in the form of an ascending scale carries the risk of bestowing upon evidence which is purely subjective a spurious scientific authority. It may, he says, mislead the jury by suggesting to it that there is an arithmetical scale or statistical basis for the strength of the comparison.'
>
> [Atkins and another v R, 2009, paragraph 11]

The appeal court judge stated that the absence of a database or specific training for the scientist did not prevent someone, with many years of experience, achieving the necessary expertise to give expert opinion. Leaving the jury to make up their own minds, based on a summary of similarities and dissimilarities with no expert evaluation, was of no help to the court in properly assessing the significance of the evidence. Experts across many areas of forensic science used scales such as the one adopted here, despite quite wide variation in the availability and quality of databases or other supporting knowledge. In such cases, it was expected that the court would interrogate the expert witness in detail on these matters during cross-examination. In this case, the trial judge had highlighted the extent and limitations of the opinion expressed, including that:

> '1. It was incapable of constituting positive identification, whilst it could positively exclude,
> 2. It involved no unique identifying feature in this case,
> 3. It was not based upon any database which could give any statistical foundation for his expression of opinion and
> 4. It was therefore, as to opinion of significance, informed by experience but entirely subjective.'
>
> [Atkins and another v R, 2009, paragraph 30]

On this basis the appeal was dismissed, effectively endorsing the way in which opinion was delivered on facial comparison at the original trial. Both the Atkins brothers were sentenced to a minimum term of 35 years in jail.

6.1.3 Opinion in Atkins

Although the analysis and interpretation of this facial comparison evidence was almost entirely subjective, apart from some measurement of features in the images, the expert witness used a qualitative scale to express his opinion. In his statement, he alluded to the prosecution's proposition – '… the allegation that …' – and, in his description of his method of analysis indicated that an alternative proposition was that the source of the CCTV image was one of the other twenty men whose images he used in his comparison. However, the validity of his specific points of comparison and whether alternative points would produce the same or a quite different outcome is not underpinned by peer-reviewed research, only by his experience. He is explicit in acknowledging the risk factors in his evaluation, particularly in terms of a database. Nevertheless, in using a scale that defines the level of support to a particular explanation for the evidence, Mr Neave was attempting to work within a logical evaluation framework, albeit one beset with the difficulties specific to facial comparison and where there must be serious doubts as to how meaningful was the form of words used in the final evaluation in relation to his observations.

6.2 Case Study 2: Ear-mark Identification

In contrast, this second case study focuses on one particular potential biometric, the ear-print, and the extent to which expert opinion on the comparison of an ear-mark at a crime scene to that of a particular individual is accepted by the court. Despite some similarities to the Atkins case, particularly in the subjective nature of the comparison process and limited database, the experts here chose not to evaluate their findings using competing propositions or on a scale of opinion. This case also reveals the importance of scientific knowledge in underpinning the work of the expert witness and the scrutiny given by the court to the reliability of expert opinion.

6.2.1 The Crime and the Evidence

Dorothy Wood was an elderly woman who was murdered by an intruder at her home in Huddersfield, United Kingdom, during the early hours of 7th May 1996. She had been suffocated with her pillow while in bed. Examination of the scene showed that the intruder had gained access by forcing open a small window above her bed with a jemmy or similar tool. Further, the glass of this window revealed some ear-prints, apparently caused by the intruder pressing his ear against it before forcing entry. This explanation was supported by the fact that the window had been cleaned some three or four weeks earlier.

Mark Dallagher was a local man who was convicted in August 1996 of a series of burglaries in the area where access had been gained in a similar manner. While in prison, he allegedly revealed information about the murder of Dorothy Wood to a fellow inmate and was consequently questioned by the police. Control ear-marks taken from Dallagher were compared to those from the crime scene by two independent experts, both of whom were satisfied that they were indistinguishable. Despite his claim of an alibi from his girlfriend, Dallagher was tried for the murder on the basis of his previous modus operandi, his conversations in prison and the ear-mark identification, which was the only forensic evidence against him. He was convicted of this offence at Leeds Crown Court in December 1998 but later appealed on the basis that the ear-mark evidence was inadmissible since other eminent forensic experts claimed that there was an insufficient body of knowledge to enable the rigorous analysis, interpretation and evaluation of such marks at a standard appropriate to a court of law.

6.2.2 Interpreting the Evidence and Challenges to the Opinion

The first expert witness to give testimony was Mr Van der Lugt, a Dutch police officer of 27 years standing, who lectured at a Dutch police college but had no formal qualifications and who had made a specialist study of ear-marks and their identification over the past ten years. He had built up a database of 300 distinct ear-prints and was satisfied that no two ear-prints were 'alike in every particular'. He told the court that it was rare for a print to be left by all of the raised parts of the ear and that, generally speaking, he would look for five or six points when making a comparison, but he emphasised that what mattered was the totality of the evidence, which he reviewed by the use of overlays. On this basis he was:

'..absolutely convinced that the prints of the defendant's left ear were identical with the prints of the left ear on the window.'

[R v Dallagher, 2002, paragraph 9]

In addition, for the right ear, he found seven points of similarity and two differences. In conclusion, he stated:

> '… that it was this defendant who had placed his ears against the window'
>
> [R v Dallagher, 2002, paragraph 9]

The second expert witness, Prof Vanezis, shared the view about the uniqueness of ears themselves and also carried out his analysis by means of overlays, though he was more cautious in relation to the extent of distortion that was possible in the ear-mark itself, due to the nature of the soft tissue of the ear. He concluded that it was highly likely that the ear-mark had been made by Dallagher and the judge summarised his opinion thus:

> '…there is a remote possibility that the impressions on the window may have been left there by somebody other than the defendant, but his firm opinion was that it was very likely that it was this defendant who made those prints, although he cannot be one hundred percent certain.'
>
> [R v Dallagher, 2002, paragraph 10]

Both experts agreed that it would be very useful if further research were done to see whether it were possible for marks from two separate ears to be produced showing apparent similarities. This, they accepted, might well be a real possibility. They also concurred that a larger database to establish standards for comparison would be desirable.

Dallagher's appeal was supported by the publication of work by Dr Champod and others (Champod *et al.*, 2001) on the current state of knowledge with regard to the individual characteristics of ear-marks and their comparison to control prints from individuals. He accepted that all ears are different but that:

> '… "a high variability between ears does not imply necessarily that a high variability is expressed in marks left by different persons" and the evidence as to that is limited.'
>
> [R v Dallagher, 2002, paragraph 11]

This expert also commented that, although the methodologies adopted by Van der Lugt and Vanezis were not unscientific, they were quite subjective and given the wide tolerances needed to accommodate pressure variation and distortion of the ear tissue, it was unclear as to how much value could be attributed to a perceived match between two marks. Given the small database available, any evaluation of such results would be of very limited significance to the court; indeed he had 'serious reservations' about the manner in which their opinions had been expressed. He concluded that the comparison of earmarks with a view to establishing identification cannot be accepted as an accepted body of knowledge within the scientific community due to the lack of empirical research and peer-review of any methodology.

The appeal court judge summed up Champod's view as:

> '… at the present time ear print comparison can help to narrow the field, and may eliminate, but cannot alone be regarded as a safe basis on which to identify a particular individual as being the person who left one or more prints at the scene of a crime.'
>
> [R v Dallagher, 2002, paragraph 12]

The defence counsel also asserted that the experts had over-reached themselves, by stating that Dallagher was the source of the marks, which was for the jury as fact-finders to decide, and that, in doing so, they presented opinion in manner biased in favour of the prosecution; for example, in this statement from Van der Lugt:

'In my opinion the unknown prints found at Miss Wood's home are from donor 1061 which is the defendant in this case. So he produced those left and right ear prints on the window.'

[R v Dallagher, 2002, paragraph 32]

Champod pointed out that this form of opinion was not justified, as it was not logically correct to say that, on the basis of the similarities observed in the crime scene and reference marks, it followed that the defendant had been the source of the mark at the scene. To reach that conclusion it would have to be shown that no other source of the mark was possible, which was not the case here.

'They should have said no more than that what they found supported to an appropriate degree the conclusion that the marks on the window were made by the defendant's ear.'

[R v Dallagher, 2002, paragraph 11]

6.2.3   The Conclusion of the Appeal

The appeal court judge concluded that the ear-mark evidence was indeed admissible as evidence, despite the doubts as to the body of scientific research underpinning the examination of ear-marks. More specifically, he asserted that the factual observations from the crime scene, the forensic examination and indeed the conclusions of the examiner were all relevant and reliable testimony for the court to hear. However, the principal issue was the value of that conclusion to the legal debate, that is, the weight the jury should attached to this evidence. In this the judge agreed with Champod that the strength of that opinion was a matter of concern and he believed that, had the fresh evidence that cast doubt on the validity of the ear-mark identification methodology been available, then the jury may have come to a different decision on Dallagher and so he found the original conviction unsafe.

As a result of this appeal a re-trial was ordered. However this was abandoned when DNA extracted from the ear-mark residues was found not to have originated from Dallagher and so he was effectively acquitted of the crime.

6.2.4   Opinion in Dallagher

The interpretation and evaluation in Dallagher was largely qualitative and conducted according to a particular methodology set by the examiner himself. Despite the allusions to databases, the opinion was conveyed in an investigative rather than an evaluative way. Although both expert witnesses at the trial acknowledged some limitations in these methodologies, their conclusions were quite categorical for the most part. Phrases such as 'absolutely convinced' and 'they were made by the same ear' and 'it was this defendant' were used by Van der Lugt while Vanezis adopted a more cautious, posterior probabilistic approach demonstrated by expressions such as 'very likely' and 'remote possibility'. Indeed, the latter expert appears to have considered an alternative proposition, namely that the marks were left by someone other than Dallagher, but expressed his opinion in separate probabilistic statements for each competing proposition, rather than as a single balanced evaluation.

In his testimony to the appeal, Champod effectively suggested that the opinion should have been presented as an evaluation of propositions based on the conclusions from the examination of the evidence and expressed as '… support(ed) to an appropriate degree …'. This was a call for evaluation based on Bayesian inference.

6.3 Case Study 3: Glass and Gunshot Residue

This third case illustrates how expert opinion may be expressed through the evaluation of competing propositions to give a balanced view on the significance of the evidence, expressed in an appropriate form of words. This case will be used to illustrate the application of logical evaluation.

6.3.1 The Crime and Trial

On 13th March 2001 there was an attempted robbery by a gang of three masked men at a post office in Droylsden, Manchester. The gang entered the post office and subsequently fired a shotgun at the glass security screen in front of the counter. When this failed to break it, they hit the screen with a sledgehammer, which only released fragments from the surface of the glass. At this point they fled from the scene in a stolen car. Brian Bowden and his father were suspected and, on searching their house, police found a variety of evidence that contributed to their arrest and subsequent trial. However, at the trial in January 2002, the father was acquitted and the jury was unable to reach a conclusion on the son who was then re-tried.

Amongst other evidence at the second trial, the prosecution once again put forward scientific findings related to materials found on a knitted balaclava helmet found at Bowden's house, which, it was asserted, came from the presence of the hat at the crime scene. Their propositions were that, as a result of Bowden wearing the balaclava during the raid, the microscopic metal particles found on it were residues from the shotgun discharge, and further, that the glass fragments, also found on the balaclava, originated from the surface of the screen when it was hit with the hammer. As a result Bowden was convicted of attempted armed robbery in July 2002.

Bowden appealed against this verdict in January 2004 on grounds not directly related to the scientific evidence but including the actions of the trial judge in directly questioning one of the expert witnesses, which was properly the job of the defence counsel. Nevertheless, the appeal considered the evaluation of the scientific evidence, in detail, before reaching its conclusion.

6.3.2 Analysis and Interpretation of the Scientific Evidence

Forensic examination of the balaclava revealed three types of transferred trace evidence:

1. Saliva stains around the mouth region. Bowden accepted that this balaclava was his and so the presence of his DNA in these stains did not contribute to the debate.
2. Glass fragments
3. Metal particles typical of gunshot residue (GSR)

At the second trial the prosecution called separate expert witnesses for the glass and particulate evidence while the defence put forward a single expert for both evidence types.

The glass evidence consisted of three fragments, all of which had refractive indices indistinguishable from each other and also from the control glass taken from the outside of the security screen. There were also no differences in chemical composition between these samples. In addition, the inner glass in the toughened, multi-laminated screen had a different refractive index and none matching this was found on the exhibit. The glass was a not uncommon type of sheet glass with a refractive index typically found in around one in a hundred windows. The expert witness added that studies had shown that many people acquire glass fragments through everyday life and these may be found on various parts of their clothing.

Elemental analysis of the metal particles recovered from the balaclava, using a technique such as energy-dispersive x-ray analysis (EDX) in a scanning electron microscope (SEM), revealed the presence of barium (Ba) and aluminium (Al). However, EDX analysis of the cartridges left at the scene showed the presence of Antimony (Sb) and Lead (Pb), as well as those two metals and all particles contained at least two or three of these elements. The presence of aluminium in cartridges was less common in the United Kingdom than in the United States and the absence of antimony in the residues on the exhibit meant that fireworks were a possible alternative source. Bowden claimed that this was indeed the origin of these residues as he had attended a fireworks party in November 2000 wearing the balaclava.

6.3.3   Propositions for Evaluation

Both sets of evidence were dealt with at source level based on physicochemical analyses. There was no specific discussion at activity level, despite both the glass and the metal residues being transfer evidence. This would involve consideration of the distribution of fragments across the balaclava in the context of the positioning of the assailants and their actions during the attempted robbery. Of course, such a forensic examination would be of more significance had full sets of clothing rather than just one item, the balaclava, been available for investigation.

To evaluate the glass and metal residue evidence we need to consider each from the perspectives of the prosecution and the defence. These were not explicitly stated during the appeal but implied by the background information presented and in the opinion expressed by the expert witnesses. For example, an appropriate set of competing and mutually exclusive propositions for the glass evidence would be:

- the glass fragments on the balaclava originated from the security screen
- the glass fragments on the balaclava originated from some other source, such as contamination from the environment

While for the metal residues evidence, comparable propositions might be:

- the metal residues on the balaclava were deposited due to the discharge of the shotgun cartridges
- the metal residues originated as material released from the explosion of fireworks.

First, it should be noted that there is no single, correct way to write these propositions, as long as they are relevant to the work carried out by the scientist and its findings and reflect questions of relevance to the court. Second, whereas the second (defence) proposition on the glass evidence is a simple negation of the source being from the post office screen, the alternative proposition for the metal particle residues specifically cites fireworks as a source of the material. Both of these are acceptable – the defence simply needs to provide a proposition, which is a mutually exclusive alternative to that of the prosecution. There may be several alternative explanations for the evidence, but only one is needed by the defence, and that may be an unspecific alternative such as that given here for the glass fragments.

It is the job of the scientist, as an expert witness, to evaluate the experimental findings on the basis of each of these propositions, to decide which explanation is more likely and to translate that outcome into a form of words that correctly conveys the weight of that evidence to the jury. Technical matters related to the analysis and to the materials themselves, as well as background knowledge acquired through the experience of the scientist or informed by that of others, for example, through published literature or surveys, may be used to reach this conclusion.

6.3.4 Evaluative Opinion: Glass

In the case of the glass fragments, the fact that the refractive index, a quantity that may be measured to a high precision, was the same, within experimental uncertainty for both the questioned and control materials, provides essential support to the prosecution case. Other factors such as the height of the screen, the force applied, the proximity of the balaclava at the time of the incident and, of course, the finding of only three fragments would all contribute to the expert's expectations of finding this glass evidence on the hat as a result of the action at the crime scene.

In contrast, what support is there for the defence proposition? This relies principally on both the quality of the refractive index analysis and therefore how close the agreement actually is, and any knowledge of the rarity of glass of this particular refractive index in the environment. In this case the expert witness called by the prosecution quoted a frequency of occurrence, based on his experience, of 'one in ninety or one in a hundred windows'. This gives some little weight to the defence case since this type of glass has been shown to be not uncommon and it is accepted by forensic experts that glass may be acquired on clothing by other, usually innocent, means. At first sight, the fact that no inner laminate glass was found on the balaclava may also lend some support to the defence assertion that the glass did not originate from that screen but the fact that the laminate itself was not ruptured by the hammer would have prevented such material being ejected by the impact. To reach his evaluative conclusion the scientist considered these factors in a qualitative way. This led to the weight of evidence lending clear support to the prosecution case, but not overwhelmingly so. Hence the opinion of the expert witness, Dr Lloyd, was:

> '... that the glass on the balaclava was moderately strong support for the view that the balaclava was worn by a participant in the robbery ...'
>
> [R v Bowden 2004, paragraph 19]

For the defence, Mr Walker provided an investigative opinion – 'consistent with' – followed by a logical evaluation that provided less support for the prosecution's case.

> 'The finding of glass on the balaclava was consistent with it having come from the Post Office, but that there were other possible explanations; the finding of the glass on the appellant was moderate evidence that the wearer had been present at the Post Office.'
>
> [R v Bowden 2004, paragraph 20]

6.3.5 Evaluative Opinion: GSR

Evaluation of the metal residues was carried out in a similar way, except that the specific alternative of the explosion of fireworks as a source of the evidence was considered. The presence of Al and Ba could be explained by either proposition but the absence of either Pb or Sb from the metal residues might be seen to favour a source other than these particular cartridges, though it was stated that individual control particles from the cartridge contained at least two or three, not necessarily all four, of these metals. The defence proposition may explain the absence of Sb. Although Al is unusual in many UK cartridges, this information is not relevant to these two propositions, as both can explain the presence of this element in the metal residues. This might not be the case if the defence proposition had related to a different type of cartridge being the source rather than fireworks. All these factors suggest that the support to the prosecution proposition, compared to that for the defence, is less strong here than was stated for the glass evidence, yet the former remains the preferred explanation for the evidence. As a result, the expert witness, Mr Blunt, concluded that:

> '... the presence of the barium and aluminium lent some support to the balaclava having been worn in a firearms incident'
>
> [R v Bowden 2004, paragraph 19]

Although both of these evaluations were carried out in a non-numerical fashion, the weighing up of the various factors against each other is, in fact, an attempt to put the outcome of the evaluation on some verbal scale corresponding to the weight of evidence. The prosecution made no comment on the cumulative effect of these two pieces of evidence; for example, by combining the two evaluative statements into one that carried greater weight. However, as a result of questioning by the judge, the defence expert did provide such an opinion. His view agreed more or less with that of Blunt, that the metal residues, on their own, provided:

> '... limited to moderate evidence that the wearer had been present at the Post Office.'

He then stated that, taken in combination, the weight of evidence moved up to provide 'moderately strong' support to the prosecution's case. There is therefore some consistency in the approach to evaluation by the forensic experts in this case, though Walker's evaluation of the glass evidence was less in favour of the prosecution's case than was that of Lloyd.

The defence expert witness was then questioned by his own counsel:

> 'You have told us about particulates; the barium and the aluminium. You told us about the glass that was found. Can you answer this yes or no? Can you as an expert say that the presence of the particulates, barium, aluminium and the fragments of glass make you scientifically certain that the mask was worn at the scene of the robbery?'
>
> [R v Bowden 2004, paragraph 21]

To which Walker replied, 'definitely not'.

The aim of this particular question and the response was to put doubt in the minds of the jury as to the scientists' evaluations. These had been carefully considered, and clearly a categorical view on the origins of the evidence, either way, was not possible. The response is not incorrect and it does not invalidate his or the others' original statements. However, it would have been preferable for him not to have responded directly to this leading question, but rather to simply reiterate his original view.

In his concluding remarks, the appeal court judge agreed that the trial judge's intervention was an error but that it did not affect the safety of the verdict and he dismissed Bowden's appeal against conviction.

6.3.6   Opinion in Bowden

In this case, opinion from all the experts was presented in terms of 'support' to a view on the evidence put forward by a particular side of the legal debate, compared to that from the other side; though this latter point is not always explicit in the statements. This is qualified by a form of words indicating the level of that support, such as 'moderately strong support', 'some support' or 'moderate evidence that'. These evaluative opinions are based on the expert's assessment of the various factors contributing to competing explanations for the trace evidence found on the balaclava. Further, for Walker, this approach also allowed him to evaluate the combination of finding both trace materials on the hat as a single weight of evidence.

In his statement on the glass fragments, this expert provided an investigative opinion by observing that the presence of the glass was 'consistent with' the balaclava having been present at the crime scene, though this is qualified by an acknowledgement that other explanations were possible. However, this does not convey the significance of the evidence to the jury. That is achieved by the evaluative statement that followed.

Finally, the cross-examination by the defence counsel reveals how even the best-prepared expert witness who has provided a carefully considered evaluative opinion, may be caught out by a barrister's leading question aimed at producing a categorical response on the evidence from the expert.

6.4   Conclusions

These cases illustrate some of the difficulties in, as well as indicating some of the solutions to, formulating opinion on scientific evidence. The logical approach based on competing propositions for the evidence, as invoked in the Bowden case, and alluded to in Atkins, has distinct advantages for the court. Although its implementation is relatively straightforward with the evidence types in the former case, in the latter there are greater difficulties when dealing with evidence in the absence of quantitative or defined characteristics and relying wholly on the expert's subjective assessment, such as in facial comparison.

To progress this further, the evaluative approach needs to be put on a more formal footing. This requires an understanding of its statistical foundations, Bayesian statistics, and how interpretation and evaluation may proceed on a more quantitative basis and be applied across a wide range of evidence types.

References

Atkins and another v R [2009] EWCA Crim 1876

Champod C., Evett I.W. and Kuchlar B. (2001). Earmarks as evidence: A critical review, *Journal of Forensic Sciences*, 46(6), 1275–1284.

R v Bowden [2004] All ER (D) 291 (Jan)

R v Dallagher [2002] All ER (D) 383 (Jul)

Further Reading

Aitken C., Roberts P. and Jackson G. (2010). Royal Statistical Society Practitioner Guide No 1: Fundamentals of probability and statistical evidence in criminal proceedings [Online]. Available at http://www.rss.org.uk/Images/PDF/influencing-change/rss-fundamentals-probability-statistical-evidence.pdf [Accessed 14 October 2015].

Edmond G., Kemp R., Porter G., Hamer D., Burton M., Biber K. and San Roque M. (2010). Atkins v The Emperor: the 'cautious' use of unreliable 'expert' opinion, *International Journal of Evidence and Proof*, 14(2), 146–159.

Halpin S. (2008). What have we got ear then? Developments in forensic science: earprints as identification evidence at criminal trials, *University College Dublin Law Review*, 8, 65–83.

Meijerman L., Thean A. and Maat G. (2005). Earprints in forensic investigations, *Forensic Science, Medicine and Pathology*, 1(4), 247–256.

Molloy J. (2010). Facial mapping expert evidence, *Journal of Criminal Law*, 74, 20–26.

O'Brien Jr W.E. (2003). Court scrutiny of expert evidence: recent decisions highlight the tensions, *International Journal of Evidence and Proof*, 7, 172–184.

7

Formal Methods for Logical Evaluation

In this chapter, the underlying statistical principles being advocated for the logical interpretation and evaluation of evidence will be described. These enable the scientist to construct conditional probabilities for the evidence under the two competing propositions, thereby arriving at a balanced view as to the evidential weight. To put this in context, we shall start by reviewing the differences between methods based on Bayesian inference and the alternative frequentist approach that has been used more commonly in some jurisdictions, particularly the United States, and by some forensic science subdisciplines. This will lead to an exposition of evaluation based on the use of the Likelihood Ratio (LR), the so-called 'logical approach'. The distinction between this method and that based on Bayes' Theorem leading to posterior odds will be highlighted. The mathematics of the key results that are required for such evaluation will be reviewed and the strategy for linking the outcome to a verbal scale for the presentation of the outcome to the court will be described.

7.1 Frequentist and Bayesian Approaches to Evaluation

7.1.1 The Frequentist Approach to Formulating Opinion

Debates about Bayesian approaches to evidence evaluation often relate to competing claims from what is termed the 'frequentist' or 'coincidence' methodology (reviewed, for example, by Curran, 2009). This alternative approach to formulating an opinion is based on the application of statistics to two aspects of the forensic interpretation; how strong is the evidence in associating the defendant with the crime scene and how rare are the characteristics of that evidence?

Forensic Evidence in Court: Evaluation and Scientific Opinion, First Edition. Craig Adam.
© 2016 John Wiley & Sons, Ltd. Published 2016 by John Wiley & Sons, Ltd.

The first of these includes the quality of matching between evidence from a crime scene and reference materials associated with the defendant. For example, this may be determined using established hypothesis-based statistical methods applied to various evidence types, such as the comparison of glass refractive index distributions using the statistical t-test, to determine the degree of confidence in the compositional similarity between the two sets of materials.

The second may be summarised as a frequency of occurrence for evidence characteristics in the environment, from which the term 'frequentist' originates; for example, 25% of randomly transferred fibres found on t-shirts are blue cotton. This leads to it sometimes also being called the 'coincidence' method since the evidence was either due to the defendant's involvement or, by coincidence, from another random source. Hence, a good 'match' for evidence with rare characteristics could be interpreted as strong evidence in support of the association of the suspect with the crime scene. However, this can lead to misinterpretation, such as in the prosecutor's fallacy – see 7.6.2 – whereby the rarity of the evidence is turned round in the minds of the jury to imply that is extremely unlikely that anyone, other than the defendant, was the source.

> 'The coincidence approach proceeds to offer evidence against a proposition by showing that the evidence is unlikely if this proposition is true. Hence it supports the alternative proposition. The less likely the evidence is under the proposition the more support that is given to the alternative.'
>
> [Buckleton *et al.*, 2005, chapter 2.1.1]

This method is quite limited in its application and, most importantly, does not take into consideration the framework of circumstances relating to the evidence. Indeed, many would regard the frequentist approach as being wrong in the sense of not informing expert opinion in a logical and complete way. At best, the frequentist approach may be regarded as a half-way house to an evaluation based on Bayesian inference, but one that cannot be applied successfully in many circumstances and that may, in some instances, mislead in court.

7.1.2   The Logical Evaluation of Evidence

In contrast, Bayesian inference carries these ideas forward by interpreting the evidence both from the defence's perspective and from the prosecution's perspective in a logical fashion by reviewing the balance of probabilities for the evidence under each of these two propositions using the likelihood ratio. For this reason, it is often called the likelihood ratio method. It also enables questions of relevance to the court to be addressed in a rigorous way, through the formulation of the competing propositions and by the incorporation of the circumstances of the case.

The likelihood ratio is the ratio of two conditional probabilities (to be defined section 7.2), and so, in itself, is not a probability. This has been a source of confusion in the courts since the word 'likelihood', on its own, is often taken as a synonym for probability; for example as in: 'What is the likelihood that the train will be late today?'

A further source of confusion amongst many users and receivers of a logical, evaluative opinion is that one can go beyond likelihood ratio and, by using the Bayes' Theorem, derive posterior odds for the prosecution and defence propositions, after consideration of the evidence, and hence obtain posterior probabilities for each of these. However, this has its difficulties and is consequently controversial, not only with the court but also with most modern adherents of the likelihood ratio approach.

7.1.3 The Debate on Formulating Opinion

The debate on how opinion should be formulated is ongoing and has something of a trans-Atlantic tension about it, with Europe and Australia fairly committed to logical evaluation, while the United States remains sceptical. Some of the issues are reviewed by Risinger (2013) while a notable opponent to the use of likelihood ratios, Bodziak, has commented in the context of footwear evidence:

> 'In contrast [with the UK and Europe], in the USA and most countries, the footwear examiner only considers the question of whether the shoe made the mark. The use of any notional or conditioning information, central to the use of the likelihood ratio, is not part of that examination.'
>
> [Bodziak, 2012]

7.2 The Likelihood Ratio Method

The logical approach to evidence evaluation is based on assessing and comparing conditional probabilities and, through the application of the following three principles, leads to the calculation of the likelihood ratio. These principles have been presented in differing ways, while retaining the essence of the framework. The following statements are based on those provided by Evett (1998).

1. Interpretation of scientific evidence is carried out within a framework of circumstances that are related to the crime itself
2. Interpretation needs to be based on consideration of at least two competing propositions
3. The role of the forensic scientist is to consider the probability of the evidence given each of the propositions to be addressed

This methodology is built on foundations of mathematical logic and whatever the complexity of the case, adherence to these principles will lead to an equitable evaluation of all evidence, scientific or otherwise. The focus is on the evidence, its interpretation and the role of the scientist in evaluating its significance to the case. The circumstances of the case provide the mathematical conditioning under which the probabilities for the evidence are generated. The expert should make these clear to the court, as they underpin the evaluation. Should these circumstances change, the probabilities and hence the evaluation, will change as well.

Following the second principle, and the discussion and examples in the previous chapters, the competing propositions are conventionally written from the mutually exclusive perspectives taken by the prosecution and defence counsel; generic propositions may be:

H_1: The defendant was responsible for the evidence at the crime scene
H_2: Someone other than the defendant was responsible for the evidence at the crime scene

Here, the alternative proposition has been taken as the negation of that provided by the prosecution. Other defence propositions are possible, as we have seen, for example, in the Bowden case in section 6.3. However, if no alternative proposition is available, then logical evaluation cannot proceed.

The conditional probabilities express the considered view of the scientist as to the explanation of the evidence E, on the basis of each proposition:

$Pr(E|H_1, I)$: The probability of the evidence E, given H_1 and I
$Pr(E|H_2, I)$: The probability of the evidence E, given H_2 and I

The evidence E is the set of observations or measurements made by the scientist on the evidential and reference materials. The additional symbol I, following the conditioning bar, represents all other conditions set by the circumstances of the case. In many instances, in manipulating the mathematics, this may be omitted but retaining it serves to remind the scientist of the importance of what it represents.

Finally, the relative magnitudes of these two probabilities, and therefore of the explanations for the evidence, are compared through taking their ratio, the likelihood ratio, LR:

$$LR = \frac{\Pr(E|H_1,I)}{\Pr(E|H_2,I)}$$

It is important to note that the propositions here must be mutually exclusive but do not need to be exhaustive; there may be other perfectly acceptable alternative hypotheses that can be selected as H_2. Since these probabilities are not exhaustive, the likelihood ratio is not a statistical odds.

The scientist will assess the probabilities, either qualitatively or quantitatively, to arrive at an estimate for the likelihood ratio. If the probability conditional on H_1, I is greater than that under H_2, I then LR will be greater than unity and hence the prosecution's explanation for the evidence should carry more weight with the court than that of the defence, and vice versa. If both probabilities are the same then $LR = 1$ and the evidence carries no weight in the debate. Theoretically, there are no upper or lower limits on the magnitude of LR and the range may be considerable; what matters is the order of magnitude of LR. Values of LR further from unity carry greater evidential weight than those closer to the neutral position. So how might a verbal expression of the evaluative opinion be expressed to the court, based on this numerical information?

7.3   Expressing Opinion Through Likelihood Ratio

The framework for devising propositions and deriving a likelihood ratio provides a uniform and consistent approach to the formulation of expert opinion. The presentation of that opinion to the court raises further challenges. The first is the format of the statement itself while the second relates to how the strength of the evaluation is translated from a numerical order of magnitude into a form of words.

7.3.1   Statements of Evaluative Opinion

In the previous chapter, some examples of evaluative statements were discussed in the context of case studies. However, none was fully expressed within the logical framework. It is important that, for the court to fully appreciate the expert's opinion, reference to both propositions should be included in the evaluation.

The following examples demonstrate suitable forms of words for evaluative statements, though other formats are possible:

A. In my opinion, the findings provide moderately strong support for the proposition that the defendant broke the window and so gained entry rather than that the glass was present on his clothing for some unknown reason, unrelated to the crime.

B. The degree of correspondence between the sole of the defendant's left shoe and the impression retrieved from the kitchen floor, in terms of pattern, size and wear, provides moderate support to the view that the footwear impression at the scene was made by that shoe, rather than by another, unknown shoe.

C. The quantity and distribution of the blood-spatter on the defendant's clothing are much more probable given the proposition that he was engaged in an assault on the victim, rather than that he had been standing close by while the assault was carried out by another, unknown person.

Further examples, given in the context of a full forensic report, and further discussion of other information relevant to the evaluation, are provided in the recent ENFSI guidelines for evaluative reporting (2015).

7.3.2   Likelihood Ratio and Verbal Equivalent Statements

Likelihood ratio lies on a single, continuous numerical scale going from a neutral outcome to one that may provide, at least theoretically, overwhelming support for one proposition. Efforts have been made to map this scale on to a series of verbal statements that accurately convey the weight of the scientific opinion to the fact-finders.

This approach puts the interpretation of all forms of evidence on the same evaluative scale and expert opinion may be given in consistent manner whatever form that evidence takes. Understandably different countries have tackled this in different ways and, as mentioned earlier, to date the United States has shown little enthusiasm for logical evaluation.

In 2009 the UK Association of Forensic Science Providers agreed a table where likelihood ratios are categorised according to their order of magnitude, with each of the six categories being allocated a verbal expression to indicate the strength of opinion (see Table 7.1). The threshold for the strongest opinion – extremely strong evidence in support of the prosecution – is set at 1,000,000. Evidential weights at this level would be applied most often to a single standard DNA profile.

The scale only applies explicitly to evidential opinion that favours the prosecution though, by taking the reciprocals of the numerical values of likelihood ratio, it may be converted into statements in favour of the defence. More recently, alternative forms of words to those at each point, expressed in a probabilistic way rather than as the degree of support to a proposition, have been recommended by ENFSI (2015). Both equivalents are given in Table 7.1.

An alternative scale, based on four points on either side of a neutral outcome, has been devised by Norgaard *et al.* (2012), for use in the nonadversarial Swedish criminal justice system. This uses a logarithmic algorithm to calibrate the likelihood ratio scale to assumptions on the numerical equivalent of 'beyond reasonable doubt' and a prior odds of unity, utilising evaluative phrases similar to those in Table 7.1.

7.4   Evaluation and Bayes' Theorem

It will now be clear that Bayes' Theorem itself is not used in the logical evaluation of evidence, as the likelihood ratio is independent of the relationships between conditional probabilities encapsulated in this theorem. However, by extending the evaluative process

Table 7.1 *A UK/European Verbal Scale for Evidence Evaluation (Based on AFSP, 2009 and ENFSI, 2015)*

Likelihood ratio range	Verbal equivalent (in terms of support to the prosecution's proposition over that of the defence)
	A neutral evaluation
LR = 1	No support for one proposition over the other or Provides no assistance in addressing the issue
1 < LR < 10	Limited or weak evidence in support or Slightly more probable than
10 ≤ LR < 100	Moderate evidence in support or More probable than
100 ≤ LR < 1,000	Moderately strong evidence in support or Appreciably more probable than
1,000 ≤ LR < 10,000	Strong evidence in support or Much more probable than
10,000 ≤ LR < 1,000,000	Very strong evidence in support or Far more probable than
1,000,000 ≤ LR	Extremely strong evidence in support or Exceedingly more probable than

through the use of the Bayes' Theorem, probabilities for the propositions themselves, which are of direct interest to the jury and court, may be calculated.

The implementation of this approach raises major difficulties within the context of the court, some of which are illustrated by the proceedings in the landmark case of R v Dennis John Adams (Chapter 8.3). First, we need to understand the mathematical relationships and the additional, conditional and unconditional, probabilities that are involved in such an evaluation.

7.4.1 Bayes' Theorem: Prior and Posterior Odds

Fundamentally, Bayes' Theorem is a mathematical relationship that links two conditional and two unconditional probabilities. Writing it in terms of some of the symbols relevant to this discussion, we get:

$$\Pr(E) \times \Pr(H_1 | E, I) = \Pr(H_1) \times \Pr(E | H_1, I) \tag{1}$$

It is worth looking carefully at the meanings of some of these quantities. The new probabilities here are:

$Pr(E)$ is the unconditional probability of the evidence

$Pr(H_1)$ is the unconditional probability of the prosecution's proposition being accepted, without any consideration of the evidence, E.

$Pr(H_1|E,I)$ is the probability of accepting the prosecution's proposition after the evidence and the circumstances of the case have been considered.

Note that, unless the two unconditional probabilities are coincidently equal, then generally:

$$Pr(H_1|E,I) \neq Pr(E|H_1,I)$$

This result is of fundamental importance in appreciating the importance of clearly distinguishing a conditioning statement from the proposition on which the probability is derived.

To see why Bayes' Theorem is potentially useful, we note that $Pr(H_1|E,I)$ is of particular interest to the fact-finders in reaching their verdict and that the theorem links this to probabilities on the evidence itself. However, to generate a directly useful relationship, we need to take two further steps. First, Bayes' Theorem may be written in a similar way for the defence proposition, H_2, to give:

$$Pr(E) \times Pr(H_2|E,I) = Pr(H_2) \times Pr(E|H_2,I) \qquad (2)$$

Then, by dividing expression (1) by (2) and cancelling the first factor in each, we get:

$$\frac{Pr(H_1|E,I)}{Pr(H_2|E,I)} = \frac{Pr(H_1)}{Pr(H_2)} \times \frac{Pr(E|H_1,I)}{Pr(E|H_2,I)} \qquad (3)$$

The second factor on the right hand side is familiar as the likelihood ratio and it is clear now why this is sometimes referred to as the Bayes' Factor. The other factor on that side is independent of the evidence E and since the propositions H_1 and H_2 are mutually exclusive, this implies that:

$$Pr(H_2) = 1 - Pr(H_1)$$

It is evident that this first factor on the right-hand side is, in fact, the odds in favour of accepting the prosecution's case prior to the consideration of any evidence and is therefore termed the Prior Odds:

$$\text{Prior Odds} = P_0 = \frac{Pr(H_1)}{Pr(H_2)}$$

In a similar way, the factor on the left hand side is also an odds on the prosecution's case; this time after the evidence has been considered. This is called the Posterior Odds, defined as:

$$\text{Posterior Odds} = P_1 = \frac{Pr(H_1|E,I)}{Pr(H_2|E,I)}$$

Finally, expression (3), which is derived from Bayes' Theorem and hence sometimes called the 'Odds' version of the theorem, may be written as:

$$P_1 = LR \times P_0 \qquad\qquad (4)$$

Posterior Odds $=$ Prior Odds $\times$ Likelihood Ratio

This result illustrates the difference between Bayesian inference, which leads to the concept of evidence evaluation via the likelihood ratio, and Bayes' Theorem, which goes a step further by showing how this may impact directly on the legal argument and the ultimate issue. The posterior odds are directly relevant to the considerations of the jury, as they provide a measure of the odds on accepting the prosecution's proposition, after the evidence has been considered through calculation of the likelihood ratio. However, as this equation shows, it also needs the prior odds, which are essentially the starting point for the court debate, prior to considering the evidence. In practice, difficulties over the prior odds limit the usefulness of the odds version of Bayes' Theorem, which has generated much debate over the past twenty-five years or so and has led to much, though not all, of the controversy around Bayesian methods in the courtroom.

7.4.2 Combining Likelihood Ratios

Nevertheless, expression (4) leads to a further concept, which is a powerful feature of both the Bayesian approach and logical evaluation using the likelihood ratio. Consider a court presented with more than one piece of evidence, scientific or otherwise. The application of this result to the first piece of evidence, through calculation of a likelihood ratio LR_1, leads to the posterior odds. This then becomes the prior odds for the debate around the second piece of evidence, using LR_2, and so on. Inclusion of each likelihood ratio essentially updates the prior odds for the case. Expression (4) therefore leads to a multiplicative combination law for the likelihood ratios corresponding to each piece of evidence:

$$P_1 = LR_1 \times LR_2 \times .... \times LR_n \times P_0$$

Hence, we arrive at a conclusion that is universally valid:

$$LR_{total} = LR_1 \times LR_2 \times .... \times LR_n$$

This demonstrates that likelihood ratios may be combined multiplicatively whether or not the odds version of Bayes' Theorem is actually used or not. It also reveals that this rule is applicable whatever the nature of the evidence, as long as a likelihood ratio may be reliably and justifiably estimated.

7.5 Prior Odds

The difficulty with prior odds is that they are based on considerations of the case without any evidence being put forward. So, how then might the initial prior odds be estimated? There are two extreme approaches to this. The first is to consider a neutral stance where innocence and guilt are equally likely – the assumption of 'equal priors'. This may seem a natural approach, though it is not in keeping with the assumption of innocence until guilt is proved beyond reasonable doubt. Equal priors implies that the prior odds are unity:

$$\frac{\Pr(H_1)}{\Pr(H_2)} = 1$$

The second view is that, with no evidence presented, the defendant has effectively been chosen at random from a population N. This would suggest that:

$$\frac{\Pr(H_1)}{\Pr(H_2)} = \frac{1}{N}$$

The difficulty here is how N is chosen. It cannot be from the whole population in the area where the crime was committed since the police do not arrest someone on a completely random basis! Rather it is the case that N represents a subpopulation of suspects that has been established in some way; for example, hypothetical scenarios might be to consider males between the ages of 18 and 40 from the local area who did not have alibis at the time of the offence or known burglars with the same modus operandi.

Prior odds may be informed by base rate statistics. Base rates represent the frequency of occurrence of particular events or attributes in a population on an everyday basis; for example, the proportion of burglars who re-offend or the frequency of finding drug traces on banknotes. Although some base rates may be required for the calculation of a likelihood ratio, others provide information that is not specifically evidence against a defendant but is relevant to the context of the case against that individual. However, courts may regard some base rate statistics as irrelevant to the legal discussion for a variety of reasons, or indeed, that their use acts against the principle of innocent until proved guilty.

Nevertheless, it is clear that the prior odds are a matter for the court and not for the forensic scientist, principally as they are not related to any aspect of the scientific evidence. Notwithstanding this, there have been examples in the past where this issue has been consciously addressed by the expert witness, for example, in the case of Denis John Adams.

The whole issue of prior odds has been discussed by Friedman (2000) who recommends that jurors take an intuitive approach and assess prior odds from the perspective of being an observer outside the judicial system. The initial prior odds would be expected to be very small, but not zero. He proposes the following statement as an example of how the judge should instruct the jury as to the starting point for the trial; effectively how to arrive at the prior odds:

> 'Members of the jury, you may not treat the bringing of the accusation, or the prosecutor's opening statement, as evidence that the accused committed the crime charged. Accordingly, now, before the trial has begun, when you have no information on the matter apart from your general knowledge of the world, if you were to ask yourself how probable it is that the accused violently assaulted his neighbor last June 25, you would, to be reasonable, have to assess that probability as being very low. This is the point from which you must begin consideration of the evidence in this case.'
>
> [Friedman, 2000]

7.6 Posterior Probabilities

Posterior probabilities are of interest, as conventionally much opinion is formulated conditionally on the findings from the evidence. Although this may be acceptable for investigative opinion, it is not appropriate for evaluation. Indeed, confusion over the role of conditioning and the meaning of a posterior probability has led to the notorious Prosecutor's Fallacy.

7.6.1 Opinion and Posterior Probabilities

Further discussion of those conditional probabilities that were defined in the expressions of Bayes' Theorem (equations (1) and (2)), will enable us to gain a clearer understanding of some of the verbal expressions of opinion discussed in Chapter 5. Earlier, in 7.4.1, $Pr(H_1|E,I)$ was defined as:

> The probability of accepting the prosecution's proposition after the evidence and the circumstances of the case have been considered

Consider the example of opinion on GSR evidence, quoted in 5.4.2:

> 'The presence of GSR on the defendant's jacket means he very probably fired the weapon'

This statement starts with the outcome from the forensic examination of the GSR on the jacket; in other words, the evidence is the condition on which the opinion is based. The opinion itself is that the defendant 'very probably fired the weapon,' which is a probabilistic view on the prosecution's proposition, H_1. This analysis confirms that this formulation of opinion is the posterior probability, $Pr(H_1|E,I)$. A similar deconstruction applies to other examples of opinion discussed in section 5.4.2.

However, equation (3) and subsequent results derived from the Bayes' Theorem have revealed that calculation of this posterior probability and the equivalent for H_2 require knowledge, not only of the likelihood ratio, but also of the prior probabilities or prior odds. In 7.5, the difficulties in dealing with prior odds were discussed. Yet those experts who commonly provide opinion in the form of a posterior probability are not working with Bayesian methods, far less are they attempting to estimate the prior odds. They are unconsciously using bits of information and ideas, both from the current case and their previous experience, possibly together with the expectations of the police or their client, to arrive at their opinion. Not only is this process not rigorous or objective, it is arguably not even a truly subjective assessment. On this basis alone, such statements as evaluative opinion do not convey the true significance of the evidence and, indeed, may mislead the fact-finder.

7.6.2 The Prosecutor's Fallacy

In 7.4.1, attention was drawn to the importance of the inequality of conditional probabilities where the condition and proposition are reversed; written here in terms of H_2 for convenience, with I omitted for clarity:

$$Pr\left(H_2|E\right) \neq Pr\left(E|H_2\right)$$

However, the precision of this mathematical expression is frequently not replicated in verbal or written language, with the consequence that the significance of the evidence is misunderstood by, or even misrepresented to, the court. Mathematically, this is called the 'error of the transposed conditional', meaning that the probability represented by the right-hand side is interpreted as that on the left-hand side. Why should this be important?

Consider evidence associating the defendant with a crime scene. The expert witness explains that an alternative explanation for the evidence at the scene would have a low probability due to its rarity in the population or environment. In other words, $Pr(E|H_2)$ where the condition is the defence proposition, has a low value:

> If the defence proposition of innocence is accepted, then the alternative explanation for the evidence is unlikely.

This may be interpreted, quite incorrectly, by some who assign this low probability to the proposition, rather than to the evidence; in other words to $Pr(H_2|E)$:

> Given this evidence, it is unlikely the defendant is innocent.

As this misinterpretation tends to favour the prosecution case, it is called the 'Prosecutor's Fallacy'. It came to prominence in the early days of DNA profile evidence, though it had existed in the courts well before that time. The fallacy may occur in debating the significance of any form of evidence, not just DNA profiles, including those where qualitative probabilities are invoked in support of the expert's testimony; for example, the statements made by the expert witnesses in R v Dallagher, quoted in Chapter 6.2.2. When transposition of the conditional occurs, in the context of source level propositions, the fallacy is sometimes termed 'Source Probability Error'. Despite a much wider appreciation of the danger the prosecutor's fallacy poses to legal debate, there continue to be examples in the courts to the present day, as we shall discover in later chapters.

7.7   Working Out Conditional Probabilities and Likelihood Ratio

Calculation of a likelihood ratio involves the determination of conditional probabilities. Although in some cases this is relatively straightforward, there are examples of where the actual numbers chosen by the scientist have proved controversial and ultimately unacceptable to the court. Although some of these will studied in detail in later chapters, for the moment it is useful to have an overview of how this calculation may be done in general terms.

The derivation of a likelihood ratio is an estimate, as ultimately it is the order of magnitude that matters, not the exact value and this is mathematically straightforward to calculate in cases where it involves only arithmetical operations. The difficult, and the controversial, aspect is in the selection of these numbers and, to a large extent, this depends on the evidence type and the nature of the propositions. It should be stressed that, although fully quantitative calculations may be possible, it is often the case that numerical data may only inform the expert's evalua-tion of these probabilities or even that they are based wholly on their experience.

The basis of the derivation is different at source level to that at activity level so each will be dealt with separately.

7.7.1   Likelihood Ratio at Source Level

At source level the LR is based on two conditional probabilities of which the numerator is normally easier to estimate. In most instances, there will be a high probability of finding the evidence, given the prosecution's view that the defendant was responsible, implying that a value of unity, or something very close to that, should be adopted. In some cases, for example, related to the quality of the correspondence between the questioned and reference materials, this may not be the case, but for the moment such possibilities will be disregarded. Thus:

$$\Pr\left(E|H_1\right) = 1$$

The magnitude of the LR is more sensitive to the value of the denominator $\Pr(E|H_2)$ and determining the probability for the alternative explanation is normally more complex, often involving assumptions and approximations. Indeed, it should be part of the scientist's task in formulating the evaluation to test the sensitivity of the likelihood ratio to these factors.

For examples where there are statistically rigorous reference databases, which are accepted both by the scientific community and the courts, and are appropriate to the evidence and circumstances under consideration, this probability will be equal to the frequency of occurrence of the evidential characteristics within the relevant population. For a full, single DNA profile, the random match probability (RMP) provides the frequency needed for this calculation. For more complex problems, for example where mixtures of DNA are involved, formal statistical methods for dealing with the calculation of likelihood ratio have been developed; for example, see Chapter 7 in Buckleton *et al.*, 2005.

For other types of evidence, where there are databases either from manufacturers, from surveys or from scientific trials or experiments, the same process may be followed. However, there will often be doubts as to the applicability of the data used and how appropriate it is. There may be instances where other sources of similar data provide quite different outcomes and the expert witness needs to convince the court of the validity of any decisions that have been made relating to such choices. Past experience has shown that courts may not be at all tolerant of this approach.

The third approach is where probabilities are based on the expert's experience, perhaps based on a mixture of hard data, casework experience and discussions with peers. These are usually fairly conservative, but are open to the challenge of being little more than guesswork, and it may be hard to provide adequate justification to the court in many instances.

Whatever method is chosen, the scientist's work should be demonstrably robust and transparent, as evidenced in the report to the court. The output from this will be a frequency of occurrence, f, for those specific characteristics of the evidence under consideration. This provides the probability for an alternative explanation based on a source of the evidence 'other than from the accused'. Thus, the likelihood ratio will be given by:

$$LR = \frac{\Pr\left(E|H_1\right)}{\Pr\left(E|H_2\right)} = \frac{1}{f}$$

For other more specific propositions put forward by the defence, a similar procedure needs to be followed. In some instances, such as fireworks being the source of metal particles in the Bowden case, discussed in chapter 6.3, activity level considerations may need to be taken into account.

7.7.2   Likelihood Ratio at Activity Level

At activity level, the source level information is usually retained but now embedded in an expression that takes account of the transfer and persistence properties of the trace evidence being considered. The detailed development of these results will not be given here (see, for example, Evett, 1984 and Adam, 2010); suffice it to say that both explanations for the transferred evidence are considered and appropriate probabilities assigned by the scientist. Expressions may be developed for many specific scenarios involving transferred evidence, but only the basic result will be quoted here. Compared to working at source level, the expert will more often rely at activity level on their experience in estimating the magnitudes of relevant probabilities. In this case, these are:

t_0: the probability of no transfer, given contact
t: the probability of transfer of a specified evidential trace, given contact
b_0: the probability of no evidential trace arising from innocent interactions
b: the probability of a specified evidential trace from innocent interactions

Thus, with f defined as in the previous section, the likelihood ratio is derived as:

$$\mathrm{LR} = t_0 + \frac{tb_0}{bf}$$

In practice, the first term is may be neglected and the magnitude effectively defined by the second term. Once again, the rarity of the trace evidence at source level is also significant to the magnitude of the LR at activity level.

7.8 Conclusions

Having justified and discussed the methodology for the logical evaluation of evidence, the next stage is to review what impact this has had in the courts. In the following chapter, some notable cases will illustrate how the frequentist and Bayesian approaches have been followed in formulating expert opinion and what has been the response from the court.

References

Adam C.D. (2010). Chapter 11, Statistics and the significance of evidence, 279–311. In Essential Mathematics and Statistics for Forensic Science, Wiley-Blackwell, Chichester, UK.

Association of Forensic Science Providers (AFSP). (2009). Standards for the formulation of evaluative forensic science expert opinion. *Science and Justice*, 49(3), 161–164.

Bodziak W. (2012). Traditional conclusions in footwear examinations versus the use of the Bayesian approach and likelihood ratio. *Law, Probability and Risk*, 11, 279–287.

Buckleton J., Triggs C.M. and Walsh S.J. (2005). *Forensic DNA Evidence Interpretation*. CRC Press. Boca Raton, Florida.

Curran J.M. (2009). Statistics in forensic science. *Wiley Interdisciplinary Reviews, Computational Statistics*, 1(2), 141–156.

European Network of Forensic Science Institutes: ENFSI guideline for evaluative reporting in forensic science [Online]. (2015). Available at https://www.unil.ch/esc/files/live/sites/esc/files/Fichiers%202015/ENFSI%20Guideline%20Evaluative%20Reporting [Accessed 24 October 2015].

Evett I.W. (1984). A quantitative theory for interpreting transfer evidence in criminal cases. *Journal of the Royal Statistical Society (Series C: Applied Statistics)*, 33(1), 25–32.

Evett I.W. (1998). Towards a uniform framework for reporting opinions in forensic science casework. *Science and Justice*, 38(3), 198–202.

Friedman R.D. (2000). A presumption of innocence, not of even odds. *Stanford Law Review*, 82, 873–887.

Norgaard A., Ansell R., Drotz W. and Jaeger L. (2012). Scale of conclusions for the value of evidence. *Law, Probability and Risk*, 11(1), 1–24.

Risinger D.M. (2013). Reservations about likelihood ratios (and some other aspects of forensic 'Bayesianism'). *Law, Probability and Risk*, 12(1), 63–74.

Further Reading

Aitken C., Roberts P. and Jackson G. (2010). Royal Statistical Society Practitioner Guide No 1: Fundamentals of probability and statistical evidence in criminal proceedings [Online]. Available at http://www.rss.org.uk/Images/PDF/influencing-change/rss-fundamentals-probability-statistical-evidence.pdf [Accessed 24 October 2015].

Dawid A.P. (2002). Bayes's theorem and weighing evidence by juries. 71–90, In R. Swinburne (Ed.). *Bayes's Theorem*. OUP. Oxford, UK.

Evett I.W., Jackson G., Lambert J.A. and McCrossan S. (2000). The impact of the principles of evidence interpretation on the structure and content of statements. *Science and Justice*, 40(4), 233–239.

Koehler J. (2002). When do courts think base rate statistics are relevant? *Jurimetrics Journal*, 42, 373–402.

Robertson B. and Vignaux T. (1995). *Interpreting Evidence*. Wiley. Chichester, UK.

Robertson B. and Vignaux T. (1998). Explaining evidence logically, *New Law Journal*, 148(6826), 159–162.

8

Case Studies in Probabilistic Opinion

The ultimate test for all approaches to the formulation of expert opinion is how it is received, and to what extent it is accepted, by the courts. Indeed, the views of the fact-finders should contribute to any review and refinement of the evaluation process. However, courts do not wish to receive expert opinion that is not admissible, relevant and reliable and this includes the methodology underpinning the formulation of opinion, as much as the scientific measurements and analysis on which the testimony is based. The aim here is to examine how the approaches discussed in the previous chapter may be implemented in practice and to illustrate some of the basic calculations. Starting with a short discussion on an unusual case dominated by probability data, we will move to one where frequentist explanations for blood and footwear mark evidence were presented and which is also amenable to logical evaluation by likelihood ratio. The case of R v D J Adams will illustrate how Bayes' Theorem itself may be applied, across both scientific and non-scientific evidence, and the issues that arose from this innovatory exercise. Finally, an example will be discussed where statistical data may be misinterpreted as favourable to the defence, under the so-called defendant's fallacy.

8.1   People v Collins 1968

Although statistics had been used in explicit numerical form in earlier cases, that of People v Collins (1968) in California is notable for the way in which the cumulative effect of probabilities was used by a mathematics expert to strengthen the court's view on witness identification evidence. The identification referred to two individuals in a distinctive car seen leaving the vicinity where an elderly woman had been robbed. A couple, Malcolm and Janet Collins, matching the witness's description, were arrested and tried for the robbery. Individual probabilities were estimated for the occurrence of six distinctive features of the identification, including the colour of the car, the colour and style of the hair of each occupant and their racial origin. On the assumption that these characteristics were independent, the probabilities were combined by multiplication to yield a frequency of occurrence for the combination observed at the crime scene. The result was a probability of one in twelve million that a couple and car, matching the witness's description, would be found by random selection from the population. On the strength of this frequentist opinion, the defendants were convicted but later the verdict was overturned at appeal, on the grounds that the trial judge was wrong to admit mathematical calculations of probability into the legal debate.

In fact, there are other more basic criticisms of this approach: there was no evidence in support of the values assigned to each probability or that they were, in fact, independent, and the accuracy of the identification witness's observations was not challenged.

At the trial, this extremely low frequency must indeed have seemed to imply that the appearance of the Collins couple was unique, particularly twenty years before DNA profiles made such low probabilities more commonplace in the courts. Nevertheless, it was argued later by Finkelstein and Fairley (1970) that, rather than quote probabilities to the court, a preferable approach to providing a weight of evidence from statistical data was to use Bayes' Theorem to generate a posterior probability of direct relevance to the fact-finders. This would be supported by a prior probability, built from background information, which potentially associated the defendant with the crime. This proposal was important, as a means for the court to attach a weight of evidence to an identification that was not categorical. However, it was to take another twenty years or so before Bayesian approaches started to impact on expert opinion in the court.

8.2   R v Michael Shirley 2003

On the evening of 8th December 1986, Linda Cook was raped and murdered in Portsmouth, United Kingdom, with injuries consistent with having her neck and body stamped on by a man's shoe. Michael Shirley, a seaman in the Royal Navy, was arrested as he admitted being in the area at the time and his account of his movements was inconsistent. At the trial in 1988, the prosecution put forward both biological and footwear-mark evidence that contributed to Shirley's conviction. Semen samples were recovered from the victim's body and, as DNA analysis was not yet possible with the limited amount of sample available, the blood group associated with the semen was found to be the same as that of Shirley. The defendant also owned a pair of shoes with a manufacturer's 'flash' logo on the sole, showing the same characteristics as a footwear-mark found on Linda Cook's body. Finally, his body bore some minor injuries to his face, arms and back, that were dated by one expert witness as having been inflicted around the time of the murder, and that Shirley could not satisfactorily explain.

In 2001, the CCRC, under ongoing pressure from Shirley's lawyers, agreed for DNA profiles to be obtained from the biological evidence that was still available. On the basis of this fresh evidence, an appeal was granted in 2003, after Shirley had served 16 years in prison. Indeed, this was the first time that the CCRC had supported a successful appeal based on the potential relevance of newly available DNA evidence.

At the trial, the scientific evidence was interpreted in a frequentist manner, as information was supplied as to the occurrence of Shirley's blood group and the sales locally of the style of shoe responsible for the marks on the body. Although likelihood ratios were not explicitly used to arrive at a summative evaluation, it is instructive to use this case as an example of the application of logical evaluation, particularly as the manner in which the weight of the footwear mark evidence was originally determined, was questioned at appeal.

8.2.1   A Logical Evaluation of Scientific Evidence

First, consider the blood group evidence. It was reported to the court that the blood group associated with the semen was common to 23.3% of the adult male population. This frequency of 0.233 may be taken as the conditional probability that someone other than Shirley was the source of the blood group and, by implication, the semen, given the defence's assertion that he was innocent. Thus:

$$\Pr\left(E|H_2\right) = 0.233 \Rightarrow LR_{blood} = \frac{1}{0.233} \approx 4$$

This is limited evidence in support of the prosecution and, on its own, of little importance to the court. The footwear mark evidence turns out to have greater probative value, however.

The evidential features of the footwear mark on the victim's body were that it was from a right foot, the size was in the range 43 to 45 and the heel of the shoe bore the characteristic 'flash' logo. No other characteristics were discussed, presumably because of the limited quality of the mark itself. Shirley's shoe size was a 44. A variety of pieces of information on sources of shoes with this logo, and on the number of such shoes in circulation in the Portsmouth area, was presented to the court to facilitate the jury in evaluating the significance of this evidence. It turns out that this was far from straightforward.

It transpired that this logo appeared on shoes from several manufacturers, in some cases as a deliberate part of the design though sometimes omitted, and in others apparently by chance. There was also the issue of whether such shoes were available for sale in Portsmouth itself. The total number of these shoes sold in 1986 in the United Kingdom was on a surprisingly small scale; and some sales figures were quoted, such as 1058 from Mark's shoes, 1721 from Melkrose and 4200 of C and A Avanti shoes, many of which did not have this logo. In summary, the judge advised the jury that a total of 51 pairs of shoes of all sizes and with the 'flash' logo, were sold in the city in that year; he added, not unsurprisingly, that this number was not 'absolutely accurate'.

On a frequentist interpretation of the marks, these figures indicated that the features observed were fairly unusual, though far from unique. On this basis, the jury members would come to their own opinion on the significance to be attached to this evidence.

From the perspective of logical evaluation, these figures inform the alternative, defence proposition for the source of the evidence, given the truth of its case. If Shirley's shoe was not the source of the mark, then it must have originated from one of the other size 43 to 45 shoes, from this set of 51 pairs of shoes bearing this logo.

On this basis, it is possible to calculate an indicative likelihood ratio, though additional assumptions have to be made. The range of uncertainty in the size of the mark, and this size range being common amongst men, mean that this aspect of the evidence carries little weight. To determine the likelihood ratio, we need quantitative data on men's shoe sizes in the United Kingdom, such as that provided by the British Footwear Association (2003). The European size range 43 to 45 corresponds to 9 to 10.5 on the UK size scale. This range comprises 41% of British men, implying a frequency of 0.41. Thus, the likelihood ratio for size is given by:

$$\Pr\left(E|H_2\right) = 0.41 \Rightarrow LR_{\text{shoe size}} = \frac{1}{0.41} \approx 2.4$$

This is effectively neutral evidence, only just being in favour of the prosecution. To estimate the likelihood ratio for the 'flash' logo, a probability needs to be derived for the defence proposition:

H$_2$: Given the truth of the defence case, the mark of the logo on the body originated from a shoe other than that worn by Michael Shirley

To calculate the probability, $\Pr(H_2|E)$, the frequency of the logo in a relevant population of men's shoes needs to be determined. As the judge confined his deliberations to the assailant being from the local area, he proposed that only men in Portsmouth need be considered. From consideration of the population and demographics, this may be estimated at around 100,000 individuals. The consequences of different men owning different numbers of shoes will be neglected; in fact, this is of little relevance if most men own similar numbers of shoes. Hence, as 51 out of 100,000 shoes have this logo and one of these pairs belonged to Shirley, the likelihood ratio for this pattern is given by:

$$\Pr\left(E|H_2\right) = \frac{51-1}{100,000} \Rightarrow LR_{\text{logo}} = \frac{1}{50/100,000} = 2000$$

Just as significant is the point, raised by the CCRC in its review of the case and re-iterated in the appeal, that by confining himself to sales of shoes only in Portsmouth, the trial judge may have underestimated how common such shoes actually were. Doubts were also raised on the validity of the sales figures citing the difficulties in obtaining reliable numbers from very many retailers. However, the appeal judge disagreed, confirming that the trial judge had given a fair overall assessment of the footwear mark evidence. It is clear from the sales figures that, as a proportion of total shoe sales, those with the logo were comparatively unusual and for the purpose of evidence evaluation this is the key point; whether men in Portsmouth bought their shoes in the city or elsewhere is a relatively minor issue.

Although LR_{size} appears neutral on its own, it may be combined with that for the logo evidence, to yield an overall likelihood ratio for the footwear evidence:

$$LR_{\text{shoe}} = LR_{\text{size}} \times LR_{\text{logo}} = 2.4 \times 2000 \approx 5000$$

The verbal equivalent scale implies that this represents strong evidence in support of the prosecution's proposition rather than that of the defence. This example shows how the use of likelihood ratio facilitates a more formal evaluation of evidence when some numerical data, here that relating to shoe size and to the population of shoes bearing the logo, is available.

8.2.2 The Outcome of the Appeal

The appeal focused on the new DNA profile evidence and its evidential weight, balancing that against the weight of the forensic evidence from the original trial. The relevant profile was agreed to be male DNA, with some features common to Shirley but having other bands besides. This was interpreted as meaning that either another male, or both another male and Shirley, had had intercourse with Linda Cook shortly before her death. Based on medical and pathological expert opinion, together with detailed accounts of Linda Cook's activities in the time leading up to the attack, the view of the appeal court judge was that the DNA profile was most probably the result of intercourse with one other male only, who was the rapist and murderer of Linda Cook, and did not include the addition of material from Michael Shirley.

In arriving at his conclusion, the appeal court judge was weighing up the forensic evidence, taking on the one hand the strength of evidence that there was only one contributor to the male DNA profile that was proved to not be Shirley, and on the other, the combination of the footwear mark evidence and the injuries to Shirley himself:

> '... it is in our judgment obvious that this piece of circumstantial evidence [the shoe-mark] cannot on its own overturn the probability that there was only one DNA contributor. It is no less clear to our minds that it cannot do so taken in conjunction with the evidence about the injuries.'
>
> [R v Shirley, 2003, paragraph 25]

This assessment may also be viewed from the perspective of likelihood ratios. The extremely high likelihood ratio for the DNA evidence, in support of the defence proposition, would be combined with that from the shoe-mark evidence, which provided a very much lower level of support to the prosecution, to yield a significant weight of evidence overall for the defence case. In deciding to overturn the conviction, the appeal judge also recognised additional scientific evidence, including that no trace of the victim's DNA was found on Shirley's shoes.

8.3   R v D J Adams 1996, 1998

Given a history of difficulties with numerical statistics in the courts, a key question for those developing evaluation by Bayesian inference was whether it would prove acceptable as a means for formulating expert opinion. In 1996, a UK court was led through a full Bayesian calculation by an expert witness, in a case that has significance for several reasons, and so is worth studying in some detail.

In R v Denis John Adams, the DNA profile from a vaginal swab was the sole evidence in support of the prosecution's case and indeed, this was the first criminal trial in the United Kingdom where this was the case. In contrast, there was a body of other, non-scientific evidence that supported the defence case. The jury was therefore faced with the task of weighing up the significance of these conflicting arguments, on the one side the quantifiable, strong evidence of the DNA, and on the other, witness identification and other evidence that pointed to the innocence of the accused. The defence strategy at the trial was to counter the probabilistic evaluation of the DNA evidence, through a similar interpretation of the witness evidence. To do this they called an eminent statistician, Prof Peter Donnelly, who proposed ways of enabling the jury to assign probabilities to each piece of nonscientific evidence, which at first sight appeared not quantifiable, and then to combine these in a logical manner. In justification of this, he stated that this was:

'... the only logically sound and consistent approach to considering situations such as this.'
[R v Adams, 1996]

With the judge's agreement, through a dialogue with the jury and with interjections from the judge, a statistical calculation, starting with prior odds, progressing through likelihood ratios and arriving at posterior odds, was carried out in the court-room. Although these terms were not used explicitly, the mathematical process was equivalent to an evaluation using the odds version of Bayes' Theorem. This was a very unusual, if not unique, approach at the time but it should be noted that the principle was accepted by the court at the trial:

'The Crown accepted that the Bayes theorem was a valid method for looking at non statistical matters in statistical terms and the judge directed the jury in relation to the Bayes theorem ...'
[R v Adams, 1996]

The detail of this is worth scrutinising, as it shows the power of the method in evaluating several quite different forms of evidence, in the same manner, and on the same scale of evidential weight. It also turned out to be a test case on whether a UK court would break the boundary existing between the approaches to the consideration of scientific and nonscientific evidence. However, first it is necessary to outline the circumstances of the case.

8.3.1   The Crime and the Evidence

On 6th April 1991 a stranger approached Miss M, as she walked home after an evening out in Hemel Hempstead, United Kingdom. He asked her the time and after briefly looking at his face she consulted her watch. At this point he attacked and raped her from behind. She later reported this attack to the police and in her statement said that her attacker was a white, clean-shaven, man with a local accent aged 20 to 25, though at a later time she estimated his age as 40 to 42 years. A vaginal swab was taken, which yielded a DNA profile, though it did not provide a match to any existing data. No progress was made until a couple of years later when Dennis John Adams, a 37-year-old white man, also from the Hemel Hempstead area, was arrested under suspicion of another sexual offence and his DNA profile was found to match that on the database from the rape of M. On the sole basis of this DNA evidence, Adams was arrested for the rape of M, in 1993.

The police set up an identification parade where the victim failed to select Adams as her assailant, although this was more than two years after the attack. Indeed, when he was committed for trial, she still failed to recognise him and stated this openly to the court. In his defence, Adams stated that he was at home with his girlfriend on the evening of the offence and she supported this claim. Hence, Adams had an alibi for the time of the attack, he did not fully match the description of the attacker and the victim herself did not recognise him.

8.3.2   A Probabilistic Analysis of the Evidence: Prior Odds

At the trial, Donnelly guided the court to estimate probabilities for the non-scientific evidence under competing hypotheses, which he proposed. This included the circulation of a supporting questionnaire to the members of the jury. The scientific evidence was considered separately and the two combined to provide the posterior odds.

The interpretation closely followed the Bayesian process of deriving the posterior odds from the prior odds, using the total likelihood ratio for the evidence. Here, the prior odds were based on two considerations; first, the random selection of the defendant from the population of potential suspects, taken to be the population of men in the local area of Hemel Hempstead, and second, an estimate that the criminal was, in fact, a local man. Local census data gave a figure of 150,000 men between the ages of 15 and 60 living within a ten-mile radius of the town. Thus, the prior odds given by random selection of the culprit from the suspect population, is given by:

$$P_0 = \frac{\Pr(H_1)}{\Pr(H_2)} = \frac{1}{N} = \frac{1}{150,000}$$

Since it is more likely than not that such an opportunistic rape was committed by a local man, though an outsider should not be excluded from consideration, a probability of 0.75 was chosen for this second factor. Hence, we obtain a total prior odds of:

$$P_0 = \frac{1}{150,000} \times 0.75 = 5 \times 10^{-6}$$

8.3.3   The Non-Scientific Evidence

Donnelly then moved on to the calculation of likelihood ratio for each piece on evidence, starting with the statement by M that she did not recognise Adams as the rapist. He dealt with this evidence by defining the questions, based on the defence and prosecution propositions, which demanded probabilistic answers:

$\Pr(E|H_2)$: If Adams is innocent what is the chance that he would not match her description?

The probability of this is clearly quite high, but not too close to unity, as there will be uncertainties in any visual identification. On this basis a value of 0.9 was proposed.

$\Pr(E|H_1)$: What is the chance of that evidence of identification if, in fact, Adams is guilty?

In contrast, the probability of failing to identify the assailant would be expected to be low, but again not very low, for the same reasons as before. This led to an estimate of 0.1. Hence, we may calculate the likelihood ratio as:

$$LR_{ident} = \frac{\Pr(E|H_1)}{\Pr(E|H_2)} = \frac{0.1}{0.9} = \frac{1}{9} \approx 0.11$$

Without using the term likelihood ratio, Donnelly expressed this to the court, as:

'What matters is the ratio of those two figures. What matters is how much more likely one thinks the evidence is if Mr Adams is guilty than if he is innocent, or how much less likely?'

[R v Adams, 1996]

The evidence of Adams' own statement of innocence was also assigned a likelihood ratio and, although this might seem an unusual exercise, it did display to the court the universal application of the Bayesian approach to evidence. Here, the two probabilities are:

$Pr(E|H_1)$: Given he is guilty, what is the probability he would in fact plead innocence?
$Pr(E|H_2)$: Given he is innocent, what is the probability he would declare his innocence?

There is little doubt that the probability for each of these propositions is certainty, that is 1 and hence:

$$LR_{defendant} = \frac{Pr(E|H_1)}{Pr(E|H_2)} = \frac{1}{1} = 1$$

This is a neutral outcome and as such carries no weight on either side of the debate. The court then moved on to the evidence of the defendant's alibi for the time of the assault. For this, the propositions have to be stated more carefully to account for the nature of the alibi, in this case that the witness was the girlfriend of the accused. Donnelly suggested the following:

$Pr(E|H_1)$: Given that the defendant is guilty, what is the chance that, whichever witness gives the alibi evidence, would give that kind of evidence?
$Pr(E|H_2)$: Given that the defendant is innocent, what is the chance that, whichever witness gives the alibi evidence, would give that kind of evidence?

It was accepted that the probability for H_2 would be greater than that for H_1 as the prosecution proposition requires complicity in lying by the alibi witness. However, neither probability should be either very large or very small, as the nature of such evidence precludes a high degree of certainty. The agreed result for the likelihood ratio was:

$$LR_{alibi} = \frac{Pr(E|H_1)}{Pr(E|H_2)} = \frac{0.25}{0.50} = 0.5$$

In other words, the alibi would be twice as likely should he be innocent, than if he were guilty.

8.3.4 The Scientific Evidence

The evaluation of the DNA evidence followed more conventional lines, though there were some complicating issues in the debate. At the time of this case, the Single-Locus Probe (SLP) technique was the standard approach to profiling and although an STR (short-tandem repeat) profile was also obtained, the judge ruled that the latter should be excluded, as the jury would not be able to deal with both sets of DNA evidence. Details on these methods are given in Chapter 10.1.

The SLP technique produced a set of nine bands on an autoradiograph that were visually compared with a control. Indeed, the expert witness dealing with the DNA evidence admitted to inking in one of the bands with a pen as it appeared less clear than the others in the profile. The random match probability for this profile was calculated by the expert witness as 1 in 297,000,000, which he 'rounded down' to 1 in 200,000,000. It was pointed out to the court that the police, at that time, conventionally expressed any such probability that was greater than 1 in 10,000,000, as just 1 in 10,000,000. The defence barrister challenged the reliability of the order of magnitude of this estimate on the grounds that one of the probes that produced two bands was based on a separate and later experiment, with the consequence that a value of only around 1 in 2,000,000 would be justified. Further, the adulteration of the evidential profile by the inking over of a band should be regarded as invalid, leading to a further reduction in this probability by a factor of 10 to give 1 in 200,000. Donnelly also expressed reservations on the estimation of the random match probability:

'I don't accept that the figure of 200,000,000 necessarily does err in the direction of the defendant. It is not clear to me what the right answer is or how far it might be wrong, but certainly I think it is quite plausible that the right answer might be in the range of 2 million rather than 200,000,000 because of the sorts of concerns I have raised.'

[R v Adams, 1996]

Despite this, the value proposed by the DNA expert witness was used in the subsequent evaluation. The conditional probabilities required for the likelihood ratio are:

$Pr(E|H_1)$: Given the prosecution's case, what is the probability that the DNA profile from the vaginal swab is indistinguishable to that from Adams?

$Pr(E|H_2)$: Given that Adams was not involved, what is the probability of such a correspondence between these DNA profiles?

Under the prosecution's proposition, the probability is accepted as certainty. For the defence's proposition, the random match probability provides the frequency of occurrence of this profile in the population. Thus:

$$LR_{DNA} = \frac{Pr(E|H_1)}{Pr(E|H_2)} = \frac{1}{1/200,000,000} = 200,000,000$$

8.3.5   Total Likelihood Ratio and Posterior Odds

Having set values for the likelihood ratios for each piece of evidence, these are then combined to produce an overall likelihood ratio for the scientific and non-scientific evidence:

$$LR = LR_{ident} \times LR_{defendant} \times LR_{alibi} \times LR_{DNA}$$
$$= 0.11 \times 1 \times 0.5 \times 200,000,000$$
$$= 11,000,000$$

Under logical evaluation, this provides extremely strong evidence in support of the prosecution's proposition as the likelihood ratio from the scientific evidence dominates. The final step in the evaluation was to calculate the posterior odds, by combining the prior odds with the total likelihood ratio, as derived in Donnelly's exposition in the court.

$$P_1 = LR \times P_0 = 11,000,000 \times 5 \times 10^{-6} = 55$$

This outcome provides the odds on accepting the prosecution's case, after consideration of the evidence, as being 55:1; or as stated by Donnelly:

'... it is much easier I think to think in terms of odds, the odds of him being guilty before the DNA evidence were 1 to 3,600,000 [see note below]. The DNA evidence has changed those and it is now 55-1, on these figures, in favour of his guilt. So the final position we arrived at with this hypothetical scenario is to a view that he is 55 times more likely to be guilty than innocent.'

[R v Adams, 1996]

Note: The figure of 1 to 3,600,000 is the posterior odds calculated, without including the likelihood ratio for the scientific evidence.

Under cross-examination by the defence counsel, Donnelly explained that if the random match probability dropped to 1 in 2,000,000, the lower limit of his suggested range, this would move the posterior odds to 0.55:1 or around 2:1 in favour of the defence proposition that Adams was innocent.

8.3.6   The Appeals

Despite the defence's strategy of logically evaluating the non-scientific evidence in the same way as the scientific evidence, Adams was convicted of rape at this trial. He appealed on several grounds including that:

'... the judge misdirected the jury as to the evidence in relation to the Bayes theorem and left the jury unguided as to how that theorem could be used in properly assessing the statistical and non-statistical evidence in the case.'

[R v Adams, 1996]

After reviewing the case at the appeal, the judge rejected the other grounds but accepted the argument on misdirection, on the basis that assessment of the relationships between different pieces of evidence and their evaluation was very much the responsibility of the jury and that Bayes' Theorem introduced an unacceptable rigidity into that activity, particularly where non-scientific evidence was involved.

'Jurors evaluate evidence and reach a conclusion not by means of a formula, mathematical or otherwise, but by the joint application of their individual common sense and knowledge of the world to the evidence before them.'

[R v Adams, 1996]

However, in granting the appeal, the judge instructed a re-trial at which the same evidence was presented and debated in the same manner as before, with the defence counsel stressing the rationale for considering the scientific and non-scientific evidence in the same way and justifying the Bayesian approach as the appropriate logical way in which to achieve this. Nevertheless, the jury returned a guilty verdict once again, that led to a second appeal by Adams, in which he claimed that the defence were obliged to counter the statistical evaluation of the scientific evidence, with a similar evaluation of the non-scientific evidence.

While the second appeal court supported the use of statistical data in the evaluation of the DNA evidence, it was critical of attempts to attach numbers to the witness identification, thereby rejecting the Bayesian method.

'However applying the Bayesian approach to non-scientific, non-DNA evidence as it was in the instant case was not to be encouraged. Juries would not be assisted in their task by reference to complex approaches which they were unlikely to fully understand and even more unlikely to apply accurately. In cases that lacked special features, expert evidence should not be admitted to induce juries to attach mathematical values to probabilities arising from non-scientific evidence adduced at trial.'

[R v Adams, 1998]

8.3.7   Review of the Issues in R v D J Adams

This case, and its sequence of trials and appeals, has highlighted many issues, some specific to the crime itself and others related to the interpretation, and more specifically the evaluation, of the all the evidence presented to the court. First, there were the difficulties in assuring the validity of the DNA profile evidence with the consequent uncertainty in its evidential value. Although, as was demonstrated, this could move the final posterior odds to favouring the defence, the fact remains that the likelihood ratio for the DNA evidence stayed a very large number and, as such, would be conveyed to the jury as providing extremely strong support to the prosecution case.

The principal purpose in adopting the Bayesian approach was to enable the jury to weigh the statistically supported scientific evidence against the subjective and contradictory witness identification evidence. The option followed by the defence was to put the latter on a quantitative basis and the appeal court report describes, very clearly, how Donnelly worked with the jury in achieving this. Though this could be criticised as mere guesswork, the outcomes were very conservative, leading to a total likelihood ratio of ~0.05, conveying only moderate support for the defence's view. The alternative, it could be argued, would have put the jury in the impossible position of either ignoring the witness identification or reaching an overall view based on gut instinct, neither of which is desirable. More fundamental is the appeal court's objection to evaluating subjective, non-scientific evidence in such a quantitative fashion.

In fact, the evaluation and contribution of the non-scientific evidence was a bit of a distraction, as it played only a minor role in the final outcome. The drivers of the posterior probability are the strength of the DNA profile evidence and the estimate of the prior odds; interestingly, this latter quantity was apparently not debated or challenged at the trials or the appeals. As was discussed in Chapter 7.5, estimation of prior odds is fraught with difficulty and there were many assumptions here, which were open to challenge. Donnelly worked on the basis of random choice from a restricted population, but that population was relatively large; for example, he did not use the age group observation from the witness, evidence of previous sex offences or the existence of alibis for others, as constraints. These would have significantly decreased the suspect population N, thereby increasing both the prior and posterior odds.

Stating competing propositions for all the evidence types provided clarity to the jury in arriving at their probability estimates and was undoubtedly an advantage from working within a Bayesian framework. Similarly, the effective use of likelihood ratios, as a means to combining the various contributions to the non-scientific evidence, demonstrates the strength of the method. However, the difficulties for the court were matters of principle, rather than the actual practice of logical evaluation.

Indeed, combining likelihood ratios through multiplication to arrive at an overall likelihood ratio for all evidence whatever its nature and source, should be welcomed. In principle, this enables the fact-finders to consider both scientific and non-scientific evidence in an equitable fashion, which is their purpose and duty. However, in this case, apart from the support of the judge, and indeed the prosecution at the outset of the first trial, none of the other courts appeared to pass a view on this particularly beneficial point, as their focus was on the derivation of the likelihood ratios themselves and the application specifically to the non-scientific component of evidence. Interestingly, if logical evaluation by likelihood ratio had been followed, rather than using Bayes' Theorem, the overall likelihood ratio, as we saw in section 8.3.5, would have delivered an opinion providing extremely strong support to the prosecution and the outcome may well have been far less controversial from the legal perspective than it turned out to be. However, as the presentation did not explicitly determine or discuss a likelihood ratio, this possibility did not arise.

Finally, the weaknesses inherent in the estimation of prior odds have consequences, of course, for the posterior odds. By providing probabilities directly concerned with the prosecution and defence propositions, the expert witness intruded into the realms of the fact-finders thereby opening his opinion to reasonable criticism. The consequences provide support to the current view that the scientist should focus on logical evaluation by likelihood ratio, as it relates to evidence alone, and leave considerations of innocence or guilt to the jury and the court.

8.4   The Defendant's Fallacy: R v J 2009

The battered body of Kelly Hyde was discovered in a river in South Wales in September 2007, three days after she had gone missing while on a walk with her dog. Close by the spot, police found the footwear mark of a trainer in the mud and they also recovered a 2.5 kg barbell weight believed to be the murder weapon. J, then a 17-year-old youth, was questioned, as he was known to have been in the area and, following a contradictory and incriminating interview, he was arrested on suspicion of the murder.

On searching his home, police found an incomplete set of barbells of the same type and manufacture as that found at the crime scene, specifically with three 2.5 kg weights missing. They also retrieved a pair on Lonsdale trainers with a sole pattern indistinguishable from the mark found on the riverbank. Further, although the shoes had been washed, tiny blood stains were found in the stitching and tongue of one of the trainers, the blood being identified as that of Kelly Hyde. J eventually admitted to being on the riverbank and that he may have trodden inadvertently on the victim's blood.

Interestingly, it fell to the defence to provide statistical data relating to the other physical evidence, in support of their case. Their barrister stated that 84,000 sets of these barbells had been sold in the United Kingdom in the previous four years. Additionally, the trainers were of a common type with one million pairs having been sold nationwide in the same period. By introducing these statistics, he was emphasising how many thousands of alternative sources there were for these two pieces of evidence, thereby attempting to weaken their significance in the minds of the jury. However, this argument is fallacious. This evidence did, in fact, strengthen the case against J compared to its absence. Indeed, the statistics did not inform the court as to how many individuals possessed both the barbell weights and these trainers; that number was likely to be very much less than either of those quoted and thereby, on a frequentist argument, considerably strengthen the prosecution's case.

The defence fallacy attempts to underestimate the significance of evidence presented in a probabilistic fashion, by misrepresenting the statistics, thereby weakening the prosecution's case. In contrast, the prosecutor's fallacy (see Chapter 7.6.2) uses a mathematical error to overestimate the strength of evidence.

8.5 Conclusion

It would appear from these examples that statistical data and Bayesian calculations have faced considerable difficulties in the courts and, despite these being only selected examples, this has very often been the case. Nevertheless, in other instances, such as some of those cases discussed in Chapter 6 and, in other examples throughout the rest of the book, effectively presented statistics and opinion, preferably formulated on competing propositions and based on logical evaluation, have been accepted, and often welcomed, by courts across many evidence types and jurisdictions. The evaluation of the DNA profile is the obvious point at which to continue this discussion in Chapter 10.

References

British Footwear Association: shoe size statistics [Online]. (1999). Available at http://www. britishfootwearassociation.co.uk/wp-content/uploads/2011/08/Footwear-sizes-2003.doc.pdf [Accessed 15 October 2015].
Finkelstein M. and Fairley W. (1970). A Bayesian approach to identification evidence, *Harvard Law Review*, 83(3), 489–517.
People v Collins, 68 Cal 2d 319 [Crim No 11176, Mar 11, 1968]
R v Adams [1996] 2 Cr App Rep 467
R v Adams [1998] 1 Cr App Rep 377
R v J [2009] EWCA Crim 2342
R v Shirley [2003] EWCA Crim 1976

Further Reading

Coutts J.A. (1998). Statistical analysis of non-DNA evidence, R v Adams (no 2). *Journal of Criminal Law*, 62, 444–446.
Dawid A.P. (2002). Bayes's theorem and weighing evidence by juries. 71–90, In R. Swinburne (Ed.). *Bayes's Theorem*. OUP, Oxford, UK.
Donnelly P. (2005). Appealing statistics. *Significance*, 2(1), 46–48.
Evett I.W., Jackson G., Lambert J.A. and McCrossan S. (2000). The impact of the principles of evidence interpretation on the structure and content of statements. *Science and Justice*, 40(4), 233–239.
Johnson P. and Williams R. (2004). Post-conviction DNA testing: the UK's first 'exoneration' case? *Science and Justice*, 44(2), 77–82.
Lynch M. and McNally R. (2003). 'Science', 'common sense', and DNA evidence: a legal controversy about the public understanding of science. *Public Understanding of Science*, 12, 83–103.
Robertson B. and Vignaux T. (1995) *Interpreting Evidence*. Wiley, Chichester, UK.
Robertson B. and Vignaux T. (1998). Explaining evidence logically. *New Law Journal*, 148(6826), 159–162.
Thompson W.C. and Schumann E.L. (1987). The prosecutor's fallacy and the defense attorney's fallacy, *Law and Human Behavior*, 11(3), 167–187.

9

Cognitive Bias and Expert Opinion

Deliberate partisanship on the part of an expert witness is recognised as a threat to reliable testimony, yet opinion delivered by an honest expert who is not consciously biased may nevertheless be contaminated by a variety of influences on the scientist throughout the analysis, interpretation and evaluation of the evidence. As a consequence, expert opinion, truthfully presented, may be unreliable and indeed inadmissible. In referring to the contaminating influence of cognitive bias on expert testimony, Edmond declared that:

> 'Courts should be cautious about admitting contaminated expert opinions until we are confident that contamination does not pose a genuine threat to reliability and proof.'
>
> [Edmond *et al.*, 2015]

In recent years, the extent and significance of human psychological influences have been studied across several areas of forensic science under the banner of cognitive bias. Consequently, mitigating strategies have been proposed to alleviate their influence on testimony. However, it is argued that such 'cures' may in fact damage the validity of testimony by limiting the scope of the scientist to engage fully with a logical interpretation and evaluation strategy.

9.1 Cognitive Bias

The mental processes underpinning human decision making are many and varied, being dependent on the individual's life experiences and consequent, unconsciously developed, mental shortcuts to logical reasoning. Such cognitive procedures, particularly when applied to the subjective interpretation of forensic findings, may lead to unwarranted and illogical inferences about the evidence, resulting in opinion that is biased. Such biased opinion is not

Forensic Evidence in Court: Evaluation and Scientific Opinion, First Edition. Craig Adam.
© 2016 John Wiley & Sons, Ltd. Published 2016 by John Wiley & Sons, Ltd.

due to any deliberate desire to mislead the court or to the result of errors or incompetence on the part of the scientist. Rather, it may be attributed to those unconscious mental shortcuts, frequently exacerbated by many factors extraneous to the immediate concerns of the examiner, yet that are absorbed through contact with other information and people concerned with the case. Cognitive bias is present in our decision-making in everyday life, in other academic and professional disciplines and is not unique to the forensic sciences. However, in that context, it may lead to significant consequences for the reliability of scientific opinion and the legal process.

The NRC report (2009) included the influence of cognitive bias upon forensic casework within its list of recommendations, specifically that the proposed National Institute:

> '... should encourage research programs on human observer bias and sources of human error in forensic examinations. Such programs might include studies to determine the effects of contextual bias in forensic practice ...'

> [NRC, 2009, recommendation 5]

9.2   Contextual Bias

In the same way as the chain of custody for forensic evidence is invoked to avoid physical contamination, and hence erroneous forensic findings, there is a need to control the contextual information to which the scientist is exposed and thereby avoid cognitive contamination, which may also lead to an unreliable outcome for the court. Control of such 'domain irrelevant information' forms part of a strategy to avoid bias in the forensic process. Indeed, such information may include the findings for other evidence types associated with a case and such influences, spreading across the range of opinion being offered to the court, can lead eventually to distortion of the outcomes for much of that opinion; the so-called 'bias snowballing effect'.

More specifically, such contextual effects may originate in the 'psychological contamination' caused by the range of other information and influences to which the forensic examiner is exposed, but that do not relate directly to the scientific examination of the evidence. These include alleged confessions from suspects, potentially mistaken eyewitness statements, close contact with the ongoing police investigation and the findings from other forensic analyses. This last influence has been described as an 'investigative echo chamber' (Saks *et al.*, 2003), as the outcomes from each piece of forensic evidence reverberate around the team, leading to a resonance around particular conclusions that may not be rigorously justified. Indeed, by taking into account evidence beyond their immediate remit when formulating opinion, the expert witness is providing additional weight to that evidence and is hence guilty of facilitating 'Bayesian double impact' (Saks *et al.*, 2003). However, there is clearly a conflict between this negative impact of case-specific information and the need for the scientist to consider the relevant circumstances of the case when formulating opinion by logical evaluation.

It has been proposed by Dror *et al.* (2015) that sources of contextual bias may be described by a five-level, hierarchical classification scheme:

1. Forensic examination of the trace evidence itself may be affected by irrelevant information.
2. Subsequent examination of reference materials may retrospectively influence the outcomes of the initial evidential investigation, so-called circular reasoning.

3. At case level, there may be further exposure to information outside of what is required for the scientific investigation.
4. The experience of the forensic examiner will inevitably lead to psychologically induced expectations, formed through previous, similar examinations, and termed 'base rate' expectations.
5. The ethos of the host institute, its organisational and cultural practices, may engender bias at any point in the analysis of the materials and in interpretation of the findings.

9.2.1 Confirmation Bias

One of the principal consequences of unwarranted contextual information is confirmation bias. This occurs when the expert seeks an outcome that confirms some initial hypothesis, often that taken by the prosecution, thereby leading to opinion that tends to support the case against a suspect. It arises in a number of ways that include expectation bias, motivational bias and anchoring. This may lead to 'tunnel vision' on the part of the forensic investigator, with explanations for the evidence that incriminate the suspect being given greater attention than alternative explanations. Confirmation bias is particularly significant when the scientist is dealing with ambiguous cases of identification evidence that rely on individual subjective judgements on the part of the examiner, or with the interpretation of trace evidence of limited quality where contextual information may tilt the outcome towards confirming the involvement of the suspect.

An obvious example where confirmation bias may be anticipated is in the verification stage of the ACE-V process for finger-mark identification (see Chapter 13.2). If the expert verifier does not work independently of the outcome of the first examiner, then being informed of the anticipated source of the mark will add emphasis to those corresponding features that form the basis of the identification, and thereby encourage the verifier to confirm that identification rather than seek alternative sources.

As a further example, the analysis of a mixed DNA profile from a crime scene stain should be completed before examining any reference profile, as awareness of any potential correspondence may bias the interpretation in favour of seeking detail to confirm the presence of that profile within the mixture, rather than forming a view on the mixture, independent of any potential contributions.

9.2.2 Expectation Bias

This occurs when the contextual information drives an expectation on the part of the scientist as to what the outcome of the analysis will be. This leads to the findings being more likely to be in agreement with other evidence rather than contradict it. Alternatively, the interpretation may be influenced by the expectations of other individuals, such as the scientist's superiors or those who have commissioned the work.

9.2.3 Motivational Bias

Within the context of the work of the forensic scientist, it is not hard see why the horror of a particular crime or a justifiable, professional motivation to contribute to the successful solution of criminal cases may override the need to be scientifically objective, and so influence the formulation of opinion towards favouring the prosecution's case. This may prove to be an issue more for those forensic examiners employed within a police service, than for those working for independent organisations. Such influences that may lead to misleading expert opinion fall into the category of motivational bias.

9.2.4 Anchoring

When a particular piece of information emerges that appears to exert an undue influence on the scientist's interpretation and evaluation of the evidence, this is termed the anchoring or focalism effect. Such information, irrelevant to the forensic examination, has the effect of setting a reference point in the mind of the examiner, which then influences the forensic findings. Although, in principle, the anchor point can lie in favour of the defence, it is more likely that it is based on other information about a suspect and hence support the prosecution's position.

9.3 Other Sources of Bias

Two other effects that may contribute to biased testimony deserve to be mentioned. Firstly, the expert witness may align with one side in the legal debate by perceiving themselves to be part of that team, which is the so-called role effect. This does not necessarily imply that the testimony is overtly partisan but rather that the interpretation of the forensic evidence is more limited where alternative explanations that may favour the defence are considered. For example, in considering transferred fibres, a null finding may be disregarded by the prosecution, though a possible interpretation might be that it would favour the defence case.

Secondly, failure by the forensic scientist to maintain contemporaneous notes on the observations and measurements made during examination of the evidence may lead to these being reconstructed at some later time when memory lapses and subsequent external influences and events may act to bias the account, rather than it being an impartial record of the work. These are termed reconstructive effects.

9.4 Fingerprint Examination: A Case Study in Bias

There have been several studies of contextual bias within fingerprint interpretation and examples of cases where bias has been identified. The mistaken identification of Brandon Mayfield as the person responsible for the Madrid train bombing in 2004, and the Shirley McKie case, which was the subject of the Fingerprint Inquiry Scotland in 2009, are cases in point. Here, we shall focus on contextual bias within these investigations, as revealed by the subsequent national enquiries; in Chapter 13, both cases will be discussed more generally.

9.4.1 The Review of the Brandon Mayfield Case 2004

Given the political significance of identifying those responsible for the Madrid train bombings in 2004, there was strong motivation within the FBI to successfully conclude this investigation. The chance AFIS identification of Brandon Mayfield's fingerprint, as a potential match for the crime scene mark, was seized upon by the fingerprint examiners who became anchored to this proposition, to the extent of strategically looking for further features within the mark that they could conclude were in correspondence to those in Mayfield's print. Such circular reasoning followed from the bias that had become built in to this investigation. The subsequent enquiry by the US Office of the Inspector General concluded that confirmation bias had contributed to the erroneous identification of Mayfield as being associated with this crime.

9.4.2 The Fingerprint Inquiry Scotland 2009

The Fingerprint Inquiry Scotland concluded that contexual bias had contributed to the incorrect identification of a finger-mark at a crime scene, as that of police officer Shirley McKie, who denied ever entering the premises. This report recommended that the then Scottish Police Services Authority (SPSA) reduce the risk of contextual bias in fingerprint identification by reviewing its procedures and introducing appropriate training for finger-print examiners. In addition, the inquiry demonstrated an awareness of domain irrelevant information, by concluding that the SPSA:

'... should consider what limited information is required from the police or other sources for fingerprint examiners to carry out their work, only such information should be provided to examiners, and the information provided should be recorded.'
[Fingerprint Inquiry Scotland, 2009, paragraph 35.139]

This inquiry also took evidence on working practices and procedures, within the Glasgow fingerprint bureau, at the time of the McKie incident in 1997. Views submitted by those from outside this bureau suggested that there was a culture of not challenging the conclusions of other examiners and considerable peer pressure to conform with that practice. Within such an environment, junior examiners regarded senior colleagues as infallible. This implied a strong motivational bias engrained within the system. It was also suggested that, when working within the sixteen point criterion, such a culture encouraged pushing an individual's judgement, when the analysis fell a little short of this threshold, so as to find further points of detail in the mark, to enable an identification to be declared (circular reasoning). Such a strategy had been encountered elsewhere within the UK fingerprint community. This was contrary to practice elsewhere, such as in the Netherlands, where the features in the finger-mark were determined before any comparison is made, and these were not amended throughout the rest of the process.

The report's recommendations also reinforced the importance of blind verification of an identification, to avoid confirmation bias at that key stage in the examination:

'A verifier should not be told of the preceding examiner's reasoning before completing A-C-E. It follows that the verifier should not be shown, for example, a photograph or comparator screen marked up to show points of similarity.'
[Fingerprint Inquiry Scotland, 2009, paragraph 36.115]

9.4.3 Bias Within Fingerprint Examination

Fingerprint identification is one of the few subdisciplines where academic research studies have attempted to investigate the influence of contextual information on the process of forensic examination. Most notable was the work by Dror *et al.*, 2006 where experienced fingerprint examiners were re-presented with marks they had each positively identified ten years previously, but this time were given fictitious contextual information relating to the mark. This exercise was undertaken within the normal casework of each examiner. Despite each being told that the mark was from the Madrid bombing and that the matched print was that of Brandon Mayfield, but that this was an incorrect identification, they were all told to ignore this contextual information when examining the evidence. The outcome was that, of the five experienced fingerprint examiners who took part, three returned a verdict of no match while another declared that there was insufficient detail for a conclusive outcome. Only one of the examiners re-stated the original finding of an identification. The conclusion drawn was that, given strong contextual information, an examiner working with a challenging finger-mark may be influenced by such factors when reaching their decision. This does not imply that the examiner has failed to follow the standard procedures or that these are at fault, rather the subjective nature of the interpretation interacts with other cognitive processes to distort the balance of the final outcome.

9.5   Mitigating Bias

Given that exposure to contextual information has been shown to play a major role in influencing scientific opinion, such effects might be mitigated, by screening the scientist from any case details that are not directly relevant to the forensic examination itself. However, this may well go against a core principle of logical evaluation which demands that, in assigning conditional probabilities for the evidence, based on the competing propositions, the scientist must take account of any relevant circumstances of the case.

By working within a case assessment and interpretation (CAI) strategy, the scientist would hope to minimise the effects of contextual bias, as the initial case pre-assessment stage sets out the parameters governing the analysis, interpretation and evaluation of the forensic evidence, including the propositions against which the outcomes are being tested (see Chapter 5.2.2). This ensures that the evaluation of the findings, by likelihood ratio, is based on principles established prior to examination of evidential materials. By following this strategy, those influences, both external and internal to the work of the examiner, that have the potential to bias the process and its outcomes should not deflect the initial strategy. However, contextual effects may still be influential in setting the strategy at the pre-assessment stage, as this will involve, not only the scientific team but also police investigators and others who possess a wider knowledge of the case and have their own personal perceptions and professional objectives. Nevertheless, this approach has been cited as good practice by the UK Forensic Science Regulator (2015).

In a broader sense, working within a structured set of procedures, such as CAI or ACE-V, can mitigate against aspects of bias, specifically where the examination is largely subjective in nature. This approach has been shown to be successful in the examination of footwear marks (Kerstholt, Paashuis and Sjerps, 2007) where a structured study revealed no evidence for bias, with evaluation reflecting more on the complexity and quality of the marks themselves. In a second study, also from the Netherlands, the potential for contextual bias in the interpretation and evaluation of bullet striations was investigated. Such examinations are made under less-structured guidelines than for footwear marks but, nevertheless, the outcome suggested, not only that the scientists were not influenced by contextual information but that they took a more cautious view in evaluation (Kerstholt *et al.*, 2010).

'Sequential unmasking' has been suggested as an approach to the mitigation of contextual bias, by Krane *et al.* (2008). Here, contextual information, including access to reference materials, would only be released to the forensic examiner after the initial analysis of the crime scene traces was complete and then provided, as and when required, in a controlled fashion to facilitate a systematic interpretation and evaluation. Responsibility for unmasking would rest with the case manager.

Both of these strategies aim to:

> '... avoid post-comparison rationalisation or circular reasoning where the decision maker begins with what they are trying to end with.'
>
> [FSR, 2015, paragraph 1.4.3]

Full documentation of the forensic process, including where background information was revealed or the initial examination was reviewed, is essential to safeguard quality and as evidence should bias be alleged at a later time.

Another approach, this time within the subdiscipline of questioned documents, has attempted to insulate the examiner from the details of the case and from those submitting the evidence. The Document Examination Unit of the Victoria Police Forensic Services Department, implemented of set of context management procedures designed to remove domain-irrelevant information from the case materials, submitted for examination (Found and Ganas, 2013). Within this pilot scheme, a context manager acted as a buffer between the submitting person, most often a police official, and the scientist. This attempted to ensure that the casework documents were examined in a context-controlled environment and, over a four-year period, no negative outcomes were noted. This study proposed that:

> 'The default position should be to assume that irrelevant context information is a potential source of error and should be excluded.'
>
> [Found and Ganas, 2013]

To avoid 'procedural bias' in comparison procedures within forensic identification, Miller (1987) demonstrated the benefits of the so-called 'blind line-up', which avoids expectations associated with reference materials known to be from a particular source (an assumed base-rate). In the context of human hair identification, rather than presenting the examiner solely with evidential hairs and the reference hairs from a suspect, with a view to asking for an opinion as to their common origin, the alternative of providing a 'line-up' of alternative sources of the hair, including that from the suspect but unidentified as such, was tested. The additional challenge of working with a line-up forced the scientist to be more discriminating and prevented confirmation bias, whereas in the context of a paired comparison the contextual information was able to more readily influence the outcome.

9.6 Mitigating Bias Versus Research on Traces

A focus on cognitive bias within forensic science, while important, should not divert attention from the continuing need for a deeper and more rigorous understanding of the techniques and methodologies for the analysis and interpretation of the crime scene traces, particularly those currently dominated by examiner-dependant subjectivity. Approaches to mitigation that insulate the scientist from the circumstances of the case, thereby turning the forensic investigation into a black-box process, may seriously risk the validity of scientific opinion delivered to the court. In support of this view, Champod (2014) has argued that mitigating bias by detaching the science from the context of the criminal inquiry will not improve the science itself in any way, and it is limitations in those methodologies, despite technical quality controls, which are ultimately more of a threat to the quality of testimony than potential cognitive bias. The benefits of exposing the scientist to contextual information, for example, relevant to formulating activity level propositions related to the evidence, outweigh the disadvantage inherent in precluding any logical interpretation and evaluation by withholding such details. Such an approach would be consistent with a move towards a more widespread acceptance of case assessment and interpretation and a focus on logical evaluation as a means of determining the weight of evidence.

9.7   Conclusions

There is no doubt that a detailed understanding of cognitive bias, across the many subdisciplines of forensic science, particularly those where there is a strong element of examiner-dependent subjectivity, is necessary to ensure valid testimony in court. However, that should not, and need not, be at the expense of an approach based on logical evaluation, including the formulation of appropriate competing propositions, where all relevant circumstances of the case are taken into consideration by the scientist.

References

Champod C. (2014). Research focused mainly on bias will paralyse forensic science. *Science and Justice*, 54(2), 107–109.

Dror I.E., Charlton D. and Péron A.E. (2006). Contextual information renders experts vulnerable to making erroneous identifications. *Forensic Science International*, 156(1), 74–78.

Dror I.E., Thompson W.C., Meissner C.A., Kornfield I., Krane D., Saks M. and Risinger M. (2015). Context management toolbox: A linear sequential unmasking (LSU) approach for minimizing cognitive bias in forensic decision making, *Journal of Forensic Sciences*, 60(4), 1111–1112.

Edmond G., Tangen J.M., Searston R.A. and Dror I.E. (2015). Contextual bias and cross-contamination in the forensic sciences: the corrosive implications for investigations, plea bargains, trials and appeals. *Law, Probability and Risk*, 14(1), 1–25.

Fingerprint Inquiry Report – Scotland [Online]. (2011) Available at http://www.webarchive.org.uk/wayback/archive/20150428160022/http://www.thefingerprintinquiryscotland.org.uk/inquiry/3127-2.html [Accessed 22 December 2015].

Forensic Science Regulator: Cognitive bias effects relevant to forensic science examinations, FSR-G-217, Issue 1 [Online]. (2015). Available at https://www.gov.uk/government/uploads/system/uploads/attachment_data/file/470549/FSR-G-217_Cognitive_bias_appendix.pdf [Accessed 12 December 2015].

Found B. and Ganas J. (2013). The management of domain irrelevant context information in forensic handwriting examination casework. *Science and Justice*, 53(2), 154–158.

Kersholt J., Paashuis R. and Sjerps M. (2007). Shoe print examinations: effects of expectation, complexity and experience. *Forensic Science International*, 165(1), 30–34.

Kersholt J., Eikelboom A., Dijkman T., Stoel R., Hermsen R. and van Leuven B. (2010). Does suggestive information cause a confirmation bias in bullet comparisons? *Forensic Science International*, 198(1–3), 138–142.

Krane D.E., Ford S., Gilder J. R., Inman K., Jamieson A., Koppl R., Kornfield I. L., Risinger D. M., Rudin N., Taylor M. S. and Thompson W. C. (2008). Sequential unmasking: a means of minimizing observer effects in forensic DNA interpretation. *Journal of Forensic Sciences*, 53(4), 1006–1007.

Miller L.S. (1987). Procedural bias in forensic science examinations of human hair. *Law and Human Behavior*, 11(2), 157–163.

National Research Council: Strengthening Forensic Science in the United States: A Path Forward, Document 228091 [Online]. (2009). Available at http://www.nap.edu/catalog/12589.html [Accessed 10 October 2015].

Saks M.J., Risinger D.M., Rosenthal R. and Thompson W.C. (2003). Context effects in forensic science: A review and application of the science of science to crime laboratory practice in the United States. *Science and Justice*, 43(2), 77–90.

Further Reading

Dror I.E. (2009). How can Francis Bacon help forensic science? The four idols of human biases. *Jurimetrics Journal*, 50, 93–110.

Kassina S.M., Dror I.E. and Kukucka J. (2013). The forensic confirmation bias: problems, perspectives, and proposed solutions. *Journal of Applied Research in Memory and Cognition*, 2, 42–52.

Part 3

Part 3

10

The Evaluation of DNA Profile Evidence

The impact of DNA profile analysis on the investigation of crime over the past thirty years has been considerable and bears comparison only with the introduction of fingerprinting eighty years earlier. However, the consequent scientific and legal issues have been significant, not only for DNA evidence itself, but also for other forms of scientific evidence that now aspire to meet the standards set by this formidable development.

In this chapter, we will discuss the interpretation and evaluation of a conventional DNA profile, from a high-quality sample, where it is accepted that the source is from a single donor. This is the conventional DNA profile-matching scenario. The analysis is at source level, where the biological material is known and the principal issue is the interpretation and evaluation of the profiles from questioned and reference materials. From its inception, the inclusion of a statistical interpretation in DNA testimony has been in effect mandatory, frequently being the principal area of debate within the court. Consequently, statistical issues form the basis of the majority of the discussion here.

In contrast, a profile from mixed sources and where some or all the contributing profiles may be only partially complete, is termed Low Copy Number DNA (LCN DNA) or, more correctly, Low Template DNA (LTDNA). This will be the subject of the following chapter, though in reality, a strong profile from a single donor and a mixed, partial profile should be viewed as two ends of a continuous scale of profile quality.

Forensic Evidence in Court: Evaluation and Scientific Opinion, First Edition. Craig Adam.
© 2016 John Wiley & Sons, Ltd. Published 2016 by John Wiley & Sons, Ltd.

10.1 DNA Profiling Techniques – A Brief History

The evaluation of DNA evidence has evolved over the past twenty-five years or more, so it is relevant to review the key techniques, and understand what they are measuring within the DNA molecule, in order to fully appreciate their impact in the court cases, which will be discussed throughout this chapter.

The first technique used in forensic casework was the Multi-Locus Probe (MLP) technique, introduced in the United Kingdom in 1987. This examines sites on the DNA molecule where probe molecules simultaneously bind to several independent fragments of DNA to produce a series of bands on the autoradiograph that resembles a barcode. The interpretation of these bands was fraught with difficulties, as it was based on the visual comparison of autoradiographs from questioned and control samples. Courts debated whether individual bands could be discerned and whether they contributed to the profile. Sufficient bands were required to justify a match and any unexplained or absent bands needed explanation.

This was superseded by the Single Locus Probe (SLP) method, sometimes called the Restriction Fragment Length Polymorphism (RFLP) technique, in 1989. This targeted specific loci on the DNA molecule with probes to produce a series of bands that comprised the profile. Once again, interpretation was based on the comparison of these bands and on the establishment of a database (of around 200 profiles) to determine the relative frequencies of each band in each ethnic group within a population. This method established the approaches to interpretation and evaluation that were later applied to results from the later STR technique, which were introduced into casework in 1996. Nevertheless, the challenges to SLP DNA evidence in the UK courts, particularly in drawing attention to the prosecutor's fallacy, mean that it plays an important role in how our understanding of the issues around the evaluation of such evidence developed during the 1990s.

The Short Tandem Repeat (STR) method determines the genotypes at a selected set of loci within the DNA molecule. These genotypes consist of either one or two alleles (short sequences of base pairs of a specific length) that are drawn from a small range of possibilities characteristic of the ethnic population. Using the Polymerase Chain Reaction (PCR) technique, the amplified DNA profile comprises well-discriminated peaks indicating the nature of the genotype, for all the loci specified in the particular methodology. In the United Kingdom, this is the Second Generation Multiplex Plus or SGMPlus system where 10 STR loci, plus the amelogenin locus for gender, are examined. In the United States 13 (12 + 1) STR loci are used within CODIS (Combined DNA Index System). This method offers many advantages over previous techniques, including the unambiguous and accurate assignation of peaks representing the alleles at each locus, the simultaneous amplification of STR regions, the sensitivity to work with small sample sizes and the ability to tailor the number of loci to the discriminating power needed for a particular population. Although this did not introduce new statistical considerations for the court, the issues around the size and nature of appropriate databases remained.

In the United Kingdom the DNA-17 profiling methodology was introduced in 2014 to supersede the SGMPlus system. From this date, all new profile data on the National DNA Database (NDNAD) is in this format that provides enhanced discrimination based on 16 STR loci plus the gender identifier while remaining compatible with earlier SGM profiles. In the United States the CODIS system is being expanded in a similar fashion to around 20 STR loci.

10.2   Databases in DNA Profiling

There are two types of database that contribute to the implementation of DNA profiling for criminal investigation.

10.2.1   Allele Frequency Databases

The first category comprises allele frequency databases for subpopulations, usually specified by ethnic origin. These data are obtained from a relatively small number of representative individuals whose DNA profiles are used anonymously to obtain approximate frequency distributions for the alleles found at each locus, to be used for the profiling process. Recent international guidelines (Carracedo *et al.*, 2013) declare that such data should be based on profiles from at least 500 individuals.

These allele frequencies allow the random match probability (see section 10.3.2) to be calculated, using a single subpopulation where the ethnic origin is known. If this is unknown, then there are three possible avenues for interpretation. Firstly, the subpopulations may be combined, in a statistically valid fashion, to create a single stratified database. Secondly, separate match probabilities may be calculated for each subpopulation and the result most favourable to the defendant adopted. Thirdly, the subpopulation appropriate to the person of interest in the investigation may be used. This last approach is currently recommended for use in the United Kingdom, as it is also generally favourable to the defendant. In all cases corrections for sampling and subpopulation effects (e.g. non-random mating) may be included.

10.2.2   Identification Databases

The second category of databases (Identification Databases) are those comprising full DNA profiles, according to the system being used (SGMPlus, CODIS, DNA-17), which are continually expanded through addition of profiles, acquired through police investigations. These may be organised at a national or regional (state) level. Such databases provide reference profiles against which an unknown profile may be compared with a view to identifying an individual who may be the source of the evidential material.

In 2013-14 the UK National DNA Database (NDNAD) Strategy Board reported that the NDNAD held profiles from 5,716,085 individuals and 456,856 profiles associated with crime scenes. For comparison, the National DNA Index (NDIS) in the United States comprised 12,917,553 profiles from offenders and arrestees plus 607,173 forensic profiles, as of January 2015, proportionally fewer than in the United Kingdom.

10.3   Interpretation and Evaluation of Conventional DNA Profiles

The interpretation of a conventional DNA profile is based on two stages. Firstly, a match to the alleles at each locus in the crime scene profile is sought, either by comparison with a reference profile from a known suspect or by utilising a profile database such as NDNAD. Secondly, where the alleles are found to correspond, the statistical basis of the evaluation is determined by using an appropriate allele database for the population under consideration. There are then three principal ways in which statistics may inform an evaluation.

10.3.1   Combined Probability of Inclusion (CPI) or Exclusion (CPE)

The (combined) Probability of Inclusion (PI) method, sometimes called the Random-Man-Not-Excluded (RMNE) approach, attempts to explain the occurrence of the observed alleles on a statistical basis, treating each allele independently. For example, if there are two alleles A and B that occur within a population with frequencies p_A and p_B, the possible genotypes and their frequencies at that single locus are given by:

Genotype	AA	AB	BA	BB
Frequency	p_A^2	$p_A p_B$	$p_B p_A$	p_B^2

Hence the PI, at the ith locus, is given by:

$$PI_i = p_A^2 + 2 p_A p_B + p_B^2 = \left(p_A + p_B \right)^2$$

This represents the probability of finding either of these alleles at that locus within the population, irrespective of genotype. For a profile based on a number of loci, N, the Combined Probability of Inclusion (CPI) is obtained by combining the PI values across all loci by multiplication:

$$CPI = PI_1 \times PI_2 \times ...... \times PI_N = \Pi_{i=1}^{N} PI_i$$

The Combined Probability of Exclusion, CPE, is given by $1 - CPI$.

10.3.2   Random Match Probability (RMP)

In contrast, the Random Match Probability (RMP) approach calculates the probability of observing a particular genotype from that population; an alternative definition is the frequency of occurrence within the population. For the example of a single locus, i, the occurrence of the heterozygote genotype AB has the probability:

$$p_i = 2 p_A p_B$$

While, for either of the two homozygote genotypes AA, BB, the probabilities of finding these in the population are:

$$p_i = p_A^2 \quad \text{or} \quad p_B^2$$

For a profile across N loci, once again these probabilities are combined by multiplication to give:

$$RMP = p_1 \times p_2 \times ...... \times p_N = \Pi_{i=1}^{N} p_i$$

Clearly, since $PI_i > p_i$, the former provides a more cautious, conservative probability, though the two numbers are measuring different things. While the RMP uses all the genetic information through the genotype, the CPI does not, and is therefore less discriminatory. So, though both methods are mathematically 'correct', given their assumptions, the use of RMP is based on a more rigorous and relevant genetic model. In the interpretation of DNA profiles, both the CPI/CPE and the RMP approaches have their supporters and both are relatively straightforward to explain to a court.

When using the RMP, corrections are usually applied for sampling bias and subpopulation structure, though from the point of view of weight of evidence, these corrections normally have little real effect.

Interestingly, although this information is usually presented as the RMP in jurisdictions such as the United States, in England and Wales the term 'frequency of occurrence' is more common as it may be more readily assimilated by the jury and avoids misunderstanding.

10.3.3   Likelihood Ratio

The RMP contributes to the Likelihood Ratio (LR) that gives a balanced, logical evaluation of the DNA profile evidence. In most instances the calculation is straightforward and given by:

$$LR = \frac{Pr(E|H_1)}{Pr(E|H_2)} = \frac{1}{RMP}$$

The use of LR for the evaluation of conventional DNA profiles has not been encouraged in the UK courts, though elsewhere, for example Australia, it appears to be common practice. Indeed there, the conversion of LR to a verbal equivalent scale generally provides a final evaluative statement for the court. Nevertheless, for anything beyond the most straightforward examples, the LR approach is to be preferred.

10.4   Suspect Identification from a DNA Database

The identification of the source of a DNA profile, taken from a crime scene stain, may be made either by comparison with that obtained from a suspect or as a result of a database search. These scenarios are not necessarily identical from the perspective of interpretation and evaluation. The interpretation of the profile evidence in the former case will follow one of the methods outlined in the previous section. However, in the latter case, significant debate has taken place over the past decades, particularly in the United States, over the correct statistical approach to interpretation following such a 'cold hit' database identification. Why should this be so? The issue is how the exclusion of the innocent profiles on the database influences the effective match probability. This may be viewed from two perspectives.

10.4.1   The Frequentist Interpretation

One approach assumes that the source of the crime scene profile A is not on the database and then looks for coincidental innocent matches to that profile. The RMP for A is calculated in the usual way as p. Hence, the probability that there will be no match to an individual profile in the database is $1 - p$ and when this progresses through a database comprising n profiles, the probability of no match being found to any profile is $(1 - p)^n$. Since p is very small this is equivalent to $1 - np$ and hence the complementary probability – that a match will be found during the trawl of the database – is np. Hence, the match probability across the population remains the RMP, p, but, in interpreting the outcome of a match from a database search, this figure should be amended to be np. This implies that the prosecution's case is weakened by evidence submitted as a result of a DNA database search. In 1996, the US National Research Council (NRC) endorsed this approach:

> 'A second procedure is to apply a simple correction: Multiply the match probability by the size of the database searched. This is the procedure we recommend.'
> [NRC, The Evaluation of Forensic DNA Evidence, 1996, p 32]

10.4.2 The Likelihood Ratio Approach

In contrast, the derivation of a likelihood ratio requires the calculation of the probability of finding a match on the database, given that the suspect is not the source of the crime scene profile. Unlike the frequentist method, this approach is based on finding a match specifically to the suspect's profile. Under the defence proposition, we first need to calculate the probability that an individual is not excluded by the search process. If the population is N and the database size n, this is given by $(N–n)/(N–1)$, since n innocent people are excluded by the search and the suspect is excluded under the defence proposition. Thus the required probability is:

$$\Pr\left(E\middle|H_2\right) = \frac{N-n}{N-1} \times p$$

Hence:

$$LR = \left(\frac{N-1}{N-n}\right)\frac{1}{p}$$

Where the database size is relatively small compared to the population, this reduces to $1/p$ while, as n becomes a larger proportion of the population, the LR actually increases above this value implying greater support for the prosecution's case. This is in contradiction to the result of the frequentist approach. However, over the past twenty years, the balance of scientific opinion has moved towards acceptance of the LR interpretation of match probability following a DNA database search. This is reflected in the view expressed in the most recent, third edition of the NRC Reference Manual on Scientific Evidence, in 2011:

> 'The need for an adjustment has been vigorously debated in the statistical, and to a lesser extent, the legal literature. The dominant view in the journal articles is that the random-match probability or frequency need not be inflated to protect the defendant.'
> [NRC Reference Manual on Scientific Evidence 3rd Ed, 2011, p. 188]

10.4.3 Database Search Evidence in Court

The impact of this debate, in the US courts, is demonstrated in the case of People v Nelson from 2002. Investigators into 'cold cases' identified Dennis Nelson, through a DNA database search, as the source of a crime scene sample recovered from the rape and murder of a young female student in 1976. Nelson had been suspected at the time but there was insufficient evidence to prosecute him. He had, however, been convicted of a later rape, which is how his DNA profile was present in the database. In 2006, Nelson appealed to the Court of Appeal of California on the grounds that the statistical basis of DNA interpretation, when the match was the result of a database search, was not accepted by the scientific community.

In its judgment the appeal court disagreed. It discussed the views of the scientific community with regard to the use of the RMP, the modified RMP and, what it termed, the use of 'Bayes' formula', including consideration of opinions expressed in other court cases. Whilst it is not clear that this court fully understood the difference between the LR approach and the calculation of posterior odds, it did conclude that:

'Bayesian techniques are inherently confusing and would be difficult, if not impossible, to explain to an average jury'

[People v Nelson, 2006]

In contrast, the appeal court concluded that scientific community overwhelmingly accepted that the 'unmodified product rule' (the RMP) was the appropriate statistical quantity to convey the rarity of a profile in the population, irrespective of context in which the match was identified. However, it added that both these RMP-based statistical measures could be presented to a court, as long as it is informed of their meanings, with the implication that the jury undertake their own evaluation of the profile on this basis.

10.5   Case Studies of DNA in the Court

From the earliest days, the challenges to DNA testimony in the UK courts have been in the interpretation and evaluation of the evidence, specifically including how the statistical aspects are conveyed to the court and the impact of that on their evaluation of the weight of the evidence. Unlike in the United Kingdom, where a balanced evaluation, incorporating likelihood ratio, was for a time seen as a step too far, the Australian courts appear content with the expert witness taking this approach. The key cases that went to appeal in the United Kingdom in the mid-1990s also highlighted the prosecutor's fallacy that has surfaced, not infrequently, in the courts here and abroad since that time. In contrast, in the United States, admissibility itself has been a greater concern, encompassing many facets of the analysis of DNA materials, as well as aspects of interpretation.

10.5.1   R v Andrew Philip Deen 1994

At Manchester Crown Court on 23rd February 1990, Andrew Deen was found guilty of the rapes of three women in south Manchester bed-sits between May 1987 and October 1988. In the case of Miss W, the crucial evidence was a DNA profile obtained from a vaginal swab. For the other two attacks, there was alternative evidence, though the convictions in both these cases relied to some extent on their similarity to that of the rape of Miss W. Deen appealed in 1993 and this appeal was granted, with a re-trial ordered on the grounds that there were two discrepant bands in the profile that had been disregarded and the judge had misinterpreted the DNA evidence to the jury.

At that time the courts were relatively inexperienced in discussing and evaluating DNA profile evidence. As well as ten bands found on the autoradiograph from the MLP technique, there was evidence of the blood group of the perpetrator from the swab material. The original interpretation by the scientist, Mr Davey, was based on an observed frequency of occurrence amongst the relevant population for each of the bands, amounting to around 0.26, plus a similar frequency for the blood group of 0.25. From these data, the RMP for the whole profile including the blood group was calculated as:

$$RMP = (0.26)^{10} \times 0.25 = 3.5 \times 10^{-7}$$

This corresponds to a probability of around 1 in 3 million that this complete profile will be found in the population.

Some debate was generated when the defence called their own expert witness, Prof Roberts, who criticised Davey's evidence. He contended that there were discrepancies with two of the ten bands on the autoradiograph, which invalidated the conclusion of a match. One of these appeared on the image from the control sample provided by Deen, yet was not on the profile from the vaginal swab, whereas the other band was present on the swab but not on the control. Following further deliberation, Roberts agreed that, although the absence of a band on the control autoradiograph could be due to excessive washing during the processing stage, the second mis-match remained unexplained, unless it was due to the swab profile originating from someone other than Deen. These discrepancies, and the emphasis the judge gave to this part of the evidence, was the first ground of the appeal.

The second concerned the manner in which the evaluation of the DNA and blood group profile frequency was conveyed to the court, through an exchange between the prosecuting counsel and the first expert witness.

'Q   So the likelihood of this being any other man but Andrew Deen is one in 3 million?
A   In 3 million, yes.
Q   You are a scientist, Mr Davey, doing this research. At the end of this trial a jury are going to be asked whether they are sure that it is Andrew Deen who committed this particular rape in relation to Miss W. On the figures which you have established according to your research, the possibility of it being somebody else being one in 3 million what is your conclusion?
A   My conclusion is that the semen has originated from Andrew Deen.
Q   Are you sure of that?
A   Yes.'

[R v Deen, 1994]

In his summing-up the judge paraphrased this opinion from Davey in the following way:

'Mr Davey says from the matching of the bands initially, he could say 1 in 700,000 in round figures. He said that further, because of the particular blood group to which Mr Deen belongs, that is multiplied to produce a figure of 1 in 3 million -- that probability -- which you may think, if it be right, approximates pretty well to certainty.'

[R v Deen, 1994]

The appeal proposed that the judge had misled the jury through reinforcing an evaluation, which was, in fact, logically incorrect. The appeal court judge in 1993 upheld the claims of the defence and a retrial was ordered.

10.5.2   Issues Raised by Expert Opinion in R v Deen

Both the grounds that led to this successful appeal originated in the nature of the expert opinion and how that was interpreted by the court. As far as the missing band on the autoradiograph was concerned, the judge failed to convey the true conclusion to be drawn from this point and from the conflicting views of the scientific experts. The concept of a profile match requires all bands to correspond between the evidential and the control samples; the absence of a single band implies no common source. Nevertheless, the judge implied that this absence could be accommodated while still holding the view that the profiles were the same. This is not correct.

The exchange on the interpretation of the profile frequency demonstrated what became known in the forensic context as the 'prosecutor's fallacy' or the 'fallacy of the transposed conditional' (see Chapter 7.6.2). The meaning of the opening question to Davey is ambiguous. Even if we accept that the word 'likelihood' was intended here to refer to a probability, was the phrase '..likelihood of this being..' meant to refer to the evidence, that is, '.. probability of the DNA profile being from..', or, as the court understood it, to the offence itself, that is, '.. probability of the offender being..'? In the first case, the question could be further clarified by not referring to the defendant (as in version 1) but to alternative sources of the profile (as in version 2), that is:

1. So, the probability of this DNA profile from the vaginal swab originating from any man other than Andrew Deen is 1 in 3 million?
2. So, the probability of this DNA profile from the vaginal swab originating from a randomly selected male in the population is 1 in 3 million?

If this was the intended meaning, then the response from the expert witness was acceptable but brief. However, the court understood this question as the second alternative:

So, the probability of the offender being any other man but Andrew Deen is 1 in 3 million?

Here, the question is directly about the probability of innocence, of accepting the defence case; however, the witness is not in a position to answer this. There is no basis for this probability being 1 in 3 million. This erroneous response is then reiterated, by the reply to the second question from counsel, which explicitly supports the guilt of Deen.

'.. the [probability]of it [the offender] being somebody else being one in 3 million what is your conclusion?'

To which he replied that Deen was the source of the DNA profile and this conclusion is emphasised by the judge in his summing up.

The fallacy arises because of the conditional probabilities. The first is where the probability of the evidence – the match of Deen's DNA profile to that from the crime scene – is considered. This may be correctly expressed as:

The probability of the evidence, *given* the truth of the defence case, is 1 in 3 million.

The second is where the probability of innocence is stated:

The probability of the truth of the defence case, *given* the evidence, is 1 in 3 million.

This is not correct, as the two probabilities are not equivalent. The court and the expert witness have transposed the conditional statement in moving from one to the other and this is logically invalid. Interestingly, it has been pointed out (Forman et al., 2003) that although there have been several cases in the United Kingdom where the prosecutor's fallacy has resulted in the reversal of a conviction based on DNA evidence, this has not occurred in the United States.

Around 1990, two other rape cases were tried and the accused men convicted, which later led to Court of Appeal hearings and both followed the line set by the R v Deen appeal. Together these cases were instrumental in setting guidelines for the evaluation and presentation of DNA profile evidence, at source level, in the UK courts.

10.5.3   R v Alan Doheny 1996

On the afternoon of 10th November 1989 a woman was assaulted, as she entered her home in Manchester by a man who punched in the face then forced her into her house. He was careful to prevent her seeing his face, though he did reveal his local accent. After threatening her with a knife, he then raped her vaginally and anally. The only physical evidence was a DNA profile obtained from semen stains on the underclothes of the victim. Although Alan Doheny fitted the limited description of the assailant given by the woman, he claimed to have a partial alibi for the time of the attack, supported by his wife and father-in-law. On this basis, and due to the match found between Doheny's DNA profile and that obtained from the semen at the crime scene, he was convicted of the crime at his trial in November 1990.

Doheny appealed on the grounds that the DNA profile evidence was not only incorrect in substance but was presented to the court in a misleading way.

10.5.4   The Doheny Trial

Evidence was presented of DNA profile analysis of the semen stain and control samples from Doheny, carried out both by the MLP and the newer SLP techniques. The match probability for the MLP profile was only 1 in 840 (based on five matching bands, each with a frequency of 0.26; a sixth was disregarded) so most of the discussion centred on the SLP result that had a match probability of 1 in 6900. In this latter case, three probes were utilised, two providing two matching bands each, whereas the third provided a single match. In addition, Doheny's blood group was the same as that identified from the stain and its frequency of occurrence was stated to be 0.14. The expert witness, Mr Davie, provided a match probability for the DNA evidence by multiplying together the frequencies for both the DNA probes and the blood group:

$$f_{DNA} = \frac{1}{840} \times \frac{1}{6900} \times 0.14 \approx 2.5 \times 10^{-8} = 1 \,\text{in}\, 40,000,000$$

When questioned about this result the following exchange took place between Mr Davie and the prosecution counsel:

'Q. What is the combination, taking all those into account?
A. Taking them all into account, I calculated the chance of finding all of those bands and the conventional blood groups to be about 1 in 40 million.
Q. The likelihood of it being anybody other than Alan Doheny?
A. Is about 1 in 40 million.
Q. You deal habitually with these things, the jury have to say, of course, on the evidence, whether they are satisfied beyond doubt that it is he. You have done the analysis, are you sure that it is he?
A. Yes.'

[R v Doheny; R v Adams, 1997]

This exchange will now be recognised as another example of the prosecutor's fallacy. The second question was not one the expert witness could answer, as it refers to the defendant not the evidence. To see why this is the case, the second question may be re-phrased as:

> Given the evidence of the matching DNA profiles, what is the probability that the evidential material came from someone other than Doheny?

This is $\Pr(H_2|E)$, yet the match probability of 1 in 40 million is, of course, the transposed conditional of this, namely $\Pr(E|H_2)$. The implication of counsel was that this very, very low number was, in fact, the value of $\Pr(H_2|E)$ and the expert witness quite incorrectly agreed with this, even when it was put again to him, even more directly, in the third question. To conclude, the judge provided a summing up, which supported this exchange, and implied that, if the jury accepted this evaluation of the DNA evidence, then Doheny's guilt was established, whatever they might feel about his alibi and any other evidence.

10.5.5 The Doheny Appeal

Both the prosecution and the defence produced two new expert witnesses, each to testify on the substance of the DNA evaluation. The first issue to be addressed was the multiplication of the profile frequencies obtained through two different techniques. For this to be mathematically valid it is essential that the two techniques can be shown to be testing the DNA in quite different ways, so that these frequencies are proved to be independent. In a written statement, Dr Debenham confirmed that research had shown that it was not possible to be certain that the two techniques will not detect the same bands or bands so close together that they are experimentally indistinguishable.

The appeal court judge agreed that this invalidated Davie's approach and that the DNA evaluation should have been based only on the SLP and blood group results, though the court could also have been told that the MLP data would, at the very least, further reduce the match probability for this profile.

Further, the exchanges with the expert witnesses introduced an estimate of the potential suspect pool, of 800,000 men. This enabled the judge to estimate the number of men within this population who, on average, would have this DNA profile. Taking the revised match probabilities, we get:

$$f_{DNA} = \frac{1}{6,900} \times 0.14 \approx 2.0 \times 10^{-5} = 1 \text{ in } 50,000$$

This gives the number of matching profiles, on average, in this suspect population as:

$$\frac{1}{50,000} \times 800,000 = 16$$

In the appeal transcript, the calculation is not given and this figure is quoted as '20 or so individuals' so some rounding must have taken place. While the judge did not believe this outcome excluded Doheny from serious consideration of guilt, particularly given the witness and other evidence, it did suggest that the previous conviction was unsafe and he granted the appeal. Given Doheny had already served eight years of his sentence and based on other considerations, the judge did not order a re-trial.

It is instructive to review these last calculations in a formal Bayesian way to calculate posterior odds. The likelihood ratio is:

$$\text{LR} = \frac{1}{f} = \frac{1}{1/50,000} = 50,000$$

This provides very strong evidence in support of the prosecution's proposition. Based on random selection from the suspect population of 800,000, the prior odds are given by:

$$P_0 = \frac{1}{800,000}$$

The posterior odds are then given by:

$$P_1 = \text{LR} \times P_0 = 50,000 \times \frac{1}{800,000} = \frac{1}{16} = 0.0625$$

Thus, the probability of accepting the prosecution's proposition, given the evidence, is 1 in 17 and the probability of accepting the defence case, 16 in 17. This is due to the 16 other men who share Doheny's profile within this suspect population and implies a posterior probability in favour of the defence of 0.94 in contrast to the original guilty verdict.

10.5.6   R v Gary Adams 1996

A similar crime took place in October 1989 in Newcastle-under-Lyme, Staffordshire, United Kingdom, when a distressed woman, called the Samaritan helpline and spoke to someone called Gary. A short while later, a man appeared at her door and sexually assaulted her in her home. The woman complained to the Samaritans but Adams provided an alibi to the police, so it was not until the following January that the victim's house was searched and semen stains on a cushion were investigated as evidence of the rape. The DNA profile extracted from this evidence was found to match that from a sample of Gary Adams' blood.

At Adams' trial, the expert witness, Mr Webster, had carried out four SLP analyses that yielded eight bands for comparison, resulting in a match probability (called 'random occurrence ratio' in the transcript) of 1 in 27 million. He stated the correspondence observed between the profiles from the crime scene stain and from Adams, then was asked, by the prosecuting counsel, about an alternative person being the source:

'A. It is possible but it is so unlikely as to really not be credible. I can calculate; I can estimate the chances of this semen having come from a man other than the provider of the blood sample. I can work out the chances as being less than 1 in 27 million.

......

Q. So, it is really a very high degree of probability indeed that the semen stain came from the same person who provided the blood sample?

A. Yes. You really have to consider the size of the group of individuals who could possibly be the source of this semen. Now, there probably are only 27 million male people in the whole of the United Kingdom so a figure of 1 in 27 million does tend to imply that it is extremely likely there is only really one man in the whole of the UK who has this DNA profile.'

[R v Doheny; R v Adams, 1997]

Once again, the use of ambiguous language and leading questions combine to facilitate the expert witness and, indeed later the judge, committing the prosecutor's fallacy. It is correct to state that the probability of the profile originating from someone other than the accused is 1 in 27 million but this cannot be turned round to relate to the probability of the source of the semen, given that the profiles match. The final answer compounds this by implying that the profile is indeed unique within the United Kingdom. This was pounced upon at the appeal hearing by Prof Donnelly who pointed out that, statistically, the correct interpretation of these data was that there was a 26% probability of there in fact being two or more men with this profile in the UK population, as the frequency of occurrence is an average value over all populations and does not always imply one unique source in all populations of 27 million (see Adam, 2010; Chapter 8.1.1).

In his summing-up, this mis-interpretation was re-iterated by the judge:

> '....it is difficult to over-emphasise the importance of the forensic evidence in this case which, if it is right, puts his semen onto [the complainant's] cushion...'
>
> [R v Doheny; R v Adams, 1997]

The principal ground of appeal, in 1996, was that the DNA evidence was reported to the jury in an 'inappropriate and erroneous' manner, though there were other grounds not relating to the scientific evidence. The appeal court judge gave some support to the view that the prosecutor's fallacy had been committed, but he believed that this did not invalidate the strength of the DNA evidence since the match probability was of such a low value. In addition, he summarised the other circumstantial evidence against Adams and stated:

> 'When to this was added the fact that his DNA profile matched the crime stain, no Jury could be in doubt that he it was who left that stain, whether the statistics suggested that there existed one other man, or ten, or even a hundred in the United Kingdom with the same DNA profile. There is no merit in the first ground of appeal.'
>
> [R v Doheny; R v Adams, 1997]

Combining the weights of the non-scientific and the scientific evidence in this way has some Bayesian logic to it, though this is not demonstrated through numerical values and does not justify the qualifier '... left in no doubt...'. The non-scientific evidence provides prior odds that are not insignificant, and when this is combined with the very large likelihood ratio provided by the DNA profile, leads to a large posterior odds in favour of the prosecution case. The appeal was therefore dismissed and the conviction confirmed.

The Gary Adams case differs from R v Doheny in that there was other evidence, apart from a matching DNA profile, supporting the prosecution's case and the match probability for the profile was substantially larger than that agreed at Doheny's appeal. The combined weight of evidence was therefore substantial enough that issues as to how the forensic evidence was evaluated and presented to the court became less significant to the appeal court judge. It is also true that the scientist in Adams' case, though lapsing into the prosecutor's fallacy, had presented most of his evidence in a more rigorous fashion that did his equivalent in Doheny.

10.5.7 Challenges to the Interpretation of DNA Profiles: US v Shea 1997

It is not surprising that challenges to DNA evidence in the US courts have centred on admissibility and the appeal in the case of US v Shea illustrates the key issues. Shea was convicted of a robbery at the New Hampshire Bank in Londonderry, New Hampshire, in

1995. Evidence against him included a DNA profile, obtained from bloodstains left at the bank from a cut on one of the robbers' hands. This matched that of Shea with a RMP of 1 in 200,000. Shea claimed three grounds of appeal:

1. The PCR technique was unreliable because of errors and omissions in the methodology
2. The RMP was inadmissible because the allele databases were too small for statistical reliability
3. The use of RMP in court may mislead the jury and this would outweigh any probative value.

The judge dismissed the first ground on the basis that the arguments presented related to the application of the PCR method in this case, rather than its inherent validity, and as such, should be dealt with through the jury's consideration of the weight of the evidence rather than its ultimate admissibility.

The court accepted that published research had shown that allele databases, constructed from a few hundred individuals across a representative population, were appropriate and that any deviations from Hardy-Weinberg equilibrium (see Adam, 2010; Chapter 8.4) or substructuring of the population could be taken into account through approximate correction factors that did not invalidate the overall approach. Any uncertainty arising from such factors would once again contribute to the weight of evidence accorded to it by the jury and estimates of relevant uncertainties should be given to the court. In fact, by this date, this argument was becoming obsolete in the US courts.

Potential jury confusion in understanding the implications of a very small RMP was considered from several perspectives. The first related to the jury's evaluation of the evidence when presented with the RMP on the one hand and an awareness of unquantifiable laboratory error rates for the analysis on the other. Shea claimed that the jury could not assimilate this evidence unless the error rate was quantified and combined with the RMP, which is not common practice. Indeed, many argue that determining such low errors rates is an impossible task. The second point is what meaning the jury took from a statement of the RMP. Shea argued that the jury would readily fall into the Prosecutor's Fallacy and take the very small magnitude of the RMP as a probability of his innocence, given the DNA profile match. Ultimately, Shea's claim was that, even if properly explained, the jury would not be able to understand such evidence. All these arguments were rejected at the appeal on the basis that, despite the potential for jury confusion, there were ample opportunities for clear explanation of RMP by the expert witness and, through cross-examination by the defence, any difficulties could be explored and resolved. In conclusion, the judge affirmed the importance of RMP in the evaluation of DNA profile evidence and that its probative value was not outweighed by the potential for the jury to be misled. Indeed, it appears that no US court has rejected the inclusion of RMP or frequency of occurrence data, on this basis.

10.6   Current Practice for Evaluating DNA Profile Evidence

10.6.1   The Impact of Doheny and Adams in the United Kingdom

Consequent upon the difficulties faced by the courts throughout the 1990s, in understanding the interpretation of DNA profiles and the ease with which several lapsed into stating opinion according to the prosecutor's fallacy, a set of guidelines was proposed by the Court of Appeal, in the ruling in the Doheny and Adams cases in 1997. These provide guidance as to the role of the scientist in the evaluation and presentation of such evidence and have been critically reviewed by Lambert and Evett (1998).

> 'The expert would properly explain to the jury the nature of the match between the DNA from the stain at the scene of the crime and the defendant's DNA and give the random occurrence ratio on the basis of empirical statistical data. Provided that he had the relevant expertise, it might be appropriate for him to say how many people with the matching characteristics are likely to be found in the United Kingdom, or any more limited relevant sub-group. That would often be the limit of the evidence which the expert could properly and usefully give. ...
> The expert should not be asked his opinion on the likelihood that it was the defendant who had left the stain at the scene of the crime ...'
>
> [R v Doheny; R v Adams, 1997]

The first issue with this statement is that the statistical terms are not always properly used. Indeed, the use of 'random occurrence ratio' is a curious mix of 'random match probability' and 'frequency of occurrence' both of which are fine, with the 'likelihood ratio', which, of course, means something quite different. The frequency of the profile and the (random) match probability are the same quantity and either of these should always be used in this context.

The suggestion that the expert might provide an estimate of the number of people with 'matching characteristics' raises more difficulties as the scientist would need to define an appropriate population. For the Doheny case, a suspect population of 800,000 implied that 16 men, other than Doheny, had the same DNA profile within that population. If populations are sufficiently high, such as that of the United Kingdom as a whole or of a large city or region, and if the profile frequency is not too low, then this will result in a small number of possible sources, which is the outcome intended by the judge. In the Gary Adams case, it was suggested that with a male population of around 27 million and a match probability of 1 in 27 million, then the implication was that there was 'only really one man in the whole of the United Kingdom who has this DNA profile'. In fact this misinterprets the meaning of the frequency of occurrence as in some populations of this size there may be no one or even two or three men with this profile. A further complication is that, if the frequency is sufficiently low then such a calculation will result in a fractional answer, so the expert opinion may be that 0.3 men in the United Kingdom have this DNA profile. What impact this would have on the jury is open to question!

Although it is logically correct to consider sources within some specified subgroup, this is moving into prior odds territory, and application of Bayes' Theorem itself, rather than the preferred interpretation by likelihood ratio. Further, for most match probabilities, estimating the absolute number within the subgroup who have that profile will almost always result in a fractional subgroup population.

The scientist's response to the final point is discussed in detail by Lambert and Evett. This is a warning to be wary of committing the prosecutor's fallacy. Here, the use of the word 'likelihood' where the judge presumably intended to imply a probability rather than the 'likelihood ratio', may lead to mis-interpretation. It is certainly the case that expert opinion should not provide the 'probability that it was the defendant who left the stain', but it is very much the role of the scientist to evaluate the evidence using a likelihood ratio, which informs a statement such as:

> The matching DNA profiles provide strong support to the proposition that the defendant's semen was the source of the crime scene stain rather than it originated from some other male in the population.

The last phrase is important as it emphasises the evaluation is based on likelihood ratio, not on a single probability, though it is all too easy to omit it and this may lead to the opinion being misconstrued as a posterior probabilistic statement on the source of the DNA profile. An alternative is to add a covering statement to the effect that the opinion is related to the strength of the evidence and not to any probability relating to the source of that evidence.

10.6.2 Current Practice in the United Kingdom

Over the past ten years or more it has been the practice in the United Kingdom for cases where a crime scene profile from a single donor is found to show all the alleles from a suspect's profile, and with no unexplainable differences, to quote an RMP of 1 in a billion, rather than that directly calculated from the actual profile for a particular case. This is in recognition of the difficulties that a court and jury might face in attempting to rationalise differing strengths of evidence, at this numerical level and beyond. This practice has recently been endorsed within the new DNA-17 methodology. Although the equivalent likelihood ratio (LR = 1,000,000,000) translates to extremely strong evidence in support of the prosecution case, the use of verbal equivalent statements has been discouraged. Indeed, as the RSS Practitioner Guide No 2 (Puch-Solis *et al.*, 2012) indicates, the extent to which UK expert testimony over recent years has fully complied with the Doheny ruling is not clear.

Some light may be cast on recent practice through the expert witness testimony quoted in two cases where the UK Forensic Science Regulator has reported on failure of quality assurance procedures during DNA analysis. These aspects of the cases of Adam Scott and R v S are discussed in section 10.8 but here the detail of the experts' statements will be examined.

After describing the exact source of the biological sample at the crime scene, in the case of S, the scientist concluded with an explanatory opinion:

> 'This DNA profile matches the reference DNA profile of [S], such that this DNA could have come from him.'
>
> [quoted in FSR-R-625, 2013]

In providing evaluative opinion, the scientist certainly showed an awareness of the Doheny ruling:

> 'My opinion as to the strength of the DNA profiling evidence is provided here for the benefit of the prosecution and defence. In the event of a not guilty plea, all the words within these square brackets should be deleted from my statement to avoid contravening the Court of Appeal ruling in R. v. Doheny (1997).'
>
> [quoted in FSR-R-625, 2013]

The expert testimony then listed the points on the verbal equivalent scale, without any reference to the numerical equivalents, and concluded with an evaluative statement:

> 'In my opinion the DNA profiling results provide extremely strong scientific support for the proposition that the DNA tested from the swab (item JAM/2), taken from the bottom rail on the outside of a front sliding door at […] Middleton, Manchester, originates from [S], rather than from another person unrelated to him.'
>
> [quoted in FSR-R-625, 2013]

This balanced evaluation is based on competing propositions at source level but does not address any activity level propositions for this case.

The other example, that of Adam Scott, did not get as far as a trial as charges were dropped when an enquiry revealed that an error within the analytical laboratory had mistakenly attributed the crime scene DNA to that of Scott. Before this mistake was identified, the scientist issued two reports, the first of which (the DNA intelligence match) addressed explanations for the source of the DNA:

> 'It is estimated that the chance of obtaining matching DNA components if the DNA came from someone else unrelated to Adam Scott is approximately one in one billion (one billion is one thousand million). In my opinion the DNA matching that of Adam Scott has most likely originated from semen.'
>
> [quoted in FSR-R-618, 2012]

The intention here was, most likely, to give the investigators early information on the results of the DNA analysis. The second report was a formal witness statement that addressed activity level evaluation, as well as that at source level. After declaring the recovered DNA profile from a vulval swab to be a mixture of that from the rape victim's boyfriend and from the suspect, Scott, he concluded that there had been some form of sexual contact between her and Scott.

> 'In order to assess the overall findings in this case I have therefore considered the following propositions:
>
> • Adam Scott had vaginal intercourse with (victim's name)
> • Adam Scott has never been to Manchester and does not know (victim's name)
>
> In my opinion, the scientific findings in relation to (victim's name) vulval swab provide strong scientific support for the view that Adam Scott had sexual intercourse with (victim's name) rather than he did not. However, given the position of the semen matching Adam Scott and an absence of semen on (victim's name) internal swabs, the findings do not specifically support vaginal penetration with ejaculation inside the vagina. They may also support vaginal-penile contact with external ejaculation or vaginal intercourse with no internal ejaculation.
>
> I have assessed the scientific findings based on the following scale of scientific support: no, weak, moderate, strong, very strong and extremely strong.'
>
> [quoted in FSR-R-618, 2012]

This conclusion is justifiably outside the post-Doheny judicial guidance, as it deals with activity level testimony and is not specifically about the source of the DNA or the biological material. The scientist has evaluated the evidence, relating to the presence or absence of the DNA on several swabs taken from the victim, against two competing propositions using their experience and scientific expertise. The weight of evidence for these findings has been provided against a verbal scale, resulting in a view of strong scientific support for the first proposition. This opinion is presented in a logical evaluation format, in the absence of numerical data. In fact, the absence of Scott's DNA on the internal swabs was later explained, as he had no association whatsoever with this rape; his DNA was found on a single sample due to the contamination of a sample tube, in the forensic laboratory.

10.6.3   Current Practice in Australia

Although the explicit use of likelihood ratios in conveying expert opinion on DNA evidence has not been welcomed by the UK courts, in Australia, it appears more generally acceptable. In the case of Forbes v The Queen, Forbes appealed against his conviction for the rape of a

17-year-old female, K. The prosecution case depended entirely on a DNA profile from the victim's clothing that matched Forbes' profile and consequently the principal grounds for the appeal was the statistical analysis, which, it was claimed, could not remove all reasonable doubt as to his guilt. The defence case included an alibi from Forbes' wife and the inability of K to identify Forbes as the assailant. Two expert witnesses explained the use of likelihood ratios in the evaluation of DNA profiles and their probabilistic basis. The transformation of the numerical LR on to a verbal equivalent scale was described to the court and for the evidence in this case, it was stated that analysis of the swab from the clothing:

> '... provided strong evidence to support the contention that the appellant's DNA is located within the crime scene sample.'
>
> [B J Forbes v The Queen, 2009, paragraph 23]

The expert witness qualified this by explaining that she could not say that Forbes' semen was the biological source of this profile or indeed that the DNA conclusively originated from Forbes. Despite the appellant claiming that this fact implied reasonable doubt as to his guilt, the appeal court judge disagreed and endorsed not only the probative value of this evidence but also the manner in which it was evaluated:

> '... evidence of the likelihood ratio produced by statistical calculations is clearly admissible and, in an appropriate case, may be highly probative evidence ...'
>
> [B J Forbes v The Queen, 2009, paragraph 40]

10.7   DNA – The Only Evidence

Given the acknowledged weight of a conventional DNA profile as identification evidence, for those cases where this is the only evidence presented by the prosecution, there are clearly difficulties for the court. As a result of several such instances where laboratory errors or the presence of the DNA on moveable objects has led to the failure of the prosecution's case, the England and Wales Crown Prosecution Service has urged caution:

> 'Where the evidence submitted by the police turns on the existence of a positive DNA match between the crime scene sample and the suspect's profile, prosecutors are advised to consider the need for evidence that supports this identification of the suspect as the offender in the case'
>
> [Crown Prosecution Service: Guidance on Expert Evidence, 2014, p. 44]

In R v Grant (2008), the issue for the court was the identification of the individual wearing a balaclava helmet who had carried out an armed robbery. The only witness evidence was his local accent and blue eyes. The balaclava had been recovered nearby after the robbery and was found to contain DNA material from more than one individual, one of whom was identified as Grant. Despite the prosecution accepting that there was no evidence that Grant had actually worn the balaclava or that another individual may have used it in the robbery and left no DNA on it, the accused was convicted at the trial. On appeal, this conviction was overturned on the basis that the trial judge was wrong not to have dismissed the case given that the sole evidence against Grant was based on his DNA on a moveable object, and could not show, beyond reasonable doubt, that he was the robber.

In a similar case against Robert Ogden in 2013, examination of a domestic burglary scene in Woolwich, London, revealed a scarf next to the smashed window, which was the entry point for the intruder. As this was disclaimed by the occupants, it was inferred that it had been left behind by the burglar. There were two small spots of dried blood on the scarf one of which was analysed and found to provide a profile match to Ogden's DNA with a RMP of 1 in a billion. No other parts of the scarf were swabbed for DNA. Ogden was not called to give evidence at the trial though he denied the scarf was his and argued that he had an alibi for the time of the crime. Despite the defence calling for the charges to be dropped for lack of evidence against Ogden, the trial judge disagreed, stating:

> 'It seems to me that the discovery of that scarf in the burgled premises with Mr Ogden's blood on it does in practical terms call for an explanation. Certainly a jury, if no further evidence is given, would be entitled to reach a verdict of guilty. Maybe some juries would, some juries would not but that is entirely within the domain of the jury and so the application is dismissed'
>
> [R v Ogden, 2013]

The appeal court judge took the contrary view, citing previous cases including Grant, and ruled that where such DNA evidence provided the sole association between an individual and a crime scene, there must be some additional evidence, however slender, that supported such a link in order for a prosecution to proceed. This was particularly true in this case where the DNA was found on a moveable object with no known association to the defendant.

10.8 Errors and Mistakes in Forensic DNA Analysis

In recent years, there have been two notable cases in the United Kingdom where mistakes at the laboratory responsible for DNA analysis have misled the police into pursuing the wrong person for a crime. These have been subject to formal enquiries by the UK Forensic Science Regulator and offer interesting insights into how the discriminating power of the DNA profile may so readily be undermined by human error.

10.8.1 Adam Scott 2012

In October 2011, Adam Scott was arrested on a charge of the rape of a woman in Manchester, United Kingdom, based solely on evidence that the DNA profile of an unknown male, from a vulval swab taken from the victim, was found to match his profile on the UK NDNAD. This action was despite Scott's partial (17/20 alleles) profile being identified on only one out of six swab samples, all of which also revealed the profile of the victim's boyfriend. The report from LGC Forensics was quite clear in linking Scott to this assault, based on his DNA being found on the victim.

In December, police, on checking on Scott's mobile phone records, found that his phone had been making a call 300 miles away in Plymouth, a few hours after the rape was committed. A detailed audit of the analytical procedures at LGC revealed that the semen sample had been processed in the same laboratory as a saliva sample from a spitting incident in nearby Exeter. However, the processing tray that had contained this sample had been re-used and the semen sample became contaminated with Scott's DNA from the remains of the saliva sample. This represented a breakdown in the laboratory quality control procedures, due to human error, as all trays should have been consigned to waste after single use. In March 2012, Scott was eventually freed from custody. The UK Forensi

Science Regulator investigated and reported on this incident, which raised serious concerns about the reliability of DNA evidence and the underpinning quality control procedures.

10.8.2 R v S 2013

During one weekend in March 2012, two businesses in different areas of Greater Manchester, United Kingdom suffered damage to their premises. In both cases, the CSI took two swabs for potential DNA identification; in the first incident, from a window (exhibits PAC/2 and /3) and in the second, from a sliding door (exhibits JAM/2 and /3). Complete single profiles were obtained from the first sample from each scene. Both were from the same source and following submission to NDNAD, an individual 'S' was identified. In consequence, the remaining samples were not analysed. 'S' admitted accidental damage to the window at the first scene, but denied being at the second. Nevertheless, he was charged with two counts of burglary.

The defence solicitor commissioned an examination of this evidence from a second forensic science provider, with a view to determining whether contamination of exhibit JAM/2 had taken place. After a detailed investigation into the analytical procedures at Cellmark, it was proposed that an error had occurred at the dilution stage at which material is transferred from one sample tube to another. In other words, the profile attributed to JAM/2 had not in fact been derived from the sample material assigned to that code at the crime scene. This view was supported by subsequent analysis of JAM/3, which identified another individual, W, as the source, followed by a second analysis of the remainder of JAM/2, which also provided a single profile corresponding to W. It appeared that human error in taking two extracts from PAC/2 and none from JAM/2 at this stage in the process was responsible for S being charged with these two offences.

Although the Regulator believed that such erroneous evidence would be unlikely to lead to court proceedings as the courts were unsympathetic to prosecution based solely on one xample of DNA profile evidence, there were concerns on the extent to which the police ight rely on such unsupported evidence when considering charging an individual.

.3 Laboratory Error Rates Versus the RMP

ears to many authorities that the incidence of laboratory error could potentially ine the evidential value of matching DNA profiles by a very significant amount, e probability of an error would swamp the RMP in any calculation. Indeed, a MP of 1 in a billion is mathematically invalid unless laboratory error rates are at ler of magnitude less than this. However, is it possible to determine an error rate atories?

lse positive (and false negative) results have been found and it would seem rrence could be quantified by laboratory audit processes. However, the dif- n the expectation that such error rates are very low indeed, it would require analyses to be audited in order to provide statistical reliability on any error , if no instances of error were found in 100 tests, at a 95% confidence ply that statistically an error rate of up to 3% could be expected across

rts, especially in the United States, have been unreceptive to any ally combine the RMP with an error rate, or even to an estimated error rate being presented alongside the RMP. One strong justification for this is that the RMP does address a proposition that is of interest to the court and as such should be provided by the expert witness. Nevertheless, difficulties with other alternative explanations for the evidence, such as laboratory error, do remain unresolved.

10.9 Conclusions

The introduction of DNA profile evidence into the criminal justice system has forced scientists and legal professionals to examine how they present and discuss expert opinion, both for such evidence and more generally. Although many of the difficulties from the early days of DNA testimony are now understood and, it is hoped, resolved, other issues, such as DNA being the sole evidence and the impact of potential errors, mistakes and contamination within the chain of custody, remain.

References

Adam C.D. (2010). *Essential Mathematics and Statistics for Forensic Science*. Wiley-Blackwell, Chichester, UK.

Carracedo A., Butler J.M., Gusmao L., Linacre A., Parson W., Roewer L. and Schneider P. M. (2013). New guidelines for the publication of genetic population data, *Forensic Science International: Genetics*, 7, 217–220.

Crown Prosecution Service for England and Wales: Guidance on Expert Evidence, DNA, 43 [Online]. (2014). Available at http://www.cps.gov.uk/legal/assets/uploads/files/expert_evidence_first_edition_2014.pdf [Accessed 18 October 2015].

FBI: CODIS-NDIS statistics. [Online]. (2015). Available at https://www.fbi.gov/about-us/lab/biometric-analysis/codis/ndis-statistics [Accessed 19 October 2015].

Forbes v R [2009] ACTCA 10

Forensic Science Regulator: Report into the circumstances of a complaint received from Greater Manchester Police on 7 March 2012 regarding DNA evidence provided by LGC Forensics, FSR-R-618, 2012 [Online]. (2012). Available at https://www.gov.uk/government/uploads/system/uploads/attachment_data/file/118941/dna-contam-report.pdf [Accessed 10 October 2015].

Forensic Science Regulator: The performance of Cellmark Forensic Services R v. [S], FSR-R-625 [Online]. (2013). Available at https://www.gov.uk/government/uploads/system/uploads/attachment_data/file/269843/cellmark_report.pdf [Accessed 19 October 2015].

Lambert J.A. and Evett I.W. (1998). The impact of recent judgements on the presentation of DNA evidence. *Science and Justice*, 38(4), 266–270.

National Research Council (1996). The evaluation of forensic DNA evidence, National Academies Press. Washington DC.

People v Nelson 48 Cal Rptr 3d 399 2006

Puch-Solis R., Roberts P., Pope S. and Aitken C. (2012). Assessing the probative value of DNA evidence, RSS Practitioner Guide No 2 [Online]. Available at http://www.rss.org.uk/Images/PDF/influencing-change/rss-assessing-probative-value.pdf [Accessed 14 December 2015].

R v Deen, Official Transcript, The Times 10 January 1994

R v Doheny; R v Adams [1997] 1 Cr App Rep 369

R v Grant [2008] All ER (D) 124 (Aug)

R v Robert Ogden [2013] EWCA Crim 1294

UK Home Office: National DNA database strategy board annual report 2013–14 [Online]. (2014). Available at https://www.gov.uk/government/uploads/system/uploads/attachment_data/file/387581/NationalDNAdatabase201314.pdf [Accessed 19 October 2015].

US v Shea 96-12-01-B, 957 F Supp 331 (1997)

Further Reading

Buckleton J., Triggs C.M. and Walsh S.J. (2005). *Forensic DNA Evidence Interpretation*. CRC Press, Boca Raton, Florida.

Foreman L.A., Champod C., Evett I.W., Lambert J.A. and Pope S. (2003). Interpreting DNA evidence – a review. *International Statistical Review*, 71(3), 473–495.

Forensic Science Regulator: Codes of Practice and Conduct for DNA Analysis, FSR-C-108 [Online]. (2014). Available at https://www.gov.uk/government/uploads/system/uploads/attachment_data/file/355357/CodePracticeConductDNAanalysisIssue1.pdf [Accessed 19 October 2015].

Forensic Science Service: Guide to DNA for lawyers and investigating officers [Online]. (2004). Available at: https://www.cps.gov.uk/legal/assets/uploads/files/lawyers'%20DNA%20guide%20KSWilliams%20190208%20(i).pdf [Accessed 19 October 2015].

Goodwin W., Linacre A. and Hadi S. (2011). *An Introduction to Forensic Genetics, 2nd Ed*, Wiley-Blackwell, Chichester, UK.

Hopwood A.J., Puch-Solis R., Tucker V.C., Curran J.M., Skerrett J., Pope S. and Tully G. (2012). Consideration of the probative value of single donor 15-plex STR profiles in UK populations and its presentation in UK courts. *Science and Justice*, 52(3), 185–190.

Kaye D.H. (2008). Case comment – People v. Nelson: a tale of two statistics. *Law, Probability and Risk*, 7(4), 249–257.

Kaye D.H. (2009). Rounding up the usual suspects: a legal and logical analysis of DNA trawling cases. *North Carolina Law Review*, 87, 425–503.

Kaye D.H. and Sensabaugh G. Reference guide on DNA identification evidence, 129–210. In Federal Judicial Centre. [Online]. (2011). *US Reference Manual on Scientific Evidence, 3rd Ed*. Available at http://www.fjc.gov/public/pdf.nsf/lookup/SciMan3D01.pdf/$file/SciMan3D01.pdf [Accessed 18 October 2015].

Koehler J.J. (1997). Why DNA likelihood ratios should account for error (even when a national research council report says they should not). *Jurimetrics Journal*, 37, 425–437.

Redmayne M. (1997). Presenting probabilities in court: the DNA experience. *International Journal of Evidence and Proof*, 187–214.

Storvik G. and Egeland T. (2007). The DNA database search controversy revisited: bridging the Bayesian-frequentist gap. *Biometrics*, 63, 922–925.

Thompson W.C., Mueller L.D. and Krane D.E. (2012). Forensic DNA statistics: still controversial in some cases: The Champion [Online]. Pp. 12–23. Available at http://ssrn.com/abstract=2214459 [Accessed 17 October 2015].

11

Low Template DNA

Techniques for extracting profiles from low template DNA (LTDNA) material were originally developed by the England and Wales Forensic Science Service, with the first casework sample being analysed in 1999. Despite the enthusiasm in the United Kingdom for
the new methodology, which led to many instances of court testimony on trace DNA evidence, other jurisdictions were slow to follow suit, with few countries reported as using it
routinely by 2008. However, engagement by the International Society of Forensic Genetics
(ISFG) and publication of a series of review papers, demonstrated the support of the international scientific community, which led to more widespread recognition of the techniques.
Among the challenges encountered in dealing with LTDNA evidence, two are of particular
significance. This first relates to the recognition by both crime scene personnel and forensic scientists of the exacting laboratory standards and scrupulous attention to the chain of
custody, required to ensure the reliability of subsequent testimony. The second lies in the
interpretation and evaluation of LTDNA, illustrated by the new debates in the courts around
what inferences may be drawn from such evidence.

11.1 Technical Issues

11.1.1 Terminology

The technique of improving the sensitivity, by increasing the number of amplification
cycles in the PCR process from the standard of 28 up to 34, forms the basis of many
methods for the analysis of small amounts of cellular material. This is the Low Copy
Number approach to DNA profiling, termed LCN DNA. However, the development of

Forensic Evidence in Court: Evaluation and Scientific Opinion, First Edition. Craig Adam.
© 2016 John Wiley & Sons, Ltd. Published 2016 by John Wiley & Sons, Ltd.

other techniques, including increasing the injection time for capillary electrophoresis and sample concentration methods, led to the generic term Low Template DNA analysis (LTDNA) being introduced to cover all methodologies where there is a very small amount of starting material. In the United Kingdom, the LCN method is used when less than 200 pg of cellular material is available.

11.1.2 Samples

Biological material found at crime scenes may fall into two categories. The first is where the source of the material is readily recognised by eye or by using a presumptive test, for example, for a bloodstain, semen stain or fragments of skin. In these cases, the expectation is that DNA analysis will provide a full conventional profile, usually from only a single donor and amenable to a standard interpretation, leading to the identity of the source. In contrast, there are very many instances where cellular material may be retrieved with no evidence, visual or otherwise, as to its biological origin. This may be observed as a generic 'crime scene stain' or through the recovery of invisible material by swabbing a surface. Often, the material may be skin cells transferred by gripping or indeed touching that surface. Hence, the term 'touch DNA' is sometimes used, though 'trace DNA' is a more appropriate term. It is vital to appreciate fully the impact of single, or indeed multiple, transfer mechanisms, the surface-specific persistence of material and the potential for contamination, when considering the interpretation of the DNA profiles retrieved in this way. There is also no reason to assume that any profiles derived from these samples originate from one donor, two donors or from more individuals. The 'shedder status' of all donors is also unknown.

Environmental factors may also play a part in determining the quality, at the molecular level, of such samples. Once it leaves its source, cellular material will naturally degrade. Exposure to elevated temperatures or humidity, and the time of such exposure, will accelerate the degradation of the molecular structure of the DNA molecule. This tends to have a greater effect on those parts identified as the higher-weight alleles in the STR profile. In addition, the donor material may be deposited where there is already other biological or chemical material. In the former case, this may lead to subsequent analysis yielding a mixed profile, possibly with one major donor, and in the latter case, chemically induced degradation of the DNA molecule may occur.

11.1.3 Technical Issues in Interpretation

The technical challenges in the analysis of LTDNA are similar to those encountered in work with conventional DNA, only much more significant. Given the wide range of unknown factors relating to the quality of a LTDNA sample, in the United Kingdom case-pre-assessment is recommended to ensure the optimum method is adopted in subsequent analysis, and quantification of the DNA material is an essential part of this.

Any DNA profile, but particularly one from a crime scene stain, may be a mixed profile with contributions from more than one individual. Using peer-agreed guidelines on peak intensities and from other observations on the profile, it is often possible to classify that mixture, for example, as due to a major donor and one or more minor donors. However, there are a number of effects, which act during the amplification process, that combine to increase the complexity of the resulting experimental profile and may contribute to significant difficulties in the process of interpretation and evaluation. These are discussed in Gill *et al.*, 2000.

Random effects during the PCR amplification become more significant when the starting material contains very small quantities of DNA. These cause a statistical stochastic variation in the experimental profile. which leads to allelic drop-out, random allelic drop-in and an increase in peaks due to stutter. In general, stochastic effects are more pronounced below the so-called 'stochastic threshold', which may be defined in terms of the amount of DNA present in the sample (e.g. 100–200 pg in the United Kingdom; one biological cell corresponds approximately to 6 pg of material). Peaks arising from these processes may be recognised in the DNA profile by running repeat samples, which is standard practice.

Stutter occurs when the PCR process produces a much smaller peak (<15% intensity) adjacent to a true allelic peak but shifted by one unit from it. Stutter occurs irrespective of the quantity of material in the sample but does increase with amplification cycles, though this effect is offset for the very smallest samples (~100 pg). However, the size of stutter peaks increases as the quantity of DNA reduces, often making them of similar size to those from a genuine minor component in a mixed profile, which produces difficulties in interpretation.

Allelic drop-out is evident when a component allele within an STR profile is absent. Of course, in an unknown profile, even from a single donor, this may not be recognised as such since, for example, an apparently homozygous allele could in fact be heterozygous. Sample degradation may also be responsible for absent or weak allele peaks, particularly for those of high molecular weight. These effects may act to produce a partial DNA profile, originating often from a single donor but missing some of the 20 alleles that would enable a conventional interpretation (SGM+) and effectively reducing its evidential value to the court.

Allelic drop-in may also arise from stochastic effects acting on traces of contaminant DNA molecular fragments, from gross contamination, or indeed from a genuine minor contributor to a mixed profile. Spurious alleles, particularly at the low molecular weight end of a profile, may even be observed in negative control samples prepared in clean laboratory conditions.

Additionally, the use of 34 PCR cycles tends to increase the imbalance in the peaks from heterozygotic alleles as the level of DNA in the sample decreases, compared to what is observed under standard conditions. Indeed, within such mixed profiles there may be examples of a peak arising from one allele at a particular locus but with contributions from more than one biological source. This may result in the 'masking' of a peak from a minor profile by a stronger peak from the major donor. Identification of this effect is usually impossible, because of the range of other factors affecting a peak intensity in these systems.

11.1.4 Quantitative Evaluation in LTDNA Profiles

Both the CPE and the RMP methods (Chapter 10.3) have been applied to the interpretation of LTDNA profiles, but neither method can be used rigorously in this context as assumptions have to be made, and this may lead to challenges to expert opinion in the courts. On the other hand, working in the context of the LR allows flexibility in setting appropriate propositions and the inclusion of probabilistic methods for dealing with the issues of stutter and drop-out. For these reasons, the use of this approach is favoured when interpreting and evaluating mixed and LTDNA profiles.

In recent years, there has been a move, headed by the ISFG, to standardise on the methods for the interpretation of DNA mixtures and LTDNA profiles, by incorporating the latest research, particularly on dealing probabilistically with drop-in and drop-out effects. A comprehensive set of recommendations was published by Gill *et al.* in 2006, followed by an update in 2012, that included the treatment of partial profiles and acknowledgement of the growth in software for the interpretation of such data. A UK response to these, in the context of working with the National DNA Database (NDNAD), was provided in 2008 by the Technical UK DNA Working Group (Gill, 2008) and more recently a further report, commissioned by the Forensic Science Regulator, set out the principles for the interpretation of complex profiles and those from LTDNA (Gill, 2012). Although there is insufficient space to discuss the details here, it is pertinent to review the main points as listed by the ISFG and discussed in Gill *et al.*, 2006:

1. The LR approach should be used for all DNA profile interpretation, as it is the only method that can rigorously deal with drop-in and drop-out effects through probabilistic models.
2. The weight of evidence that contributes to the expert testimony should follow from the LR calculation.
3. Estimates of the drop-in and drop-out probabilities should be made using data from validation studies that are appropriate to the experimental method employed.
4. All calculations should be made using appropriate software to avoid errors and mistakes. Software resources are available from the ISFG website.
5. If the justice system does not 'appear to support' the explicit use of likelihood ratios in testimony, the expert witness should nevertheless use this approach in the case notes.
6. In addition to a number of recommendations related to dealing with the inclusion of alleles based on their peak heights or areas, there are specific comments on including consideration of stochastic effects, allelic drop-in and allelic drop-out in the interpretation of LCN DNA profiles.

Finally, the 2012 publication concluded with a number of additional recommendations that included further research on stochastic effects and software tools, further validation studies appropriate to experimental methodologies, enhanced anti-contamination procedures throughout the chain of custody and additional expert witness training to focus on the accurate presentation of opinion.

11.2 Importance of the Chain of Custody: Queen v Sean Hoey 2007

The acquittal of Sean Hoey on fifty-eight counts including the murder by bombing of twenty-nine people in Omagh, Northern Ireland in 1998, proved to be an important milestone in the presentation of LCN DNA as admissible evidence in the courts (see also Chapter 1.6.8). Until this high-profile and politically sensitive case, testimony based on this technique had not been scrutinised by the UK courts to any great extent. The DNA profiles were obtained from bomb fragments that were retrieved from the crime scenes in 1998 and 1999 when awareness of the need for a strict chain of custody when dealing with trace evidence or the implications specifically for LCN DNA analysis, were not as fully recognised as they later became. Consequently, the prosecution were unable to convince the court of the reliability of the DNA analyses, as the questioning of police, forensic and expert witnesses at the trial, progressed. During the court testimony, many instances were revealed where the management of the crime scene, the retrieval and storage of evidence as well as the laboratory examination, fell short of what was required for more established trace evidence such as fibres, far less for the more stringent procedures essential for trace DNA exhibits. To quote two examples:

> 'It came to light that a Ms Cooper, then a SOCO … gave evidence that she was wearing protective clothing at this scene when in fact she was wearing nothing of the kind, as photographs taken at the scene fortunately revealed.'
>
> [Queen v Hoey, 2007, paragraph 50]

> 'She agreed that when the exhibits in this case were initially examined in the laboratory in 1998/99 there were no programmes in place within the laboratory to cater for the special examination and cleaning regimes necessary for the examination of items that might yield LCN DNA profiles.'
>
> [Queen v Hoey, 2007, paragraph 58]

Indeed, the judge expressed his surprise that the forensic scientists had expected these DNA profile results to be of evidential value to the court while knowing of the shortcomings throughout in the chain of custody. He was also concerned about the reliability and scientific basis of the LCN technique itself, given that it had quite limited use across other countries at the time and that the only validation appeared to be two articles written by the expert witnesses themselves. Although he based his final verdict on the contamination issue, he also stated:

> 'I have devoted a little space to this subject because of my concern about the present state of the validation of the science and methodology associated with LCN DNA and, in consequence, its reliability as an evidential tool.'
>
> [Queen v Hoey, 2007, paragraph 62]

He concluded that the standard of evidence presented at the trial did not reach the standard of 'beyond reasonable doubt' required for a guilty verdict and the defendant was acquitted of all charges.

11.3   The Caddy Report 2008

Following from the Hoey case, the newly appointed UK Forensic Science Regulator set up an inquiry under Prof Brian Caddy to report on the science of LTDNA analysis. The Caddy Report, published in 2008, provided a reference point for the standards that were required to be in place, in order that the legal process could have reassurance as to the validity and reliability of the methodology. In addition to setting out a number of recommendations, including quantification of the total yield of DNA retrieved, the report endorsed the techniques based on 28 and 34 PCR cycles and the stochastic threshold of 200 pg. It also defined the term Low Template DNA analysis to encompass all methods that sought to obtain a profile, of which the Low Copy Number approach is one example. In considering the interpretation and evaluation of such profiles in expert testimony, the report stated its opinion that:

> '… any LTDNA profile should always be reported to the jury with the caveats: that the nature of the original starting material is unknown; that the time at which the DNA was transferred cannot be inferred; and that the opportunity for secondary transfer is increased in comparison to standard DNA profiling. There may perhaps be some exceptions …'
>
> [Caddy Report, 2008, paragraph 7.4]

'… when DNA profiles match as a result of LCN DNA profiling, the significance of the match should be reported on the probability that the two DNA profiles match only. As the results were obtained from LCN it is inappropriate to comment upon the cellular material from which the DNA arose or the activity by which the DNA was transferred.'

[Caddy Report, 2008, paragraph 7.5]

These very clear guidelines were intended to provide guidance to the expert witness delivering opinion to the court on LTDNA evidence.

11.4 Case Studies in LTDNA opinion in the UK Courts

To illustrate the range of issues that have arisen in the UK courts, in relation to LTDNA testimony, a number of case studies will be presented and discussed, each highlighting a specific aspect of interpretation and evaluation.

11.4.1 Partial Profiles

In May 2005, James Garside and Richard Bates were convicted, for the second time, of the murder of Garside's estranged wife Marilyn, Bates having been hired by Garside to carry out the killing. Marilyn Garside had been stabbed repeatedly in the neck and chest at her mother's house in Romford, United Kingdom and DNA profiles obtained from bloodstains around the doorway and on the garden gate were crucial evidence. This trial led to an appeal on the basis that the DNA evidence should not have been admitted, as it was based on partial profiles.

Samples taken from seven locations around the door and gate all provided mixed partial profiles that included at least one male, in addition to peaks attributable to the major profile from the victim. The court focused on the interpretation of two samples in particular; one from the front door handle, the other from the gate post. These showed eight alleles that matched Bates' profile but the other twelve were absent, in all but three cases this was attributed to masking by peaks from the major profile. These three were referred to as 'voids'; a statement that is true only if the prosecution's hypothesis, that Bates' profile does in fact contribute to this stain, is accepted. On this basis, the drop-out mechanism explains the absence of these alleles. However, from the defence perspective, there is no particular expectation of finding these alleles, as Bates' DNA was not present in the stain, so the term void is inappropriate.

Two expert witnesses provided differing evaluations of these profiles. The prosecution called Dr Evett, who calculated a match probability based only on those eight alleles allegedly attributed to Bates. This implied taking a neutral view of the 'absent' and 'masked' alleles, equivalent to setting their probabilities to unity. This gave a match probability of 1 in 610,000, which, though very much larger than for a full profile, still represented very strong evidence for the prosecution. Prof Balding who was called by the defence, believed that this approach was incorrect because the absence of any of these three alleles could be interpreted as exculpatory evidence, by implying the absence of Bates' DNA as contributing to this profile. The defence counsel urged that, since this implied that no reliable statistical interpretation was possible, the DNA analysis of these stains should not be admitted as evidence. The trial judge disagreed with this and allowed the evidence to be presented to the jury, on the expectation that they would undertake their own evaluation in the light of the reservations put forward by Balding.

The appeal court judge confirmed that the provision of a rigorous and complete calculation of match probability was not an essential prerequisite for the admissibility of DNA profile evidence. There was no reason in principle why a partial profile should not be admitted as evidence, as indeed all SGMPlus profiles were 'partial' as they were based only on alleles at a selection of ten loci within the molecule. Although there may be instances where the number of missing alleles becomes so great that the match probability becomes sufficiently large to lead to exclusion of the evidence due to its low probative value, the appeal court ruled that:

> 'We can see no reason why partial profile DNA evidence should not be admissible provided that the jury are made aware of its inherent limitations and are given a sufficient explanation to enable them to evaluate it.'
>
> [R v Bates, 2006, paragraph 30]

On this basis, and as the DNA evidence formed only part of the prosecution's case against Bates, the appeal was dismissed.

11.4.2   Quantities of DNA; Interpretive Issues on Transfer

Following the murder by stabbing of Peter Hoe in Eston, Teesside, United Kingdom in October 2006, the brothers David and Terence Reed were convicted of the killing, at the Crown Court, ten months later. Despite the defence being based on alleged alibis for the Reeds, DNA profile evidence obtained from trace cellular material on two plastic knife handles found near Peter Hoe's body was crucial for the prosecution case. A knife, fitting one of these handles, was found in a drain at the house. Although the defence did not challenge the proposition that the Reed brothers were the source of the DNA profiles on the handles, they did dispute the alleged value of this evidence to the charge of killing Peter Hoe. Initially, the general reliability of DNA evidence, obtained using the LCN process, was challenged, but this was withdrawn, before the appeal hearing itself, following a review by experts for the defence team. Despite this, there was discussion on this issue, in particular on when a legal challenge could realistically be made to LCN DNA evidence.

This court focused on the minimum amount of cellular material needed for a LCN profile to be deemed valid, based on the threshold at which stochastic processes may overwhelm a rigorous interpretation of the profile. It was agreed that this value lay between 100 pg and 200 pg but that the scientific community could be no more precise than that. Consequently, the appeal court ruled that:

> '... a challenge to the validity of the method of analysing Low Template DNA by the LCN process should no longer be permitted at trials where the quantity of DNA analysed is above the stochastic threshold of 100–200 picograms in the absence of new scientific evidence.'
>
> [R v Reed and Reed, 2009, paragraph 74]

For amounts of material within that range, it was anticipated that evidence could be admitted on an individual basis where expert advice and more recent scientific advances were provided in justification. It was suggested, however, that such instances would be rare. No observation was made on admissibility where quantities lay below that threshold range. The appeal court also confirmed that match probabilities could be presented from LCN DNA profiles as long as the quantity of material was above this stochastic threshold.

The substantive debate, around these DNA profiles, focused on issues of transfer and activity at the crime scene and the reliability of the science underpinning any evaluation on this basis. The expert testimony was given by Valerie Tomlinson, an experienced forensic biologist, who had not only supervised all the laboratory examination of exhibits but who had spent three days examining the crime scene. The two knife handles – exhibits AC/3 and AC/4 – were found close to the victim's body; the former had no visible bloodstains on it while the latter had been in contact with blood on the floor. Neither handle matched any others found in Hoe's house. Both exhibits provided sufficient cellular material for three aliquots, of which two were used for the analyses. The total yield was not quantified at the time but later the amount in the third aliquot was measured and this indicated that there had been 1000 pg of DNA on AC/3 and 2500 pg on AC/4, both well above the limit for legal validity. Two DNA profiles of similar quality were found on handle AC/4, one of which was attributed to Peter Hoe, the other to David Reed, whereas AC/3 revealed a satisfactory single profile identified as that of Terence Reed.

Tomlinson's testimony discussed the interpretation and evaluation of this evidence based on issues of primary and secondary transfer, persistence and alternative explanations for the DNA evidence on the knife handles. She proposed that, although the biological source of the cellular material could not be identified, and despite the not unexpected absence of fingerprints on the handles, the most likely source was through hand contact. She could not say how long the material had been present on the handles though, given the limited degradation evidenced by the quality of the DNA profiles, it was unlikely to have been there for any length of time. She enumerated several explanations for the findings:

1. The DNA arose through primary transfer from the Reed brothers when they brought the knives to the house and that they were holding them when they broke. The DNA profile evidence was consistent with this interpretation.
2. Someone else brought the knives to the house, then primary transfer occurred when the Reed brothers innocently touched them. She believed this explanation was unlikely.
3. The material resulted from secondary transfer following contact between the Reeds and other people who had then handled the knives and taken them to Hoe's house. This would have to have occurred over a short timescale and involved quite substantial contact with the knife handles by the Reed brothers to account for the amount of DNA and the quality of the profiles observed.
4. Material from David Reed had transferred to Peter Hoe on an earlier occasion when they were known to have shaken hands and Hoe then transferred that to the handle AC/4. This did not explain the profile from Terence Reed found on AC/3.

Finally, she stated her summative view based on these explanations:

> 'In all the circumstances, the most likely explanation for the DNA of the Appellants being on AC/3 and AC/4 was that they were brought to Peter Hoe's house by the Appellants and that they were handling them when they broke.'
>
> [R v Reed and Reed, 2009, paragraph 89]

The defence were critical of the lack of any valid and accepted scientific basis to some of Tomlinson's statements, particularly on transfer processes, persistence and issues around time. The wording of her final evaluation was heavily criticised as '… in effect a direction from an expert to convict.'

It was claimed that there was no way such detail about the activity of the Reeds could be deduced from the DNA evidence alone. The defence case at appeal was supported by testimony from two expert witnesses who were critical of this interpretation, as going beyond what could justifiably be said. The appeal court judge, however, considered that the experience of Tomlinson was more relevant to the circumstance of this case than was that of the other expert witnesses. Indeed, the judge regarded the scenes of crime experience of this witness as being important in informing her interpretation of the DNA transferred to the knife handles, though she needed to be cautious in expressing those aspects of the evaluation where the underpinning scientific arguments were less strong. His judgment accepted her approach to the evaluation of this evidence and ruled that:

> '... we consider that the science is sufficiently reliable for it to be within the competence of a forensic science expert to give admissible evidence evaluating the possibilities of transfer in DNA cases where the amount is over 200 picograms and when there is a sufficient evidential basis from the profiles and other material ... for it to be done.'
>
> [R v Reed and Reed, 2009, paragraph 122]

Tomlinson's enumeration of the alternative scenarios and her balanced qualitative evaluation of their probabilities was commended by the appeal court judge. However, he did rule that, as there was no reliable scientific basis to her final comment that the Reeds 'were handling [the knives] when they broke', this part of her evidence was not admissible. Nevertheless, he stated that the 'impermissible gloss' this added to the main body of the evidence was not significant enough to have affected the verdict of the jury at the trial and the appeal was dismissed.

11.4.3   Very Low Quantities of DNA

A series of arson attacks, linked to animal rights activism, were carried out against college buildings in Oxford, United Kingdom in 2006. Following a trial in 2007 at which the jury failed to reach a verdict, Mel Broughton was convicted of conspiracy to commit arson, at a retrial in 2009, but appealed on grounds that included the admissibility of DNA evidence where the amount of cellular material was very low.

The evidence in question was a set of DNA profiles obtained from the stalks of matches found at one of the crime scenes. The amount retrieved could not be directly measured but was estimated to provide no more than 100 pg of material in each analysis, at the lower limit of the range deemed acceptable. The analytical methodology was not the standard LCN approach involving 34 cycles, but a complex combination of processes based on the 28 cycle STR amplification with the addition of a variant called 'Identifiler', followed by so-called clean-up procedures and the use of a 'consensus approach' to combine the resulting profiles. This enabled an interpretation based on a single profile containing 20 alleles, all of which were common to Broughton's profile, and with only two additional alleles visible in some of the contributing results. These were not from Broughton but attributed to contamination and stutter. This allowed the statistical evaluation to be based on a single SGMPlus profile, identical to that of Broughton, with a match probability of one in a billion. The possibility of more than one donor was not considered. The forensic scientist, Miss Hammond, did add to her testimony the proposition that, if there was any error in the interpretation of any one of the component profiles, then the statistical interpretation became invalid.

The thrust of the arguments put by the expert witnesses, called by the defence, were summarised by the appeal court judge and included:

'... the consensus approach was flawed in that it was overly subjective; that the quantity of DNA recovered was so low as to be below the stochastic threshold; and that when dealing with such low levels of DNA, stochastic effects become very much more common ...'

[R v Mel Broughton, 2010, paragraph 29]

It was confirmed at the appeal that the earlier ruling from Reed and Reed did not preclude evidence from samples of DNA, of less than the stochastic threshold, being admitted to court. Indeed, that ruling included the statement:

'Below the stochastic threshold the electrophoretograms may be capable of producing a reliable profile, if for example there is reproducibility between the two runs.'

[R v Reed and Reed, 2009, paragraph 48]

The validity and reliability of the analytical methodology was endorsed by other expert witnesses. In particular, the fact that Broughton's alleles consistently appeared in the set of profiles contributing to the final result, was, in the view of the appeal court judge, evidence of its reliability.

Although the appeal court ruled that the trial judge had been correct to admit this DNA evidence, it disagreed on his guidance to the jury, that they should simply exercise caution if they doubted Hammond's interpretation, preferring that, in this case, all the DNA testimony should be disregarded. On this basis Broughton's appeal was successful. However, at the second retrial, in July 2010, Broughton was found guilty and the ten-year sentence confirmed.

11.4.4   Opinion Without Statistics

Although it formed only a relatively minor part of the evidence that led to the conviction of Ashley Thomas, in June 2010, for possession of a prohibited firearm and causing grievous bodily harm with intent, the admissibility of trace DNA profile evidence from the weapon formed one of the grounds for his appeal in the following year. The incident, described as an altercation, occurred near a nightclub in Luton, United Kingdom, and as a result Opey Akinboro sustained a gunshot wound to the groin. A trace bloodstain on the pistol, recovered from the scene, was subjected to both SGMPlus and LCN techniques, as the quantity of material was very low. The resulting DNA profile was reviewed by two expert witnesses who concluded:

- DNA from at least three people contributed to the overall profile
- No single contributing profile could be described as a major component
- As the quantity of DNA was estimated to be around the 100–200 pg level, stochastic effects needed to be considered in its interpretation
- The amplification process had gone well and no alleles were below an acceptable threshold
- Significant stochastic effects at the high molecular weight end of the profile, in particular the D2 and FGA loci, precluded the identification of a major contributor to the overall profile

- All the component alleles from Thomas' DNA profile were present in the profile from the stain
- The nature of these results implied that statistical evaluation was not possible

The two expert witnesses, however, disagreed on the weight to be attached to this evidence and it was alleged that this made the evidence unreliable and hence inadmissible.

Miss Cornelius based her evaluation on consideration of two mutually exclusive propositions:

H_1: Ashley Thomas was a contributor and some of the DNA recovered was from him
H_2: Ashley Thomas was not a contributor and none of the DNA recovered was from him

Support to H_1 was provided by all the alleles attributable to Thomas being observed within the mixed profile. In the event of H_2 being true, few matching alleles would be expected in the crime scene stain and, as finding all these twenty alleles by chance within such a profile was a 'rare' event, the evidence lent little support to this second proposition. Scientific support for this assertion was provided by unpublished simulation experiments, not seen by her, but which were consistent with her personal experience over many years. In her summative evaluation, Cornelius stated that:

> '... in my opinion, the DNA profiling evidence provides support for the view that some of the DNA recovered was from Ashley Thomas, but I am unable to quantify the level of this support.'
>
> [R v Thomas, 2011, paragraph 14]

In conclusion, she agreed that there would be other, different mixtures of DNA from different donors, which would produce a mixed profile, similar to that from this stain. In his summing up, the judge indicated that, under cross-examination Cornelius had concurred with the implication that the DNA evidence had limited significance, and further:

> '... she agreed that the bottom line was that she could give no statistical evaluation of what the word rare meant and she accepted that her findings really did not enable her to say that the defendant had handled the Baikal pistol.'
>
> [R v Thomas, 2011, paragraph 17]

The second expert witness was Dr Syndercombe-Court who was of the view that a more appropriate evaluation was that Thomas could not be excluded as a source of DNA material within the crime stain because, despite all twenty alleles being observed, it was impossible to say that they all came from the same source. This view suggested that the opinion of Cornelius had over-stated the weight to be attached to this evidence. However, it should be noted that, at the time, the England and Wales Forensic Science Service preferred not to use statements such as 'could not be excluded' as jurors were inclined to interpret this in terms of providing some support to the prosecution's case!

In ruling on the admissibility of this evidence, the appeal court judge stated that the absence of a statistical evaluation did not preclude any scientific evidence, including DNA profiles, being admitted to the court as long as the validity of the experimental results was accepted, as both experts agreed was the case here. In addition, precedent indicated that underpinning research, such as the work referred to by Cornelius, could be unpublished or conveyed through the expertise of individuals and on these bases he ruled that her evidence was admissible and the appeal was not granted.

Two further points discussed by the appeal court are worth emphasising. Firstly, as a result of cross-examination it emerged that, despite their opening statements, the actual difference in opinion between the two experts was slight, or as the judge stated, 'almost a distinction without a difference'. Secondly, he expressed some concern that, while Cornelius was able to state that her evidence provided support to the prosecution, she was unable to quantify the level of that support on any scale or relate that to the probability of the random occurrence of all of Thomas's alleles in a mixed profile, which she, nevertheless, described as a 'rare' event.

These issues have continued to be debated in later cases, including most notably, in the combined appeals of R v Dlugosz, R v Pickering and R v MDS (2013). Here, the appeal court judge summarised that:

> '… all three appeals proceeded on the basis that the DNA evidence was given without any of the experts being able to provide a random match probability … It was a further feature of each case, as is common in Low Template DNA cases that it was not possible to tell when the DNA was deposited or how it had been deposited … or the origin of the DNA …'
>
> [R v R v Dlugosz; R v Pickering; R v MDS, 2013, paragraph 4]

In response to all these cases, Pope and Evett commented:

> 'Scientists are not trained to provide qualitative assessments of evidential weight of DNA mixtures, and no system exists for assessing the robustness of such assessments'
>
> [Pope and Evett, 2013]

In other words, if statistical evaluation proves impossible, then the expert witness is unable to provide an opinion on the weight of evidence and the court should not expect one to be given.

11.4.5   Experts Differ in Opinion

The grounds for the appeal by Steven Hookway and Gavin Noakes, against their conviction for violent robbery at a Tesco supermarket in Middlesbrough, United Kingdom, in 2007, were that DNA evidence should not have been admitted and that the judge's summing up was misleading. Swabs taken from the nearside interior door handle (KTI51) and from the driver's seat-belt release (KTI36) of the stolen Mercedes car, in which they made their getaway, were analysed using LCN techniques, as cellular material was expected to be present only at trace level. Both the defendants admitted that their DNA may have been present, as they claimed to have been in the car on an earlier occasion, but denied taking part in the robbery. The interpretation of the profiles may be summarised as:

> KTI51: This revealed a mixed profile with at least two and possibly three contributors and including all the component alleles from Hookway.
> KTI36: This was also a mixed profile with at least two contributors with a possible trace of a third. All the anticipated alleles from the car's owner were present and, once they were removed, the remaining major alleles could be attributed to Noakes.

Expert witness, Dr Sharpe judged that Hookway's profile was the main contributor to KTI51 and she therefore felt able to assign a match probability of 1 in a billion and her evaluation was that it provided extremely strong scientific evidence for the prosecution. She made a similar statistical evaluation for Noakes' profile in KTI36.

However, the defence called a second scientist, Claire Stangoe, who stated that she would have attempted to obtain a profile using the standard STR method, prior to considering whether the LCN approach was necessary, but confirmed Sharpe's approach was valid. She agreed with most of the qualitative interpretation provide by the prosecution's expert but differed in her evaluation. Stangoe did not regard the component peaks from either Hookway or Noakes to be at a sufficiently high level, within the mixed profile, to be regarded as amenable to statistical interpretation, particularly because of the uncertainties around the contribution from a possible third individual. In her view, it was possible that there was a random combination of components from three individuals that produced a profile identical to that of the defendant. Her evaluations of the DNA profiles from both these exhibits, were similar to, but of significantly less evidential weight than, those from Sharpe:

> '... whilst I agree that Stephen Hookway could have contributed the majority of DNA to this result, and in my opinion the result does provide support for the assertion that DNA from Mr Hookway is present, in my opinion, it is inappropriate to assign this statistic [1 in a billion] to this finding.'
>
> [R v Hookway, 2011, paragraph 20]

Both experts agreed that the other's interpretation was valid but that their views differed. The appeal court judge confirmed that this was not a case where the two experts differed in whether the evidence incriminated or exculpated the defendants; rather it was that they provided conflicting opinions that lent different levels of significance to the prosecution's case. It was a matter for the jury to decide on their own view as to what weight to attach to the DNA evidence, in the light of these two expert opinions. The appeal was dismissed.

Despite this legal view that the jury could decide on the basis of these two evaluations, it is clear from the statistical perspective that the views of the two experts were of considerably different evidential weight and, in a case where DNA evidence could make a crucial impact on the legal argument, it is hard to see that this view from the appeal court judge would assist matters. At its core, this case reveals how a decision, on whether a set of component peaks in a mixed profile may be regarded as originating from one source, can lead to an evaluation that may, on the one hand, 'provide support' or on the other, 'provide extremely strong support' to the prosecution. While the latter statement provides a clear weight of evidence, the former does not. This raises the question of how a jury might weigh these two options against each other in any logical way. Although this may appear an impossible task, the legal position remains that the jury should come to an evaluation of all evidence in the context of the case overall.

11.5 LTDNA in Jurisdictions Outside the United Kingdom

Although the initial development and use of LTDNA techniques, and its presentation as evidence in the court, originally took place in the United Kingdom, other jurisdictions eventually followed suit. Challenges to its admissibility, both on grounds of novelty and reliability as well as to its interpretation, were raised in the appeal courts; in some instances this provided new insights as to the difficulties such evidence might encounter within the legal process. It is instructive to review some of these by briefly looking at some key examples from the United States and Australia.

11.5.1 United States

Surprisingly, LCN DNA evidence was relatively slow in being included as testimony across the United States, with only over 100 examples quoted as having been admitted as evidence by 2014 and, as of October 2014, it had yet to be presented to a US Federal Court (US v Johnny Morgan, 2014). It is not unexpected that both Frye and Daubert hearings have taken place over the past few years, as applicants seek to have such evidence declared inadmissible at their trial. At district and state court level such hearings have proved largely unsuccessful.

In 2004 Earl Davis was arrested for bank robbery and the murder of an armoured car guard who was transporting money to a bank in Hyattsville, Maryland. Key evidence from the prosecution was a series of DNA profiles obtained from the swabbing of firearms and vehicle steering wheel covers recovered from the crime scene. These exhibits provided profiles of varying quality that were asserted by the prosecution to implicate Davis and others accused of this crime. For a number of reasons, including the prosecution seeking the death penalty, Davis' submission for a Daubert hearing on this DNA evidence, on the grounds of its being obtained by non-validated LCN methods, did not take place until March 2009.

At this hearing the prosecution claimed that, as the techniques used in this work were the same as applied to conventional DNA profiling, this was not in fact a novel method. The defence proposed that it was the amount of cellular material examined and the existence of a stochastic threshold that defined the LCN method and claimed that the scientific community was not agreed on what constituted this threshold, with some suggesting less than 500 pg, whereas others advocated a threshold around 125 pg.

However, following further debate, it was resolved that the defence's interpretation of the quantity used in these analysis as being 100 pg was in error and that it was probable that the correct figure was ten times greater. On this basis, the court did not need to adjudicate on whether the method met the Daubert criteria, as it was convinced that this was a conventional DNA analysis.

In 2010, a Frye hearing into the admissibility of LCN DNA evidence was published by the New York Supreme Court. The applicant, Hemant Meganth, was accused of the murder of Natasha Ramen who had been scheduled to appear as a witness against him for an earlier offence. Crucially, swabs taken from Meganth's automobile revealed DNA profiles 'consistent with' that of Ramen, thus associating her with his vehicle. The defendant submitted that, as LCN methods had been used to obtain these profiles and were of unproven reliability, such evidence was inadmissible under the Frye criterion.

The analyses had been carried out at the Office of Chief Medical Examiner (OCME) in new laboratories, equipped specifically to the highest standards required for LCN work. The laboratory had also carried out extensive validation studies and these had been externally reviewed and confirmed as reproducible and reliable. The court decided that, as the basic procedures were fundamentally the same as those used when working with conventional samples, the LCN technique was deemed reliable and accepted by the scientific community. It was, in fact, just an extension of the standard method and there was no precisely definable threshold in moving from one technique to the other. Hence issues relating to the interpretation of LCN DNA profiles should not affect the admissibility of the evidence but rather be dealt with by a court when considering the weight of evidence to attach to it.

Interestingly, a few years later, a New York district court held a Daubert hearing on similar matters in the case of Johnny Morgan who was accused of possessing a firearm after being convicted of a felony, following an incident in 2012. At issue was whether a gun, found on the pavement, was dropped by Morgan. LCN DNA profiles from three swabs taken from the gun were compared with that of Morgan; the defence argued against the validity of this evidence.

As validation of the LCN DNA methodology used by the OCME was based on samples of 25 pg, prepared from two known contributors, it did not follow that the analysis could be applied to a degraded, mixed source sample of only 14 pg, as was the case here. The judge responded that, since he was content that the basic methodology was correct, issues relating to the interpretation of casework samples such as these would be accounted for in the weight assigned to the evidence and not to its admissibility. Each of the characteristics of casework samples had been tested in the earlier validation studies by OCME, including its sensitivity to amounts as low as 6 pg. The prosecution countered a specific challenge to the amount of DNA material in this sample by putting forward an expert view that it was the stochastic effects rather than the absolute quantity of cellular material that mattered. These effects were taken account of in the interpretation and evaluation of the profiles and did not constitute part of the core method itself. Specifically, the DNA subcommittee of the New York Commission on Forensic Science was quoted as saying that:

> '... there is no lower limit below which LCN testing cannot be performed, though it declined to determine whether there is a lower limit below which OCME could not test based on OCME's validation studies and protocols.'
>
> [US v Johnny Morgan, 2014, p33]

Other matters, related to analysis, were also deemed to be interpretative issues that influenced the weight of the evidence and did not raise doubts as to the scientific validity of the LCN DNA method as implemented by OCME. Hence the judge ruled the evidence admissible under Daubert.

11.5.2 Australia

The first Australian case to use LCN DNA evidence was also one that captured substantial public interest. It involved the disappearance and alleged murder of a British tourist, Peter Falconio, and the assault of his girlfriend Joanne Lees, as they stopped at the roadside while driving through the outback in the Northern Territory, in 2001. Falconio had left their van to speak to another driver who had requested they stop. Lees subsequently heard a gunshot and saw a man she later identified as Bradley John Murdoch, pointing a gun at her. He forced her into his vehicle and handcuffed her but she then escaped and hid in the scrub, after which the assailant moved the Kombi van off the road into the scrub further along the road. Peter Falconio's body was never found.

The crucial forensic evidence related to DNA profiles from a bloodstain on Lees' t-shirt and from swabs taken from the steering wheel and gear stick knob in the Kombi van. The prosecution's case was that these linked Murdoch to the crime.

Initial analysis was carried out locally using conventional PCR techniques. The blood-stain provided a conventional profile identical to that of Murdoch and this evidence was not contested. A partial profile was obtained from the gear stick that included only alleles from

Murdoch's profile but with a high match probability of 1 in 678. The swabs from the steering wheel and gear stick were taken to the United Kingdom to be examined by Dr Whitaker, using the new LCN DNA technique.

The steering wheel profile was interpreted as including contributions from at least three individuals with both the victims and Murdoch not excluded as sources. However, even if DNA from these three was present, not all the alleles were accounted for, so another fourth contributor should be included. Whitaker's evaluation was that the complexity of the whole profile precluded any meaningful comparisons and it therefore had no value to the court. On the other hand, the gear stick revealed two sources, including a minor contribution from Falconio, with the remaining alleles all present in Murdoch's profile. In his evaluation Whitaker stated:

> 'I have calculated that the combination of DNA bands, which match the profile of Bradley John Murdoch (and which are not shared with Peter Falconio) would be expected to occur in approximately one in nineteen thousand of the United Kingdom Caucasian population. This result would provide very strong evidence of association between Bradley John Murdoch and the gear stick.'
>
> [Queen v Murdoch, 2005, paragraph14]

He added that the total profile was what would be expected, had both men driven the van.

This testimony was challenged on grounds that the novel technique of LCN DNA was inadmissible in the Australian courts and that the prosecution could not demonstrate that contamination had not led to invalid results. However, the appeal court judge was not convinced by these arguments. He accepted the evidence of Whitaker as to the research underpinning the development of LCN DNA analysis in the United Kingdom and its relationship to conventional methods, its validation based on known profiles and its reliability, including its expanding use in casework both inside and outside the United Kingdom.

> 'I am satisfied that LCN has a "sufficient scientific basis" and general acceptance within the relevant scientific community to render results achieved by LCN "part of a field of knowledge which is a proper subject of expert evidence".'
>
> [Queen v Murdoch, 2005, paragraph 44]

The judge observed that there were no challenges to the technique from within the scientific community worldwide and dismissed the first ground of appeal, stating:

> 'The body of knowledge and general acceptance with which the fundamental principle is concerned are not limited to a body of knowledge or general acceptance within the confines of the Australian boundaries.
>
> [Queen v Murdoch, 2005, paragraph 41]

On the issue of contamination, Whitaker explained that both general contamination from the environment during the chain of custody of the samples and specifically cross-contamination between evidential samples within the laboratory were important considerations. In particular, in this case, the complexity of that chain of custody that involved two laboratories and intercontinental travel, as well as procedures at the crime scene itself, implied that potential contamination was a relevant issue. However, the appeal court judge ruled that this did not affect the admissibility of the LCN DNA evidence. It was up to the jury to decide, on the testimony it received, as to whether contamination was an issue that would impact on the reliability and probity of the evidence. On this basis the appeal was dismissed. Murdoch was convicted of these offences in 2005, though he continued to claim his innocence. However, in 2014, he withdrew a subsequent appeal against this conviction.

11.6   Conclusions

Although LTDNA evidence is largely now admitted to the courts, the debate on its interpretation and evaluation is ongoing, with some of the key difficulties highlighted through recent cases. Some of the issues, particularly those concerned with source-level testimony from mixed and partial profiles are likely to be resolved, at least in part, with further research and increased use of validated software tools. However, there remain difficulties where no statistical interpretation is deemed possible. In contrast, at activity level, the onus falls on the expert's skill and experience to provide reliable opinion, based on competing propositions and taking into account the full circumstances of the case.

References

Caddy B., Taylor G.R. and Linacre A.M.T. (2008). A review of the science of low template DNA analysis [Online]. Available at https://www.gov.uk/government/uploads/system/uploads/attachment_data/file/117556/Review_of_Low_Template_DNA_1.pdf [Accessed 21 October 2015].

Gill P., Brenner C.H., Buckleton J.S., Carracedo A., Krawczak M., Mayr W.R., Morling N., Prinz M., Schneider P.M. and Weir B.S. (2006). DNA commission of the International Society of Forensic Genetics: Recommendations on the interpretation of mixtures. *Forensic Science International*, 160, 90–101.

Gill P., Brown R.M., Fairley M., Lee L., Smyth M., Simpson N., Dunlop J., Greenhalgh M., Way K., Westacott E.J., Ferguson S.J., Ford L.V., Clayton T. and Guiness J. (2008). National recommendations of the Technical UK DNA working group on mixture interpretation for the NDNAD and for court going purposes. *Forensic Science International: Genetics*, 2, 76–82.

Gill P., Guiness J. and Iveson S. (2012). The interpretation of DNA evidence (including low-template DNA), report for the Forensic Science Regulator [Online]. Available at https://www.gov.uk/government/uploads/system/uploads/attachment_data/file/143745/interpretation-of-dna-evidence.pdf [Accessed 21 October 2015].

People v Hemant Meganth [2010] 917/2007 Frye Hearing

Pope S. and Evett I.W. (2013). Complex DNA mixtures as evidence, *Law Society Gazette* [Online]. Available at http://www.lawgazette.co.uk/law/practice-points/science-of-mixed-results/5036961.fullarticle [Accessed 31 March 2016]

R v Bates [2006] EWCA Crim 1395

R v Mel Broughton [2010] EWCA Crim 549

R v Dlugosz; R v Pickering; R v MDS [2013] EWCA Crim 2

Queen v Sean Hoey [2007] NICC 49

R v Hookway and another [2011] EWCA Crim 1989

Queen v Murdoch [2005] NTSC 76

R v Reed and another; R v Garmson [2009] EWCA Crim 2698

R v Ashley Thomas [2011] EWCA Crim 1295

US v Davis [2009] 602 F. Supp 2d 658 (D Md 2009)

US v Johnny Morgan [2014] Southern District of New York, Case 1:12-cr-00223-GHW

Further Reading

Balding D.J. and Buckleton J. (2009). Interpreting low template DNA profiles. *Forensic Science International: Genetics*, 4, 1–10.

Gilbert N. (2010). DNA's identity crisis. *Nature*, 464(18), 347–348.

Gill P., Whitaker J., Flaxman C., Brown N. and Buckleton J. (2000). An investigation of the rigor of interpretation rules for STRs derived from less than 100 pg of DNA. *Forensic Science International*, 112, 17–40.

International Society for Forensic Genetics (ISFG): Forensic software resources. (2016). [Online]. Available at http://www.isfg.org/Software [Accessed 31 March 2016].

Jamieson A. (2011). LCN DNA analysis and opinion on transfer: R v Reed and Reed. *International Journal of Evidence and Proof*, 15(2) 161–166.

Meakin G. and Jamieson A. (2013). DNA transfer: Review and implications for casework. *Forensic Science International: Genetics*, 7, 434–443.

Puch-Solis R., Roberts P., Pope S. and Aitken C. (2012). Assessing the probative value of DNA evidence, RSS Practitioner Guide No 2 [Online]. Available at http://www.rss.org.uk/Images/PDF/influencing-change/rss-assessing-probative-value.pdf [Accessed 14 December 2015].

12

Footwear Marks in Court

As expert testimony, the evaluation of footwear mark evidence has proved over recent years to be one of the most interesting and controversial whether from the perspective of admissibility or from that of evaluation. In this context, there are several competing views as to how opinion should be developed and indeed on what interpretive basis that should be done. These include establishing whether there is a 'match' or 'no match', interpreting the degree of correspondence using statistical data or, alternatively, approaching the evaluation in the context of competing propositions. In all of these cases, the nature of the process for examination of the marks includes much that is qualitative and some that is quantitative, and although there is some agreement across jurisdictions as to the procedures for the examination of footwear marks, there is divergence on how interpretation and evaluation should be carried out.

In this chapter, the core principles underpinning this area of work will be presented, approaches to evaluation will be discussed in the context of cases, including the landmark case in the United Kingdom of R v T and the progress made towards agreeing scales and verbal forms for conveying that expert testimony will be examined.

12.1   The Analysis and Interpretation of Footwear Marks

The examination of footwear marks is based on the identification of class characteristics and individualising traits from an image of the crime scene mark and the comparison of these to a similar examination of reference marks. The class characteristics include the size, or more often a narrow size range, for the footwear, observations regarding the outline shape of the mark and, most importantly, features within the outsole pattern. For many types of shoe,

Forensic Evidence in Court: Evaluation and Scientific Opinion, First Edition. Craig Adam.
© 2016 John Wiley & Sons, Ltd. Published 2016 by John Wiley & Sons, Ltd.

particularly the sports shoe or trainer, this pattern may be very complex and distinctive, including a manufacturer's logo amongst many other features. Individualising, or more accurately potentially individualising, traits comprise two types. The first is the wear pattern on the outsole, which arises from the combination of the gait and walking habits of the wearer, the mechanical properties of the footwear sole materials themselves, the length of time of wear and the nature of the surfaces on which the wearer has walked. These factors may lend individuality to the wear pattern but this may be offset by the limited clarity and quality of the footwear mark itself and the evolving nature of these features with time. For these reasons, wear may be of limited use in practical casework. The second is damage to the outsole due to random, accidental events during the wear period, including gouges and tears to the sole material and inclusion of stones and other material within grooves in the outsole pattern. Once again the potential for individualisation is limited by the changes that may take place to such traits with ongoing use and such features would be of most value when the damage is significant and the time factor and circumstances are known.

On the basis of these observations, the scientist arrives at a view as to whether the number and quality of the characteristics are sufficient to determine whether the crime scene mark and the reference mark may have a common origin; if not, an inconclusive opinion would be returned. Possible outcomes include categorical statements on the identification or exclusion of a common origin, with a range of intermediate opinions based on some probabilistic statement reflecting the strength of support or otherwise for a common origin. In arriving at an intermediate outcome the contributions from class and potentially individualising features in the mark would play a key role.

Studies have revealed that, in most casework, crime scene marks are most commonly distinguished by class characteristics, and wear features contribute little to the interpretation and evaluation. There are, however, notable occasions, particularly with older shoes, where accidental damage characteristics play a significant role in interpreting the evidence.

Completing the interpretation of the evidence and reaching an evaluation for the court is a less well-defined process and this is where procedures may diverge according to examiner, laboratory and jurisdiction. Although quite detailed qualitative processes for footwear mark examination have been provided (e.g. Bodziak, 2000), the lack of a consensus on any quantitative measures of how individualising features contribute to evaluative opinion was a significant criticism of the methodology in the NRC report (2009). As with other types of mark or impression evidence, the issue of uniqueness or whether there is a need to have some assessment of other possible sources of the questioned mark, apart from that associated with the suspect, are central to the evaluation. Although there are many examples where the focus has been on 'establishing a match', evaluation has been achieved increasingly through frequentist statements or, in some cases, using likelihood ratio.

12.2   Match Opinion: R v D S Hall 2004

12.2.1   The Crime and the Evidence

Peggy Jo Barkley-Dube was murdered at her home in Sault Ste. Marie, Ontario, Canada in May 1999 by being repeatedly attacked with a sharp weapon. She had not been sexually assaulted and the crime scene had the appearance of a break-in. After an extended investigation, David Scott Hall, was arrested, largely on grounds of circumstantial evidence. The only traces of physical evidence found at the scene were four spots of Hall's blood, separately located at different places in the house, and shoe-marks, from the same type of shoe, imprinted on the deceased's blood in both the dining room and kitchen. Although Hall had an alibi for most of the evening of the murder, there was a one-hour period that he could not reliably account for. He claimed that while he had visited Barkley-Dube earlier the same day, he had banged his finger, opening up a cut causing his blood being found at her home. He denied being responsible for the shoe-marks though he admitted to owning a pair of Wilson running shoes such as those that caused the marks. A shop CCTV camera had identified him a short time before the murder apparently wearing shoes such as these, though he later denied that was the case. Hall was convicted of second-degree murder in October 2000, largely on the shoe-mark evidence.

Hall appealed in 2004 on grounds that the probative value of the shoe-marks had been greatly exaggerated by the jury in their deliberations, due to the actions of the judge, and that the evidence was inadmissible due to its novelty.

12.2.2 Footwear Mark Evidence and Opinion

The expert witness, from the Ontario Provincial Police, confirmed the extent of his training and experience in the examination of footwear marks, before describing to the court the techniques he used to lift the shoe-mark at the crime scene. He then produced test impressions from the Wilson shoes recovered from Hall's house, which he had compared with the crime scene marks. Using photographs and diagrams, he identified class characteristics, such as the size and make indicated by the pattern, as well as wear features and accidental characteristics that assist in individualising the mark. He concluded by stating that the impression found at the scene corresponded in many respects to that obtained from the Wilson shoe worn by the accused. Interestingly, the judge qualified this opinion by ruling that he, the expert, could indeed testify as to the similarities between the two impressions but could not give an opinion on whether Hall's shoe was in fact responsible for making the mark found in blood at the crime scene.

However, Hall's counsel claimed that this expert evidence was not necessary as the jury could readily interpret the shoe-mark evidence themselves without expert guidance. This was not accepted by the appeal court judge who pointed out that a lay juror might not see or properly interpret the significance of subtle wear marks or features due to accidental damage and that the expert's opinion was essential for a proper evaluation of this evidence. Once again, the defence view was that the weight and authority of expert opinion would lead the jury to over-estimate the significance of the shoe-mark evidence to the prosecution's case, thereby prejudicing the defendant's case. There was a risk that they would accept it uncritically. As stated by the defence counsel:

> 'The judge didn't caution them about not giving it undue weight. The way this opinion was left to the jury, it was almost impossible for them to come to an independent opinion. It would have simply overwhelmed them.'
>
> [Makin, 2004]

To this, the judge at appeal noted that, unlike other forms of evidence, the presentation of a shoe-mark comparison is not difficult for a lay person to interpret critically, with guidance. He added:

> 'The basis for this expert's opinion was capable of evaluation by the jury. They could examine the photographs and charts and independently consider whether the similarities identified by

the expert were in fact similarities. This was not the kind of expert evidence which carries with
it an aura of "mystic infallibility".'

[R v Hall, 2004]

The 2004 appeal was unsuccessful and Hall's conviction was confirmed.

12.2.3   Review of Expert Opinion in R v Hall

In reviewing this evidence and the expert opinion, two points are notable:

First, the view of the court was that expert opinion was essential to the jury in their
deliberations, yet the judge was clear on the limitation he placed on the expert as regards
his evaluation. The role of the jury was to understand and assimilate this testimony on the
similarities between the marks, prior to coming to a view as to whether the crime scene
marks were in fact made by the defendant's shoe. This was to be achieved without any
further guidance from the expert.

Second, the evaluation is presented solely as establishing a match and qualifying the
strength of the comparison between the questioned mark and that produced from Hall's
shoe. There is no mention in the appeal court document that alternative explanations for the
evidence were presented or data on the frequency of occurrence of this model and size of
Wilson running shoe were provided. In contrast, a contemporary newspaper report of the
trial itself stated

'A partial imprint of a running shoe left when the killer stepped in his victim's blood took on
even more importance once police discovered that only a couple of thousand pairs had been
sold in Canada.'

[Makin, 2004]

It appears that this fact did not contribute to the deliberations of the appeal court.
Interestingly, in contrast to the trial judge, the judge at a bail appeal in 2000 summarised
the shoe-mark evidence as follows:

'This…forensic evidence makes the Crown's case very compelling. We have the evidence of
an expert, someone who made a scientific study, who says that the print in the victim's blood
came from a pair of shoes owned by the accused and found in the accused's father's residence.
Putting it another way, the shoe fits the print.'

[R v Hall, 2002]

This reveals that his view on the significance of the evidence went much further.

12.3   The Likelihood Ratio Approach to Evaluation of Footwear Marks

How then may the likelihood ratio method of evaluation be applied to footwear marks?
First what is the evidence E? This is the outcome of the examination of the crime scene
mark and relevant reference marks which is based on the observed correspondence of the
features discussed in section 12.1, taking into account any uncertainties assessed as
relevant by the examiner.

The propositions of interest to the court relate to the source of the evidence and may be written as:

H_1: The suspect's shoe was responsible for the mark
H_2: A source other than the suspect's shoe was responsible for the mark

In assessing the probability of E based on the prosecution's proposition, the scientist will take into account any variation in the marks produced from a particular shoe consequent on factors such as surface properties and contact dynamics. Under the defence proposition, the scientist requires knowledge of other potential sources of footwear with similar characteristics that may produce marks that correspond to that produced by the suspect's shoe. To provide the probabilities necessary to calculate this likelihood ratio, survey information or an appropriate database of footwear marks is needed, as well as some understanding of uncertainties in the process of examination.

12.4   Standardising Scales for Expert Opinion

Over the past ten years, attempts have been made to standardise the scales of expert opinion for shoe mark evidence and, although quite detailed documents have been compiled to guide the expert witness, there persist some significant divergence of views on how opinion should be developed and presented. Examples of European and US scales are presented as equivalent in Table 12.1; this is for convenience, and no direct matching of the boundaries is implied by either organisation. These scales apply more generally to other sources of marks and impressions, such as those from vehicle tyres.

12.4.1   SWGTREAD Scales of Opinion

In the United States, the consensus is on presenting posterior probabilistic statements, based on the degree of correspondence between the crime scene and reference marks. The current SWGTREAD (2013) scale of conclusions was preceded by an earlier version (2006), which focused on defining terminology. Prior to this, a scale of statements for the court was provided in the treatise by Bodziak (2000). These are framed in a similar fashion to those in SWGTREAD (2006), though the focus is very much on the degree of correspondence, with only occasional statements about other sources of footwear, and no reference is made to any need for database or frequentist information in arriving at a conclusion.

The scales include an inconclusive outcome that may arise either from there being no discernable features in the mark or the examiner reaching a view that any features present are of insufficient quality to arrive at any other conclusion. There are points corresponding to the categorical outcomes of the identification or elimination of the mark. These are somewhat at odds with the posterior probabilistic conclusions defining the other intermediate points but are very much in the tradition and working ethos of examiners of marks and impressions.

The SWGTREAD (2013) scale encourages the examiner to comment on alternative sources for the mark when arriving at an opinion but the logical process underpinning this and how it is incorporated into the final testimony is unclear. Indeed, it is stated that no

Table 12.1 *Scales of Evaluative Opinion for Footwear Mark Evidence (based on ENFSI (2006); SWGTREAD [2013])*

ENFSI Scale point	ENFSI 'LR'	ENFSI 'post-probabilistic'	SWGTREAD outcome	SWGTREAD criteria
1	Identification	Identification	Identification	Sufficient class and individual characteristics
2	Very strong/ strong support for the prosecution's proposition	Very probably	High degree of association	Sufficient class and some individual traits
			Association of class characteristics	Sufficient class characteristics
3	Moderately strong/strong/ limited support to the prosecution	Probably	Limited association of class characteristics	Some associative class characteristics
4	Inconclusive	Inconclusive	Lacks sufficient detail	No features or insufficient quality
5	Very strong to limited support to the defence proposition	Likely not	Indications of non-association	Some dissimilar traits but insufficient for exclusion
6	Elimination	Elimination	Exclusion	Sufficient class and/or individual traits are dissimilar

statistics should be used in this process. However, this scale is much clearer as to the relationship between the quality and quantity of class and individualising characteristics that are expected at each point on the scale, though the detail is left to the individual examiner. For example, phrases such as 'sufficient quality and quantity' and 'association of some class characteristics' are used without further explanation. As an example, where a high degree of association is noted, that is justified by:

> 'The questioned impression and known footwear…must correspond in the class characteristics of design, physical size, and general wear. For this degree of association there must also exist: (1) wear that, by virtue of its specific location, degree and orientation make it unusual and/or (2) one or more randomly acquired characteristics.'
>
> [SWGTREAD, 2013]

In the SWGTREAD table, an extended statement is provided for each point on the scale. For example, if the expert reaches a conclusion implying a high degree of association between the marks, then the following would form the basis of the opinion:

> 'In the opinion of the examiner, the characteristics observed exhibit strong associations between the questioned impression and known footwear or tire; however, the quality and/or quantity were insufficient for an identification. Other footwear or tires with the same class

characteristics observed in the impression are included in the population of possible sources only if they display the same wear and/or randomly acquired characteristics observed in the questioned impression.'

[SWGTREAD, 2013]

12.4.2 ENFSI Scales of Opinion

In contrast, the European Network of Forensic Science Institutes (ENFSI) has debated extensively on the fundamental approaches to formulating opinion on footwear mark evidence. In consequence, two competing scales were presented in 2006 representing different views within the community on how such evidence should be evaluated. The first was derived from logical evaluation by likelihood ratio, based on competing propositions, whereas the second provided posterior probabilities, verbally similar to those on the SWGTREAD scale but derived from Bayes' Theorem with a prior odds of unity. Within ENFSI, a significant group of members argued that, in many countries, the expectation in the court was that the expert would respond directly to a question on the source of a footwear mark, and that this could only be achieved through posterior probabilistic statements. However, the use of the 'full Bayes' rule' and the assumption of a prior odds proved controversial with many scientists. The development of these scales is discussed in detail in ENFSI (2006).

These scales include six levels of opinion, compared to seven on that provided by SWGTREAD (2013) and the points are explicitly numbered, though this appears to be no more than a reference index. Despite being based on probabilistic considerations, both scales include points justifying the categorical outcomes of identification or elimination of the mark. Despite the quite different basis and meaning of the 'LR' and 'probabilistic' forms of opinion statements in this scale, the intention is that the two expressions at each level are taken as equivalent. Further, the verbal scale based on likelihood ratio does not correspond completely to that given in Table 7.1 since it incorporates a 'leap of faith' in defining the highest level of support to the prosecution's case as 'identification'. Working with both these scales requires information on the frequency of occurrence of other footwear able to produce the mark, as well as consideration of the quality of the comparison itself.

A more recent document reveals how the European view has moved on from that in 2006. ENFSI (2015) appears now to fully endorse logical evaluation, using likelihood ratio, over a range of evidence types, including that of footwear marks. This will be discussed in section 12.8.

12.5 Challenges to Opinion on Footwear Evidence: R v T 2010

The England and Wales appeal court judgment in the case of R v T has claimed some notoriety, as initial reaction to it from the UK forensic science community suggested that future expert opinion across most evidence types, save only for DNA profiles, would be severely curtailed to simple qualitative remarks along the lines of 'could have made the mark'. This furore was evidenced by the rapid publication of a number of articles from eminent scientists, from across the globe, providing detailed critiques of this judgment. As it turned out, the Crown Prosecution Service (CPS) confirmed that the judgment was intended specifically for footwear marks and, indeed, it does not appear to have impacted strongly on more recent cases.

The judgment is redacted, nevertheless sufficient detail is provided for the expert testimony and the process whereby the scientist arrived at his opinion, to be discussed.

12.5.1 Outline of the Footwear Mark Evidence in R v T

The defendant T was tried for murder and convicted, primarily on the basis of footwear mark evidence. At the appeal, one of the grounds was the reliability of the expert evidence on footwear marks and the manner in which it was conveyed to the jury. This point was examined in detail by the appeal court and, in doing so, it raised issues related to the use of likelihood ratios in arriving at expert testimony where 'the statistical data available were uncertain and incomplete'.

The footwear marks were retrieved by the forensic scientist, Mr Ryder, following standard experimental and interpretive procedures. He told the court that his assessment of any correspondence or difference between the questioned and reference marks was made against two competing propositions:

H_1: The shoe in question has made the mark
H_2: The shoe has not made the mark

He observed in this case that:

1. The pattern and size of the trainers were the same as the mark and the pattern was one most frequently found in casework.
2. The wear on defendant's shoes was greater than on that which had made the mark; this could be due to wear subsequent to the mark being made but there was no evidence to test this hypothesis.
3. Some of marks showed damage characteristics, yet no such damage was evident on the defendant's shoes. This could be explained by:

    a. Artefacts on the floor
    b. Features on the trainers that had worn away with subsequent use
    c. The presence of a stone, for example, that had become dislodged with use

Consequently, Ryder arrived at the following opinion based on this examination:

> 'Overall it is my view somewhat unlikely that the observed correspondence would have been obtained as a result of mere coincidence had the recovered footwear not made the marks in question…. there is at this stage a moderate degree of scientific evidence to support the view that the [Nike trainers recovered from the appellant] had made the footwear marks'
>
> [R v T, 2010, paragraph 24]

There were three reports with similar conclusions presented to the court by Ryder and all were verified by colleagues. None of these reports presented any statistical information or calculations, despite the declaration of competing propositions and the phrasing of the opinion, suggesting that a likelihood ratio approach had been adopted.

In cross-examination by the defence counsel, he was asked about the occurrence of this particular type of trainer and data was presented on the sales of this shoe by Nike, and of sports shoes generally in the United Kingdom, over the period 1996–2006. The statistical information was that 786,000 such trainers were sold, which contributed to a total sports shoe population of 300,000,000. Of these around 3% were of size 11, the same as the shoe responsible for the mark. Additional sources of this pattern included counterfeit shoes and those sold by Footlocker. The effect of these data was to indicate that the proportion of such shoes in the population was relatively small, despite his earlier statement that the pattern was a 'common type' found in casework. These points and the apparent contradiction with the strength of the evaluative opinion, were emphasised by the judge in his summing up.

12.5.2 The Expert Witness' Notes

In preparation for the appeal, the contemporaneous notes kept by Ryder during his work were examined and found to contain some statistical detail and calculations, which appeared to justify the opinion of moderate evidence in support of the prosecution's proposition, yet had not been presented or discussed during cross-examination at the trial. The substance of these related to the use of the likelihood ratio method to combine the weight of evidence associated with each attribute of the footwear mark comparison, and reference to the Forensic Science Service (FSS) footwear mark database of patterns, used to provide a frequency of occurrence for the particular pattern observed in this case.

The detailed methodology of these calculations will be given here and summarised in Table 12.2. The class and individualising features of the mark were separately assessed using likelihood ratios and combined by multiplication in the usual way. The relationship between the propositions and these calculations is unclear and will be discussed later. In each of the following, it is assumed that the probability of observing the evidence given the prosecution's proposition is certainty, hence $\Pr(E|H_1) = 1$.

1. Pattern

To estimate the probability of the evidence under the defence proposition, Ryder used the FSS casework database that had been built up over many years and consisted of 8,122 patterns. In extracting the statistical data appropriate to this case he appears to have considered shoes added in 2005–2007 where around 20% exhibited this pattern.

Table 12.2   Comparison of LR Calculations in R v T (based on the data provided in R v T [2010])

Attribute	According to case-notes Paragraphs [35]–[37]	LR	Under cross-examination Paragraphs [42], [44], [104]	LR
Pattern	20% of shoes recently in the FSS database, comprising 8122 shoe-marks from casework, are of this pattern	5	786,000 Nike shoes produced from a population of 300 million sports shoes manufactured over the past 5 years	400
Size	3% of men's shoes in the United Kingdom are of size 11 but allowing some margin for uncertainty on size	10	3% of men's shoes in the United Kingdom are of size 11	33
Wear	Estimated from around half of shoes lacking such wear marks	2	Estimated from around half of shoes lacking such wear marks	2
Damage	Some contradictions in the observations imply neutral evidence	1	Assumed neutral	1
Opinion	Moderate evidence	100	Very strong evidence	26400

This provides the justification for his comment on its commonality. Hence, the LR for the pattern evidence is given by:

$$\text{LR}_{pattern} = \frac{\text{Pr}(E|H_1)}{\text{Pr}(E|H_2)} = \frac{1}{0.2} \approx 5$$

2.   *Size*

Here, survey data from the SATRA manufacturers' organisation indicated that 3% of men wore UK size 11 shoes. However, it was considered that some flexibility should be allowed for wear, style and other factors that might contribute some uncertainty to the estimation of exactly size 11 shoes. This would reduce the LR from that obtained from strict use of the 3% value. Hence, the LR for the size evidence rounded down to 10, according to:

$$\text{LR}_{size} = \frac{\text{Pr}(E|H_1)}{\text{Pr}(E|H_2)} = \frac{1}{0.03} = 33 \approx 10$$

Note that there is an arithmetical error in paragraph [36] of the appeal where the frequency is incorrectly entered in the formula as '0.333' resulting in an illogical argument as to how the final likelihood ratio is estimated.

3.   *Wear*

Ryder took a cautious line on evaluating the wear he observed in the footwear mark, for the reasons already mentioned. He estimated that it was typical of around half the footwear he examined, providing a LR of:

$$\text{LR}_{wear} = \frac{\text{Pr}(E|H_1)}{\text{Pr}(E|H_2)} = \frac{1}{0.5} \approx 2$$

4.   *Damage*

Once again, the random damage was evaluated on the basis of contradictions in the observations leading to a largely neutral outcome, where the probability given the defence proposition was estimated to be only a little less than unity:

$$\text{LR}_{damage} = \frac{\text{Pr}(E|H_1)}{\text{Pr}(E|H_2)} = \frac{1}{1} \approx 1$$

The total likelihood ratio was therefore:

$$\text{LR}_{evidence} = \text{LR}_{pattern} \times \text{LR}_{size} \times LR_{wear} \times \text{LR}_{damage} = 5 \times 10 \times 2 \times 1 = 100$$

Hence using the table of verbal equivalents, the final, conservatively estimated opinion of 'moderate evidence in support of the prosecutions' proposition' was arrived at. Mr Ryder stated that the outcome of this calculation was used:

> '..to confirm an opinion substantially based on his experience and so that it could be expressed in a standardised form.'

> [R v T, 2010, paragraph 38]

12.5.3 Evaluation Using an Alternative Database

At this point, it became clear that the significance of the evidence is different when evaluated on the basis of the database using in the previous section, compared to when the statistical data, discussed under cross-examination at the trial and given in 12.5.1, are used. In particular, although the size factor contributes in a similar way, the likelihood ratio for the pattern evidence is quite different.

1. Pattern

The database used here was essentially manufacturers' information on total sales of sports shoes and in particular Nike trainers that corresponded to this outsole pattern. Hence the frequency of occurrence of this pattern amongst all sports shoes provides:

$$\Pr\left(E|H_2\right) = \frac{786000}{300000000} = 0.00262$$

$$LR_{pattern} = \frac{\Pr(E|H_1)}{\Pr(E|H_2)} = \frac{1}{0.00262} = 382 \approx 400$$

When the appellant's counsel raised this aspect in detail at the appeal, he extended his argument by including the likelihood ratios for the other characteristics of the footwear mark, though he did not allow for any uncertainty in assigning a size 11 to the crime scene mark. These results are summarised in Table 12.2. The overall likelihood ratio of 26,400 would imply a verbal opinion of 'very strong support' for the prosecution's proposition.

Thus, from the legal perspective not only did the expert witness not reveal the statistical basis and methodology used in arriving at his stated opinion but when the data he discussed under cross-examination is used, a quite different strength of evidence emerges. The appeal court ruled that the statistical evidence was inherently unreliable, that the jury had not been told the exact basis on which the expert witness had arrived at his conclusive opinion and overall the process had not been transparent. On this basis the appeal was upheld and the conviction was quashed.

12.5.4 The Summary by the Appeal Court Judge

The real issue according to the appeal court judge was whether, following from positive observations as to the similarities between a crime scene footwear mark and a reference mark from the defendant's footwear, the scientist could then provide a 'probabilistic' evaluation, what the basis of that might be and how it might be expressed.

The appellant had submitted that the expert could assess the degree of match between questioned and reference marks but was not permitted to interpret such a comparison. The judge agreed that this may often be the case and in those circumstances:

> 'The use of the term "could have made" is a more precise statement of the evidence; it enables a jury better to understand the true nature of the evidence than the more opaque phrase "moderate [scientific] support"'

> [R v T, 2010, paragraph 73]

However, the judge stated that sometimes the expert could go further in the evaluation than that and expressed support for the US (SWGTREAD) scale of evaluation, in particular.

The use of Bayesian inference and likelihood ratios was not rejected for all evidence types, as the basis of an evaluation, since the judge appeared to accept that this approach was acceptable in the evaluation of DNA profiles. The difficulty for footwear mark evidence was in the robustness of any database used in such an evaluation.

> 'If there was a sufficient database in footwear cases then an expert might be able to express a view of the probability of the mark being made by the footwear … '
>
> [R v T, 2010, paragraph 91]

However, in the context of the databases referred to in this case, he was quite firm in dismissing any statistical basis or numerical process as part of the evaluation. He was clear that any evaluation should be subjective and based on experience; the word 'scientific' should not be used in reporting this to the court:

> ' … if that phrase is put before the jury, it is likely to give an impression to the jury of a degree of precision and objectivity that is not present given the current state of this area of expertise.'
>
> [R v T, 2010, paragraph 96]

The judge repeatedly condemned any mathematical input into the evaluative process, on the grounds that it was invalid given that input from different databases resulted in different answers.

> 'We are satisfied that in the area of footwear evidence, no attempt can realistically be made in the generality of cases to use a formula to calculate probabilities. The practice has no sound basis.'
>
> [R v T, 2010, paragraph 86]

He concluded that:

> 'In our judgement, an expert footwear mark examiner can therefore in appropriate cases use his experience to express a more evaluative opinion where the conclusion is that the mark "could have been made" by the footwear. However no likelihood ratios or other mathematical formula should be used in reaching that judgement for the reasons we have given.'
>
> [R v T, 2010, paragraph 95]

12.6   Discussion of R v T

There are several major issues raised by this case that relate both to the scientific and statistical basis used for the evaluation of footwear marks, and to the manner of presentation and discussion of such evidence, by the expert witness and the court.

12.6.1   Terminology, Probabilities and Statistical Methodology

The transcript in R v T illustrates yet another example of the difficulty, faced by those participating in the legal discussion, in distinguishing between logical evaluation based on LR, and the use of Bayes' Theorem to generate posterior odds ('the Bayesian method'). This issue was discussed in 7.1.2.

Although the brief propositions declared by the expert witness in 12.5.1 and the definition of likelihood ratio by the judge, stated at the beginning of paragraph [33] (i) in the ruling, are satisfactory, the re-iteration of this towards the end of that paragraph is incorrect. The judge appears to have lapsed into the prosecutor's fallacy in referring to the probabilities of the competing propositions themselves.

This underlines the importance of the formulation of these propositions and the subsequent probabilities, in particular of that relating to the defence proposition, as these are of crucial significance to conveying the meaning of an evaluation. The scientist is concerned with the probability of the evidence, in this case the observations relating to the comparison of the questioned and reference marks, and not to the origin of the mark itself. Thus, we might consider, for example:

> Given the prosecution's proposition that the defendant's footwear was responsible for the crime scene mark, what is the probability of observing the outcome of the mark comparison?

By stating erroneous probabilities, such as that for 'the defendant's shoe made the crime-scene mark', the opinion moves from a logical evaluation to a posterior probability focused on the strength of mark comparison being directly related to the strength of the prosecution's case. This may lead to confusion in the court about the verbal scales of opinion being used and invalid comparisons of terminology across the ENFSI and SWGTREAD scales given in Table 12.1, for example. At one point Mr Ryder is quoted as directly comparing his LR scale to that from SWGTREAD:

> 'Both [scales], he [Ryder] said, expressed a judgment based on the skill and experience of the examiner in interpreting the observations. "Moderate support" corresponded to "could have made" in the US scale.'
>
> [R v T, 2010, paragraph 67]

As far as the overall approach to evaluation is concerned, the expert witness was trying to use logical evaluation based on likelihood ratio within a practitioner context that was largely devoted to posterior probabilities and in a court that did not fully understand the distinctiveness of these methodologies. Indeed, the judgment itself fails to distinguish correctly between the former and the use of Bayes' Theorem. Consequently, a number of erroneous statements were made on all sides, which contributed to the confusion over the reliability of this testimony and in the appeal court ruling itself.

12.6.2 Footwear Databases

The formulation of the defence proposition is also highlighted in this case, as it raises the issue of which statistical information and databases are appropriate. For example, by simply negating the prosecution's proposition, the implication is that all other sources of footwear except for those worn by the defendant, are being considered. This is not a realistic scenario even if this shoe population is narrowed down to sports' footwear. There are likely to be makes and models of shoes with specific physical characteristics, sold in the locality at the right time and at the right price, which, for a variety of reasons, may appeal particularly to those intent on criminal activities, and others that would definitely not be worn. Here, the context and circumstances of the case are relevant and this has been discussed independently of, and indeed prior to, the R v T case, by Champod *et al.* (2004).

These authors suggest avenues to define alternative databases. For example, it may be more appropriate to consider only those shoes that have left marks at crime scenes, perhaps only in recent times and in the same locality (a crime-related (CR) database). Alternatively, rather than consider only the footwear marks themselves, perhaps the appropriate database would comprise marks from all footwear worn at such crime scenes, here including those for which marks were not identified (offender-related (OR)). A further possibility would be marks from the shoes of all those in the locality who came to the attention of the police during the investigation (an innocent suspects (IS) database). In addition, the environmental nature of the crime scene or time of year may influence that choice or indeed the type of crime itself. The issues around selecting the 'right' or the 'best' database and their implementation has been discussed, post-R v T, by Biedermann *et al.* (2012).

The size of such a database itself is not a major issue. It is more important to understand the nature and limitations of whatever database is available, whether it is representative and use it to inform the estimation of probabilities. Despite what was stated at the appeal, DNA allele databases are based on a far smaller number of individuals than the several thousand examples of footwear marks in the FSS database. The difference here is in the nature of the information provided by the database and how it is used subsequently.

On this basis it would appear that the approach followed by Ryder in his contemporaneous notes, in particular his choice of database, was more appropriate than using the statistical data on country-wide shoe manufacture, which were used to support his opinion under cross-examination.

12.6.3   Was the Jury Told the Basis of the Expert Opinion?

The verdict on the presentation of the expert evidence and its transparency are more straightforward to deal with. The difficulties appear to have arisen in the cross-examination of Ryder by the defence counsel, though it is unclear why they would wish to draw attention to data that would strengthen the case against their client. When data on the distribution of Nike trainers in the United Kingdom was put to him, Ryder could have steered his reply back to the actual statistical information he had used in his evaluation and explained why it was, in his view, the appropriate statistical basis for his testimony. Instead, he responded directly and used the small proportion of this style of Nike trainer within the whole sports shoe population as providing support for his initial opinion. This was in spite of this contradicting his earlier statement on the relative commonality of the pattern. Thus, not only was the jury oblivious to the true methodology outlined in his contemporaneous notes but they were also drawn into a separate set of statistical information that the exchange with counsel implied was in support of his overall opinion. As the appeal judge stated:

> 'If evidence of the full figures [from Ryder's notebook] had been put before the jury then, …, it might reasonably have affected the decision of the jury to convict.'
>
> [R v T, 2010, paragraph 108]

Further, the presentation of this evidence through the three reports, the testimony and its cross-examination was not transparent to anyone, as the methodology remained unrevealed in the contemporaneous notes. Ryder's justification for this was that the likelihood ratio and contributing statistical data were only used to support an opinion based on his experience since he regarded these data as not being sufficiently 'exact and precise' to be the sole basis of his evaluation. He added that their standard practice, rather surprisingly, was not to include statistical calculations, such as those from his notes, in the reports submitted to court.

12.6.4   The Appeal Court Ruling: Bayes, Mathematics and Formulae

The reaction of the forensic science community to the R v T ruling was initially focused on statements from the judge about the use of statistical and mathematical methods in evaluation and the implications on their future work for the courts. Despite the fact that these fears were to some extent alleviated by a review statement from the England and Wales CPS (Squibb-Williams, 2010), several authoritative publications followed that challenged many of the statements and points of discussion at the appeal. Some of these have already been discussed in the previous sections but here some of the generic mathematical issues will be briefly addressed.

The extensive discussion around the wording of opinion, including that used by Mr Ryder in his reports, and the terminology of the ENFSI and US practitioner scales, as well as a frequent focus on the expert's view as to whether 'the defendant's shoe was responsible for the mark' is evidence of an underlying uncertainty, or possibly even misunderstanding, amongst those involved about the meanings both of Bayesian inference and of the statements on these scales. This is a major issue within evaluation and has been discussed extensively elsewhere (e.g. Chapter 5.4).

Similarly, the repeated comments on the inappropriate use of formulae and mathematical calculations, reveal a misconception as to the purpose and use of a statistical or mathematical framework as part of evaluation. The likelihood ratio method provides a framework that allows the use of numerical or, indeed non-numerical, information. The formula is simply the mathematical representation of the logical framework but does need to be applied in a fashion that is sensitive to the nature of the data and to its limitations. Most importantly it shows how evidential weights may be combined by multiplication across different evidence types. This point is discussed by Robertson *et al.*, who conclude:

> 'If the Court were to say that the expert was not to use a logical procedure, rather than a 'mathematical formula', the flaw in its reasoning would be obvious.'
>
> [Robertson *et al.*, 2011]

Although these important issues were raised by R v T and are subject to continuing discussion, the CPS view was that the ruling should be interpreted in a narrower sense. The ruling related 'solely' to the FSS footwear database and the reliability of other databases was not addressed. Where the statistical nature of another database, for any evidence type, is considered reliable, then the use of statistical methods of evaluation was not precluded. At the heart of this is robust and effective case management to ensure that:

> '..experts are … transparent about the statistical data and methods used in coming to their conclusions.'
>
> [Squibb-Williams, 2010]

Case management should ensure the admissibility and hence the reliability of evidence submitted to the court. This includes full transparency of the process by which the final evaluation is reached. Despite these reassuring comments on logical evaluation, the CPS concluded:

> 'Footwear comparison evidence remains admissible and experts can still give subjective, evaluative opinion based on their experience and examinations'
>
> [Squibb-Williams, 2010]

12.7 Footwear Mark Evidence After R v T: R v South 2011

12.7.1 The Crime and Evidence

Sergio South was convicted of burglary in September 2010, following a break-in at a student house in Bournemouth, United Kingdom. The principal scientific evidence against him was a footwear mark on scattered envelopes at the crime scene, which provided moderately strong evidence that his sport trainer was responsible for the mark. He also had previous convictions for similar thefts. In his defence, he cited an alibi for the time of the theft from an associate who, the prosecution divulged, had convictions for many previous offences of dishonesty. South appealed on the grounds that this information should not have been admitted by the judge on the basis of 'non-defendant bad character' evidence. At the appeal, the footwear mark evidence was re-visited by the defence barrister, in light of the recent ruling in R v T.

12.7.2 Evaluation of the Footwear Evidence

The expert witness, Mr Jones, confirmed that his expertise in footwear analysis had been accumulated over eighteen years. In this case, the defendant's size 9 trainer was consistent with that responsible for the mark, which was size 8 to 9, but not a large as size 10. The class features of the pattern, in particular a zig-zag bar pattern and curved tramline, were similar to those on the trainer and an individualising wear pattern, which agreed in alignment and degree of wear, also was present. Jones added that, in his experience, burglars frequently wore sports trainers and he had come across this particular type of footwear in around 2% of the cases he had dealt with in the past. He consequently was of the opinion that this mark provided moderately strong evidence in support of the prosecution's proposition that South's trainer was the source of the crime scene mark.

At the appeal the judge reported a statement from the defence barrister, Mr Claxton, challenging the admissibility of this evidence:

> 'Mr Claxton told us that, in cross-examination, Mr Jones had said that this expression [moderately strong evidence] reflected a statistical probability of the footprint having been made by the shoes of the Appellant which was considerably more than a 50% probability, because the linguistic phrases used, such as "weak or limited support" or "extremely strong support", were based on probability which was itself based on a logarithmic scale.'
>
> [R v South, 2011, paragraph 28]

On this basis the defence alleged that Jones, in his oral evidence, had gone beyond what the appeal court had ruled in R v T, as he had given:

> '... an impression of a degree of precision and objectivity which is not present given the current state of expertise.'
>
> [R v South, 2011, paragraph 29]

In response, the appeal court judge dismissed this contention, confirming that by giving evidence based on his experience and in a way that enabled the jury to come to a view as to whether the defendant's trainers had made the mark, the expert witness had not breached the guidelines set in R v T.

12.7.3   Review of the Expert Opinion

In reviewing the delivery of this expert opinion it is clear that, although the interpretation of the shoe-mark was carried out and explained in a similar level of detail to that in R v T, the expert was careful to be concise in his evaluation. He provided a minimum of numerical data and did not imply that his evaluation was based on calculations or any hard statistical information other than that gleaned through his professional experience. He was not subjected to any detailed cross-examination as to his methodology or asked directly how he arrived at his final evaluation, except for the additional conclusion attributed to him in the quotation from the defence barrister. Assuming the barrister was accurate, it does appear that the witness went beyond his brief by providing an estimate for a posterior probability – 'considerably more than 50%' – which appears to be plucked out of the air. By doing so, he links the likelihood ratio, as reflected in 'moderately strong evidence', directly to the prosecution's proposition that the footprint was made by the appellant's shoes, written mathematically as:

$$Pr(H_1 | E) \gg 0.5$$

To derive this probability from the likelihood ratio requires knowledge of the prior odds. To explore this statement further, we need to numerically estimate the likelihood ratio. Assuming this is based only on the frequency of occurrence of the size, pattern and wear described by the scientist, we can use men's shoe size statistical data, the frequency of 2% quoted for the pattern and, in the absence of any real information on the wear, neglect that aspect. Given that 42% of men have shoe sizes in the range 8 to 9 (BFA, 2003), this gives:

$$LR_{footwear} = LR_{size} \times LR_{pattern} = \frac{1}{0.42} \times \frac{1}{0.02} \approx 125$$

This justifies the evaluative statement of 'moderately strong evidence' made by the expert witness, though he did not state all these figures or imply that this calculation had been carried out. Inclusion of the wear factor would strengthen the justification for this evaluation. To estimate the posterior probability, based on the ENFSI (2006) suggestion of equal priors, we can use equation (4) in Chapter 7.4.1, which may be rearranged to give:

$$Pr(H_1 | E) = \frac{1}{1 + (LR \times P_0)^{-1}} = \frac{1}{1 + (125 \times 1)^{-1}} = 0.992$$

This result shows that the expert witness was correct in stating that this was 'considerably more than a 50% probability', though he was over-stepping the mark by doing so, and was fortunate not be have been more closely interrogated on how he arrived at this statement. He was presumably attempting to expand on the meaning of the evaluative opinion by saying that it implied a better than evens probability of guilt but this requires an assumption of prior odds which is outside his responsibility to the court. His final point about the verbal equivalent being logarithmically related to the likelihood ratio is true and was a further attempt to add to his core evaluation, but this was not directly relevant, and indeed was another hostage to fortune as far as his testimony was concerned.

12.8   ENFSI Recommendations on Logical Evaluation 2015

These recent ENFSI guidelines demonstrate, not only how the logical evaluation method may be applied across a range of evidence types, including footwear, but also how the interpretation and evaluation should be presented within the expert witness' report and the nature of the supporting information that is required.

> 'This framework for evaluative reporting applies to all forensic science disciplines. The likelihood ratio measures the strength of support the findings provide to discriminate between propositions of interest. It is scientifically accepted, providing a logically defensible way to deal with inferential reasoning.'
>
> [ENFSI, 2015, 2.4]

For those who advocate logical evaluation, this document is a significant advance on the ENFSI position in their 2006 guidelines.

Two exemplar cases, in the formulation of opinion for footwear mark evidence, are provided in the report. The first of these uses a laboratory footwear mark database, constructed from 2600 casework examples, and the experience of the examiner in working with such casework marks, to estimate the contributing factors to an overall LR. The propositions are those based on the prosecution and defence perspectives and the examiner provides detailed background and literature references in the report to underpin the discussion.

The LR is calculated from four factors: pattern type in the database, size/mould type, general wear and specific wear features. The numerical result is quoted in the evaluation and conveyed as the appropriate verbal equivalent. In many ways, this follows the practice adopted in R v T, except in the emphasis given to the clarity and detail of the explanations and the coherence and justification provided for the arguments in the ENFSI example.

The second case is dealt with in a less quantitative fashion, as the interpretation is based more strongly on a range of potentially individualising, accidental wear features – 'acquired features' – rather than on the class characteristics of the mark, though these do correspond in the marks concerned. Here, the short time delay between the crime and the retrieval of the shoes, the high quality of the mark and the presence of ten acquired features, lead to an extremely low probability of the observations of similarity between the crime scene and reference marks, under the defence proposition. The expert provides an estimate of this as 'in the order of less than one in a million'.

> '… the results are in my opinion in the order of a million times more probable given the seized shoe made the mark than given an unknown shoe made the mark.'
>
> [ENFSI, 2015, p 92]

The formal statement of opinion is made using the verbal equivalent of the LR, only:

> 'The degree of correspondence between the sole of John Brown's left shoe and the impression at the scene in terms of pattern, size, wear and acquired features, provides extremely strong support for the proposition that the footwear impression at the scene was made by his shoe, rather than by a different, unknown shoe.'
>
> [ENFSI, 2015, p 96]

Further justification for this high level of support to the prosecution proposition, is provided:

'In the present case, the presence of 10 acquired features (with a high level of complexity) in correspondence between the mark and the print would be exceptional to observe on impressions made by two different soles.'

[ENFSI, 2015, p 97]

So, although the numerical probability appears to be stated somewhat arbitrarily, the justification is provided by this supporting statement based on the expert's experience, and the citation of relevant research papers, that it would be 'exceptional' to observe such features by chance, on marks made by two different shoes. In this way, a logical evaluation may be implemented on a largely non-numerical basis.

12.9   Conclusions

It is clear that formulating expert opinion on footwear marks, using logical evaluation and the likelihood ratio, is not only possible but now appears to be the recommended approach for those working under ENFSI. Nevertheless, it remains controversial in some jurisdictions where posterior probabilistic evaluative statements are preferred and cases, such as R v T, reveal the potential difficulties faced by the scientist in explaining and justifying the logical evaluation methodology and its outcomes to the court.

References

Biedermann A., Taroni F. and Champod C. (2012). How to assign a likelihood ratio in a footwear mark case: an analysis and discussion in the light of R v T. *Law, Probability and Risk*, 11, 259–277.

Bodziak W.J. (2000). Footwear impression evidence, detection, recovery and examination 2nd Ed. CRC Press. Boca Raton, Florida.

British Footwear Association (BFA): SATRA report on men's shoe sizes [Online]. (2003). Available at http://www.britishfootwearassociation.co.uk/wp-content/uploads/2014/03/Footwear-sizes-2003.doc.pdf [Accessed 20 December 2015].

Champod C., Evett I.W. and Jackson G. (2004). Establishing the most appropriate databases for addressing source level propositions. *Science and Justice*, 44(3), 153–164.

ENFSI Working Group, Marks Conclusion Scale Committee, Chair: H Katterwe. (2006). Conclusions scale for shoeprint and toolmarks examinations. *Journal of Forensic Identification*, 56(2), 255–279.

ENFSI guideline for evaluative reporting in forensic science [Online]. (2015). Available at https://www.unil.ch/esc/files/live/sites/esc/files/Fichiers%202015/ENFSI%20Guideline%20Evaluative%20Reporting [Accessed 24 October 2015].

Makin K. The case of the bloody shoe print. *The Globe and Mail*, Toronto [Online]. (22 Nov 2004). Available at http://www.theglobeandmail.com/news/national/the-case-of-the-bloody-shoe-print/article4091741/ [Accessed 12 January 2016].

National Research Council: Strengthening Forensic Science in the United States: A Path Forward, Document 228091 [Online]. (2009). Available at http://www.nap.edu/catalog/12589.html [Accessed 10 October 2015].

R v Hall [2002] SCC 64

R v Hall [2004] Court of Appeal of Ontario C35369

R v South [2011] EWCA Crim 754

R v T [2010] EWCA 2439

Robertson B., Vignaux G.A. and Berger C.E.H. (2011). Extending the confusion about Bayes, *Modern Law Review*, 74(3), 430–455.

Squibb-Williams K. (2010). Crown Prosecution Service statement on Footwear database analysis by experts using Bayesian statistics [Online]. Available at http://www.csofs.org/write/MediaUploads/News/CPS_Annoucement.doc [Accessed 26 October 2015].

SWGTREAD: Standard Terminology for Expressing Conclusions of Forensic Footwear and Tire Impression Examinations [Online]. (2006). Available at http://www.swgtread.org/images/documents/standards/archived/swgtread_10_terminology_conclusions_200603_201302.pdf [Accessed 13 January 2016].

SWGTREAD: Standard for Terminology Used for Forensic Footwear and Tire Impression Evidence [Online]. (2013). Available at http://www.swgtread.org/images/documents/standards/published/swgtread_15_terminology_evidence_201303.pdf [Accessed 26 October 2015].

Further Reading

Aitken C. and thirty other authors. (2011). Guest editorial: Expressing evaluative opinions – a position statement. *Science and Justice*, 51(1), 1–2.

Berger C.E.H., Buckleton J., Champod C., Evett I.W. and Jackson G. (2011). Evidence evaluation: A response to the court of appeal judgment in R v T. *Science and Justice*, 51(2), 43–49.

Koehler J. If the shoe fits they might acquit: The value of forensic science testimony. Faculty Working Papers, paper 23 [Online]. (2011). Available at http://scholarlycommons.law.northwestern.edu/facultyworkingpapers/23 [Accessed 4 April 2016].

13

Fingerprints and Finger-Marks – Identifying Individuals?

Fingerprint evidence has been accepted by the courts for over one hundred years and has been very much revered as the ultimate evidence, associating an individual with a crime scene. Over recent years, questions have been raised about the scientific basis of this, the most important of the so-called 'forensic identification sciences'. In this chapter we shall review the methodology of fingerprints and fingerprint identification and, in particular, how the expert examiner evaluates and presents testimony to the court.

To ensure clarity throughout this discussion, the ridge pattern on a finger-pad will be called the fingerprint, whereas the pattern left by deposition of trace sweat residues at a crime scene will be called the finger-mark, or often just the mark.

13.1 Fingerprint Identification on Trial

The fact that no two individuals have been found to have the same fingerprint, is the foundation of their alleged uniqueness and this is a fair basis on which to utilise the complete or full fingerprint as a biometric measure. However, the same conclusion cannot necessarily be drawn from the comparison between the crime scene marks originating from those two individuals' fingers, given the large variation in the quality of latent marks, both full and partial, that may be produced from a finger under different conditions of contact, on different surfaces and revealed through many different enhancement and imaging methods. There is a continuum of quality from the image of the finger-pad itself, through the scanned or inked print and the enhanced full print, down to a degraded, distorted, partial, latent mark from a crime scene.

Forensic Evidence in Court: Evaluation and Scientific Opinion, First Edition. Craig Adam.
© 2016 John Wiley & Sons, Ltd. Published 2016 by John Wiley & Sons, Ltd.

Hence, the claim that there is an infallible set of procedures that enables the expert to deliver categorical opinion to the court, that a mark has been identified as coming from an individual or that a suspect has been excluded as the source of the mark, has now come under serious scrutiny from academic researchers, legal authorities and governmental agencies.

The rapidity and assurance with which the criminal justice system accepted fingerprint evidence, largely without question, may appear surprising in retrospect, given the challenges made in more recent times to those new developments in forensic analysis that often make fairly modest claims. However, the opposite was true for fingerprints; as Saks has commented:

> '...fingerprint identification presented the courts with a novel claim (infinite individuality) in an astonishingly strong form (infallibility)...'

> [Saks, 1998]

To see how challenges to fingerprint evidence have shaped changes in the profession, in the courts and in academia, by encouraging new scientific developments, we need to start with the procedures by which the mark and the print are compared.

13.2 ACE-V: A Scientific Method?

The sequence of protocols, namely analysis – comparison – evaluation, was first proposed by Huber in 1959 in an attempt to formalise the process of forensic identification, specifically in the context of document examination. This was later adopted by the fingerprint community as providing a description of the process, already established, in the examination of fingerprint evidence. The fourth stage of verification was included later and, in 1999, the acronym 'ACE-V' emerged in testimony from David Ashbaugh, at a Daubert hearing in the case of United States v Mitchell. Since then, the fingerprint examiner communities worldwide have come to regard this as their own methodology and one that provides scientific underpinning to fingerprint testimony in court.

ACE-V encompasses the four stages in the process of examining, interpreting and evaluating the comparison of a latent finger-mark against, most commonly, the fingerprint from a suspect. Detailed process maps have been provided by NIST in their expert working group report (NIST, 2012). The initial examination of the friction ridge impression forms the analysis stage. Here the three levels of detail within the mark and the print are inspected. These comprise the ridge flow and pattern class (level 1), the identification of points of second-level detail commonly termed minutiae (level 2) and any fine detail on ridge shape and pore positions (level 3). The examiner decides at this point whether the totality of information provided by both impressions – but effectively driven by the quality of the mark – is sufficient to proceed to the next stage or whether the process is terminated and a verdict of insufficient detail is returned, which is the first outcome.

In the comparison phase the three levels of detail are worked through in sequence and, in each case, points of similarity and any points of difference between the mark and the print are noted. At the evaluation stage, the examiner uses the evidence already accumulated, to arrive at a conclusion that may be one of three further outcomes. Firstly, the examiner may be unable to reach a conclusion at all, most commonly due to the quality and quantity of features available in the mark. In this case, no further detail would be provided in testimony regarding the detail of the examination and the outcome declared inconclusive. Secondly, the suspect print may be excluded, categorically, as the source of the mark. This would follow from any inexplicable differences in ridge flow or ridge detail between the two impressions. Thirdly, the examiner can declare that the mark is identified, on the basis of sufficient individualising characteristics. The exact meaning of this final outcome and how it is conveyed in testimony has been the subject of debate over recent years.

At the final stage, the work of fingerprint examiner is verified by at least one other examiner, though whether this amounts to a fresh, blind examination or an inspection and moderation of the work of the first examiner, appears to depend on local practice.

The ACE-V method has been criticised as being simply a set of protocols rather than a scientific methodology. It is notable that the rise of the ACE-V acronym and the increasing emphasis it has received within the fingerprint community has coincided with increasing criticism of the scientific basis of fingerprint examination, both from the academic community and from public bodies:

> '... merely following the steps of ACE-V does not imply that one is proceeding in a scientific manner or producing reliable results.'
>
> [NRC, 2009, p. 142]

It is also apparent that to progress through the ACE-V protocols the examiner has to make judgements and decisions that are highly dependent on training, experience and a range of external factors that may influence these, including those under the heading of contextual bias (Chapter 9.4). Hence at every stage human factors can have a direct impact on the outcome of the process.

There are two substantive issues for discussion in trying to understand how the expert witness testimony follows from the outcome of the ACE-V process. The first relates to how the fingerprint examiner makes decisions at various points throughout the stages and what objective criteria, if any, may be applied. The second issue is how the outcome of identification is conveyed to the court as expert opinion.

13.3 Evaluation Criteria

13.3.1 Thresholds for Categorical Evaluation

Ever since the introduction of forensic fingerprinting techniques almost 120 years ago, there have been attempts to put the methodology on some kind of quantitative and scientific basis. From the early work of Galton onwards, statistical justification for the uniqueness of a fingerprint has been sought and most approaches to this have been based on counting points of second-level detail; those are the minutiae, such as the ridge ending and the bifurcation, within the print. Although the full pattern in a print is much more than just these few characteristic points, their nature and position within the pattern enable the distinctiveness of the pattern to be reduced conveniently to a manageable set of parameters. It was clear, from the earliest days, that the inclusion of more minutiae within this set allowed greater distinctiveness and that larger populations of suspects demanded that more minutiae be considered to justify the uniqueness of the print within that population. In this way the total number of minutiae, as points of comparison identified as being present in both the print and the mark, has come to be used as a quantitative measure of the degree of similarity in fingerprint examination. This is now also called the 'Empirical Standard Approach' (ESA) to reaching an opinion on fingerprint identification.

13.3.2 The Balthazard Model

As an example of such a statistical model that of Balthazard (see Adam, 2010) illustrates how a very simple approach may yield what later models suggest, is a very conservative estimate of the individuality of a fingerprint, based solely on counting minutiae. This assumes that when a minutia forms, the ridge either terminates or bifurcates and this can happen in either direction along the ridge. There are therefore four possible outcomes that are assumed to be equally probable. Hence the probability of finding a particular combination of n minutiae is given by:

$$\Pr(n) = \left(\frac{1}{4}\right)^n$$

For this to be a unique combination within a population of N digits requires this to be equal to $1/N$ and hence by re-arrangement, we obtain:

$$n = \frac{\text{Ln}(N)}{\text{Ln}(4)}$$

Evaluation of this equation for a population of 60 million people (600 million digits) provides an estimate of 15 minutiae as sufficient for individuality within this population. This model does not use any information on the class of the pattern or, more importantly, the relative spatial positions of these minutiae across the pattern. Nevertheless, it is noteworthy that this estimate is of the same order of magnitude as that used worldwide in those jurisdictions that utilise points-based criteria. In any case, it should be emphasised that neither this, nor any other statistical model, constitutes proof of the uniqueness of a fingerprint or indeed of any finger-mark made by that digit.

13.3.3 Identification Thresholds and the Points Standard in the United Kingdom

In the early twentieth century, the Metropolitan Police in London regarded the identification of 12 points of second-level detail, with no unexplainable discrepancies, as providing the quantitative measure necessary to support the conclusion that a particular individual's digit was the source of a mark. Under those conditions, Edmond Locard had stated, in 1914, that 'the certainty of identity is beyond debate'. Later, in 1924, this standard evolved into 16 points when a historical example was reviewed (though later discredited), which appeared to suggest the inadequacy of the 12-point standard. In 1953, following a murder case where there were doubts as to the admissibility of fingerprint evidence based on two marks, neither of which met the 16-point standard, it was agreed that if two marks from the same individual were presented as evidence then the threshold for each could be lowered to 10 points. Much later, the community of fingerprint examiners in the United Kingdom agreed that, exceptionally, if the case was sufficiently important and the expert eminent and widely experienced, then evidence of identification based on fewer than 16 points could be presented in court. Indeed in 1978 the UK National Conference of Fingerprint Experts also confirmed that:

'... if there were 8 points of resemblance present, that was sufficient to establish identity beyond all reasonable doubt.'

[quoted in Evett and Williams, 1996]

Over the following years two classes of fingerprint opinion emerged in the United Kingdom: standard testimony on identification based on 16 points of comparison, and 'non-provable' identification based on 8 to 15 points of comparison that provided leads to the investigators but were not sufficient, unless in exceptional circumstances, to be used in court.

It has never been suggested that 16 points provides a theoretically or experimentally proven threshold to determine a conclusive identification. Rather, it represents such a high level of similarity in minutiae detail between the mark and the print, such that any challenge to a identification in court is extremely unlikely.

However, following work by Evett and Williams, commissioned by the UK Home Office and published in 1996, the threshold points system, for justifying the categorical testimony of identifying a individual as the source of a crime scene mark, was abandoned in England and Wales in June 2001 (Scotland followed in 2007). This study revealed significant variation in the number of points identified by different examiners across a series of example finger marks. Hence, the threshold based on points was replaced by the opinion of a qualified fingerprint examiner on the identification of a sufficient number of similarities, including quantitative minutiae information, and no discrepancies between the mark and the print and endorsed by the independent verification of that view by two other, similarly qualified experts. In this move the focus shifted from minutiae exclusively, to a broader examination in terms of ridgeology. In this, the United Kingdom was following the precedent of the United States, which had abandoned the points system in 1973 and moved to this holistic approach.

13.3.4   The Basis of the Non-Numeric (Holistic) Approach

In formulating an opinion, without the sole use of a numerical threshold for arriving at and justifying an identification, the examiner uses all the observable information contained within the crime scene mark, and hence this is often called the 'holistic' approach. It is a necessary prerequisite to this methodology that there are acceptable standards of training and competency testing of fingerprint examiners, and that standard procedures, such as ACE-V, are adhered to.

Having decided that there are no dissimilarities between the suspect print and the crime scene mark, all features, including the counting of minutiae, will be assessed between the two images to determine whether the mark is characterised to a sufficient degree of individuality and an identification will be declared:

'... when the examiner observes a level of agreement (across the three levels of legible features) that exceeds the highest level of correspondence he observed through his/her training and experience in comparisons involving non-matching entities.'

[Champod and Chamberlain, 2009]

The examiner will then conclude that, for a digit from any other individual to be the source of the crime scene mark, is so improbable as to be impossible. At this point there is, what has been termed, a 'leap of faith' as the probabilistic mental processes by the examiner during the evaluation stage cross an undefined threshold to the categorical certainty of opinion to be presented to the court. Note that this opinion is reached without any reference to, or need for, an explicit determination of a number of matching minutiae within the mark. If the expert is asked under cross-examination for a statement on the number of points of agreement in any particular case, the reply should be clear that, under the holistic methodology, there is no standard criterion, with the identification of each mark being dealt with on an individual basis.

This, however, is not the final stage in the process. The holistic approach commonly requires independent examination of the same mark by two other experts under the same protocols as for the first examination. All three examiners need to agree on the outcome before this may be conveyed as testimony to the court.

13.3.5   Identification Thresholds in Other Jurisdictions

Almost all countries have used the empirical, standard approach in support of fingerprint testimony in the past, but over recent years, many have moved to the holistic methodology. In the United States in 1973, a working group of the influential International Association for Identification (IAI) came to the view that a points system had no basis and should be abandoned.

> '... no valid basis exists ... for requiring that a pre-determined minimum number of friction ridge characteristics must be present in two impressions in order to establish positive identification.'
>
> [Polski, Smith and Garrett, 2010]

The term 'valid' was later replaced in 1995 by 'scientific' and 'characteristics' by 'features'. This view was later endorsed by the NRC Report, in 2009.

In Canada and Australia, there were similar moves away from a points-based to a holistic approach for identification. However, mainland Europe remains divided on this issue with most of Scandinavia and the United Kingdom following the precedent set by the United States, whereas central and southern Europe adhere to numerical criteria in the range of 10 to 16 points (see Table 13.1).

13.3.6   R v Buckley 1999

In March 1997, a masked man overcame an elderly woman, in the north of England, and stole a number of her possessions, including a pension book and building society pass book. Some items were later found abandoned in an alleyway by police and forensic examination revealed a finger-mark with 9 points of second-level detail on the cover of the pension book. Other evidence led to Buckley being suspected of the crime and when the mark was identified as his fingerprint, he was arrested, tried and convicted of aggravated burglary.

In support of his opinion, the expert witness stressed his experience, his examination of the similarities and dissimilarities between the mark and the print and his breadth of knowledge of the literature and work of other examiners. In conclusion, he confirmed that the:

> '... possibility of the disputed print and the control prints being made by different people could in his judgment be effectively ruled out.'
>
> [R v Buckley, 1999]

Table 13.1 *Fingerprint Threshold Identification Criteria for Some Countries (information adapted from Appendix C in Polski, Smith and Garrett, 2010)*

Country	Numeric threshold for identification (points)
South Africa	7
Hungary	10
Denmark	10
Netherlands	10–12
Poland	12
France	12
Italy	16–17

Countries with non-numeric threshold criteria
Australia
Canada
Finland
Norway
Sweden
United Kingdom (all countries)
United States

During cross-examination he stressed that his testimony was a professional opinion rather than a scientific conclusion.

Buckley appealed his conviction on grounds that included his claim that the fingerprint identification was inadmissible as evidence, as it was based on fewer than 16 points of comparison. The appeal court judgment alluded to previous cases, which suggested contradictory precedents on this issue with 10 points being excluded in 1996, whereas 12 points were admitted in two cases around the same time. They were also aware of the recent developments in evaluation criteria, for example in the work of Evett and Williams, and the probable move in England to a holistic approach. The legal position of fingerprint evidence was confirmed to be:

> '... admissible as a matter of law if it tends to prove the guilt of the accused. It may so tend, even if there are only a few similar ridge characteristics but it may, in such a case, have little weight. It may be excluded in the exercise of judicial discretion, if its prejudicial effect outweighs its probative value.'
>
> [R v Buckley, 1999]

Thus, if there are more than eight points of comparison and the judge is satisfied as to the experience and expertise of the expert and there are sufficient ridge characteristics, with sufficient quality and clarity in the mark and its size is adequate, then the analysis of the mark may be admitted as evidence. Consequently, the points threshold used by fingerprint examiners at that time, was not necessarily also the condition for admissibility by the court. Interestingly, the judge concluded with a statement that appeared to contradict the categorical statement preferred by the fingerprint community and emphasised the opinion nature of such expert testimony:

> 'In every case where fingerprint evidence is admitted, it will generally be necessary for the judge to warn the jury that it is evidence opinion only, that the expert's opinion is not conclusive and that it is for the jury to determine whether guilt is proved in the light of all the evidence.'
>
> [R v Buckley, 1999]

On this basis the appeal by Buckley was refused.

13.4   Evolution of the Basis of Fingerprint Opinion in the Court

Whichever methodology is used to arrive at an identification, the confidence with which the examiner arrives at the outcome is the same; the difference is in the philosophy of the method employed. The range of evaluative outcomes is broadly similar across jurisdictions, though there are minor differences in how opinion, other than identification and exclusion, are categorised. These are summarised, against the four outcomes described in 13.2, in Table 13.2.

In terms of evidential value, fingerprint evidence in the UK and US courts and elsewhere, is normally provided either as a categorical statement as to identification, or exclusion, or as making no contribution to the legal debate. In the last case, this outcome may be due to the ridge flow and ridge characteristics being insufficient for the examiner to conclude that the threshold for either of the categorical outcomes has been reached. This does not in fact necessarily mean that the evidence is of no value but, under current practice, an opinion would not be conveyed to the court. From one perspective, this is understandable since there is no rigorous way in which the examiner may deduce the weight of such evidence. On the other hand, to present factual information on ridge detail between the mark and the reference print from the comparison process, without providing an evaluation, could seriously mislead the jury.

In 1979, the IAI effectively forbade any further probabilistic statement on a fingerprint examination:

> '... any member ... who provides oral or written reports, or gives testimony of possible, probable or likely friction ridge identification shall be deemed to be engaged in conduct unbecoming ...'
>
> [Polski, Smith and Garrett, 2010]

Following a fresh review of more recent research, the IAI published a series of updated statements in 2009 some of which confirmed, whereas others modified, earlier views. These include confirmation that, in their view, friction ridge skin is biologically unique and persists unchanged throughout life. However, the IAI also concluded that it is not possible to prove that the same ridge skin pattern would not be observed in any two individuals, thereby backing away from asserting the uniqueness of any fingerprint. They also withdrew any phrases from testimony that could imply absolute certainty in that opinion and now asserted more flexible grounds for the expert opinion:

> 'Based on the training, experience, and knowledge of the friction ridge examiner, an opinion of source attribution may be provided when such an opinion can be derived, given the quantity, quality, and specificity of the friction ridge detail.'
>
> [Polski, Smith and Garrett, 2010]

Table 13.2 *Evaluation Outcomes in Different Jurisdictions (adapted from FSR, 2015; SWGFAST, 2013)*

	UK	US	Comment
Identification	Sufficient quality and quantity of ridge flow and characteristics; no unexplainable differences	Individualisation	Sufficient features in agreement; likelihood of a different source is remote, a practical impossibility.	SWGFAST also state that identification is synonymous with individualisation; both imply a categorical statement as to the source of the mark.
Exclusion	Sufficient features of disagreement; the impressions did not originate from same source	Exclusion	Sufficient features of disagreement	These are equivalent
Inconclusive	The quality and quantity of ridge flow/characteristics are insufficient for identification or to confirm an exclusion	Inconclusive	Mark cannot be identified or excluded; lack of similar or dissimilar features; lack of completeness in the known print	These both confirm that a comparison can be made but the level of information is insufficient to reach a categorical opinion
Insufficient	The mark is of poor quality; ridge flow/characteristics in the mark are of low quantity and/or poor quality	Mark deemed of no value	Insufficient quality of features; the mark is not considered beyond the analysis stage	There is a difference in the statement of opinion but the evaluations are equivalent

13.5   A Critical Summary of Fingerprint Identification

The processes and procedures in forensic fingerprint analysis have been, and continue to be, criticised at a variety of levels, despite the historical success of such evidence. Such criticism is founded on both the lack of a rigorous scientific basis, for what some might wish to call fingerprint science, and on the absence of a logical and probabilistic framework for the evaluation of fingerprint evidence and court testimony. Three distinct lines of argument have been outlined by Neumann, Evett and Skerrett (2012).

Despite the ACE-V protocols, the procedures in any examination are driven by the individual expert and so lack reproducibility, will vary from one examiner to another and are not well-documented. Therefore, even though two examiners may both correctly assert that they are using ACE-V, they may be employing different cognitive processes. Despite improvements in standardisation and in the training of examiners, this issue remains.

Although there is a substantial body of evidence, from many quarters, that any full fingerprint may be distinguished from any other in a categorical fashion, this becomes untenable once the quality of the crime scene mark reaches some indefinable level, in terms of reduction in size, resolution and increased level of distortion. Hence, there is no validity in any general statement as to the uniqueness of crime scene marks. This implies that, in evaluation, the weight of evidence will be consistently over-stated in court testimony. Hence, the fundamental issue of the nature of the evaluation of fingerprint evidence remains unresolved.

Finally, there is no accepted approach to quantifying the reliability of fingerprint identification outcomes and to testing claims of a zero or small error rate, despite examples of erroneous testimony in the courts. Ideally, there should be an error rate for the mark in question rather than a generic error rate for fingerprint analysis, as that would be significantly reduced by the proportion of high-quality marks included in the survey. Despite some studies in this area, there is no rigorous scientific basis that would enable courts to assess the reliability of fingerprint evidence.

13.6   Challenges to Fingerprint Testimony

13.6.1   R v P K Smith 2011

In February 2007, Hilda Owen was assaulted with a hammer and murdered at her home in Skegby, Nottinghamshire, United Kingdom. Her body was found two days later by a neighbour, Peter Smith, who was first regarded as a witness but then arrested for the murder, as Mrs Owen had recently made a will in his favour. There was little physical evidence to associate Smith with the activities at the crime scene, save for an indistinct finger-mark found in blood on the door handle, which turned out to play a significant part in Smith's trial.

The mark was initially classified as having insufficient detail to progress through ACE-V. However, a year later and after Smith's arrest, the same fingerprint officer reviewed the mark and concluded, on the basis of ridge flow, with no discrepancies and 12 points of detail, that he could identify the source as Smith's left forefinger. His only record was a brief note of this outcome. He informed the court of his holistic evaluation, that:

'In forming my opinion I have considered the amount of detail, its relative position and sequence and general quality. I have no doubt that the area of friction ridge detail indicated in the photograph was made by [the Appellant].'

[R v Smith, 2011, paragraph 19]

Despite the defence mounting a challenge to this evidence by calling on alternative expert opinion, Smith was convicted of murder. In 2011, Smith appealed against this verdict on the grounds of new expert opinion on this finger-mark. The key issues before the appeal court were:

Although the identification had been verified independently by two other examiners, sufficient contemporaneous records, including charts indicating the mark-print comparison, were not made by either the examiner or the verifiers.

The prosecution did not accept the expert status of the principal defence witness at the trial as she had been trained partly in the United States and not through the United Kingdom's police fingerprint bureau training regime.

The fresh evidence from two other fingerprint experts, both of whom had careers in English fingerprint bureaux, cast substantial doubt on the outcomes of analysis and comparison, as described by the original group of examiners. There were three areas of conflict between them:

1. Which lines comprised ridges and which furrows in the pattern on the mark from the door handle and whether pore features were visible. This point was of fundamental importance to the comparison process.
2. Whether the mark was, in fact, due to a double touch, with a second set of ridges overlaying part of the first set. This fact led to differences of opinion between the two sides as to the identification of points of agreement and disagreement between the mark and the print.
3. Whether the left side of the mark was sufficiently clear for any comparison to be made. One of the defence experts stated that he had found 10 points of dissimilarity in this area while the original examiners believed it was insufficiently clear for any comparison to be made.

While it did not contribute to the appeal court ruling, the judges were critical of the standards of record-keeping and court presentation by the relevant fingerprint bureau. They were also concerned that the only independent fingerprint experts in United Kingdom who were acceptable to the police, were retired officers or members of other forces in the country.

'It is not unsurprising that the points we have raised identify practices which differ so markedly in England and Wales from modern forensic science practice in other areas of forensic science.'

[R v Smith P K, 2011, paragraph 61]

The appeal court judge concluded that there was clear conflict between the two groups of experts on the interpretation of this evidence and that this had not been put before the jury at the original trial. If all the disputed details of interpretation had been presented, it may well have been the case that the jury would have accepted the testimony from the defendant's expert witnesses that Smith's finger was not the source of that mark. On that basis, the appeal was upheld and the conviction quashed. However, following a re-trial in November 2012, Smith was found guilty and sentenced to a minimum of 29 years in prison.

This case is notable in highlighting the need for the maintenance of accurate records of fingerprint examinations, the difficulties in operating the ACE-V protocols in a consistent way because of their subjective nature and the disputes in court that can occur between experts, even with categorical evidence such as fingerprint identification.

13.6.2 Shirley McKie and the Scottish Fingerprint Inquiry 1997–2011

The Shirley McKie case is notorious in demonstrating a successful challenge to the infallibility of fingerprint evidence, where the honesty and integrity of one member of the police force, was set against the identification of a mark agreed by the fingerprint examiner establishment. The mark in question presented itself on a doorframe inside the house of murder victim Marion Ross in Kilmarnock, Scotland on 8th January 1997. The victim had been stabbed in the neck with a pair of scissors. During the police investigation, two latent finger-marks were found that are central to this discussion: the first (Y7) was found on the bathroom doorframe, and later attributed to police officer Shirley McKie, the second (QI2) was found on a tin containing money in the house of the principal suspect, David Asbury. The latter mark was initially identified as originating from Ross and associated Asbury with the tin, believed to have originated from her house. This evidence was crucial in Asbury being convicted of the murder in 1997.

The identification of mark Y7 was controversial from the start as McKie stated that, from her arrival at the scene on 9th January until the mark was retrieved on 14th January, she was under instruction not to enter Ross's house and that she had obeyed that order. Accordingly, she insisted that she was not the source of the mark. McKie was tried in April 1999 for perjury, effectively amounting to an allegation that she had lied about not entering the house, when in fact the finger-mark proved she had done so. Much of the trial was taken up with debate on the identification of Y7 with competing contributions from the fingerprint examiners from the Scottish Criminal Records Office (SCRO) and independent experts recruited by the defence.

This debate has been summarised by the Fingerprint Inquiry Scotland (FIS) Report in 2011, as follows:

From the prosecution perspective:

- The mark Y7 had been identified, independently by four examiners from the SCRO, as McKie's left thumb print, being based on 16 corresponding points of second-level detail across the bottom of the mark
- They all excluded the top section of the mark on quality grounds and thereby set aside any apparent discrepancies in ridge detail from that part of the mark with the corresponding area of the thumb print
- The source of Y7 was McKie's left thumb

From the defence perspective:

- Apart from five points of second-level detail, which were accepted as being within tolerance, the remainder of the prosecution's 16 points, in the bottom of the mark, were either unreliably identified as such or beyond acceptable tolerance.
- It was incorrect to exclude the top section and the discrepancies in ridge detail should be taken into account in the comparison and evaluation
- These differences alone lead to McKie being excluded as the source of the mark

In his summing up at the trial, Lord Johnston highlighted the conflicting expert evidence on fingerprint Y7 and the need for the jury to decide which they found reliable. In doing this, he rather surprisingly stated that the jury were entitled to assess the mark and McKie's print with their own eyes and make their own comparisons, effectively ignoring or over-riding the expert opinion. He added, crucially, that they should consider the expert's views on the top section of the print and whether their reasons for accepting it in, or excluding it from, the comparison were justified. In doing so, he drew attention to the logical reasoning by which the defence experts included it, as against the prosecutions' justification based on the more nebulous concept of judgement.

After retiring for only one hour and twenty-five minutes, the jury returned a unanimous verdict of not guilty, so exonerating McKie. This verdict on the attribution of Y7 was endorsed by the FIS where the debate on the fingerprint detail went into even greater depth and included different independent experts from those at the trial.

Despite this legal outcome, the SCRO held to their position on the identification and it took seven years of campaigning and legal action before McKie received compensation for treatment she had received as a result of this accusation. Nevertheless, a public judicial inquiry was set up to fully investigate all aspects of this case and, in particular, the role played by the SCRO. This inquiry produced the FIS Report in 2011.

So what of David Asbury? He successfully appealed in 2002 against his conviction for murder, on the grounds that the mark on the tin had been wrongly identified as that of Marion Ross. This second misidentification was also reviewed by the FIS and the opinion of independent examiners sought on mark QI2. This single mark was overlaid on ridge detail attributed to Asbury, in addition to features from the image printed on to the tin itself. In his conclusion, following extensive discussion and cross-examination of the expert witnesses from both sides, the FIS chair commented that:

> 'There was little, if any, common ground among the witnesses.'
>
> [FIS Report, 2011, paragraph 26.79]

His view was that only three points of detail could be agreed across both the mark and Ross's print, but that fell well short of the 16-point standard required at the time. Additionally, the overall level of clarity of the mark implied that an identification was not possible under the holistic approach.

> 'My conclusion is that SCRO were in error in identifying QI2 as having been made by Miss Ross. There was a misidentification of QI2 Ross.'
>
> [FIS Report, 2011, paragraph 26.95]

The FIS report produced ten key findings and ten recommendations. These included some of widespread significance to the fingerprint community. Of those specifically related to this case, it concluded that the mis-identifications were attributed to human error alone and that no 'sinister' implication should be drawn from the occurrence of two such errors in the same case. More generally, it was concluded that the fingerprint examiners' methodology fails to deal adequately with complex marks, that the examiners themselves are poorly equipped to deal with testimony other than the provision of the categorical identification of a mark and that both the experts and the courts need to give consideration to the difficulties that may arise when working at the limits of the methodology itself.

For the future, the FIS recommended that:

> 'Fingerprint evidence should be recognised as opinion evidence, not fact, and those involved in the criminal justice system need to assess it as such on its merits.
> Examiners should discontinue reporting conclusions on identification or exclusion with a claim to 100% certainty or on any other basis suggesting that fingerprint evidence is infallible. Examiners should receive training which emphasises that their findings are based on personal opinion; and that this opinion is influenced by the quality of the materials that are examined, their ability to observe detail in mark and print reliably, the subjective interpretation of observed characteristics, the cogency of explanations for any differences and the subjective view of 'sufficiency'.'

[FIS Report, 2011, Chapter 42]

These recommendations all conform with the views expressed in other cases and by many of those who have studied and critically reviewed fingerprint examination, the ACE-V methodology, the criteria for evaluation and the presentation of testimony from both scientific and legal perspectives.

13.7 Identifying a Mark from a Database

13.7.1 AFIS Versus Manual Systems

It is frequently the case that a potential suspect's fingerprints are identified following a search through a ten-print database. This would normally be accomplished with the aid of (I)AFIS ((Integrated) Automatic Fingerprint Identification System) computer software, such as that used by the UK police fingerprint bureaux, as IDENT1. The output from this process is a list of prints from individuals, ranked according to some quantitative criteria related to the comparison of the ridge detail between the mark and the print, which is intended to guide the fingerprint examiner to those prints that require human examination, according to the ACE-V process. From this point, the task is, to some extent, similar to that traditionally encountered when the examiner was presented with ten-prints from a series of suspects. In such a manual process, these would have been selected according to other criteria, often unrelated to the nature of the prints themselves or indeed to other forensic evidence in the case, and hence it is highly unlikely that there would be any detailed, minutiae-related similarities amongst this set of prints. On the other hand, the AFIS list is derived from the specific pattern of ridge detail on the mark itself leading to a high degree of similarity across the set and, increasingly so, as the size of the database increases. For this reason alone, the chances of an incorrect identification are higher from an AFIS-assisted process.

Consequently, the interaction of the machine and the examiner leads to a methodology that is not directly comparable to the human-only procedures, and may actually require different (higher) threshold standards for arriving at an identification. In addition, before the introduction of AFIS, the concept of the identification of a crime scene mark, in the absence of any other evidence, by a 'cold hit' process was not possible. Of course, in this case, the source of the mark may not even be on the database, so the human analysis stage is of crucial importance in arriving at a valid outcome. These and related issues have been discussed by Mnookin and Dror (2010) who summarise:

'Its achievements notwithstanding, we believe that by failing to think through all the consequences of the use of AFIS for latent identification, not only is latent fingerprint identification not living up to its full potential but also that *the chances for incorrect identifications have increased.*'

[Dror and Mnookin, 2010]

The most high-profile example of AFIS misidentification was the case of Brandon Mayfield in 2004.

13.7.2   The Madrid Bombing Case (Brandon Mayfield) 2004

The terrorist attack on commuter trains in Madrid, Spain, in March 2004 resulted in the deaths of 191 people and injuries to over a thousand others. Cyanoacrylate fuming of a bag of detonators, connected to the incident, revealed a latent finger-mark (LFP17), which was regarded as key evidence in the search for the perpetrator. A week later, following from a request from the Spanish National Police (SNP), the FBI ran LFP17 thorough their IAFIS system and found a cold hit against a print from Brandon Mayfield, a civil and immigration lawyer in Portland, Oregon who had also served as a former US army lieutenant. This print had been included on the database following his arrest for burglary, twenty years before. It was also known that he was Muslim convert following his marriage to an Egyptian. His was one of twenty ten-prints on the IAFIS list of possible matches. Each was scrutinised by an experienced examiner and the identification of the left index finger of Mayfield, as the source of the mark, was confirmed by two other experts. When details of this identification were passed back to the Spanish authorities, the surprising response was that the fingerprint examiners in Spain had returned a verdict of 'negativo' against Mayfield being the source, so contradicting the view from the FBI. Despite this, the FBI continued their surveillance of Mayfield and their attempts to accumulated evidence against him. In mid-May, the SNP identified the true source of the mark as an Algerian, Ouhnane Daoud, who was living in Spain. Consequently the FBI withdrew their identification of Mayfield and he was released from detention.

As a consequence, an inquiry by the US Office of the Inspector General (OIG) was initiated to determine amongst many other things, the cause of this finger-mark misidentification and the response of the FBI. In an extensive report, the following key factors were identified:

- There was claimed to be an 'unusual similarity' in the ridge flow and in the positions of ten minutiae identified in both LFP17 and the print from Mayfield's left index finger, though the resolution of the mark was of relatively poor quality.
- The nature of some of these minutiae was different between the two prints; for example, a bifurcation in one and a ridge ending in the other.
- The combination of these ten minutiae of limited spatial resolution together with the enormous size of the FBI database led to Mayfield's print appearing high on the IAFIS list. As the OIG Inquiry concluded:

'The Mayfield case demonstrates the need for particular care in conducting latent print examinations involving IAFIS candidates because of the elevated danger of encountering a close non-match.'

[Office of the Inspector General, 2006, IV A]

- The FBI examiner was guilty of 'circular reasoning' (see Chapter 9.4) in that, having found a potential source on ten points of similarity, further minutiae on the mark were sought in an attempt to strengthen the case for an identification outcome.
- The examiner also gave undue weight to a comparison between what turned out to be distortion in LFP17 and alleged third level detail in Mayfield's print.
- Explanations for discrepancies found between the mark and the print were contradictory and invalid; for example, despite continuity of ridge flow across the whole of the mark, the absence of any similarities across the top of the mark was attributed to a superposition of a second mark.
- Verification by a second examiner was not carried out 'blind', though this was not believed to have contributed to the misidentification.
- Although the evaluation followed the recommended holistic approach, use of the alternative ESA criteria would not have prevented misidentification in this case, despite the initial comparison using only ten minutiae.
- The FBI criteria within ACE-V may have encouraged examiners to progress an identification rather than the alternative outcome of inconclusive evidence.

This case highlights many of the weaknesses in the fingerprint identification process within the ACE-V-holistic system.

13.8 Admissibility of Fingerprint Evidence

Not unsurprisingly, fingerprint evidence has been subject to scrutiny in the US courts on admissibility grounds ever since the arrival of the Daubert Trilogy criteria. Indeed, many welcomed what was regarded by some as an overdue appraisal of the scientific basis of this leading example of the forensic identification sciences. Indeed, the difficulties for both sides in dealing with a Daubert hearing on fingerprint evidence were predicted by Saks who provided a *précis* of the issue as:

> 'A vote to admit fingerprints is a rejection of conventional science as the criterion for admission. A vote for science is a vote to exclude fingerprint expert opinions.'
>
> [Saks, 1998]

Two cases are notable, not only as examples of a legal challenge to the alleged invalidity of an established form of forensic evidence, but also as the forums for debate between the majority of professional fingerprint examiners on the one hand, and those who challenge the scientific basis of the forensic identification sciences in general, and fingerprinting in particular, on the other.

13.8.1 US v Byron Mitchell 2004

Following an armed robbery in Philadelphia in 1991, in which Mitchell was accused of driving the getaway car, fingerprints on the gear stick and driver's side door, were the only evidence associating him with the crime. During a protracted series of trials and appeals, Mitchell raised new evidence which he claimed cast doubt on the admissibility of fingerprint evidence in general. The report, from this appeal court in 2004, reviews the whole of this extended legal argument, the essence of which is related here.

First, the court declared that it did not have to decide to which area of specialised knowledge fingerprint identification belonged, only that the evidence in this case was 'highly probative and substantially outweighs any danger of unfair prejudice to defendant'. Second, it confirmed that the sole question before the court was whether the examination of a latent mark would assist in the identification of an individual. To this end, the court agreed that both the prosecution and the defence could call upon any expert in latent fingerprints to give testimony or indeed to say whether or not fingerprints were reliable sources of information. However, beyond that purpose, the court ruled:

> '... to exclude evidence as to whether or not [latent fingerprint identification is] scientific, technical, or whatever. It has no relevance before the jury here.'
> [US v Byron Mitchell, 2004, p. 16]

This invokes the Kumho Tire ruling that expert forensic evidence does not need to be specifically scientific to be admissible. The court also stated that it would:

> '... take judicial notice that human friction ridges are unique and permanent throughout the area of the friction ridge skin, including small friction ridge areas, and further that human friction skin arrangements are unique and permanent ...'
> [US v Byron Mitchell, 2004, p. 17]

In combination, these statements provide strong legal endorsement, not only of the admissibility of fingerprint evidence, but of the strong belief in its worth to the legal process.

13.8.2   US v Llera Plaza 2002

In contrast, the appeal court ruling in another case resulted in a front-page headline in the New York Times, in January 2002:

> 'Judge Rules Fingerprints Cannot Be Called a Match'
> [Newman, 2002]

This article reported on the appeal by Carlos Ivan Llera Plaza and two others, prior to their trial on drugs and murder charges, that fingerprint evidence should not be admitted, as it did not satisfy the Daubert criteria. In its ruling, the court agreed that expert testimony may:

- describe how latent marks and control, rolled prints from individuals were obtained
- present such images in magnified form before the court, identifying minutiae and ridge detail
- mark-up and explain any similarities observed between the mark and the control print from any particular individual

The defence may call on another expert to comment and provide their own opinion in the same way. However, neither examiner may testify as to whether any individual was, or was not, the source of the crime scene mark. This final, evaluative statement was declared inadmissible as evidence.

Unsurprisingly this ruling, though it was not binding on other courts, caused consternation within the judicial system and in the fingerprint community, hence the newspaper interest. Unusually, the appeal court judge, Justice Pollock, found reason to revisit his ruling and only two months later, published a second document reversing this final point, thus restoring traditional fingerprint evidence to full admissibility.

It is apparent that, in both rulings, most of the principles of fingerprint science remained intact. Neither the uniqueness nor the permanence of the print itself was challenged and the principles of the first two stages of ACE-V were accepted. The issue was whether the evaluation and verification stages provided a reliable outcome (under Daubert/Kumho Tire) irrespective of the quality of the crime scene mark. Do the subjective assessments by the examiner imply that the outcome is unreliable, as was concluded in the first ruling, or do the use of objective criteria in such assessments, nevertheless, ensure reliability, as the judge decide in his second ruling? In consideration of this issue, Judge Pollock considered testimony on the training and testing of fingerprint examiners as well as reviewing studies of error rates in identifications. In conclusion, he justified the reversal of his earlier decision by stating that:

> '... there is no evidence that certified FBI fingerprint examiners present erroneous identification testimony, and, as a corollary, that there is no evidence that the rate of error of certified FBI fingerprint examiners is unacceptably high'
>
> [US v Llera Plaza II, 2002]

13.9   Towards a Probabilistic Evaluation of Fingerprint Evidence

Although the comments of Locard are often quoted as providing the basis for a categorical, points-based evaluation of fingerprint evidence, it is less well known that he included a further statement on evaluation, should a lower number of matching points be observed:

> 'If a limited number of characteristic points are present, the fingerprint cannot provide certainty for an identification, but only a presumption proportional to the number of points available and their clarity'
>
> [Locard 1914, translated and quoted in Champod, 1995]

The interpretation of this quite prescient remark is that, rather than a categorical verdict of inconclusive, evaluation for such marks, should be based proportionately on the quantity (and quality) of common features between the mark and the reference print; in other words a sliding scale, or preferably, a probabilistic evaluation. There are two principal issues with fingerprint evidence where a probabilistic interpretation would bring immense benefits:

First, the re-interpretation in probabilistic terms of the categorical thresholds for identification and exclusion. This is of importance in providing scientific underpinning and rigorous justification for such opinions

Second, the retrieval of evidential value from currently inconclusive evaluations. This is of considerable use in practice, as it would enable potentially relevant evidence to come before the court.

In a recent series of papers, Neumann and coworkers (2006; 2012) have described the methodology for, and demonstrated the feasibility of, providing a probabilistic evaluation using likelihood ratio for casework finger-marks and, in particular, in addressing the second of these benefits.

It should be clear from the start that this process is quite different to, and separate from, the identification of a potential source of a mark, using an AFIS system. Initially, the fingerprint examiner makes an identification decision on the source of the mark from the database of reference prints. It is assumed that this is based, amongst other factors, on the close relative positions of selected minutiae in both the mark and the print. In order to determine the evaluation on a probabilistic rather than a categorical basis, a likelihood ratio for this identification is calculated based on the following methodology.

The competing propositions may be stated as:

H_1: the mark was made by the finger that made the reference print
H_2: the mark was made by some other, unknown finger

The evidence E is the examiner's conclusion that the minutiae configuration observed in the mark corresponds to the same configuration in the print, within the measurement uncertainty. The measurement uncertainty encompasses both within-finger and between-finger variability. The former includes random distortions in the mark made repeatedly by the same finger; the latter includes real variation in minutiae positions between similar but distinct fingerprints patterns from the population. The two conditional probabilities to be calculated are:

$\Pr(E|H_1)$: the probability that the minutiae configuration observed in the mark is indistinguishable from the same configuration in the print, within the measurement uncertainty, given that the mark was made by the finger which made the reference print.
$\Pr(E|H_2)$: the probability that the minutiae configuration observed in the mark is indistinguishable from the same configuration in the print, within the measurement uncertainty, given that the mark was made by some other, unknown, finger.

The calculation of these two probabilities requires experimental survey data, and hence the outcomes are dependent on the choice and extent of these databases.

For the numerator of the LR, the key information is the within-finger variability, which represents the range of distortion found in the marks produced when the finger impacts on the surface. Estimates of this may be derived experimentally for some limited conditions and then mathematically modelled. This provides a measure of the quality of the match. The denominator of the LR requires a database comprising a sample of the range of typical minutiae configurations amongst the population of fingerprints. This provides a measure of the rarity of the minutiae configuration selected on the mark. In the feasibility study, this database comprised around 12,000 prints. In both cases, the variability in the positions of the minutiae in both the mark and the print, as marked up by the fingerprint examiners, were included.

Unlike the original identification, the likelihood ratio calculation is based solely on minutiae matching; in this study the numbers of minutiae k ranged from 3 to 12 and the minutiae configurations were handled in the calculation by linking them to form polygons.

The main conclusions provided strong grounds for further development of this approach for the evaluation of identified crime scene marks.

- As anticipated, the median value of LR increased with k
- The identification of a known mark with $8 \le k \le 12$ resulted in $10^{10} \le LR \le 10^{13}$; this is comparable to the weight of evidence provided by a standard, high quality SGMPlus DNA profile.
- For the lowest values of k, $10^3 \le LR \le 10^5$ so providing, for the first time, an estimate of the weight of evidence from a mark identification based on only 3 or 4 minutiae.

Despite the success of this feasibility study there is much more research to be done before this approach becomes accepted within the scientific community, far less amongst fingerprint examiners. In addition, this does not mean that such a revolutionary change in fingerprint evaluation would then be accepted by the courts. It is likely that there would be many years of discussion and debate to resolve consequent legal issues and difficulties.

> 'In the immediate future, we do not see that the current practice of presenting categorical opinions will change. But longer term we expect an evolution towards a framework that is similar to that which underpins DNA evidence'
>
> [Neumann *et al.*, 2012]

13.10   Conclusions

Despite the criticisms directed at fingerprint evidence over recent years, the fact remains that crime scene marks routinely identify individuals and associate crime scenes, to the satisfaction of courts across the globe. Nevertheless, contemporary fingerprint examiners are much more aware of the limitations of their subdiscipline both in methodology and in providing opinion. Current developments in the logical evaluation of fingerprint evidence have the potential, both to underpin this established field with a valid scientific basis, and to enable those lower-quality crime scene marks, which would either be disregarded or more ominously wrongly interpreted at present, to contribute reliably to the legal debate.

References

Adam C.D. (2010). Chapter 8.2, Probability and the uniqueness of fingerprints, 198–200 in *Essential Mathematics and Statistics for Forensic Science*, Wiley-Blackwell, Chichester, UK.

Champod C. (1995). Edmond Locard – Numerical standards and "probable" identifications. *Journal of Forensic Identification*, 45, 136–145.

Champod C. and Chamberlain P. (2009). Fingerprints. In J. Fraser and R. Williams (Eds.). *Handbook of Forensic Science*. 57–83. Willan Publishing, Cullompton, Devon, UK.

Dror I. and Mnookin J.L. (2010). The use of technology in human expert domains: challenges and risks arising from the use of automated fingerprint identification systems in forensic science. *Law, Probability and Risk*, 9(1), 47–66.

Evett I.W. and Williams R.L. (1996). A review of the sixteen points fingerprint standard in England and Wales, *Journal of Forensic Identification*, 46(1), 49–73.

Fingerprint Inquiry Report – Scotland [Online]. (2011). Available at: http://www.webarchive.org.uk/wayback/archive/20150428160022/http://www.thefingerprintinquiryscotland.org.uk/inquiry/3127-2.html [Accessed 22 December 2015].

Forensic Science Regulator: Codes of practice and conduct, Fingerprint comparison. Appendix FSR-C-128 [Online]. (2015). Available at https://www.gov.uk/government/uploads/system/uploads/attachment_data/file/415108/128_FSR_fingerprint_appendix__Issue1.pdf [Accessed 7 November 2015].

Huber R.A. (1959). Expert witnesses: in defence of expert witnesses in general and of document examiners in particular, *Criminal Law Quarterly*, 2(3), 276–295.

Neumann C., Champod C., Puch-Solis R., Egli N., Anthonioz A., Meuwly D. and Bromage-Griffiths A. (2006). Computation of likelihood ratios in fingerprint identification for configurations of three minutiae. *Journal of Forensic Sciences*, 51(6), 1255–1266.

Neumann C., Evett I.W. and Skerrett J. (2012). Quantifying the weight of evidence from a forensic fingerprint comparison: a new paradigm. *Journal of the Royal Statistical Society A*, 175(2), 371–415.

Newman A. (11 January 2002). Judge rules fingerprints cannot be called a match, New York Times [Online]. Available at http://www.nytimes.com/2002/01/11/national/11PRIN.html [Accessed 4 November 2015].

NIST: Latent print examination and human factors: improving the practice through a systems approach: The report of the expert working group on human factors in latent print analysis, NIJ [Online]. (2012). Available at http://www.nist.gov/oles/upload/latent.pdf [Accessed 7 November 2015].

NRC: Strengthening forensic science in the United States: a path forward, Document 228091 [Online]. (2009). Available at http://www.nap.edu/catalog/12589.html [Accessed 10 October 2015].

Office of the Inspector General, US Dept of Justice: A review of the FBI's handling of the Brandon Mayfield case; executive summary [Online]. (2006). Available at http://www.justice.gov/oig/special/s0601/exec.pdf [Accessed 4 November 2015].

Polski J., Smith R. and Garrett R., for the IAI Standardization Committee: The Report of the International Association for Identification, Standardization II Committee [Online]. (2010). Available at https://www.ncjrs.gov/pdffiles1/nij/grants/233980.pdf [Accessed 4 November 2015].

R v Buckley [1999] All England Transcripts, 143 SJ LB 159

R v Smith P.K. [2011] EWCA Crim 1296

Saks M.J. (1998). Merlin and Solomon: Lessons from the law's formative encounters with forensic identification science. *Hastings Law Journal*, 49(4), 1069–1141.

SWGFAST: Document #10, Standards for examining friction ridge impressions and resulting conclusions (latent/tenprint) [Online]. (2013). Available at http://www.swgfast.org/documents/examinations-conclusions/130427_Examinations-Conclusions_2.0.pdf [Accessed 7 November 2015].

United States v Llera Plaza and others II, Cr No 98-362-10, 11, 12 [E D Pa, March 2002]

United States v Mitchell, Cr No 96-407-1 [E D Pa, 2004]

Further Reading

Ashbaugh D.R. (1999). *Quantitative-Qualitative Friction Ridge Analysis: An Introduction to Basic and Advanced Ridgeology*. CRC Press. Boca Raton, Florida.

Champod C. and Evett I.W. (2001). A probabilistic approach to fingerprint evidence. *Journal of Forensic Identification*, 51(2), 101–119.

Giannelli P.C. (2002). Fingerprints challenged! *Criminal Justice*, 17, 33–35.

Kaye D.H. (2003). The nonscience of fingerprinting: United States v Llera-Plaza. *Quinnipiac Law Review*, 21(4), 1073–1088.

Moenssens A.A. (2003). Fingerprint identification: reliable forensic science? *Criminal Justice*, 18, 30–37.

National Institute of Justice: The Fingerprint Source Book [Online]. Available at: https://www.ncjrs.gov/pdffiles1/nij/225320.pdf [Accessed 4 November 2015].

Wax S.T. and Schatz C.J. (2004). A multitude of errors: the Brandon Mayfield case, *The Champion*, September-October, 6–16.

14

Trace Evidence, Databases and Evaluation

The power of trace evidence, in associating crime scenes through its transfer and persistence properties, is demonstrated particularly strongly by those materials that are amenable to quantitative characterisation by physicochemical analysis, and for which identification and interpretive databases are available. In these cases, logical evaluation by likelihood ratio should be the standard approach in preparing testimony for court. The interpretation and evaluation of such materials falls into the category of 'Type B evidence'; so-called by Berger *et al.* (2011) in their response to the court of appeal judgment in R v T (2010) (See Chapter 12.5). This chapter will discuss some of the most common and well-studied examples, notably glass, fibres and gunshot residue (GSR).

What makes these forms of evidence especially distinctive is that interpretation and evaluation may very often need to be given at activity as well as at source level and, for both of these, databases may be used in arriving at an opinion. The likelihood ratio approach enables complex contextual information and conditioning to be incorporated in the evaluation process that allows the expert witness to respond, at least in theory, to the specific questions being addressed by the court. However, this requires at least a semi-quantitative understanding of transfer and persistence mechanisms to inform the expert's interpretation, and information on these may be limited.

14.1 Analytical Methodologies for Glass, Fibres and GSR

In all cases of trace evidence, the methods of identification, retrieval and subsequent handling of the sample are crucial to the final interpretation and evaluation of the analytical results. Expert testimony should include statements that the evaluation is predicated on the

---

Forensic Evidence in Court: Evaluation and Scientific Opinion, First Edition. Craig Adam.
© 2016 John Wiley & Sons, Ltd. Published 2016 by John Wiley & Sons, Ltd.

limitations consequent on the sampling of exhibits. The amount of sample preparation prior to analysis will vary according to technique and in some cases, such as the microscopic examination of fibres, a tape lift may be examined directly.

14.1.1 Glass Analysis

The primary technique for characterising glass fragments is measurement of refractive index (RI), often supported by elemental analysis using the Energy Dispersive X-ray (EDX) facility in a scanning electron microscope (SEM). This latter technique may well be superseded at some future time by the greater sensitivity, elemental range and superior quantification power of the ICP-OES and ICP-MS techniques, though these have yet to impact seriously on casework. Statistical tools, such as the t-test, may be used to group fragments from one exhibit and to compare results from questioned and reference samples, which, together with frequency of occurrence data, often from an in-house database, leads to an evaluation at source level. The categorical impact of using the t-test, by providing a match or no match outcome, is a weakness of this approach, though its simplicity is nevertheless a benefit in practice.

14.1.2 Fibre Analysis

Fibre analysis incorporates a wider range of techniques, the choice of which depends on the complexity of the materials under examination. However, in all cases, light microscopy would be the starting point as this enables, not only visual assessment and size measurements, but also the identification of, and grouping by, the chemical class (polymer type) of the fibres, through the observation of the birefringent colour under cross-polarised light microscopy (XPLM). This measurement may be supplemented by FTIR spectroscopy if necessary and, if an objective measurement of the colour of an individual fibre is required, this may be achieved using microspectrophotometry. All these techniques are non-destructive but, for the separation of complex mixture of dyes, a destructive technique such as TLC or other chromatographic method may be required. Widely available reference databases may be used for the chemical identification of fibres from both birefringence and FTIR spectra. Comparison and interpretation is often achieved by a qualitative assessment of these data, though there are statistical tools available, for example to compare the visible absorption spectra produced by microspectrophotometry.

14.1.3 GSR Analysis

In contrast, the chemical, or more accurately elemental, analysis of GSR is concerned with the largely spheroidal, metal particles of typically 1 to 10 μm and larger in size, together with clusters of these, which are released following the detonation of the ammunition primer in the firearm. Conventionally, these are imaged and analysed by EDX analysis in the SEM, often in an automated instrument. Using EDX the analysis is, at best, semi-quantitative, though the result is usually confined to a list of the major and minor constituent elements in the sample. Comparison and interpretation is therefore not done on a statistical basis, but rather by categorising samples into similar compositions and relating these to known types of ammunition, such as the common 'type 1' Pb-Ba-Sb residue and the variants of 'type 2', Pb-Ba-Sb-Al and Pb-Ba-Al. The type 1 composition has been claimed to be unique to GSR, though this categorical assertion is no longer supported, and the phrase 'characteristic of GSR' is often used in presenting opinion where a full complement of major elements, such as in type 1 or other key compositions, is present in the residue. This reflects the possibility of an alternative, non-GSR source. Similarly, where only some of the key elements are present, empirical studies have suggested the terms 'indicative of GSR', or 'consistent with GSR', is more appropriate. In quantifying the amount of residue, the number of GSR particles may be linked to expressions such as 'low level', implying, say, one to three particles, or 'very high level' where more fifty particles are present.

14.2   Databases for Source and Activity Levels

14.2.1   Source Level

Databases for the chemical identification of polymer fibres from birefringence or infrared spectra have been mentioned already. For glass fragments, similar but more generic indications as to the source of the evidence may be deduced from the refractive index; for example, whether it is window glass or bottle glass. From the elemental composition of a GSR, the chemical class of the ammunition may be deduced.

Alternative explanations for the evidence at source level require survey data on its frequency of occurrence and these interpretive databases are less well-established, outside those built up over the years by some individual laboratories; for example, the glass refractive index database from casework samples set up by the FBI or its equivalent within the, now disbanded, England and Wales Forensic Science Service. In some cases, manufacturers may be able to supply data, for example, on fibre production, or information is available piecemeal, supported by the knowledge and experience of the forensic scientist. Critical assessment of whether any particular database is appropriate to current circumstances or to the question being addressed, may limit the use of such information, however. For example, one FBI glass RI database was generated over a period of many years since 1964.

Of course, such databases are intended to support the alternative explanation put forward under the defence proposition, the most common being the random acquisition of the material by chance from the environment. Transferred fibre studies of clothing in the population, for example, indicate how the frequency of occurrence depends on the type of fibre, its colour and indeed, the geographical location of the study itself. Other explanations are more specific, particularly where the material has more focused usage rather than being part of everyday life. For example, in the interpretation of metal particulates alleged by the prosecution to be GSR, the defence proposition may rely on alternative sources of chemically similar material such as firework explosive residues, particulates from car brake linings or solder residues.

14.2.2   Activity Level

At activity level the information supplied by databases, surveys and casework-based experiments is essential in underpinning interpretation and evaluation. These provide indications of the transfer and persistence of the trace material on relevant surfaces, and under appropriate conditions and time span. Ideally, these would inform the estimation of transfer probabilities for use in a logical evaluation. Unfortunately, unless specific casework experiments are carried out, published studies can usually only contribute to the expert's evaluation in a generic fashion. Interestingly, persistence studies have shown some common features across different types of trace evidence. Persistence times are important, for example, where there is a known time interval between an incident and the examination of clothing. Generally, persistence under everyday conditions is found to depend more on the host garment or surface, than on the nature of the transferred material, and models, based on either exponential decay curves or a two stage process, have often been found to describe the amount of material retained as a function of time.

Over the past forty years or so, and increasingly in recent years, the published literature on such work has become more extensive and it is pertinent to summarise briefly the scope of these studies.

14.2.3 Glass

The fracture and transfer of glass fragments and its persistence on clothing and hair have been the subject of many studies that have resulted in a good base of knowledge relating, for example, to the effects of impact conditions, fragment size and surface properties. In addition, there have been transfer and persistence studies and other research to establish glass fragment populations arising from other processes in the environment. These include publications on glass populations in hair and headwear, clothing from the population in general, and from those engaged in criminal activity, as well as on shoes. These, together with the frequency of occurrence databases already mentioned and the availability of statistical models for interpretation, based on Bayesian inference and incorporating transfer and persistence parameters, mean that much of the methodology for the logical evaluation of glass transfer evidence is now in place. However, much of this remains in the research literature and there are few examples in casework.

14.2.4 Fibres

In contrast to glass, the situation for fibre evidence is more complex and intractable due to the huge range of fibres, fabrics, contact conditions and surfaces available, as well as the variety of environmental interactions and conditions affecting the persistence of transferred material. Nevertheless, there continue to be many studies published of indicative populations of transferred fibres, from many sources, on a variety of types of clothing, on footwear and on car interiors, in addition to specific studies on the mechanisms underpinning transfer and persistence. These studies generally agree that, although finding a very low number of transferred fibres or fibres of a very common type, such as blue polyester, is not unlikely, it is very much more unusual for a larger group of such fibres to be found by chance. Thus the evidential value in this case will be much more significant.

14.2.5 GSR

In addition to those studies that have attempted to characterise and classify GSR by chemical composition and morphology, research has also demonstrated that alternative sources of metal particulates which may be similar to some GSR materials, can originate from automobile maintenance activities, specifically from brake-pads; from cartridge operated industrial tools, from other metal manufacturing processes and from the airborne and other residues formed during firework displays. Although residues from this last source have been shown to be retained well on clothing, studies in those areas are mostly qualitative and are of relevance to the evaluation of only some GSR compositions. Of course, it is also relevant to consider alternative sources of GSR itself, for example from law enforcement professionals and others who handle firearms for legal purposes. Although there is an awareness of this, research on transfer and persistence from such sources appears limited. Nevertheless, examples of the evaluative reporting of GSR evidence are included in the ENFSI guidelines (2015).

14.2.6 Statistical Models and Case Pre-Assessment

Following from the pioneering work of Evett (1984), statistical models have been developed to deal with the transfer and persistence of trace evidence; the basic approach was described in Chapter 7.7.2. These have evolved to include increasingly more complex transfer scenarios, either generically or for specific forms of evidential material. A good example of the use of such a model, in the context of the evaluation of glass evidence, may be found in the ENFSI Guidelines (2015). These form the foundations upon which future developments into casework interpretation and evaluation may be undertaken, although how these would be implemented in practice and what the courts' response might be to scientific opinion heavily reliant on complex statistical calculations, remains to be seen.

Nevertheless, such models may also inform the forensic process in support of case pre-assessment (Chapter 5.2.2) where the scientist devises a forensic strategy, including interpretation and evaluation, prior to carrying out experimental work. For most forms of trace evidence at activity level, the scientist's experience and understanding, informed by empirical studies, currently play a significant role in estimating the evidential value, consequent on various analytical outcomes. There is potential for relevant and tested statistical modelling to contribute beneficially to this approach to forensic casework.

14.3 Glass Evidence in Court

Legal discussion on glass evidence has reflected both source level and activity level issues as well as how an evaluative opinion is formulated and presented to the court. These issues will be illustrated by the following cases.

14.3.1 R v Abadom 1983

Steven Abadom appealed in 1983, at Newcastle-upon-Tyne Crown Court, against his conviction for robbery on the grounds that the statistical information used by the expert witness was inadmissible as it was not based on work of which he had first-hand knowledge. The scientific evidence was glass fragments recovered from the defendant's shoes that were alleged to have originated from the window broken during the robbery.

As the fragments were found both on the upper part of the shoes and embedded in the sole, this was declared to be 'consistent with the incident', a comment we would now interpret in terms of activity at the crime scene. The refractive index of the fragments was indistinguishable from that of reference glass from the window and this conclusion was supported by elemental analysis, which also revealed that the glass composition was typical of modern window glass. The expert witness emphasised the precision of the measurements and stated that 4% of the total glass examined in his laboratory was of this refractive index. Indeed, if only window glass in the database was considered, this value would be lower. In giving opinion, he stated:

> 'Well, considering that only 4% of controlled glass samples actually have this refractive index, I consider there is very strong evidence that this glass from the shoes is in fact the same as the glass from the window. In fact it originated from the window.'
>
> [R v Abadom, 1983]

Although an expert witness called by the defence did not challenge this evidence directly, he attempted to weaken this opinion, thereby committing the defendant's fallacy, by arguing that, as there were between 20,000 and 40,000 tons of such window glass in existence, it was not at all uncommon. The appeal court argued that statistical information was essential to a proper evaluation of the evidence and it was appropriate for the expert to include that, using profession judgement as to its quality and relevance, irrespective of its source. As always, the jury would decide ultimately on the significance of the expert's testimony, in conjunction with all the other evidence. The appeal was rejected and Abadom's sentence confirmed.

14.3.2   R v Lewis-Barnes 2014

Jermaine Lewis-Barnes was apprehended near to the scene of the theft of a holdall from a vehicle in Wood Green, London, in July 2011. Despite not being in possession of the bag itself, which was found nearby, the appearance of glass fragments on his hooded top, glistening in the police torch-light, led directly to his arrest on suspicion of having broken the car window and stealing the holdall. On forensic examination, over seventy-five fragments were recovered from the clothing, several of which were found to be indistinguishable, on the basis of refractive index and chemical composition, from the glass of the car window. The expert witness report gave the opinion that:

> '... these findings provided strong support for the proposition that the appellant was in close proximity to the car window as it was breaking, or came into subsequent contact with the broken glass from that window.'
>
> [R v Lewis-Barnes, 2014, paragraph 4]

Lewis-Barnes admitted to putting his head through the broken window as he claimed to have arrived at the scene to find the vehicle and was curious about it. He denied being responsible for the damage and stealing the holdall. Following the guilty verdict at his trial, Lewis-Barnes appealed on the grounds that the judge had misdirected the jury by asking them explicitly whether the finding of that number of glass fragments was consistent with the defendant's explanation, given that the expert witness had given no indication as to which of his two explanations for the evidence was more probable.

However, the appeal was rejected on the basis that the jury was entitled to act on the judge's direction and reach their conclusion in light of all the evidence in the case and indeed that it was 'common sense':

> '... that the jury did not require expert evidence in order to reject, as untrue, the suggestion that the appellant had somehow acquired multiple fragments of broken glass on his top merely by looking into the car.'
>
> [R v Lewis-Barnes, 2014, paragraph 14]

A clearer statement from the expert witness as to relative strengths of the two alternative explanations for this amount of glass on the hooded top, may have assisted the court in this issue.

14.3.3 R v L and Others 2010

In March 2008, three masked assailants broke the double-glazed French window of a house in Cheshire, United Kingdom and demanded valuables from the occupant who was assaulted during the incident. The robbers then made off in the victim's car, which was stopped by police, later that evening, and the three occupants, Jamieson, Taylor and L, were arrested. At their trial, scientific evidence was presented on glass fragments recovered from their hooded tops and from reference glass taken from the floor below the broken windows.

In his testimony, the expert, Mr Sutton, confirmed that the two panes of glass in the glazing unit were chemically different to each other and that glass retrieved from the defendants' clothing was indistinguishable from the reference glass from the crime scene, as determined by both refractive index and chemical composition measurements. He added that both types of glass were of an unusual composition and therefore uncommon in casework. In his evaluation, Sutton provided different statements on the glass evidence taken from each of the three defendants.

For Taylor, this evidence provided 'extremely strong' support to the proposition that he had been in contact with the broken glass *at* the crime scene, whereas for Jamieson there was 'very strong' support for the same view, the difference presumably being due to the number and distribution of glass fragments found on the clothing of each of them. In contrast, for L where two fragments, one from each type of glass in the window, had been identified on his top, Sutton's opinion was that this provided very strong evidence for the proposition that 'there was contact with breaking or broken glass *from* the scene'. This is in clear contrast to his view that the glass evidence placed the clothing of the other two defendants at the crime scene itself.

At appeal, one of the grounds raised by the appellants was that the judge had incorrectly summarised the detail of the expert testimony for the glass evidence found on L, by stating that there was contact in his case 'at the scene' rather than with glass 'from the scene'. The appeal court acknowledged that the trial judge had indeed made an error in his initial summing up but that he had corrected himself following intervention from the defence. Indeed, this had emphasised the difference in expert opinion with regard to L and the other defendants, though the significance of this distinction was for the jury to decide. The appeal was rejected and the guilty verdicts on all three were confirmed.

14.3.4 People v Smith 2012

Darnell M Smith was tried in September 2010 on a count of burglary at a cafe in Springfield, Illinois. Witnesses had heard the breaking of glass and observed the intruder, whom they later identified as Smith, crawling out from the broken glass panel in the cafe door. When he was apprehended later, while walking in the neighbourhood, police observed traces of glass fragments on his arm. This was the sole physical evidence linking Smith with the crime scene.

The crime scene technician confirmed that she had retrieved reference glass samples from the door (exhibit 26) and packaged Smith's clothes and footwear together as a second exhibit, number 27. Forensic scientist, Kimberly Bradley, confirmed that this material was indeed glass and measured refractive index and other properties. From exhibit 27 a number of glass fragments were retrieved, though it was impossible to determine from which item in the package they originated. The three largest fragments were extracted but two of these were found to be distinguishable from the reference glass of the basis of colour. The remaining fragment could be analysed only by refractive index due to its small size and, on this basis, it was found to be 'similar' to the reference glass from the cafe. In arriving at her evaluation, Bradley used her laboratory's refractive index database comprising over 2500 casework samples. On this basis, she described exhibit 26 as being 'uncommon glass' and concluded:

> '... to a reasonable degree of scientific certainty, that the glass standard and the third fragment had a "good probability of common origin".'
>
> [People v Darnell M. Smith, 2012, paragraph 57]

When asked, under cross-examination, why the strength of her opinion was limited to 'good probability', rather than say 'high probability', she replied that, irrespective of the frequency of occurrence in the database, with only one refractive index measurement she was unable to attach a higher significance to her findings.

Although she had more, smaller fragments from the clothing available, Bradley did not examine any of these, as:

> 'Under laboratory procedures, if one found a glass fragment that was similar in all measurable properties to the standard and if none of the remaining fragments had a greater number of measurable properties, there was no need to go on ...'
>
> [People v Darnell M. Smith, 2012, paragraph 59]

In his appeal, Smith alleged that the strength of evidence was insufficient to prove him guilty beyond reasonable doubt. For the glass evidence, he asserted that Bradley was unable to say for sure whether the single glass fragment came from his boots or his clothing and indeed whether it originated from the café door. The appeal court judge disagreed, citing the statements affirming the chain of custody of exhibit 27 and confirming that the glass certainly originated from Smith when he was arrested. The expert's opinion implied a sufficient weight of evidence for the court and he added:

> 'Granted, Bradley could not say "for sure" that the two had a common origin, but a "good probability" is more than "may" or "may not."'
>
> [People v Darnell M. Smith, 2012, paragraph 148]

On this basis the trial court's judgment was upheld.

14.3.5   Review of the Evaluation of Trace Glass Evidence

Those cases from the United Kingdom illustrate the move over the past thirty years, from a mostly source level interpretation to one that more explicitly embraces activity level. In Abadom, the focus is on matching the questioned glass to that from the crime scene and providing some frequency of occurrence in support of an evaluative statement. A logical evaluation, based on $f=0.04$, would yield a likelihood ratio of 25 and moderate support to the prosecution's proposition, rather than the very strong support stated by the expert at the time. In addition, there is no basis for the assertion that the source of the glass was indeed the crime scene window, as was claimed here.

In all cases, at source level, the importance of frequency of occurrence databases appears to be widely recognised and used to inform opinion; for example, in R v L the glass is 'unusual' implying as a minimum 'strong support', whereas in Smith the glass was 'uncommon' leading to a 'good probability of common origin'.

Of course, the weight and detailed expression of opinion should also take account of activity, something mentioned only in passing in Abadom. In R v L, for the two defendants where larger amounts of glass were retrieved from their clothing, the expert's proposition extended to them being in contact with the broken glass at the crime scene, whereas for L the presence of just two fragments was taken to support only contact with broken glass from this source. It was left for the court to decide whether this provided any view in support of L being at the crime scene.

The importance of the expert providing an evaluation based on those propositions of most use to the court is reinforced by the testimony in Lewis-Barnes where two quite distinct explanations for the glass evidence were included, but no view was provided to enable the court to distinguish between them on their significance.

In Smith, the expert was unable to provide any opinion on activity, due to the action of the CSI in bundling all the clothing and footwear into one package. In addition, the methodology used in her laboratory precluded her, we must presume, carrying out any statistical comparison between the questioned and reference materials, as she was able to measure the RI for only a single fragment. This also constrained her final opinion, despite the input from her laboratory database.

For recent cases from the United Kingdom, the influence of logical evaluation is evident from the references to propositions, though the extent to which any of these examples were fully evaluated in this way, including at activity level, is not clear and it is more probable that these opinions were based on informed experience.

In contrast, the testimony of Bradley is formulated as a posterior probability, reminiscent of the use of a scale of opinion, and the phrase '… reasonable degree of scientific certainty …' has no real foundation in statistics or scientific rigour.

The evaluation of glass evidence using likelihood ratio is not fully evident from these past cases, though this is now encouraged in Europe; for examples, see ENFSI (2015).

14.4   Fibre Evidence in Court: R v Dobson 2011, R v Norris 2013

Stephen Lawrence was eighteen when he was attacked and stabbed to death by a gang of youths at a bus stop in Eltham, London in 1993, in what was believed to be a racially inspired crime. Despite the efforts of the police, insufficient evidence was found for a prosecution and a private prosecution brought by Lawrence's parents in 1996, resulted in the acquittal of Gary Dobson and two others. However, by 2010, fresh forensic evidence became available, which resulted in the arrest of David Norris, and a motion from the DPP to the appeal court to quash the acquittal of Dobson in 2011, so that he and Norris could be tried together for the murder. Both were found guilty in January 2012. Central to these convictions was transferred fibre evidence that linked Dobson and Norris to the murder scene.

Initial forensic examination, in 1993, had focused on fibre transfer from the assailants' clothes to those of the victim, as this was believed to be the best strategy given the delay in securing the defendants' clothes. However, this met with little success since those transferred fibres that were retrieved, had provided only weak evidential support to the prosecution's case. By 2006, the potential for transfer in the opposite direction was realised, with the consequence that tape-lifts, from the examination of clothes from Dobson and Norris made in 1993, were subjected to detailed microscopic and microspectrophotometric investigation. These revealed a variety of fibre evidence and some tiny blood flakes, which potentially associated both defendants with the murder scene.

14.4.1 Fibre Evidence: Dobson

Dobson's Grey/Yellow Bomber Jacket LH/5

Four rare, red-orange polyester fibres and seven, quite common, pink-orange cotton fibres were found on this jacket that were all microscopically indistinguishable from reference fibres taken from the polo shirt of the victim. In addition, there were two quite rare green-blue acrylic fibres with characteristics corresponding to those on the cuffs and waistband of Stephen Lawrence's jacket. Finally, there were five grey cotton fibres judged to be of no evidential significance. Interestingly, one of the pink-orange fibres produced a visible absorption spectrum characteristic of blood, similar to that found on a bloodied fibre from the polo shirt.

Recovered from the debris, within the exhibit bag containing this jacket, was a discrete blood flake with two blue acrylic fibres embedded in it. These fibres corresponded to fibres from Stephen Lawrence's cardigan (SP/2). The implication was that the fibres had been carried in a liquid blood droplet during transfer. Testing this blood flake and others within the exhibit bag produced DNA profiles matching that of Stephen Lawrence. This initiated a further examination of the jacket specifically for blood flakes. Forty-three were found, which, when aggregated, produced a partial DNA profile of limited evidential value. However, a tiny bloodstain on the collar yielded an almost complete profile matching that of Stephen Lawrence.

Dobson's Multicoloured Cardigan ASR/2

The cardigan provided additional, though less abundant, fibre evidence. Three quite rare blue-green acrylic fibres were identified, which were microscopically and instrumentally indistinguishable from those of the victim's jacket. In addition, transferred fibre evidence was retrieved from Stephen Lawrence's clothing, specifically three common blue wool fibres and one common turquoise blue fibre, which corresponded to fibres on Dobson's cardigan. However, these were assigned much less evidential weight:

> '… because [the cardigan] is made up of so many colours and shades of wool that there must be a greatly increased chance of finding matching wool fibres on an item selected at random compared to finding a wool fibre from an item which contains only one shade of wool.'
>
> [R v Dobson, 2011, paragraph 50]

The expert witness, provided an evaluative opinion taking into account the totality of fibre evidence on the jacket (LH/5), which included specific statements as to its weight at source and at activity level. For the former he stated:

> 'Extremely strong scientific support for the assertions that the evidential fibres found within the material recovered from the grey jacket (LH/5) originated from the clothing of Stephen Lawrence, rather than being due to chance matches…'
>
> [R v Dobson, 2011, paragraph 51]

He was more cautious at activity level, though he endorsed primary transfer as the most-probable mechanism, basing his conclusion on the numbers of fibres recovered that he deemed to be higher than he would have expected if there had been secondary transfer and far more than from tertiary transfer:

> '... the presence of the fibres provides at least moderately strong scientific support for the assertion that they arrived as a result of primary contact with the clothing of Stephen Lawrence rather than having arrived by an indirect route.'
>
> [R v Dobson, 2011, paragraph 51]

Opinion regarding the fibre evidence related to Dobson's cardigan was more limited. The fibres found on the victim's trousers 'lacked significance', whereas those on the cardigan itself provided 'strong evidence' for Stephen Lawrence's jacket being their source; there was 'moderate support' for the proposition their presence was attributable to direct transfer.

In combination, it was stated that the evaluation of the blood and fibre evidence:

> '... provides extremely persuasive evidence to link the wearer of the grey jacket (LH/5) to the attack itself and/or to contact with the perpetrators soon afterwards'
>
> [R v Dobson, 2011, paragraph 52]

The defence position was to attempt to cast doubts on these findings through allegations of cross-contamination and poor continuity of evidence over the years of the investigation. However, in anticipation of this, the prosecution provided a detailed rebuttal of these points and this was accepted by the court.

14.4.2   Fibre Evidence: Norris

Here, the fibre evidence and its evaluation was similar to that presented against Dobson. Although, in total, fewer fibres were found, their evidential value was still significant. In addition, mitrochondrial DNA evidence, obtained from two short hairs retrieved from Norris's jeans, provided a match to Stephen Lawrence, albeit with a match probability of one in a thousand. Examination of Norris's purple sweatshirt (DC/7) revealed six green fibres providing a match to the victim's trousers and one red fibre indistinguishable from his polo shirt. In his evaluation, the forensic scientist stated that, in relation to source attribution, his opinion was based:

> '... on the colour, type and physical properties of these fibres, and their relative rarity...when taken together this combination of fibres provides at least strong support for the assertion that they came from items of clothing relating to Stephen Lawrence rather than being chance matches.'
>
> [R v Norris, 2013, paragraph 18]

In respect of the mechanism of transfer, his opinion was very much more cautious, as due to the short duration and nature of the attack he would not expect large numbers of transferred fibres and so, as the judge later summarised, secondary transfer remained a possibility.

> 'In my opinion the presence of these fibres provides at least moderate scientific support for the assertion that they arrived as a result of primary contact with the clothing of Lawrence rather than having been deposited via an indirect route.'
>
> [R v Norris, 2013, paragraph 18]

Indeed, Dobson's request for an appeal in 2013, included his allegation that the prosecution's emphasis had moved from primary to secondary transfer during the trial and after he had given evidence, which had precluded him responding to this issue. However, this was dismissed by the judge as there was no 'alternative innocent explanation' for the fibre evidence, other than Dobson's involvement in the murder of Stephen Lawrence.

14.4.3 Review of the Evaluation of the Fibre Evidence

The evaluation process in this case is based on the formulation of propositions, at both levels, and the final opinion is conveyed in accordance with the use of likelihood ratio, though the detailed implementation of this is not apparent from the court discussion.

Source Level

Using both the qualitative and quantitative experimental results on the fibre evidence, the conclusion was reached that they were indistinguishable in terms of chemical composition, physical dimensions and colour. Any statistical aspect of that analysis was not discussed in court. Then, using survey information, published data and their own experience, the experts reached a qualitative view as to the frequency of occurrence of each type of fibre, on the basis of all these characteristics, as expressed by terms such as 'rare' or 'quite common', but no numerical data was supplied to the court. This was then evaluated against the propositions:

H_1: The evidential fibres found within the material recovered from the exhibit originated from the clothing of Stephen Lawrence

H_2: The evidential fibres found within the material recovered from the exhibit originated by chance

Note that these propositions included the results for all the types of transferred fibres identified on the specified exhibit so, in considering $Pr(E|H_2)$, the estimates for each type of fibre would effectively be multiplied together, since, if they originated by chance, each event would assumed to be independent of the other. The consequence of this is a verbal evaluation of 'extremely strong support' for the fibres on Dobson's jacket and cardigan and 'at least strong support' for the smaller range of fibres on Norris's sweatshirt.

Activity Level

At activity level, three propositions were effectively considered, though the latter two – secondary or tertiary transfer – appear to have been bundled together in some way.

H_1: the fibres transferred to the exhibit as a result of primary contact with the clothing of Stephen Lawrence

H_2: the fibres transferred to the exhibit as a result of by an indirect route, specifically secondary or tertiary transfer

In considering this evaluation, parameters such as the known nature and duration of the assault, the surface properties of the clothing, including the propensity to shed fibres, the number and distribution of the transferred fibres and the time and conditions of the recovery and handling of the exhibits themselves, would have been considered. Given the uncertainties in most of these parameters and, where the number of fibres recovered was very small, the possibility of secondary transfer, it is not unexpected that the strength of opinion is less that that expressed at source level. So, based on the expert's knowledge and experience of fibre transfer, the opinion for the case of Dobson was 'at least moderately strong scientific support', whereas for Norris it was only 'moderate support' for H_1.

However, for Dobson's jacket the combination of the fibre with the blood evidence increased the level of support at activity level to 'extremely persuasive evidence' in favour of the more specific proposition:

H_1: The wearer of the grey jacket was linked to the attack itself and/or to contact with the perpetrators soon afterwards

Overall, these testimonies are excellent examples of current practice, in providing a balanced opinion regarding trace evidence.

14.5 Gunshot Residue (GSR) Evidence in Court

Interestingly, the three cases to be discussed here originate from the United Kingdom. Although GSR analysis is still used in the United States at the state level, the decision by the FBI not to continue to accept requests for such work from 2006, due to lack of demand, may be indicative of reduced interest countrywide.

14.5.1 R v Wooton and Others 2012

The shooting of Police Constable Stephen Carroll in a police car while attending to a call-out in March 2009, was attributed to a terrorist plot to kill a serving officer in the Police Service of Northern Ireland, undertaken by those opposed to the peace agreement. Visual identification and a variety of circumstantial evidence, together with scientific evidence including DNA and gunshot discharge residues, led to the trial of John Wootton and Brendan McConville for the murder in 2012. The issues around the GSR evidence were complex as metal residues were found, often in small quantities, across a variety of exhibits and locations. In addition, the testimony of the scientists called by the prosecution was challenged by the defence expert, both in terms of the quality of the analytical work and their evaluation of the results. Here the focus will be solely on the source of residues found on one item of clothing associated with the crime.

A bullet and its copper jacket were retrieved from the police car, together with spent brass cartridge cases (LH7) found nearby. Later an AK47 rifle was recovered, wrapped and hidden in a back yard. Forensic examination revealed this to be the murder weapon and reference GSR material was obtained, both from test-firing the rifle and from the cartridge cases near the crime scene.

Crucially, attention focused on a brown jacket (HGS3) retrieved from the boot of Wootton's car, which was associated with McConville through DNA found on its collar, though he denied that he owned it.

Elemental analysis of the residues on the cartridges (LH7) revealed the presence of antimony (Sb), tin (Sn) and mercury (Hg) in the particulates. The expert witness, Ms Shaw, explained that the presence of all three elements was deemed characteristic of GSR (type 7 according to her classification), and this composition of the material was given greater evidential weight than when only some of these elements were found. Residues, swabbed from the gun barrel itself, showed only Sb and Sn, with Hg being absent due, it was suggested, to its comparative volatility. In contrast, examination of the jacket yielded many particles, particularly across the front and the sleeves comprised of Sb/Sn, often in equal proportion, with some also containing lead (Pb) and copper (Cu). The court reported that:

> 'The particles [on the coat] were very unusual ones and apart from mercuric ammunition she knew of no alternative source that could be identified. The particles were of a spherical appearance. … This morphology was consistent with the particles having a firearm source. … These were, in Ms Shaw's view, indicative of Type 7 residues.'
>
> [R v Wooton and others, 2012, paragraph 60]

Shaw regarded the term 'consistent with' as equivalent to 'indicative of' and she added that the high levels of residues suggested that the jacket may have been wrapped around the gun when it was fired. Later, Shaw described her investigation of alternative sources of Sb/Sn alloys, which were limited to pewter artefacts and lead-free solder, as most other sources included additional elements not found in the jacket residues. However, in both these materials, the Sn concentration is very much higher than that of Sb, leading to the conclusion that no alternative source for such particles could be identified. Her conclusion was that:

> 'The relative levels of the elements in antimony/tin on the particles on the jacket and the absence of an alternative non firearm source suggested that they were more likely to have originated from a firearms source than not. They were consistent with the GSR adduced by the last ammunition fired by the murder weapon but not exclusive to it.'
>
> [R v Wooton and others, 2012, paragraph 62]

In other words, the murder weapon was a possible source, but it was not proven that it was the only possible source of the residues on the jacket. Under cross-examination, she was challenged as to how certain she was of this evaluation. She replied that she could not be 100% certain about the origin of the particles but provided an estimate of her confidence in her opinion:

> 'It is very difficult to put a figure on it but certainly greater than 95% that there is no other source to which I have found to date from the particles with high levels of antimony and tin apart from mercuric ammunition.'
>
> [R v Wooton and others, 2012, paragraph 64]

Mr Doyle, called as an expert by the defence, considered that the residues on the coat may have originated from at least three types of ammunition and that the absence of any Hg called into doubt the testimony from Shaw. In any case, a reliable interpretation of her findings was hampered by the complexity of the analytical data. He quoted research papers in support of his argument that Hg would be expected to be detected in at least some of the particles released from a gun using mercury fulminate primer, particularly given the quantity of residues on the jacket. However, under cross-examination, he was unable to offer an alternative source of ammunition that could produce residues of this chemical composition, other than mercury fulminate.

Doyle proposed that such a complex set of analytical data across several exhibits was better evaluated by likelihood ratio based on propositions such as:

H_1: The antimony-tin residues on the jacket were the result of the discharge of this AK47 rifle when Carroll was killed

H_2: The antimony-tin residues originated from a different source to this event

Alternative explanations for the defence proposition included the separate discharge of a firearm to that which killed Carroll or some other non-firearms source. On his own consideration of the analytical results, he concluded that, on this basis, the GSR evidence did in fact provide more support to the defence case (H_2) than to that of the prosecution (H_1).

This approach was repudiated by Shaw and her colleague who stated that the likelihood ratio approach could only be applied where there were sufficient statistical data, including appropriate databases that were accepted by the community of scientists in this area of work. She considered that an 'evaluative or likelihood ratio approach' was not suitable for the formulation of an expert opinion on GSR evidence and that she preferred an 'investigative approach'. The court was reminded of the ruling in R v T (2010), in the context of footwear evidence (Chapter 12.5), which the judge deemed relevant to this case, but added that the absence of a database did not preclude an evaluative opinion being provided by the expert witness.

In his summing up on this point, the judge re-iterated that residue particles, containing tin and antimony, were only indicative of GSR but that there was some research, supported by the experience in other similar cases in Northern Ireland, where mercury was found to be absent in residues produced using mercury fulminate primer, even when a significant quantity of GSR is found. Thus, the court was satisfied that the evidence on the coat 'was very probably firearms related' and, as no credible alternative explanation had been proposed, in the light of all the other evidence, the conclusion was that these particles were GSR which resulted from the activity during the murder of Stephen Carroll.

On the basis of this and much other evidence, some of which was also firearms related, both Wootton and McConville were convicted of the murder of Stephen Carroll in March 2012. Despite an appeal in 2014, this conviction was upheld.

14.5.2   R v Gjikokaj 2014

The prosecution case in the murder of career criminal Cima Sogojeva, an Albanian living in London, was almost entirely circumstantial with the only forensic evidence being firearms related. Sogojeva had been shot and stabbed to death at his London flat in October 2008. The suspect who was later tried and convicted of the offence in 2012, was Lundrim Gjikokaj, a Kosovan national, who had borrowed a substantial sum of money from Sogojeva and, it was alleged, killed him to avoid repayment. Gjikokaj claimed to have visited the victim on the day of the murder in order to repay part of the loan but said that Sogojeva had been alive when he left.

The crucial firearms evidence related to cartridge cases found at the flat, others discovered later in a drain near to where Gjikokaj's hire car had been parked, and two particles of metal residue retrieved from inside the car itself, eighteen days after the incident. Gjikokaj had continued to use the car for nine days after the incident before it was impounded by the police. In addition, he owned a number of guns, supposedly for self-defence, although the actual weapon used to kill Sogojeva did not feature at the trial. Examination of Gjikokaj's clothes eleven days after the incident failed to find any metal particulates.

Analysis of material from the victim's body and clothing identified high levels of material assigned as Type 2 GSR, with other particles of Type 1. Of the two particles from the car, the one on the near-side seat was found to be Type 1, whereas the other, from the front door handle, was Type 2. In his testimony, the expert witness, Dr Moynehan, confirmed that both these compositions of GSR are very common and that there were, in his view, three possible explanations for their presence in the car:

'i. The presence of particles was consistent with the appellant being at the flat at the time of the murder.
ii. There had been innocent contamination.
iii. The particles were there by sheer chance'

[R v Gjikokaj, 2014, paragraph 29]

Moynehan confirmed that he was unable to provide an evaluative opinion based on these three scenarios, due to the evidence comprising only two particles of GSR, which was deemed insufficient for a reliable evaluation. He added that, given the time lapse, he would not have expected to find any residues on the defendant's clothing, and that any on the car would decrease significantly with time.

Two other factors emerged which might have had some relevance to these competing explanations. Firstly, the proximity of the drain to Gjikokaj's parked car was proposed as supporting the first of these. Secondly, it emerged that, a few days beforehand, the defendant had been involved in a minor traffic accident in Reading where he and his car had been in contact with a police officer who happened to be attached to the county police tactical firearms group. This fact could be cited in support of the second explanation.

At appeal, counsel for the defendant argued that the evidence from Moynehan was inadmissible, as it had no reliable conclusion, and so did not present any probative value to the court. The judge explained that an expert witness may provide both 'primary scientific opinion', meaning factual information based on scientific examination of the evidence, as well as an 'evaluative scientific opinion'. Both have value to the court and, in this instance, the first of these was plainly admissible, as it prevented any assertion from the defendant that there was no scientific evidence that could connect him with the crime, since this GSR evidence:

'… was consistent with the appellant being there and he could not therefore claim that the absence of forensic evidence showed he could not have been there and fired the shot.'

[R v Gjikokaj, 2014, paragraph 35]

The real question addressed at appeal was how the jury was expected to deal with this primary scientific opinion. The appeal court supported the trial judge who suggested the jury should not attempt an evaluation where the expert himself was unable to do so. If the jury was satisfied that the cartridge casings in the drain were linked to Gjikokaj and that the Reading incident had no significance then, by aggregating all this evidence together, the appeal court agreed that they could conclude that:

'… the [GSR] evidence was consistent with the appellant being present when the gun was fired at the deceased'

[R v Gjikokaj, 2014, paragraph 43]

As the remaining grounds of appeal were also rejected, Gjikokaj's conviction was confirmed.

14.5.3 Review of the Evaluation of GSR Evidence

These two contemporaneous cases highlight some of the difficulties in the interpretation and evaluation of GSR evidence. Firstly, there is the use of the chemical composition of the residues as a means of classification, but not one that is necessarily exclusive to a firearms' source. This was straightforward in Gjikokaj, but less so in Wootton, due to the unusual composition and the technical debate between the experts over recent research into the effects of the volatility of mercury and its impact on their interpretation. This influenced the investigation of alternative explanations for the evidence, which, in Wootton, related to other possible, non-firearms sources of that particular, unusual composition, whereas, in Gjikokaj, the presence of only two particles, implied alternatives that were consequently through chance encounters with GSR material. In Wootton, the impact of the experience of the expert and her expert community was significant to the interpretation and evaluation.

Both cases reveal the variety of approaches to reaching and stating an evaluative opinion that are currently being used. Indeed, in Wooton, Doyle explicitly preferred a logical evaluation that allowed him to deal with the complexity of information, whereas Shaw believed that this 'statistical' approach was unworkable in the GSR context. Nevertheless, in her evaluation she quoted what appeared to be an arbitrary figure of 95% intended to be the level of statistical confidence she had in her opinion. In Gjikokaj, Dr Moynehan gives three explanations for the evidence – one of which contains the unhelpful word 'consistent' – but goes no further due, he claimed, to the evidence comprising only two particles.

Seven years previously, the application of Bayesian inference was crucial in the evaluation of a single particle of GSR evidence, in the second appeal by Barry George against his conviction for the murder of television personality, Jill Dando, in London, in 1999.

14.5.4 R v George 2007

The case against Barry George was founded largely on identification evidence and the finding of a single particle of GSR in the inside pocket of a jacket found at his home, a year after Dando's murder. At the original trial, and at his first appeal, despite the expert opinion emphasising the very low significance of this finding, the court concluded that, since the residue was indistinguishable chemically from that at the crime scene, it was relevant and its weight a matter for the jury's judgement.

Following a review of this evidence by Dr Ian Evett and his colleagues, and the support of the CCRC, the second appeal was presented with a fresh evaluation based on competing propositions:

H_1: Mr George is the man who shot Ms Dando
H_2: Mr George had nothing to do with the incident

Based on their experience, this group of experts had formulated likelihood ratios, using estimated, order-of-magnitude probabilities and invoking the principles of case assessment and interpretation. For the three instances, where differing amounts of residues may be found, their probability estimates were:

For E being the finding of no GSR particles: $Pr(E|H_1) \approx Pr(E|H_2) \approx 0.99$

For E being the finding of one or a few particles: $Pr(E|H_1) \approx Pr(E|H_2) \approx 0.01$

For E being finding of many particles: $Pr(E|H_1) \approx Pr(E|H_2) \approx 0.0001$

As these probabilities remained the same under both propositions, the outcome was that, under any of the scenarios, the likelihood ratio would be unity, implying a neutral weight of evidence and contributing nothing to the legal debate. This fresh evidence persuaded the appeal court that the summing up of the GSR evidence had misled the trial jury and George's conviction was quashed.

14.6   Conclusions

The interpretation and evaluation of many forms of trace evidence has the potential to contribute significantly to the legal debate, due to the presence of both source and activity level information, which may enable the expert witness to respond directly to many questions of interest to the court. However, to do this successfully requires a balanced logical evaluation based on competing propositions, which accurately reflect the needs of the court and for which the expert possesses the knowledge and tools to deliver. Although there is a good body of research available to support this approach in casework, this is only just beginning to influence some practitioners and much work remains to be done, both in the research field and in the effective dissemination and application of these developments.

References

Berger C.E.H., Buckleton J., Champod C., Evett I.W. and Jackson G. (2011). Evidence evaluation: A response to the court of appeal judgment in R v T. *Science and Justice*, 51(2), 43–49.

ENFSI guideline for evaluative reporting in forensic science [Online]. (2015). Available at https://www.unil.ch/esc/files/live/sites/esc/files/Fichiers%202015/ENFSI%20Guideline%20 Evaluative%20Reporting [Accessed 24 October 2015].

Evett I.W. (1984). A quantitative theory for interpreting transfer evidence in criminal cases. *Journal of the Royal Statistical Society (Ser C: App Stats)*, 33(1), 25–32.

People v Darnell M. Smith 968 NE 2d 1271 (2012)

R v Abadom [1983] 1 All ER 364

R v Dobson [2011] EWCA Crim 1256

R v George [2007] EWCA Crim 2722

R v Gjikokaj [2014] EWCA Crim 386

R v L and others [2010] EWCA Crim 1232

R v Lewis-Barnes [2014] EWCA Crim 777

R v Norris [2013] EWCA Crim 712

R v Wootton and others [2012] NICC 10

Further Reading

Akulova V., Vasiliauskiene D. and Talaliene D. (2002). Further insights into the persistence of transferred fibres on outdoor clothes. *Science and Justice*, 42(3), 165–171.

Bennett S., Roux C.R. and Robertson J. (2010). The significance of fibre transfer and persistence – a case study. *Australian Journal of Forensic Sciences*, 42(3), 221–228.

Brozek-Mucha Z. (2014). On the prevalence of gunshot residue in selected populations – An empirical study performed with SEM-EDX analysis. *Forensic Science International*, 237, 46–52.

Bull P.A., Morgan R.M., Sagovsky A. and Hughes G.J.A. (2006). The transfer and persistence of trace particulates: Experimental studies using clothing fabrics. *Science and Justice*, 46(3), 185–195.

Caddy B. (Ed.) (2001). *Forensic Examination of Glass and Paint*. Taylor and Francis. London.

Coulson S.A., Buckleton J.S., Gummer A.B. and Triggs C.M. (2001). Glass on clothing and shoes of members of the general population and people suspected of breaking crimes, *Science and Justice*, 41(1), 39–48.

Curran J.M., Hicks T.H., and Buckleton J.S (2000). *Forensic Interpretation of Glass Evidence*. CRC Press. Boca Raton, Florida.

Curran J.M., Triggs C.M., Buckleton J.S., Walsh K.A.J. and Hicks T. (1998). Assessing transfer probabilities in a Bayesian interpretation of forensic glass evidence, *Science and Justice*, 38(1), 15–21.

Garofano L., Capra M., Ferrari F., Bizzaro G.P., Di Tullio D., Dell'Olio M. and Ghitti A. (1999). Gunshot residue: further studies on particles of environmental and occupational origin. *Forensic Science International*, 103, 1–21.

Grima M., Butler M., Hanson R. and Mohameden A. (2012). Firework displays as sources of particles similar to gunshot residue. *Science and Justice*, 52(1), 49–57.

Grima M., Hanson R. and Tidy H. (2014). An assessment of firework particle persistence on the hands and related police force practices in relation to GSR evidence. *Forensic Science International*, 239, 19–26.

Hicks T., Vanina R. and Margot P. (1996). Transfer and persistence of glass fragments on garments. *Science and Justice*, 36(2), 101–107.

Jackson F., Maynard P., Cavanagh-Steer K., Dusting T. and Roux C. (2013). A survey of glass found on the headwear and head hair of a random population vs. people working with glass. *Forensic Science International*, 226(1–3), 125–131.

Lambert J.A., Satterthwaite M.J. and Harrison P.H. (1995). A survey of glass fragments recovered from clothing of persons suspected of involvement in crime. *Science and Justice*, 35(4), 273–281.

Marnane R.N., Elliot D.A. and Coulson S.A. (2006). A pilot study to determine the background population of foreign fibre groups on a cotton/polyester T-shirt. *Science and Justice*, 46(4), 215–220.

Morgan R.M., Cohen J., McGookin I., Murly-Gotto J., O'Connor R., Muress S., Freudiger-Bonzon J. and Bull P.A. (2009). The relevance of the evolution of experimental studies for the interpretation and evaluation of some trace physical evidence. *Science and Justice*, 49(4), 277–285.

Romolo F.S. and Margot P. (2001). Identification of gunshot residue: a critical review. *Forensic Science International*, 119, 195–211.

Roux C., Chable J. and Margot P. (1996). Fibre transfer experiments onto car seats. *Science and Justice*, 36(3), 143–151.

Roux C. and Margot P. (1997). The population of textile fibres on car seats. *Science and Justice*, 37(1), 25–30.

Roux C., Langdon S., Waight D. and Robertson J. (1999). The transfer and persistence of automotive carpet fibres on shoe soles. *Science and Justice*, 39(4), 239–251.

Schwoeble A.J. and Exline D.L. (2000). *Forensic Gunshot Residue Analysis*. CRC Press. Boca Raton, Florida.

Scientific Working Group for Gunshot Residue (SWGGSR): Guide for primer gunshot residue analysis by scanning electron microscopy/energy dispersive x-ray spectrometry [Online]. (2011). Available at http://www.swggsr.org/ [Accessed 15 November 2015].

Torre C., Mattutino G., Vasino V., and Robino C. (2002). Brake linings: A source of non-GSR particles containing lead, barium and antimony. *Journal of Forensic Sciences*, 47(3), 494–504.

Wallace J.S. (1998). Discharge residue from mercury fulminate-primed ammunition. *Science and Justice*, 38(1), 7–14.

Wallace J.S. (2008). *Chemical Analysis of Firearms, Ammunition and Gunshot Residue*. CRC Press. Boca Raton, Florida.

Wiggins K., Drummond P., Hicks T. and Champod C. (2004). A study in relation to the random distribution of four fibre types on clothing (incorporating a review of previous target fibre studies). *Science and Justice*, 44(3), 141–148.

Wolten G.M., Nesbitt R.S., Calloway A.S.R., Loper G.L. and Jones P. (1977). Final report on particles analysis for gunshot residue detection, Aerospace Corporation, El Segundo, CA, ATR-77, 7915-3 [Online]. (1977) Available at https://www.ncjrs.gov/pdffiles1/Digitization/43632NCJRS.pdf [Accessed 15 November 2015].

15

Firearm and Tool-Mark Evidence

Among the identification sciences, the examination of marks and impressions due mechanical damage, which includes the substantial subset of firearms evidence, is one where there remains considerable potential for fundamental research. Based on the fields of physics, materials, mathematics and computer science, this would aim to replace largely qualitative methodologies with ones based on quantitative measurements and criteria, leading to a probabilistic evaluation of the evidence. Over the past years, debates in the courts have revealed the difficulties faced by the forensic examiner in the interpretation and evaluation of firearms and tool-mark evidence; in particular, in justifying the often categorical identification of the source of a mark, supported by assertions as to its unique nature.

In this chapter the focus will be primarily on those marks and impressions associated with the use of firearms, partly because of the volume of such evidence, particularly in the US courts, and partly because of the attention devoted to it in the literature, though much of the discussion applies also to the wider field of tool-mark evidence. In this chapter, this term will be used as the generic name for this subdiscipline of forensic science.

15.1 Pattern Matching of Mechanical Damage

The forensic identification of firearms, by examining discharged bullets and cartridges, forms a subset of the more generic discipline of tool-mark identification. The principles and much of the practice that underlie this field of work are similar, though the examination of such marks, as a means of identifying the weapon of origin, is probably the most common casework application and potentially the one where objective measurements may contribute to the forensic process.

Forensic Evidence in Court: Evaluation and Scientific Opinion, First Edition. Craig Adam.
© 2016 John Wiley & Sons, Ltd. Published 2016 by John Wiley & Sons, Ltd.

The source of crime scene tool-marks is the frictional damage caused by the motion of one surface against another, as in the passage of a bullet along the rifled barrel of a gun or a chisel scraping against a window frame. Alternatively, this may be due to the direct impact of one surface against another by the application of an external force, for example, the firing pin impacting on a bullet cartridge or the jaws of pliers acting on a metal wire. The former leads to indented striation lines on the bullet or window frame, whereas the latter is identified as a characteristic impressed mark on the surface. The expectation is that these marks will include identifiable class characteristics, due to the design and manufacture of the firearm or tool, as well as to the nature of the surface and forces on impact. In addition, some individual traits may be identified, for example, arising from wear, damage or corrosion effects, on which the assumption of uniqueness may be based. A further assumption is that these marks are reproducible, though not necessarily identical at the microscopic level, and that, over time, some evolution in the fine detail may be observed.

For bullet examination, in particular, many of the class characteristics are amenable to direct measurement, as they include the calibre (diameter) of the bullet itself, as well as the number and dimensions, both width and depth, of the lands and grooves within the design of the rifling in the barrel and its angle/direction of twist. In some instances the examiner may need to consider so-called subclass features, often due to some modification of the manufacturing process, such as a change of tooling, or from a step-change in the history of a firearm following from dismantling and cleaning, which does not impact on the macroscopic class characteristics but that does lead to minor, systematic, observable changes to the mark itself. It is clear that the ability to distinguish between class, subclass and individual characteristics is a crucial skill of the forensic examiner.

The practical examination of all tool-mark evidence is founded on qualitative microscopic examination, detailed observation and the use of the comparison microscope to align and review the crime scene and reference marks. The focus is on the comparison of allegedly unique marks and statistical data on the rarity of particular classes of mark is not formally considered. The interpretation and evaluation of the findings is subjective and based on the experience of the expert examiner. Such manual examination is based largely on the two-dimensional image of the mark; more recent developments use laser-scanning techniques to provide a three-dimensional representation by including depth information, though that is still not standard practice.

15.2   The Interpretation and Evaluation of Tool-Mark Evidence

Since the vast majority of tool-mark evidence from firearms is from the United States, this will be discussed first, followed by a shorter exposition of recent practice in the United Kingdom.

15.2.1   US Opinion

Guidance from the Association of Firearm and Toolmark Examiners (AFTE) defines four evaluative outcomes following from the examination of the evidence. Although there are no quantitative criteria underpinning the interpretation stage, some qualitative indications are provided to guide the examiner and provide justification for the final evaluation. These are based on the publication in 1998 of a statement by the Association in its journal (Murdock,

1998) and a subsequent minor update to the wording in 2011. Not all examiners work to or are necessarily aware of this document.

1. *Identification*

This outcome provides a categorical assertion as to the common origin of two marks based on their surface contours being in 'sufficient agreement'. This requires the individual characteristics, observed in the questioned and reference marks, to agree to a greater extent than experience would suggest would be the best case if they did not have a common origin and to demonstrate consistency typical of other cases where the marks are known to have a common origin.

> 'The statement that "sufficient agreement" exists between two toolmarks means that the agreement of individual characteristics is of a quantity and quality that the likelihood another tool could have made the mark is so remote as to be considered a practical impossibility.'
> [Murdoch, 2011]

On this basis, the expert would state the opinion in a form such as: The questioned bullet has been identified as having been fired from the suspect's firearm.

On close examination, there is a discrepancy between this categorical statement of opinion and the probabilistic reference to alternative sources – '…. likelihood … so remote… a practical impossibility' – given in the AFTE guideline. The assertion that this provides an absolute identity of the source has been the subject of some debate.

2. *Inconclusive*

Where the class characteristics are in agreement, yet there are insufficient quality and quantity of individual traits to justify an identification, the expert opinion should be inconclusive. Indeed, there may be some conflict in the observed individual traits, but that falls short of providing sufficient grounds for arriving at an elimination evaluation. In this instance, a typical opinion may be:

> 'Specimen Q1 is a bullet that has been fired from a barrel rifled with six (6) grooves, right twist, like that of the K1 pistol; however, from microscopic examination, no definitive conclusion could be reached as to whether the Q1 bullet was fired from the barrel of the K1 pistol.'
> [Bunch *et al.*, 2009]

Although this evaluation has not eliminated the reference firearm (K1) as the source of the striations on the bullet (Q1) and hence this finding may have some significant probative value, this cannot be quantified in any way under current practice so, under these guidelines, this neutral opinion from the expert tends to undervalue the evidence.

3. *Elimination*

In many ways the most straightforward evaluation is provided when there are discrepancies between the class characteristics observed in the questioned and reference marks, as this implies that a common source is impossible. Thus, this observation eliminates the suspected source as the origin of the questioned mark and this will be reflected in the expert opinion; for example: As there are differences in the class characteristics, the questioned bullet was not fired from the suspect's weapon.

4. Unsuitable for comparison

The quality and quantity of any features observed in the marks are insufficient to justify any detailed comparison of the evidence and so no expert opinion is possible.

15.2.2 UK Opinion

In contrast, in the UK practitioners have adopted scales of opinion based on probabilistic statements, formulated on qualitative assessment, though not precluding assertions of identification and elimination. This is in line with the ENFSI (2006) scale of conclusions for marks and impressions, which was discussed, in the context of shoe-marks, in Chapter 12.4. The forms of words may include both references to propositions and the use of background statistical information in formulating opinion, as well as posterior probabilistic statements as to the source.

For example, in R v Chattoo and others (2012), the firearms expert examined the weight of individual pellets and other characteristics of the questioned and reference shotgun cartridges. He then stated that this specific type of cartridge had not been found previously in casework at his laboratory and that the average weight of the pellets was on the low side of the size distribution commonly encountered and recorded in the laboratory's reference collection. On this basis, his opinion was that:

> '... this finding provides supporting evidence for the proposition that the cartridge [recovered from the shotgun] and the cartridges recovered from 97 Norgreave Way have originated from the same source.'
>
> [R v Chattoo and others, 2012, paragraph 28]

In R v Roden and another (2008), the expert testified on his comparison of the rifling marks on the bullets taken from the victims' bodies, with others known to have been test-fired into a tree by a friend of the defendants. The gun was initially unavailable but, when later retrieved from a river, was too corroded to be discharged.

> 'His conclusion was that the three bullets [taken from the victims] had been fired down a similar filed barrel and a microscopic examination showed that the rifling characteristics were the same in the case of those bullets and the bullets fired into the tree.'
>
> [R v Roden and another, 2008, paragraph 16]

He then provide some background information on the occurrence of class characteristics found in this style of rifling, which was not unique to this particular make and type of weapon, before concluding with a statement that:

> 'In his view the evidence strongly suggested that the same gun had been used to fire all the bullets that he had examined.'
>
> [R v Roden and another, 2008, paragraph 16]

15.3   Critical Review of Tool-Mark Evaluation

Along with other areas of the forensic identification sciences, the examination of tool-mark and firearms evidence was criticised in the NRC report (2009); this reinforced earlier comments in a publication from the Council (NRC: Ballistic Imaging, 2008), which highlighted shortcomings in the discipline. These criticisms focus on some of the fundamental aspects of the examination, interpretation and evaluation of this evidence:

> 'The validity of the fundamental assumptions of uniqueness and reproducibility of firearms-related toolmarks has not yet been fully demonstrated.'
>
> [NRC: Ballistic Imaging, 2008, p 81]

> '… the decision of the toolmark examiner remains a subjective decision based on unarticulated standards and no statistical foundation for estimation of error rates.'
>
> [NRC, 2009, p 154]

These generic criticisms, directed against assumptions of uniqueness, reproducibility, the absence of objective criteria and lack of any statistical basis for interpretation and evaluation, are common to all the forensic identification sciences and, coupled to the formulation of an opinion, which includes the categorical identification of the source of a mark, combine to provide support to those who argue that the current practice is unscientific, unreliable and ultimately inadmissible in court. In addition to these fundamental issues, there are also areas of dispute within the current methodology.

Despite the guidance provided by the AFTE, there remain no protocols for the examination of tool-mark evidence, which would enable all scientists to carry out the same investigations on the evidence, assign the same weightings to their observations and interpret their findings according to proscribed thresholds, ideally linked to a probabilistic scale of opinion. Particular difficulties have been identified in four areas of this work (Schwartz, 2005).

The set of individual characteristics in a particular mark is composed of features, each of which may not be unique. This means that the source of a mark may be wrongly assigned on the basis of observing only a corresponding subset of these characteristics. Subclass traits may be confused with individual characteristics, as wear may cause these to change over time in some cases, whereas they may persist in others. There is no method to distinguish subclass from individual traits so the examiner must use subjective criteria, based on their experience in identifying the nature of the features in the mark. This may also lead to an incorrect identification. Finally, it is recognised that all tool-marks from a particular source will change over time, so a correct assignation may be made where there yet remain small discrepancies between the questioned and reference marks. However, it is also possible that the source may be misattributed, if the examiner mistakenly identifies such traits as due to time-related wear rather than originating from an alternative source.

Despite a variety of attempts at estimating error rates for firearms identification, the experimental design and interpretation in many of these studies are often disputed amongst those engaged in them. Primarily, it is difficult if not impossible, to generate error rates in the context of casework examination. For those simulated exercises, it appears that examiners differ most frequently at the boundary between an inconclusive and an identification opinion; two outcomes of quite significant distinctiveness to the court.

Of course, a scale of opinion that includes categorical assertions as to the source of the mark is at odds with the methodology, which, despite its shortcomings, is based on largely subjective observations that provide a qualitative yet continuous scale on which to develop an interpretation. Further, alternative explanations as to the source of a mark are not considered in any way and the absence of any appropriate databases preclude this contributing to the evaluation of the evidence, except subconsciously through the limited experience of the examiner. Hence, probabilistic interpretations of tool-mark evidence based on statistical considerations have not been attempted in casework in the United States and only to a limited, informal degree elsewhere.

15.4 Consecutive Matching Striations

For striated tool-marks, such as those produced on a bullet from the rifling within the barrel of the firearm, the method of counting consecutive matching striations (CMS) attempts to provide a quantitative, objective measure of the degree of matching between questioned and reference marks. In comparing any tool-mark with a reference mark from a different source, some random matching striations will be found; indeed, such a random striation count has been found to be higher on average to that found in comparison with a mark from the true source. However, if consecutive matching striations are counted, this quantity has been shown to discriminate well between the true source and alternatives, as long as the required numerical threshold is set sufficiently high. Empirically derived threshold values of one group of eight or two groups of five CMS are often quoted for two-dimensional marks, whereas these fall to six or three, respectively in the three-dimensional case. In firearms examination the CMS should be determined from striations identified as individual characteristics in the mark, with class and subclass traits being discounted.

This statistical parameter applies, of course, only to striated marks and not to those arising from impact conditions. Further, it is not wholly objective as it relies on the subjective judgement of the examiner in identifying relevant striations in the first place and, in particular, in distinguishing these from any subclass characteristics that may be present. The statistical basis of CMS may also be difficult to explain to the court. It has been suggested that tool-mark examiners may use CMS in support of testimony based on conventional subjective assessment, though there is little evidence of this in court proceedings and, indeed, some examiners have demonstrated limited understanding of the concept under cross-examination.

15.5 Databases

The most basic database of use in forensic ballistics is one that enables identification of the type and manufacturer of a weapon from the pattern and numerical measurements of class characteristics in the mark; for example, the General Rifling Characteristics database used by the FBI. Similar databases exist for ammunition. In the United Kingdom, the National Ballistics Intelligence Service (NABIS) database has a more generic function, acting as a repository for both technical and other information related to gun crime thereby providing intelligence to assist investigation.

Over the past twenty years or so computer-based systems for the comparison and linking of both two, and now three, dimensional images of marks on both bullets and cartridges have been developed, most notably using the Integrated Ballistic Identification System (IBIS) software products from Ultra Electronics Forensic Products Inc and implemented to work as part of the National Integrated Ballistic Information Network (NIBIN) operated within the US Department of Justice. This uses a database, generated through the input by law enforcement organisations, of images of bullet and cartridge marks recovered from crime scenes and from suspect weapons. By running a search of a new crime scene mark against this database, potential links may be made between weapons and crimes across the country. This system does not identify the source of a mark, rather it provides a short-list of similar images to aid the investigator and potentially associate crimes and offenders. Attempts have been made, for example in New York State, to legally require all new fire-arms to be registered on the system but this has not yet expanded beyond the individual state. The imaging and software limitations, currently in the system, preclude discrimination on the basis of individual characteristics where large numbers of weapons, with similar class and subclass characteristics, are in the database and this led the NRC report in 2008 to conclude that:

> 'A national reference ballistic image database of all new and imported guns is not advisable at this time.'
>
> [NRC: Ballistic Imaging, 2008, p 239]

However, there do not appear, to date, to have been any attempts to use these databases as an aid to the evaluation of firearms evidence by providing statistical data, such as the frequency of occurrence of particular class or individual characteristics for bullets or cartridges, to inform a logical evaluation of ballistics evidence.

15.6   Tool-Marks and Evaluation by Likelihood Ratio

Given the criticisms of current methods for interpretation and the formulation of expert opinion, it might be expected that the development of an approach leading to a balanced logical evaluation, based on Bayesian inference, would inevitably be a preferred alternative. Despite some recent attempts to demonstrate the feasibility of this, there is little evidence of it receiving more widespread attention or having had any impact on casework.

For the example of firearm cartridge evidence, competing propositions, at source level, may be:

H_1: the questioned cartridge case was fired from the suspect's weapon
H_2: the questioned cartridge case was fired from an unknown weapon and not that retrieved from the suspect.

Thus, by evaluating the usual conditional probabilities, a likelihood ratio may, in theory, be calculated. The evidence, E, is some measure of the characteristics of the marks on the cartridge fired from the appropriate weapon. How this should be quantified has been the subject of recent studies. For example, Bunch (2000) suggested using the maximum CMS count and justified this with probability histograms for typical CMS counts made under the two propositions. In a critical appraisal, he concluded that the subjectivity in counting striations, bias and difficulties in explaining the methodology to the court were likely to preclude its use in casework.

More recently, Bunch and Wevers (2013) sought to promote a likelihood ratio approach starting from an agreed list of characteristics, observations and other information about the exhibits, on which to base the interpretation and evaluation. These then led the examiner to estimate the necessary probabilities based on experience and other data where available. The outcome would be an opinion based on the verbal equivalent to the total likelihood ratio. This has some value in encouraging the use of Bayesian inference and the formulation of opinion based on competing propositions, despite its reliance on qualitative criteria and the experience of the expert.

In contrast, Riva and Champod (2014) discuss an approach where the evidence, E, is based on the three-dimensional topographical contour of the mark, as measured by laser profiling of the exhibits, in this case the firing pin and breech face impressions on a cartridge. Comparison algorithms then reduce the data to similarity scores that feed into the calculation of the required probability densities. The study utilised firearms having the same class characteristics so the resulting likelihood ratios derive solely from the individual traits imparted from each weapon. The statistical distributions of those individual characteristics, both from within a single firearm and between a range of different weapons, all with the same class characteristics (79 examples of SIG Sauer 9 mm Luger calibre pistols), formed the mathematical basis on which to generate the likelihood ratio. The results revealed a very high discriminating power and low rates of misleading outcomes. This study demonstrates the feasibility of the method but its further development may be limited by the immense task in building up the statistical databases necessary for casework.

15.7 Firearms Evidence in the US Courts

There is no shortage of appeal court cases, particularly post-Daubert, where the admissibility and evaluation of tool-mark evidence in the context of firearms has been debated. Despite this, such opinion has not been deemed inadmissible by any court in the United States over recent years. However, no convergent view has emerged as to the limitations that should be applied, though, particularly over the past 10 years or so, many courts have been unwilling to accept the categorical identification of the source without some qualification. In contrast, there appears to have been little dispute in the United Kingdom when such evidence has been presented, albeit much less commonly. By way of illustration, three almost contemporary cases from the US courts will be discussed here.

15.7.1 United States v Hicks 2004

Texas farmer, Richard Hicks, had a reputation for leading police officers into car chases across country. In December 2000, at an hour after midnight, one such patrol car, staffed by the Lamance brothers, followed a white truck into a field whereupon James Lamance was shot dead by a single gunshot and the truck made off. Believing it to having been driven by Hicks, officers broke into his house and arrested him on suspicion of murder. Following a search of his property, a Marlin 30-30 rifle was retrieved and, together with some 30-30 shell casings found at the crime scene, was forwarded for forensic examination. The bullet that killed Lamance passed through his head and was never found.

At the State Court trial, firearms expert, John Beene, testified categorically that:

'... the bullet casings in the field were fired from the .30-30 rifle found in Hicks's son's bedroom'

[United States v Hicks, 2004, paragraph 24]

Nevertheless, there was no other physical evidence presented in support of the case against Hicks, neither he nor his truck had been conclusively identified at the crime scene and forensic pathology testimony expressed some doubts as to whether this weapon was in fact responsible for Lamance's death. Consequently Hicks was acquitted by the jury.

Soon afterwards, Hicks was re-arrested on grounds of defying a restraining order that banned him possessing firearms or ammunition, following an earlier incident involving his ex-wife. Consequently, he faced a second trial in 2003 at a Federal District Court on these new charges, at which he was found guilty. At the subsequent sentencing hearing, evidence was presented, which resulted in Hicks' conviction for the second-degree murder of officer Lamance and he was sentenced to 15 years in prison. Following this, Hicks appealed on several grounds including the admissibility of the firearms evidence.

Hicks criticised those aspects of Beene's methodology, which, he believed, implied it fell short of the scientific standards required under Daubert. Under cross-examination Beene was unable to describe some of the technical detail of his work, relating to the characteristics of the marks themselves. He admitted that he did not test-fire other 30-30 weapons with a view to determining whether individual features in the questioned marks were in fact unique to Hick's weapon. Finally, Hicks' counsel alleged that Beene had been unable to provide essential supporting statements relating to testing, standards, error rate and the scientific literature underpinning the methodology.

In response, the appeal court did not address directly most of these points, preferring to fall back on other evidence, which, it asserted, showed that such opinion was indeed admissible. It accepted Beene's testimony that both the methodology and the literature produced by the AFTE demonstrated the reliability of firearms examination, including the comparison of cartridges, and his statement:

'... that the error rate of firearms comparison testing is zero or near zero.'

[United States v Hicks, 2004, paragraph 32]

It observed that the comparison of spent shell casings, with reference casings from a suspect weapon, was an established technique that had been in use for decades and concluded:

'We have not been pointed to a single case in this or any other circuit suggesting that the methodology employed by Beene is unreliable.'

[United States v Hicks, 2004, paragraph 31]

It is clear from this that the court accepted, without qualification, the categorical opinion presented by Beene at the original trial. Consequently, the court rejected the appeal, including these specific grounds, and affirmed the conviction and sentence given to Hicks.

15.7.2   United States v Darryl Green *et al.* 2005

Darryl Green, Jonathan Hart and Edward Washington who were members of a violent street gang, the Esmond Street Crew in Boston, were accused of the shooting and wounding of Richard Green in September 2000. The firearms evidence comprised two sets of discharged .380-calibre shell cases, one set found at scene of the incident, the other in a nearby street where a separate shooting had taken place a week earlier, together with a loaded Hi Point pistol, also .380 calibre, discovered in a front yard associated with the gang in Esmond Street a year later. In his testimony in 2005, the expert witness, Sergeant

Detective O'Shea, gave his opinion that all of these shell cases were discharged from the same firearm, that weapon was the Hi Point pistol retrieved from Esmond Street, and further, that this identification was:

'to the exclusion of every other firearm in the world'

[United States v Green *et al.*, 2005]

The defendants' counsel raised a pre-trial motion to exclude this testimony on the grounds of inadmissibility, despite it having been reviewed earlier at separate Daubert hearing.

O'Shea had followed the conventional methodology in his examination, though he had restricted the comparisons to reference casings fired from the recovered firearm only and to four other examples of discharged Hi Point casings held by the police department, as a means of establishing class characteristics. Nevertheless, the hearing undertook a detailed audit of both his forensic examination and his standing as a firearms examiner, leading to several critical conclusions by Judge Gertner.

It was established that, although he had worked in the ballistics unit for seven years and claimed to have undertaken hundreds of examinations, O'Shea had received very limited training, had not been tested for his proficiency and neither he nor the Boston laboratory were certified by the AFTE. When questioned, he was unable to cite any publication on error rates in firearms' examination though he quoted a figure of 'around one and a half percent' for false positive identifications.

The judge accepted that there were many tool-marks on a cartridge that originated from the firing pin, the breech face and from scratching as the cartridge was discharged from the gun, but that, even if it assumed these are unique, there were significant issues as to how these are distinguished by the examiner and how their training, experience and the methodology they applied, would influence the outcome of the examination. The potential changes to the characteristics of a weapon over time were of particular importance in this case, as the gun had been found over a year after the recovery of the cartridges at the crime scene, and it was acknowledged that, for a cheap weapon made of softer steel such as the Hi Point, such wear would be more significant. Further, there was no evidence that O'Shea had used the FBI reference publication of general rifling characteristics to establish the class characteristics in this particular weapon. In using additional, in-house reference casings from other Hi Point pistols, O'Shea had not undertaken a 'blind-trial' examination, as he knew which were the crime scene exhibits, and he had not considered whether the guns, from which the laboratory casings had originated, were manufactured at the same time or place as the suspect weapon. This could introduce bias, as he had not evaluated the comparison in the context of alternative sources of the marks.

The judge was particularly scathing of the record keeping by the expert in his work. He had taken no notes, photographs or recorded measurements during the original examination and it was only shortly before the Daubert hearing that he had recorded some photographic images in support of his opinion but he admitted these were of limited quality. Indeed, the judge commented that the court was unable to see the relevant characteristics in these images, even when O'Shea had pointed them out. O'Shea also conceded that there were some minor discrepancies that he had chosen to discount in arriving at his opinion.

When cross-examined on the criteria he had used in interpreting the marks, O'Shea repeated generic statements akin to those in the AFTE methodology and, when it came to defining 'sufficient agreement', he cited the use of the CMS approach though he was vague on its criteria and application. Following further questioning on the detail of his examination, it was clear that the final opinion was based on a highly subjective assessment of the evidence.

The court also heard testimony from an expert for the defence, David Lamanga, who focused attention on to some of the key weaknesses in the prosecution's evidence:

- the issue of wear over time, particularly with the soft steel used in this particular firearm
- the non-repeatability of the fine detail of marks from cartridges discharged from the same gun
- the neglect of the depth of the marks (the three-dimensionality) in O'Shea's examination
- the absence of standards distinguishing between class, subclass and individual features

In conclusion, Lamanga criticised O'Shea's final evaluative conclusion, as not one that would be made by a 'responsible scientist', adding:

> 'The legitimate way to render an opinion is a statistical opinion. The probability of a match, not 'I've made an absolute match to the exclusion of all other firearms just because I find a few matching striations,' for example.'
>
> [United States v Green *et al.*, 2005]

In conclusion, Judge Gertner agreed that, although the comparison of tool-marks was not traditional science, it was based on observations and had some empirical basis. The methodology was potentially reliable but, in this case, the poor record keeping by O'Shea precluded anyone attempting to reproduce his results and this impacted on their reliability. Interestingly, the judge was less critical of the absence of clear testimony on error rates, lack of proficiency testing and certification of the expert, since she accepted that as long as the results of the expert's examination – the images of the questioned and reference marks – were available for the court to view and understand, then, on balance, the testimony was admissible.

> 'If the jurors cannot see and understand the testimony, it amounts to nothing more than "trust me" testimony …'
>
> [United States v Green *et al.*, 2005]

She expressed concern about the long-standing use of ballistics testimony in the courts, in light of the issues raised in this case. Nevertheless, she agreed to admit O'Shea's evidence, with limitations on its interpretation and evaluation.

> 'It may well be that each firearm produces a unique signature transferred onto a shell case and that it is possible to identify that signature using scientifically valid methods. The question is whether the approach used by the expert in this case allows for that identification "to the exclusion of every other firearm in the world."'
>
> [United States v Green *et al.*, 2005]

The results of the examination may be presented in testimony and the expert may tell the court about his observations in light of these results and be subjected to cross-examination. However, no conclusion could be given and, specifically, she forbad the absolute identification of the source of the mark to the court in terms such as 'to the exclusion of every other firearm in the world'.

15.7.3   US v Glynn 2008

Chaz Glynn, a member of the New York 'Bronx Bloods' gang, was accused of ordering the murder of a rival drug dealer. At his first trial in June 2008, it was alleged that Glynn had supplied the gun used in the killing, and forensic ballistics evidence was crucial in associating his weapon with shell casings retrieved from the crime scene. However, the jury became deadlocked and a retrial was ordered. During this process, the defendant's counsel requested a hearing to exclude the testimony from the prosecution's ballistics expert, Detective James Valenti, on grounds of insufficient reliability under Rule 702 of the Federal Rules of Evidence.

In the report of the hearing, the court argued that, if it concluded such evidence was reliable, it then needed to decide whether the degree of confidence expressed in the expert's opinion was admissible, given the subjective nature of the interpretation and evaluation. This was important because:

> '... once expert testimony is admitted into evidence, juries are required to evaluate the expert's testimony and decide what weight to accord it, but are necessarily handicapped in doing so by their own lack of expertise. There is therefore is a special need in such circumstances for the Court, if it admits such testimony at all, to limit the degree of confidence which the expert is reasonably permitted to espouse.'
>
> [United States v Glynn, 2008]

In cross-examination Valenti admitted that the process was qualitative and the conclusion was up to the individual examiner, based on their experience and judgement as to when there was sufficient agreement between the marks. On this basis, the court concluded that such a methodology 'lacked the rigor of science'. However, despite the New York City Police Laboratory adhering to the AFTE guidelines, which were described as being subjective and having some inherent vagueness, the fundamental assumptions and basic methodology for firearms examination did not lead to the examiner 'working on a hunch' but, the court asserted, were 'plausible' and provided 'a good working assumption for most practical purposes'.

Despite this lack of scientific rigor and the uncertainty inherent in the methodology for examination and interpretation, it was evident that firearms evidence was sufficiently reliable, and therefore admissible, based on support for the methodology from the experience of professional forensic examiners and its historical use. Nevertheless, past cases had shown that there was a tendency for expert opinion to exaggerate the certainty with which an identification was claimed or for the court to be informed of zero error rates associated with the process. For these reasons, it was necessary to alert the jury to the limitations inherent in such opinion by constraining the range of evaluative opinion proffered by the expert.

In this instance, Valenti had stated that:

> '... a bullet recovered from the victim's body and shell casings recovered from two related crime scenes came from firearms linked to Glynn ... to a reasonable degree of ballistic certainty'
>
> [United States v Glynn, 2008]

Such an opinion was overstating the degree of confidence possible, given the limitations in the methodology. It was proposed that an acceptable alternative, intended to move the weight of the evaluation down from certainty, by using more probabilistic language, would be:

> It is more likely than not that 'a bullet recovered from the victim's body and shell casings recovered from two related crime scenes came from firearms linked to Glynn'

At the first trial, the court had permitted a variant of this, namely:

> It is at least more likely than not that 'a bullet recovered from the victim's body and shell casings recovered from two related crime scenes came from firearms linked to Glynn'

However, this latter opinion was overturned by the appeal hearing, in favour of the preceding statement, on the basis that the inclusion of 'at least' made the opinion more vague than it would be without it. Though acceptable to the court, this nebulous, probabilistic phrase is not founded on any objective criteria whatsoever and appears to be an arbitrary way of introducing an element of doubt into the expert's conclusion. On this basis Glynn was convicted at the second trial and sentenced to life imprisonment.

15.8   Concluding Comments on Firearms Cases

There is a significant contrast in outcomes between Hicks and the other two cases, despite the appeal in Green being only one year later. This is indicative of the growing criticism of firearms testimony in the courts. In Green, Judge Gertner was critical of the expert and the methodology, though ultimately she allowed a statement of identification, but only if it was not qualified by an emphasis on absolute certainty and the court was able to view the images to allow it to reach its own evaluation. In Glynn, the appeal court regarded firearms experts as prone to giving exaggerated opinion and demanded that assertions of identification be qualified by probabilistic language, though the suggested phrasing does not appear to have any statistical basis whatsoever.

In contrast, in those few cases from the United Kingdom where similar firearms testimony has been given, the expert witness has used probabilistic phrases akin to those on subjective scales of opinion, thereby avoiding the difficulties with categorical statements experienced in the US courts. However, in neither jurisdiction have competing propositions or Bayesian inference appear to have been adopted when formulating firearms opinion.

References

Bunch S.G. (2000). Consecutive matching striation criteria: a general critique. *Journal of Forensic Sciences*, 45(5), 955–962.

Bunch S.G., Smith E.D., Giroux B.N. and Murphy D.P. (2009). Is a match really a match? A primer on the procedures and validity of firearm and toolmark identification. *Forensic Science Communications*, 11(3) [Online]. Available at https://www.fbi.gov/about-us/lab/forensic-science-communications/fsc/july2009/review/2009_07_review01.htm [Accessed 14 November 2015].

Bunch S. and Wevers G. (2013). Application of likelihood ratios for firearm and toolmark analysis. *Science and Justice*, 53(2), 223–229.

ENFSI Working Group, Marks Conclusion Scale Committee, Chair: H Katterwe. (2006). Conclusions scale for shoeprint and toolmarks examinations. *Journal of Forensic Identification*, 56(2), 255–279.

Murdock J. (committee chair) (1998). Theory of identification as it relates to toolmarks. *Association of Firearm and Toolmark Examiners Journal*, 30(1), 86–88.

Murdock J. (committee chair) (2011). Theory of identification as it relates to toolmarks: revised. *Association of Firearm and Toolmark Examiners Journal*, 43(4), 287.

National Research Council, Cork D.L., Rolph J.E., Meieran E.S., and Petrie C.V., (Eds.) (2008). *Ballistic Imaging*. National Academies Press. [Online]. Available at http://www.nap.edu/catalog/12162.html [Accessed 15 November 2015].

National Research Council: Strengthening Forensic Science in the United States: A Path Forward, Document 228091 [Online]. (2009). Available at http://www.nap.edu/catalog/12589.html [Accessed 10 October 2015].

R v Chatto and others [2012] EWCA Crim 190

R v Roden and another [2008] EWCA Crim 879

Riva F. and Champod C. (2014). Automatic comparison and evaluation of impressions left by a firearm on fired cartridge cases. *Journal of Forensic Sciences*, 59(3), 637–647.

Schwartz A. (2005). A systematic challenge to the reliability and admissibility of firearms and toolmark identification. *Columbia Science and Technology Law Review*, 6, 1–42.

United States v Glynn, 578 F Supp 2d 567 (SDNY 2008)

United States v Darryl Green and others, 405 F Supp 2d 104 (2005)

United States v Richard Hicks, 389 F 3d 514 (5th Cir 2004)

Further Reading

Bernstein D.S. (6 January 2006). Bad Ballistics, *Boston Phoenix* [Online]. Available at http://www.bostonphoenix.com/boston/news_features/this_just_in/documents/05177319.asp [Accessed 14 November 2015].

Biasotti A.A. (1959). A statistical study of the individual characteristics of fired bullets. *Journal of Forensic Sciences*, 4(1), 34–50.

Chu W., Thompson R.M., Song J. and Vorburger T.V. (2013). Automatic identification of bullet signatures based on consecutive matching striae (CMS) criteria. *Forensic Science International*, 231(1–3), 137–141.

Federal Judicial Centre: US Reference Manual on Scientific Evidence, 3rd Ed [Online]. (2011). Available at http://www.fjc.gov/public/pdf.nsf/lookup/SciMan3D01.pdf/$file/SciMan3D01.pdf [Accessed 13 October 2015].

Giannelli P.C. (2007). Daubert challenges to firearms ("ballistics") identifications, 2007, Faculty Publications, paper 154 [Online]. Available at http://scholarlycommons.law.case.edu/faculty_publications/154 [Accessed 14 November 2015].

Giannelli P.C. (2011). Ballistics evidence under fire. *Criminal Justice*, 25(4), 50–53.

National Institute of Standards and Technology (NIST): Forensic Database Firearms and Toolmarks Table [Online]. (2013). Available at http://www.nist.gov/oles/forensics/forensic-database-firearms-and-toolmarks-table.cfm [Accessed 15 November 2015].

Nichols R.G. (2007). Defending the scientific foundations of the firearms and tool mark identification discipline: responding to recent challenges. *Journal of Forensic Sciences*, 52(3), 586–594.

Schwartz A. (2008). Challenging firearms and toolmark identification – Part One. *The Champion*. October, 10–19.

Tobin W.A. and Blau P.J. (2013). Hypothesis testing of the critical underlying premise of discernible uniqueness in firearms-toolmarks forensic practice. *Jurimetrics Journal*, 53,121–142.

Tontarski Jr. R.E. and Thompson R.M. (1998). Automated firearms evidence comparison: A forensic tool for firearms identification – an update. *Journal of Forensic Sciences*, 43(3), 641–647.

Ultra Electronics Forensic Technology [Online]. (2015). Available at http://www.ultra-forensictechnology.com/ibis [Accessed 23 December 2015].

16

Expert Opinion and Evidence
of Human Identity

Within the forensic identification sciences, there are many evidence types that have been used for human identification, with varying degrees of success. These alleged biometrics include ear-marks, bite-marks, facial mapping and gait analysis – the identification of the characteristic body movements of individuals. Ear-marks occur in quite specific crime scene contexts. Bite-mark evidence, on the other hand, is more common and has been included together with identification of individuals by the direct examination of human dentition, in the field of forensic odontology. Facial mapping and gait analysis are more recent techniques that have become increasingly significant due to the ease with which recorded images, for example, from CCTV cameras, are now available and the development of digital image manipulation tools to facilitate analysis. Nevertheless, all these areas of work are justifiably subject to the same criticisms made of other identification sciences, namely weak underpinning science, rogue experts, subjective interpretation and arbitrary, not to say over-enthusiastic, evaluation. Many of these issues have been the subject of debate in the appeal courts and elsewhere and this forms the basis for the discussion in this chapter.

16.1   Introduction to Ear-Marks

The use of ear-mark evidence in the courts appears to have been relatively routine in a few jurisdictions, such as Switzerland and the Netherlands, whereas in others, including the United Kingdom and the United States, it has been restricted to a few high-profile and controversial cases, which have led to fundamental debates on its scientific basis and the nature of admissible opinion

Forensic Evidence in Court: Evaluation and Scientific Opinion, First Edition. Craig Adam.
© 2016 John Wiley & Sons, Ltd. Published 2016 by John Wiley & Sons, Ltd.

The fundamental forensic problem is the attribution of the source of a mark suspected to have been formed when an individual's ear is pressed, with unknown force, against a surface, commonly a windowpane. The key issues lie in understanding the factors affecting the production of the mark from the physical structure of the ear itself, the nature of the comparison process, the distribution of characteristics of the mark in the total population of ear-marks, in other words how common is any particular questioned mark, and how an opinion is formulated from the interpretation of these factors. Unfortunately, the inherent difficulty in dealing rigorously with these issues means that, in practice, the interpretation and evaluation of ear-mark evidence is carried out on quali-tative data assessed in a largely subjective manner, leading often to a greatly exaggerated certainty in the outcome including the categorical identification of the source of the mark. Claims of uniqueness are often made but whether this applies to the ear itself or a crime scene mark made by that ear, is often unclear and the significance of this difference frequently appears to be lost in court debates.

In an excellent critical review of the field of ear-mark evidence, Champod *et al.* (2001) discuss the scientific challenges to be overcome in providing a rigorous underpinning to the forensic process and how an opinion may be formed using Bayesian inference. A major contribution towards this goal has come from the EU-funded FearID project based in the Netherlands (see, e.g. Meijerman *et al.*, 2004; Alberink and Ruifrok, 2007). However, the fruits of such recent research are yet to penetrate into legal debate and, over the past few years, cases reaching the appeal courts appeared to have dried up.

In key past cases, the courts have taken a critical view of ear-mark evidence, certainly in both the United Kingdom and the United States, in particular by seeking to limit the weight of evidence and forbidding categorical opinion on the identification of a mark.

16.2   R v Kempster 2003, 2008

Mark John Kempster was convicted at Southampton Crown Court, United Kingdom, in March 2001 on four counts of domestic burglary. At one of these incidents, the key physical evidence was an ear-mark on the window pane, adjacent to the one that been forced open. Kempster admitted doing some recent building work for the homeowner but denied the burglary. The court was told that the windows were cleaned monthly.

At the trial, reports on the ear-mark evidence were received from two expert witnesses, though only Ms McGowan, the expert witness for the Crown, gave her testimony in person and was subjected to cross-examination. McGowan was a fingerprint officer who had over four years' experience in ear-mark examination and had completed a course led by Van Der Lugt who had given evidence in the Dallagher case in 1998 (Chapter 6.2.1). She stated that no two ears are the same and, following her comparison of the mark with control prints from Kempster, she concluded that the crime scene mark had been made by the same per-son as made the controls. In her cross-examination, she was asked by the defence counsel if the mark could have been made by someone other than Kempster, particularly a close relative such as a cousin; to which she replied, categorically:

'No, in my opinion, I don't believe it could have been made by anybody else.'

[R v Kempster, 2003, paragraph 10]

In contrast, the opinion of the second expert was not categorical but structured, as if formulated by considering competing propositions and evaluated by likelihood ratio:

> '… the combination of exact size and shape of the ear-print and … four distinctive features present, all of which are replicated in one or more of the control samples of Mr. Kempster's ear-print, lead me to the conclusion that they offer extremely strong support for the view that Mark John Kempster was responsible for the ear-print found on the kitchen window… '
>
> [R v Kempster, 2003, paragraph 11]

Kempster did not deny that the mark might be his but rejected the accusation that it associated him with the burglary. Following the guilty verdict, Kempster appealed on the grounds that the ear-print evidence was unreliable, and without any scientific basis, and further, that had opinion been sought from another expert witness for the defence, then the jury's decision may have been different; as such, these mirror the grounds in Dallagher's successful appeal.

16.2.1 The First Appeal 2003

As in the Dallagher case, the appeal court admitted testimony from Prof Champod, though he did not directly examine the evidence, but rather focused on its evaluation, given the observations and outcomes made by McGowan in her report. He emphasised that the resolution and detail in an ear-mark was far less than in the ridge detail of a finger-mark, that there was a lack of research underpinning the comparison methodology and databases of ear-prints were quite limited in scope. On evaluation, he made three key statements in his report and in cross-examination:

1. Ear-mark evidence could be used to exclude a suspect as the source of the impression
2. Expert opinion should not extend to comments on a positive comparison between a crime scene mark and a control
3. If a statement of comparison were to be admitted then it should be limited to an expression such as 'the questioned ear-print was consistent with a known impression' or something similar

The third point was rejected by the court as it believed that the expert should not be constrained in their testimony on the subject of positive comparison and that the jury would decide on the weight of evidence in light of the whole legal debate. McGowan reiterated the categorical opinion she gave at the trial, reinforcing it by reference to 'checking her findings' against what the appeal court recorded as '… a national database of ear-prints held in Durham', though the nature and extent of this does not appear to have been discussed by the court.

The appeal court accepted that any evidence from Champod would have been admissible at the trial but did not agree that this would have affected the final view of the jury, as Kempster did not deny that the mark was his and there was additional supporting evidence against him. Thus, in contrast to the Dallagher case, the appeal was rejected.

16.2.2 The Second Appeal 2008

Following a referral by the CCRC, a second appeal was heard in May 2008, which admitted fresh evidence on the interpretation and evaluation of ear-marks from Dr Ingleby, an applied mathematician who had worked on the FearID research project into forensic ear-mark analysis. He examined the work done by Ms McGowan and made two principal criticisms:

First, detailed examination of the crime scene mark and the control print revealed that the match was not precise, as had been claimed by McGowan, and the differences were not attributable to pressure induced distortion or movement of the ear against the window.

Second, the quality of the mark revealed only gross detail– principally the main cartilaginous folds of the ear – with only two small anatomical features that he termed minutiae, being present and that these were at a slightly different separation in the mark from in the print. Thus, from his appraisal of both the quantity and quality of detail, he disagreed with McGowan that the mark and the print necessarily shared the same origin.

In response, McGowan confirmed that she believed the small differences were indeed due to pressure effects; in particular, the difference in the separation of the two minutiae was only in the range 2.3 to 2.5 mm and this depended on the exact positions at which the measurements were made. In addition, she regarded the nature of these features – the notch and the nodule – as unusual and commented that they were 'identically placed'.

The judge concluded that ear-mark evidence was relevant and admissible and that, even with only the presence of 'gross features', it may provide a 'match', implying an identification of the source. However, for this to be the case there would have to be a precise alignment of these characteristics within the limits of uncertainty due to pressure and other factors. He agreed with Ingleby that this would not always be the case and appeared to justify this by his own inspection of the images and overlays:

> '… we are struck by the gross similarity of the shape and size of the ear-prints used for the comparison, and by the close similarity of the notch and the nodule on each. This, in our view, establishes that the ear-print at the scene is consistent with having been left by the appellant. But having examined the comparisons of the gross features, it is also apparent to us that they do not provide a precise match.'
>
> [R v Kempster, 2008, paragraph 28]

On this basis, sufficient doubt remained on whether Kempster was the source of the mark and hence this evidence did not justify the guilty verdict, on this count, at the original trial. The appeal was upheld but Kempster remained in jail, serving his sentence for the remaining three burglaries.

16.2.3 Conclusions From R v Kempster

So what can be concluded from the outcomes of these two appeals? There is much agreement between them on the admissibility and evaluative scope of testimony on ear-mark evidence. Indeed, there is some alignment of views between the limits of evaluation outlined by Champod at the first appeal, with the conclusions of the judge at the second appeal. In dissenting from Champod's view, the judge appeared to base his ruling on other factors in the case rather than directly challenging any aspect of the expert testimony. Having had his attention drawn to small differences between the mark and the control print, the judge's personal inspection of the images at the second appeal appeared to influence his final decision that a 'precise match' of gross features was necessary to infer an identification. If similar testimony had been presented at the first appeal, the outcome may have been quite different. However, whether the interpretation and evaluation by a lay person, here the judge, should be able to influence the final outcome or potentially override the considered conclusions of an expert witness, may be a matter for concern and a major factor in our understanding of how courts may deal with many forms of identification evidence.

This case also illustrates how the non-expert tends to approach this forensic process exclusively in terms of 'looking for a match' without appreciating some of the fundamental factors that need to be considered when reaching an evaluation. First, there is the confusion between ears and ear-marks. At the trial, McGowan was quoted as stating that 'that no two ears were the same', whereas at the second appeal this statement was quoted as 'that no two ears left the same mark'. The first of these is arguably true, though whether that has any forensic consequence is debatable, whereas the second is clearly not universally correct. The second point relates to whether there is any substantive evidence underpinning claims that features on ear-marks are common or rare and the relevance to this of any databases. Despite a reference to the latter at the first appeal, the impact of this on the evaluative process does not appear to have been picked up by the court. The Durham database was in fact set up at the National Training Centre (NTC) for the United Kingdom by practitioners from across the EU, and such databases were described by Champod *et al.* in 2001 as 'a gallery of images without a forensic structure'.

16.3   State v Kunze 1999

Apparently, the sole case to date in the United States, where an appeal court has had to confront ear-mark evidence, occurred only shortly before the first Kempster appeal and around the same time as that of Mark Dallagher. David Wayne Kunze was tried and convicted in 1996 for the murder of James McCann and the attempted murder of his son Tyler in Clark County, Washington State. Both had been bludgeoned around the head with a heavy weapon, during what appeared to be an attempted robbery at their home. Despite his appearance conflicting with a description of the assailant given to the police by Tyler, Kunze was suspected as his ex-wife had recently told him that she planned to marry James McCann. The only physical evidence against Kunze was the discovery of an ear-mark on the outside surface of McCann's bedroom door which the prosecution alleged associated Kunze with the crime scene.

16.3.1   The Frye Hearing

Prior to the trial, Kunze appealed on the grounds that ear-mark identification evidence was inadmissible and a pre-trial (Frye) hearing was ordered. Michael Grubb from the State Crime Laboratory who had interpreted the evidence, admitted having no previous experience with ear-marks, although he had much experience of other forms of impression evidence. He claimed that identification from ear-marks was accepted by the scientific community:

> '... the earprint is just another form of impression evidence ... other impression evidence is generally accepted in the scientific community.'
>
> [State v Kunze, 1999]

He agreed that he had not read any studies of ear-marks or had knowledge of the occurrence of different shapes of ear within the population; he concluded that:

> 'Mr. Kunze could be the source of [the latent] impression, and even further, I believe it's likely that the impression from [the] crime scene is Mr. Kunze's ear and cheek print.'
>
> [State v Kunze, 1999]

At the hearing, thirteen scientific and practitioner witnesses were called to testify whether the field of ear-mark identification was accepted by the scientific community and under-pinned by scientific research. Only two confirmed or implied that it was; one being Van der Lugt who stated that judges in the Dutch courts accepted the principle of identification from ear-mark evidence and that, in general, the sub-discipline was accepted by his scien-tific peers, although he did not refer to any relevant published literature. In contrast, four others provided a contrary view and seven were unaware of the status of the field within the forensic community.

Professor Moenssens added that he did not know of any studies that had scientifically validated the identification methodology or indeed proved that ears are unique; he agreed that a comparison exercise can be carried out, but that:

> '... the question is whether that comparison means anything.'
>
> [State v Kunze, 1999]

Several experts from the FBI agreed that they were unaware of that organisation doing any work with ear-marks from crime scenes. Nevertheless, apparently going against the view of the majority of these experts, the judge agreed to admit the ear-mark evidence and con-firmed that in his view, ear-mark identification by a process of visual comparison:

> '... is based upon principles and methods which are sufficiently established to have gained general acceptance in the relevant scientific community.'
>
> [State v Kunze, 1999]

16.3.2   The Trial

In addition to Grubb, Van der Lugt gave testimony at the trial on his own examination of the images. He found some features of the ear and the mark that were in complete correspondence and a few others where there were differences, but stated that these could be explained by pressure effects. He conceded that the level of correspondence needed to establish a match was quite subjective, there being no agreed criteria. Finally, he was asked if he had an opinion on the probability that Kunze was the source of the crime scene mark:

> 'A: I think it's probable that it's the defendant's ear is the one that was found on the scene.
> Q: How confident are you of the opinion that you just expressed?
> A: I'm 100 percent confident with that opinion.'
>
> [State v Kunze, 1999]

In other words, he was certain that it was probable the Kunze was the source of the mark, not certain of the source itself. From the jury's perspective, this is not a clear evaluation and it has the potential to mislead the court. Following his conviction, Kunze appealed, once again on the admissibility of the ear-mark evidence.

16.3.3   The Appeal

The appeal court judge summarised that the correspondence of class characteristics between a mark and a control print may lead to expert opinion such as, that the suspect 'cannot be excluded' as the source or that he 'could have made' the crime scene mark or that the mark 'is consistent with' the control impressions. The evaluations of Grubb and Van der Lugt, in this case, implied a stronger association of the mark with Kunze than that suggested by these statements and hence they must have identified at least one individualising trait, in addition to class characteristics, in order to justify that opinion. To do so they had to be using scientific, specialised or technical knowledge and so the argument moved to establishing whether such a field existed and was accepted by the community.

Following a review of the testimony of the thirteen experts at the pre-trial Frye hearing, and considering precedents, the appeal court judge concluded that the existence of any significant dispute as to the validity of forensic evidence in a scientific community, implied non-acceptance of that evidence by the community. This was clearly true for ear-mark identification and thus such opinion was inadmissible in court. However, this ruling applied to the identification of the source of a mark based on individualising features and not to the presentation of factual observations on the mark itself, to the court. Hence, the expert witness could explain the methodology and acquisition of the images of the mark and of any control prints and these could be presented to the court for their own visual interpretation, with comments on any observable similarities and differences provided by the expert. If class characteristics were in correspondence, then opinion could be given that the suspect was not excluded as the source of the crime scene mark; opinion on inclusion was not permitted. This would be the limit of opinion admissible by the court. It follows, though not explicitly stated, that opinion on exclusion, due to non-correspondence of class characteristics, was admissible.

Thus the appeal was upheld, the verdict on Kunze was quashed and a retrial ordered. However, following the declaration of a mistrial by the judge due to an improper statement by the prosecutor during the second hearing, the prosecution abandoned any attempt at a third trial due to lack of evidence and the charges against Kunze were dropped in 2001.

16.4   Review of Ear-Mark Cases

There are substantial similarities between the courts' final views in these two cases, although the terminologies and arguments differ. The comparison of gross features or class characteristics, leading to an opinion on exclusion or non-exclusion, was accepted as admissible evidence. However, in neither case are these traits or the precision of agreement that is needed, defined; the interpretation is based on the experience and judgement of the expert. To progress towards an identification or to a probabilistic scale of opinion, the Kempster case emphasised the precision of correspondence of gross features, with some reference to additional traits, whereas in Kunze, the focus was on the number and quality of individualising features that needed to be considered in the evaluation; precision was not explicitly mentioned. Generically these are both driving the process in a similar direction. However, not only are the methodologies described in quite different terms, with no definitions of relevant characteristics in the mark, but at all stages the interpretation is based on a qualitative assessment of data with no universally accepted criteria. Further, alternative explanations for the mark, based on a knowledge of the characteristics of an appropriate population of ear-marks, do not contribute to the evaluation in any explicit fashion.

16.5 Introduction to Bite-Mark Evidence

Although the examination of dentition as a means of human identification at post-mortem is common practice, as it is based on widespread acceptance of its uniqueness as a biometric, the same principle cannot be extended to a bite-mark formed by a much smaller number of teeth, indented into material ranging from foodstuffs to human skin and tissue. Even if those teeth themselves represented a unique structure, some of that representation would be lost in the mark due to the elastic and behavioural properties of the material and the nature and action of the forces during the bite itself. Despite this, there have been quite diverse views from the forensic odontology profession as to how the interpretation and evaluation of bite-mark evidence may be conveyed to the court and whether either the active dentition or the mark itself may be regarded as unique. Indeed, a survey by Pretty (2003) revealed that 91% of respondents agreed with the former view, whereas 78% supported the latter statement. Many of the issues around the scientific basis of bite-mark analysis, its reliability and its evaluation as expert opinion, have been debated in and out of court, particularly in the United States, over the past forty years and were subject to scrutiny in the NRC report (2009), which concluded that, although such evidence could make a contribution to legal discussion:

> '... the scientific basis is insufficient to conclude that bite mark comparisons can result in a conclusive match'
>
> [NRC, 2009, p 175]

Nevertheless, it added that it was a reasonable assumption to conclude that bite-mark examination could reliably exclude an individual, as the source of the mark.

In addition, there are competing and sometimes contentious procedures for the examination of bite-marks, based either on the direct comparison of the mark with a model of the dentition or by two dimension overlays or the use of computer-based images, and there are some instances where statistical data, of uncertain provenance, has been included in support of expert opinion. This is despite the absence of large-scale population studies to inform the examiner on the diversity and uniqueness of bite-mark patterns. All of this contributes to doubts as to the reliability of bite-mark testimony, and specifically on the limitations to expert opinion. Nevertheless, bite-mark evidence has been accepted fairly consistently in US courts, with many cases where opinion has claimed conclusive identification of the source of the mark.

16.6 The ABFO Guidelines and Expert Opinion

Bite-mark testimony has included examples of the typical posterior probabilistic phrases used elsewhere. These include 'consistent with' and 'probably made', as well as 'positive identification' or 'match', often invoked with little consistency as to how these followed from the expert's observations or clarity on their precise meanings.

The American Board of Forensic Odontology (ABFO) recognised, during the 1980s, that standards for the examination, interpretation and evaluation of bite-mark evidence needed to be established and these were in place in 1986, though the scoring system, devised to provide an objective mapping of the observed features on to an evaluative opinion, was later withdrawn, pending 'further research'. These guidelines define the terminology, process of examination and documentation, as well as the experience an individual needs to achieve to be professionally recognised. They include descriptions of typical class characteristics and individual traits, the observation of which should form the basis for the systematic examination of a bite-mark. A decision tree is provided to facilitate the examiner arriving at an evaluative opinion, though this is based on purely qualitative considerations. Importantly, it includes consideration of whether the control impression is from an open or closed population. The bite-mark examiner needs to address two questions:

First, is human dentition the source of the mark?

Three outcomes for an opinion on this question may be provided based on examination of the mark itself and of any observed class or individual characteristics. These are:

1. Human teeth created the mark
2. The impression is 'suggestive of a human bite-mark'; however, the detail in insufficient to provide more definitive outcome
3. Human teeth are not the source of the mark

Second, what is the opinion regarding the source of the bite-mark?

Opinion on the source should be presented in a form of words indicated by a five-point scale, with the qualification that the opinion is given 'to a reasonable degree of dental certainty':

1. Categorical opinion: the source of the control mark is the biter
2. The source of the control mark is the 'probable biter'
3. The source not excluded as the biter
4. Categorical opinion: the source is excluded as the biter
5. The outcome of the examination is inconclusive

In cases where the population of possible sources is not defined (an open population), the categorical outcome as to the identification of the source (point 1) is not permitted as a valid opinion. Such opinion is only appropriate where a finite population of sources (a limited number of suspects) has been examined. In all cases, the interpretation and evaluation should be reviewed by a second recognised expert prior to submission as testimony. Despite these guidelines, justification for the selection of a particular point on this scale is based on an unspecified and qualitative assessment of class and individual characteristics. The meanings of the probabilistic terms in these guidelines are nebulous – what exactly is meant by 'a reasonable degree of dental certainty' – and therefore may be misleading to the court.

16.7 Bite-Mark Cases in the United States

To illustrate debates around bite-mark testimony in the US courts, some notable cases will be discussed, albeit that they mostly demonstrate historic practice originating from several decades ago, but which nevertheless reveal the concerns expressed much more recently in the NRC report (2009).

16.7.1   People v Marx 1975

Walter Marx was found guilty of the voluntary manslaughter of his landlady Lovey Benovsky by strangulation in 1975. The body had post-mortem knife wounds and, more significantly, an 'elliptical laceration of the nose' believed by the coroner to be a bite-mark, presumably inflicted by the murderer. At his trial, the prosecution alleged that Marx was the source of this mark and this was supported by expert testimony. However, Marx appealed his conviction on the grounds that such evidence was inadmissible.

Before discussing this evidence in detail, the circumstances and methods employed in acquiring and examining the bite-mark need to be outlined. Mrs Benovsky died on 2nd February 1974 and the first records of the mark were photographs taken at autopsy two days later. The body was then interred and subsequently exhumed to allow cast impressions in rubber-based material to be made of the mark on 23rd March, shortly after impressions were taken of Marx's teeth to create a positive cast in dental stone. The comparison of the mark with the control was therefore based on a three dimensional analysis.

Three dentists provided testimony for the prosecution and all were clear that this was a novel case, given the depth of the bite-mark and their consequent ability to 'use a virtually unprecedented three-dimensional approach' in the analysis. They stated that this would strengthen their opinion on the evidence and indeed all three concurred in providing categorical identification of the source of the mark.

16.7.2   The Appeal

The debate at the appeal centred around the fundamental question of whether the identification of an individual was possible from dentition and, more specifically, whether in this case there was sufficient evidence for such a match and for the elimination of all other sources. The court appeared to accept the first point since even the defence had conceded that such identification was acceptable practice, though whether they were distinguishing between dentition and a mark made by a sub-set of those teeth is not clear. The experts acknowledged that there was no established scientific basis for the identification of individuals from bite-marks and the judge commented that their testimony:

> '... reflects their enthusiastic response to a rare opportunity to develop or extend forensic dentistry into the area of bite mark identification.'
>
> [People v Marx, 1975, A1a]

Given that all involved accepted that the use of these techniques, and hence the methodology employed in this examination, was novel and so could not, at that time, be generally accepted by the scientific community, the expectation might have been that the testimony would fail legal acceptability under the Frye criteria. However, the judge argued that this was not the case, as the individual techniques themselves were not novel or untested and the results of the analysis – including the basic data, models, photographs and images – were all physically presented in court for all concerned to verify the opinion of the experts for themselves and indeed to assign a different weight to that evaluation should they wish. Thus, it was implicit that the court could bypass the expert and indeed interpret the evidence without possessing any of the expert's knowledge and experience. The expression of the experts' opinion was not challenged or discussed at the appeal.

A further ground of appeal related to the alleged use of mathematical probabilities and formulae by the experts in arriving at their opinion, contrary to the ruling also in California, in People v Collins (see Chapter 8.1). However, the judge accepted the expert's statement that all discussions on probabilities were in general terms, that no numbers were involved and that the purpose was to convince himself that the combination of unusual features in Marx' dentition were such as to make the possibility of there being other sources of such a mark very unlikely. On this basis the appeal was rejected and Marx' conviction upheld.

16.7.3 State v Garrison 1978

The use of statistical information in presenting an opinion and its admissibility was to the forefront in another case involving death by strangulation, this time of a young woman in Arizona in 1976. Bobby Jo Garrison was convicted of the murder of Verna Marie Martin whose body had been mutilated by bite-marks. At his trial, testimony from forensic dentist, Homer Campbell Jnr, related how he had compared indentation impressions, made with a model of Garrison's dentition impacted on wax, with the marks and, based on the identification of ten points of similarity, he stated:

> 'My conclusion was that the bite marks on the deceased, and the bite marks produced by the model that I received, were consistent, the marks were consistent with those being made by the teeth that I received.'
>
> [State v Garrison, 1978]

Strictly, such opinion implies non-exclusion of Garrison as the source of the marks and so has limited weight. However, this evaluation was apparently strengthened when he added:

> '... the probability factor of two sets of teeth being identical in a case similar to this is, approximately, eight in one million, or one in one hundred and twenty-five thousand people.'
>
> [State v Garrison, 1978]

In his appeal, Garrison sought to have this latter testimony disregarded as unreliable, claiming that Campbell had stated:

> '... that there is an eight in one million probability that the teeth marks found on the deceased's breasts were not made by appellant.'
>
> [State v Garrison, 1978]

Although this is a clear example of the prosecutor's fallacy, the appeal court did not appear to recognise it as logically incorrect, but instead focused only on the use of numerical probability in the evaluation. In doing so, the Supreme Court of Arizona reached a majority decision to reject the appeal, with two judges dissenting.

As Campbell had simply quoted the probability from a published source, the majority view was that this proved the reliability of the figures and thus its admissibility. If they had consulted this reference, it would have been clear that the work referred to complete dentition and not to bite-mark impressions. The dissenting judges provided a more detailed set of arguments in support of their view. First, they concluded that, as he in fact did not generate the figures himself, was unaware of the formula used or could not explain the weighting of each variable, Campbell was 'totally out of his field when the discussion turns to probability theory'.

Second, they suggested that Campbell had misquoted his reference and the probability was actually 8 in 100,000. In either case, based on the local county population being 465,000, they concluded that these statistics would imply either 3.7 or 37 people with bite-marks indistinguishable from those of Garrison. These figures reveal how misleading it could be to a jury to have seemingly tiny probabilities quoted in support of expert opinion.

Third, they disputed whether the product rule was appropriate in combining the probabilities associated with each characteristic in the mark to arrive at the final figure for its frequency of occurrence, as some characteristics may not be independent. Finally, they disagreed that this published figure could be applied to Campbell's data, as he had claimed to have disregarded some of the ten factors in reaching his conclusions and this, combined with doubts on weightings and the product rule, meant that the correct probability would be considerably less than his declared figure. On this basis they dissented from the majority view by interpreting the law in quite the opposite fashion.

16.7.4   State v Stinson 1986

In November 1984, Ione Cychosz was found dead in her back yard. She had been raped, beaten severely and her body had sustained several bite-marks inflicted before she died. On the basis of circumstantial evidence and the testimony from two expert witnesses that he was the source of the bite-marks, Robert Lee Stinson was convicted of the murder at his trial, the following year. Stinson appealed this verdict, principally on grounds of the admissibility of the bite-mark evidence.

The appeal court confirmed the expert status of Dr Johnson, a dentist and clinical pathologist, and Dr Rawson, a forensic odontologist and chairman of the Bite Mark Standards Committee of the ABFO. It endorsed the view of the trial court that the analysis of bite-mark evidence was an accepted and recognised area of science where there were 'adequate controls and standards' and concluded that the presentation of such evidence by an expert witness was of invaluable assistance to the jury, adding that:

> 'By looking directly at the physical evidence used, the models and the photos, the jury was able to judge for itself whether Stinson's teeth did in fact match the bite marks found on the victim's body.'
>
> [State v Stinson, 1986]

In his testimony, Johnson stated that his examination was based on direct comparison and the use of overlays of cast impressions of the bite-marks and Stinson's dentition. Interestingly, Stinson had a twin brother, Robert Earl, from whom a cast impression was also procured and later eliminated on the basis of significant class differences. Due to having several examples of the bite-mark on the body, Johnson not only claimed to be able to eliminate distortion effects in his comparisons but also that he could identify key individual traits repeated across some of the marks. After what was claimed to be an 'exhaustive examination' of the evidence, he concluded:

> '... to a reasonable degree of scientific certainty, that the bite marks on the victim were made by Stinson.'
>
> [State v Stinson, 1986]

Rawson carried out an independent review of Johnson's work and was impressed by both the quality and quantity of the evidence with which he had to work. He confirmed that Johnson had worked to ABFO standards (his evaluation was point 1 on the ABFO scale) and concurred with his opinion, adding that the evidence was 'overwhelming'.

On this basis the appeal court confirmed the trial verdict and concluded:

'The reliability of the bite mark evidence in this case was sufficient to exclude to a moral certainty every reasonable hypothesis of innocence.'

[State v Stinson, 1986]

However, Stinson continued to protest his innocence and in 2005 the Wisconsin Innocence Project took up his case. Through DNA profile testing of stains on the victim's clothing and a review of the bite-mark evidence, they succeeded in proving that Stinson was not the rapist and killer of Cychosz, although it was not until January 2009 that he was freed from prison and exonerated. In April 2012 Moses Price Jnr was charged with this crime on the basis of the DNA evidence.

16.7.5   Bite-Mark Testimony in the Courts

In retrospect, there is now a significant record of wrongful convictions from bite-mark evidence, most notably where a positive identification has been given, which has later been shown to be invalid. There have also been examples of similar testimony, in support of the prosecution, where the conviction has been confirmed at appeal, yet the expert's opinion has been subject to further scrutiny on grounds of admissibility, its scientific foundations, the statistical basis of the evaluation and other factors. In addition, there have been cases of substantial disagreements between experts and a growing body of publications critical of much of the sub-discipline, in particular in providing a categorical identification of a source. From the perspective of the courts, the suggestion from judges that, as long as the factual outcomes from the forensic examination are made available to the court, which allow the jury to make their own interpretation of the evidence, then bite-mark testimony is admissible, is a cause for concern. This overrides one of the key skills and duties of the expert witness, which is to provide interpretation and evaluation, whereas transferring that task to un-trained and inexperienced jury members has potentially quite dangerous consequences for justice.

16.8   Body Biometrics: Facial Mapping and Gait

Traditionally, evidence of visual identification has been admitted in court, whereby a witness of fact has identified an individual from memory, for example, as a suspect in a line-up. In more recent times, expert advice has been sought where recorded images have been available, for example, from CCTV cameras where the image quality has been poor or facial features are obscured, yet characteristics of body movements (gait) may be discerned. This has led to expert opinion on gait and facial mapping (recognition) being admitted and sometimes challenged in court. In Chapter 6.1, the case of the Atkins' brothers, convicted on facial mapping evidence, was discussed. Their challenge to the use of an arbitrary scale for the evaluation was rejected on appeal but as we shall see, this is not always the outcome.

16.8.1   R v Hookway 1999

An early example of facial mapping evidence proved crucial in the conviction of Stephen James Hookway, for the armed robbery of a bank in Salford, United Kingdom in July 1997. The identification of Hookway, as one of five gang members in stocking masks, was the sole evidence against him, and his appeal in 1999 contended that the testimony of the expert witness, Richard Neave, was not, on its own, sufficient to sustain a guilty verdict.

Neave and his assistant worked from still photographs of the robbery and reference images taken of Hookway. They considered the proportions and morphology of the facial features, using overlays to aid comparison, and took account of the flattening effect of the mask itself. Neave concluded that Hookway's features were 'totally consistent' with those of one of the bank robbers and stated that in his opinion this provided:

> 'very powerful support for the assertion that the offender was the appellant'
>
> [R v Hookway, 1999]

He then qualified this assertion by claiming that this was not a categorical identification and that within the Manchester area there could well be one or two others with a similar appearance, including Hookway's brother, so he could not exclude the possibility that the bank robber was someone else. Under cross-examination, he provided details of his observations, which led to this conclusion.

The defence did not challenge the credentials of the expert witness or the validity of the techniques of facial mapping, preferring to focus on the absence of any relevant database to support the evaluation. Since this implied, as Neave had accepted, that the possibility of another man being the source of the masked image was not excluded, they asserted that such evidence on its own was insufficient to convict. In rejecting the appeal, the judge stated that, given the testimony was admissible and had been the subject of adequate debate in the court, its weight was ultimately a matter for the jury to decide. In formulating an opinion, the use of 'total consistency' to justify 'very powerful support' for a proposition, in the absence of any justification for the population statistics quoted in support of any alternative proposition, make this testimony unconvincing.

16.8.2   R v Otway 2011

Twenty seconds of CCTV footage showing a man at a filling station walking from a blue Honda car that was later to be used for the shooting of Mark Daniels in a Manchester street, provided crucial evidence which helped to convict Elroy Otway of the murder. Although the images were clear, the individual's face was not visible, so identification by analysis of the man's gait and comparison to reference sequences taken of Otway at a police station, were used as the basis of expert testimony.

At Otway's trial in 2009, the defence challenged the admissibility of a witness statement from podiatrist, David Blake, on the following grounds:

- The comparison of images was something that could be done by the jury themselves, without expert advice
- There was no statistical database on which to evaluate the significance of any opinion
- There was no scientific basis or measurements to support the methodology
- There was no 'sufficiently recognised body' of experience to underpin gait analysis

Blake's account of the field, in his report, convinced the judge that gait analysis was a sufficiently organised body of knowledge, that he was qualified to give expert opinion and was fully aware of the range of both common and more unusual gait characteristics. In rejecting the defence's challenge, the judge agreed that Blake could provide an account of the similarities in gait between Otway and that displayed in the CCTV images, in order to assist the jury in their own evaluation of the visual evidence. However, Blake could not give his own evaluation in terms of a probabilistic statement on Otway being the driver of the car.

Nevertheless, Otway raised the same issues as grounds for his appeal in 2011. Through a similar set of arguments, the appeal court judge arrived essentially at the same conclusion and rejected the appeal. One further claim, that while Blake was qualified to identify features of an individual's gait, he was not qualified to compare such characteristics between two people, was dismissed as untenable. The limitations of such expert opinion however were firmly reinforced:

> 'We agree ..., however, that Mr Blake's ability safely to express his ultimate conclusion in terms of probability of a match, even probability based on Mr Blake's clinical experience, was insufficiently established. It is important that juries are not misled to an over-valuation of comparison evidence.'
>
> [R v Otway, 2011, paragraph 22]

It was emphasised that, in general, the admissibility of such 'podiatric' evidence should be dealt with on an individual basis, to ensure that the testimony stays within the area of expertise of the particular expert, and that the court makes clear the limitations it sets on the scope of the evaluation. This statement reconciles this appeal with that in the case of the Atkins brothers.

16.9   Conclusion

Despite the apparent diversity in the nature of all these biometric identifiers, there has been some convergence within the courts as to how expert opinion should be presented. Admissibility has not been a major issue, with the courts preferring to include such evidence, even if it is accepted to be of limited reliability. However, the interpretation and formation of an evaluation has been more problematic, with courts often setting limits on how far the expert may go, beyond stating observations and providing advice on interpretation to the jury; the absence of interpretive databases contributing to this difficulty. Once again, the impetus to allow a proper evaluation by the expert is thwarted by the visual nature of the evidence itself. It is all too easy for the court to fall back on allowing the significance of the evidence to be decided by the non-expert jury, through their own inspection and comparison of images, relying only on advice and guidance from the expert witness.

References

Alberink I. and Ruifrok A. (2007). Performance of the FearID earprint identification system. *Forensic Science International*, 166(2–3), 145–154.

American Board of Forensic Odontology (ABFO) Diplomats Reference Manual, section III [Online]. (2015). Available at http://www.abfo.org/resources/abfo-manual/ [Accessed 13 November 2015].

Champod C., Evett I.W., Kuchler B. (2001). Earmarks as evidence: a critical review. *Journal of Forensic Sciences*, 46(6), 1275–1284.

Meijerman L., Sholl S., De Conti F., Giacon M., van der Lugt C., Drusini A., Vanezis P. and Maat G. (2004). Exploratory study on classification and individualisation of earprints. *Forensic Science International*, 140, 91–99.

National Research Council: Strengthening Forensic Science in the United States: A Path Forward, Document 228091 [Online]. (2009). Available at http://www.nap.edu/catalog/12589.html [Accessed 10 October 2015].

People v Marx [1975] 54 Ca. App 3d 100

Pretty I.A. (2003). A web-based survey of odontologist's opinions concerning bitemark analyses. *Journal of Forensic Sciences*, 28(5), 1–4.

R v Hookway [1999] EWCA Crim 212

R v Kempster [2003] EWCA Crim 3555

R v Kempster [2008] EWCA Crim 975

R v Otway [2011] EWCA Crim 3

State of Washington v David Wayne Kunze [1999], 22338-4-II

State v Garrison [1978] 585 P 2d 563 (Ariz)

State v Stinson [1986] 134 Wis 2d 224

Further Reading

Clement J.G. and Blackwell S.A. (2010). Is current bite mark analysis a misnomer? *Forensic Science International*, 201(1–3), 33–37.

Deitch A. (2009). An inconvenient tooth: Forensic odontology is an inadmissible junk science when it is used to "match" teeth to bitemarks in skin. *Wisconsin Law Review*, 1205–1236.

Earprint Burglary Conviction Tossed: Justice Denied, the magazine for the wrongly convicted [Online]. (2008). Available at http://justicedenied.org/issue/issue_41/jd_issue_41.pdf [Accessed 13 November 2015].

Giannelli P.C. (2007). Bite mark analysis, Faculty Publications, Paper 153 [Online]. Available at http://scholarlycommons.law.case.edu/faculty_publications/153 [Accessed 13 November 2015].

Halpin S. (2008). What have we got ear then? Developments in forensic science: earprints as identification evidence at criminal trials. *University College Dublin Law Review*, 8, 65–83.

Innocence Project: Descriptions of bite-mark exonerations [Online]. (2015). Available at http://www.innocenceproject.org/docs/Description_of_Bite_Mark_Exonerations.pdf [Accessed 13 November 2015].

Pretty I.A. and Sweet D.J. (2001). The scientific basis for human bitemark analyses – a critical review. *Science and Justice*, 41(2), 85–92.

Pretty I.A. and Sweet D.J. (2006). The judicial view of bite-marks within the United States criminal justice system. *Journal of Forensic Odonto-Stomatology*, 24(1), 1–11.

Pretty I.A. and Sweet D.J. (2010). A paradigm shift in the analysis of bitemarks. *Forensic Science International*, 201, 38–44.

Rawson R.D., Vale G.L., Sperber N.D., Herschaft E.E. and Yfantis A. (1986). Reliability of the scoring system of the American Board of Forensic Odontology for human bite marks. *Journal of Forensic Sciences*, 31(4), 1235–1260.

Vale G.L., Sognnaes R.F., Felando G.N. and Noguchi T.T. (1976). Unusual three-dimensional bite mark evidence in a homicide case. *Journal of Forensic Sciences*, 21(3), 642–652.

17

Questioned Documents

The work of the questioned document examiner (QDE) encompasses many aspects of written and printed documents, several of which will be considered in this chapter. The focus, however, will be on those that comprise the majority of such evidence in the courts, which is establishing the source of handwriting and signatures, though comments will also be made on the examination of indented writing and other less common investigations.

At the heart of the examination of handwriting and signatures lie the principles, only verifiable if sufficient writing is available, that no two people write in exactly the same way and no person writes in the same way twice. Thus, the uniqueness of each set of writing, the need to assess variability in an individual's writing and a detailed knowledge of the variety of writing styles across a population, form the basis for the process of the comparison of questioned writing with a set of reference writing and hence the formulation of an evaluative opinion for the court. The reliability of this opinion depends not only on the validity of this methodology and but also on the competence of the practitioners in their implementation of it. These factors may lead to competing testimonies from expert witnesses and challenges to the evidence in the court, particularly in the United States, post-Daubert. An excellent discussion of the principles and current practice of questioned document examination is given by Allen (2016).

The broad scope of the work and the potential range of special circumstances in any particular case, mean that the examination of questioned documents is arguably in a league of its own within the mainstream forensic sciences. For example, in addition to the passage of time, writing is affected by ill-health and extreme age (Gale v Gale, 2010), assistance with writing leads to 'guided-hand signatures' (Barrett v Benn and others, 2012) and the expert may be asked to provide testimony on the speed of writing on a document (R v Maynard and

Forensic Evidence in Court: Evaluation and Scientific Opinion, First Edition. Craig Adam.
© 2016 John Wiley & Sons, Ltd. Published 2016 by John Wiley & Sons, Ltd.

others, 2002). Beyond conventional handwriting, evidence may be in the form of graffiti (R v Previte, 2005), hand printing (US v Saelee, 2005) or indeed printing in English by an individual whose native script is Japanese (US v Fujii, 2000).

To understand how such a wide range of testimony is developed and delivered to the court we need to examine some key cases. However, before doing so, the methodology of the forensic examination of writing needs to be explored further.

17.1 Handwriting and Signature Comparison – A Scientific Methodology?

The over-arching process guiding the comparison and analysis of questioned handwriting and signatures is well-defined, though there are differences in the detail of examination for these two types of evidence. Given a sufficient amount of questioned and reference writing, the examiner will attempt to identify a range of characteristics and their natural variability in both sets of writing. For handwriting, these characteristics would normally be related to individual letters and their combination into words, whereas for signatures a more flexible approach is needed to accommodate the wide variety of forms such writing might take. The comparison procedure then follows, to establish whether each trait falls within or outside the natural variability across the two sets and this enables the formation of a view as to whether these traits are similar or dissimilar between the questioned and reference writings. Finally, an evaluation stage weighs the similarities against the dissimilarities to enable the examiner to arrive at an opinion as to whether the writer of the reference writing is also the source of the questioned writing and to present that opinion in a form of words which reflects the weight of the evidence.

So is this a scientific methodology? This is certainly a clear, logical procedure that may be followed by all trained examiners and, at each point, the examiner adopts a hypothesis testing approach in reaching a conclusion. However, throughout the examination, decisions must be made for which there are no accepted quantitative criteria that would render this an objective process, and indeed there may be substantial flexibility in the qualitative assessments made by individual examiners. These include the following specific questions:

1. How much material comprises an adequate sample for establishing natural variability?
   Questioned writing may vary considerably in length and range of characteristics; there may be only a single questioned signature; the reference writing may be limited in scope, may not comprise an appropriate range of letters or characters or may not be contemporaneous. The QDE may decide that there is an insufficient quantity and/or quality of reference writing to proceed with the analysis and return an inconclusive opinion; the threshold for this may differ between examiners. The assessment of natural variability is a subjective process without definable reference criteria.
2. What features of the writing should be used in the comparison process and should some of these carry more weight than others?
   The features will often be specific to the content of the questioned sample and their selection is up to the individual examiner; the quantity and quality of these characteristics will vary between examinations and examiners. Features will include both class characteristics and the detailed appearance and formation of individual letters.

3. What criteria are used to reach a view on similarity or dissimilarity?

Since the assessment of variability is qualitative, the comparison of characteristics must also be qualitative and based on the examiner's own criteria; despite the continuous nature of variability the implication is that the QDE may arrive at a categorical view on similarity or otherwise for each characteristic in the writing.

4. How are these similarities and dissimilarities aggregated into an opinion?

In some cases, where either predominates, a clear view may emerge on identifying or excluding the writer of the reference material, as the source of the questioned document. Yet the QDE needs to adopt criteria to support a categorical opinion on the source such as confirming no significant dissimilarities; this is particularly important where the style and characteristics of the writing are commonly encountered in the population. In other cases, these attributes need to be combined to arrive at an opinion and this process is entirely subject to the judgement of the examiner, for example in formulating opinion based on many similarities and some dissimilarities.

5. How is the opinion presented to the court?

Categorical opinion is often provided in cases of handwriting and signature analysis, for example using the phrase 'conclusive evidence' for or against a proposition. Other outcomes are usually mapped on to a scale of opinion and, although several scales are used, there is no agreement on a standard number of points or forms of words. An inconclusive opinion may follow from either there being insufficient material on which to proceed with an examination or from a neutral outcome arising at the comparison stage of the analysis. Expert opinion is normally given in relation to the source of the evidence and logical evaluation, based on Bayesian inference, is not common practice. Having said that, there has been a move away from an interpretive process whereby the observations lead towards a specific conclusion, to some conscious attempt to balance these against competing explanations. Nevertheless, it is rare for the QDE to comment directly on the occurrence of a style of writing in the population, reinforcing the assumption of the uniqueness of handwriting and signatures.

This lack of definable criteria, despite the scientific framework underpinning the examination of handwriting and signatures, may lead to different evaluative outcomes for different QDEs working on the same evidence and to difficulties in justifying those outcomes. Before discussing examples, some further understanding of how the QDE conveys opinion to the court is needed.

17.2   Scales of Expert Opinion

In expressing opinion to the court the QDE may often give a categorical statement of attribution or exclusion; for some, this is the only testimony they may wish to give, or that the court will accept, and is represented by a three-point scale with the inclusion of an inconclusive point. In many cases, however, testimony that is not conclusive still may be of use to the court and the expert must formulate a statement that reflects the degree to which the evidence may support any particular proposition, reflecting their confidence in the outcome. Given the subjective nature of the comparison and analysis process and the absence of any quantitative measures, a scale with many points of gradation would not be

Table 17.1   *Scales of Evaluative Opinion for Handwriting and Signature Evidence (The categories do not necessarily correspond horizontally across the table)*

9-point scale* (SWGDOC, 2013)	7-point**	5-point scale (Ellen, 2006)	3-point scale (Categorical opinion)
Identification	Identification	Conclusive evidence did	Conclusive evidence did
Strong probability	Highly probable		
Probable		Supporting evidence did	
Indications	Probable		
No conclusion	Inconclusive	Inconclusive	Inconclusive
Indications did not	Probable did not	Supporting evidence did not	
Probably did not			
Strong probability did not	Highly probable did not	Conclusive evidence did not	Conclusive evidence did not
Elimination	Elimination		

* Based closely on that proposed by McAlexander *et al.* (1991)
** Such as that used by Mr Holland in Jarrold v Isajul *et al.* (2013)

appropriate. However, most QDEs do utilise a relatively coarse scale calibrated with verbal statements that may be used to convey the weight of evidence to the court, though there is no universal agreement on either the number of points or the form of the verbal statements attached to them and indeed the examiner may work to a scale specified by a third party. It appears that scales ranging from five to nine points have been used commonly across jurisdictions in recent years (see Table 17.1).

One argument for providing opinion, other than that which is conclusive, is that there will be other evidence presented to the court under consideration and, if the balance of opinion from the QDE is that the handwriting evidence, for example, supports that other testimony then that would be how it should be verbally presented. This then defines the five-point scale where additional points, referring to 'supporting evidence' in favour or against the proposition, are included.

For those scales with more than five points, the gradations are written in qualitative probabilistic terms that represent the degree of confidence that the QDE has in the validity of their conclusion, based not on statistical considerations but on scientific principles and their experienced judgement. A nine-point scale has been specified in the SWGDOC Standard Terminology for Expressing Conclusions of Forensic Document Examiners (2013) where additional, but limited, guidance is provided to enable the QDE to select the appropriate scale point. These include comments such as when 'strong probability' is used it implies that the examiner is 'virtually certain' of an identification or elimination conclusion with only 'some critical feature' absent, whereas more doubt in the mind of the QDE might lead to a statement such as:

'It is my opinion, on the basis of examination of the defendant's handwriting, that he is probably the source of the questioned material.'

Nevertheless, it is acknowledged that some QDEs may not wish to work with the three intermediate levels of probability offered by this scale, thereby reducing it to a seven-point or even to a five-point scale. It is not clear that such fine distinctions would have any real impact on the court's deliberations on this evidence; would the jury appreciate that the statement given above was two scale points below an identification of authorship? Indeed, the use of such extended scales has been criticised in the courts, for example in US v Starzecpyzel. It follows that a five-point scale is often the most useful and effective in court though it should be noted that this may take either the 'supporting evidence' or 'probably' verbal format.

As Ellen (2006) has pointed out, in formatting their evaluative statement, the QDE should give some consideration to clarity of expression by balancing a probabilistic state-ment of attribution against one on an alternative source, for example:

> 'There is supporting evidence that the defendant was the source of the questioned handwriting but the possibility of its originating from someone else should not be excluded.'

Despite these scales, as we shall see, in practice examiners frequently use variants and combinations of the terms given in Table 17.1. The SWGDOC (2013) guidelines also wisely provide advice on the avoidance of other terms that may be misinterpreted by the court. Not unexpectedly, these include 'could have', 'consistent with', 'possible' as distinct from 'probable', 'reason to believe', 'qualified identification' and surprisingly, 'inconclu-sive'. SWGDOC notes that 'no conclusion' is preferable to 'inconclusive', which it believes may be misconstrued by the court, though there is no evidence that this particular difficulty has emerged in the United Kingdom.

To illustrate how the QDE presents testimony to the court and how competing opinions are resolved, some pertinent examples of cases reaching the appeal courts in Australia and in the United Kingdom will be reviewed.

17.3   Jarrold v Isajul and Others 2013

The Jarrolds emigrated to Australia from Wales, but lived largely apart, both in the United Kingdom and in Australia, separating in 2006. However in 2006, Mr Jarrold sold the Australian property keeping all the proceeds, as he alleged he had obtained a signed power of attorney dated 5th June 2006, from his wife, authorising him to do so. She agreed that, at a meeting earlier that year in Wales, he had asked her to sign such a document but that she had refused. In 2012 Mrs Jarrold took her ex-husband and a number of others involved in the house sale, including the state registrar of land titles, to court, claiming one half legal interest in the pro-ceeds from the sale of this property and alleging that Mr Jarrold had forged her signature on the power of attorney. The trial was concerned with a number of circumstantial issues, in addition to the forensic examination of the signature on the document, the examination of which was hindered as the original document was lost, only a photocopy being available. This precluded a full analysis of the fluency and fine detail of the ink line in the signature.

Three QDEs contributed testimony on the signature: Dr Strach (following from his colleague Mr Westwood) was called by Mrs Jarrold, Mr Holland by the Registrar and Mr Lacroix by Mr Jarrold. All three experts were provided with samples of writing from Mr and Mrs Jarrold, both signatures and handwriting, and asked to consider, not only whether the questioned signature originated from Mrs Jarrold herself, but also whether it had been forged by Mr Jarrold. All three examiners reached different conclusions and under cross-examination other issues affecting the weight to be attached to their testimonies, were debated.

17.3.1   Dr Strach's Testimony

This examination had been started by a colleague, Mr Westwood, and then passed to Strach after a preliminary report had been written. He confirmed that there were a large number of dissimilarities between the questioned and reference signatures, leading to the conclusion that the former was an 'abnormal version' of Mrs Jarrold's style of signature and hence that it was 'unlikely to have been written' by her. In support, he stated that:

> '... the presence of differences, in particular when present in large number and/or as repeated differences, is of paramount importance in arriving at a scientific and logical conclusion'
>
> [Jarrold v Isajul *et al.*, 2013, paragraph 596]

He added that the questioned signature was not produced by a tracing technique but rather it had been formed by freehand imitation. On the basis that someone else had forged her signature, he stated that the evidence:

> '... was supportive of the proposition that the signature could be attributed to Mr Jarrold but ... that this was far from a certain conclusion.'
>
> [Jarrold v Isajul *et al.*, 2013, paragraph 38]

Under cross-examination it was suggested that, due to Westwood's initial work, Strach had not undertaken an independent examination of the documents and that his testimony was biased, as he had carried out the work after reading Westwood's report that had come to a similar conclusion. The judge observed that, although Strach had indeed examined the evidence himself and had made more extensive observations, he had arrived at largely the same conclusions and his report contained passages based largely on those from the earlier report. He concluded that this testimony had been:

> '... affected by a lack of independence and that he [Strach] had formed the view that Mr Westwood's conclusions were correct before he had conducted his own examination of the primary evidence. I have taken these findings into account in assessing the weight to be attributed to his conclusions ...'
>
> [Jarrold v Isajul *et al.*, 2013, paragraph 631]

17.3.2   Mr Holland's Testimony

This expert provided two reports, the second almost a year after the first and based on a wider range of reference writing. The two reports reached quite different conclusions. After initially concluding that it was 'highly probable' that Mrs Jarrold was the originator of the questioned signature, his revised opinion was that it was 'highly probable' that she was not. He justified this dramatic change of view on the difficulties in establishing the range of variation from a limited supply of control writing, stating that:

> '... the provision of additional samples had enabled him to conclude that the dissimilarities were not in fact variations common with other signatures, but rather differences, meaning that it was 'highly probable' that the questioned signature was written by someone else.'
>
> [Jarrold v Isajul *et al.*, 2013, paragraph 639]

As he formulated his evaluation on a seven-point scale, this change amounted moving from point 2 to point 6 on that scale. In the first report he did add that, without examining the original signed power of attorney, he could not provide a 'definite opinion'. He also stated that it was 'highly probable' that Mr Jarrold was not the source of the signature, due to 'significant dissimilarities', whereas later, he amended this to being unable to reach an opinion on that question.

Under cross-examination, the justification for his significant change of view was challenged and it was questioned whether any opinion at either of these scale points was valid, given it was reached from working on a photocopied document.

The judge praised the independence of Holland in confirming a view that was contrary to that of the Registrar who engaged him, but noted that he did not comment in his first report on any limitations to his opinion resulting from the small sample size of reference writing. He concluded:

> 'In assessing the weight to be attributed to Mr Holland's evidence, I consider it to be relevant that Mr Holland's final conclusions are the opposite of those expressed in his first report. The fact that Mr Holland changed his opinion inevitably invites the question, how much confidence can be placed in his present conclusions, if even a 'highly probable' conclusion is susceptible of being reversed on the basis of new evidence?'
>
> [Jarrold v Isajul *et al.*, 2013, paragraph 654]

17.3.3   Mr Lacroix's Testimony

A preliminary report from the third expert witness concluded that there was 'qualified support' for the proposition that the questioned signature originated from Mrs Jarrold. However, in his final report, produced shortly after a meeting between the three handwriting examiners, he stated that his opinion was that the evidence was inconclusive as to the authorship of the signature. Lacroix mapped his evaluation on to a five-point scale going from very strong evidence for the proposition to very strong evidence against it. He justified this conclusion (point 3 on his scale) on the basis of all the control writing available to him and on the limitations imposed from working from a photocopy of the questioned document.

> 'There is an elementary information deficit with respect to the nature of lines, pressure and the flow and direction of movement, all of which constitute crucial elements for an analysis to determine the origin of a given specimen of handwriting and signatures.'
>
> [Jarrold v Isajul *et al.*, 2013, paragraph 661]

He expressed a similar opinion on the proposition that the signature had been forged by Mr Jarrold. Under cross-examination, it was suggested that Lacroix lacked experience, that he had made some errors and overlooked some detail in his examination of the documents. Whilst acknowledging that he was less experienced than the other two experts, the judge did not agree that he lacked sufficient expertise to fulfil his role as a documents examiner.

17.3.4   The Appeal Court Judge's Conclusion

In summarising the testimony from all three, the judge concluded that the balance was towards Mrs Jarrold not being the author of the signature. However, that implied that it was forged and that could only reasonably have been done by Mr Jarrold. However, the evidence for that was less convincing, adding that:

> '... a lack of similarities between Mr Jarrold's handwriting and the questioned signature, however, tends to tell against the conclusion that the signature was forged.'
>
> [Jarrold v Isajul *et al.*, 2013, paragraph 695]

As far as weight of evidence was concerned, all three had commented on the limitations imposed from working with a photocopy, particularly in using the full dynamic range of the scale in any evaluation. In addition, the judge considered that all three examiners had lost some of the confidence of the court in formulating and communicating their conclusions, and that needed to be reflected in the significance attached to their testimony: the lack of independence shown by Strach, the dramatic change in opinion expressed by Holland and the errors and mis-observations of Lacroix. When combining the forensic evidence with other circumstantial evidence in the case, the judge declared that Mrs Jarrold had not satisfied the burden of proof that was required.

> 'The expert evidence, taken together, does not displace the very grave doubts I have regarding the lay evidence relied on to prove that Mrs Jarrold did not sign the power of attorney. Expert evidence must not be considered in isolation but along with all of the evidence. Proof cannot be found 'as a result of a mere mechanical comparison of probabilities'.'
>
> [Jarrold v Isajul *et al.*, 2013, paragraph 701]

Some of the 'lay evidence' concerned the meetings and circumstances around the time of the alleged signing of the power of attorney and apparent contradictions in the statements and evidence provided to the court during the trial. On this basis, Mrs Jarrold appealed and, at the hearing in 2015, it was established that the judge had misinterpreted her phone bill thereby incorrectly casting doubt on parts of her testimony. This appeal was successful and a re-trial was ordered.

17.4   Gale v Gale 2010

The death in May 2007 of Vera Gale initiated a probate action between her two children over the authenticity of three codicils to her will, allegedly signed by the deceased in 2002, 2004 and 2005. In her later years, Mrs Gale had suffered from Alzheimer's disease and had shown increasing signs of mental confusion during that time. The codicils related to the intention to leave her house and contents solely to her daughter, rather than the whole estate being split equally between the siblings. Gale's daughter shared the house with her mother. The signature on all codicils was witnessed by Mrs Gale's cleaner and by a man who occasionally acted as her driver. Her daughter sought to prove the authenticity of these codicils at a hearing in the Chancery Division of the High Court of England and Wales in 2010, at which her son claimed that his mother did not have the testamentary capacity at that time to execute them. In addition, there were a number of relevant handwritten notes from Gale, including document 574(9) dated 2005, specifying conditions for herself and daughter while living together in her house. A major part of the debate focused on forensic examination of all of these documents.

The court established from medical evidence that around early 2002 Gale was mentally capable of making decisions about her will, whereas by February 2004 this was not the case. After cross-examination in court, the judge ruled that evidence from both the witnesses to her signatures was unreliable and little confidence could be placed on the presence of their signatures on the documents.

17.4.1   ESDA Analysis

The 2004 codicil was subjected to ESDA examination and revealed indented writing, which corresponded to that on document 574(9), the note handwritten in 2005 by Gale. This implied that the codicil had been underneath this latter paper when Gale produced the writing. However, careful examination of the ESDA trace revealed that where the ink writing on 574(9) and the indentations crossed, it was the dark line corresponding to the indentation that was broken and the ink line, which predominated. This implied that the writing was added after the indentations, in other words after 2005 and contrary to the date of February 2004 on the codicil. It should be noted that this testimony was not delivered as a categorical evaluation rather that it was 'likely' that this was the explanation for these observations; the weight of this evidence was possibly enhanced by the judge's view that the QDE, Mr Handy, was a 'careful and impressive witness'. A second expert witness, Miss Marsh, was largely in agreement with this conclusion.

17.4.2   Signature Analysis

The analysis of the signatures on the three codicils was concerned with two issues: firstly, were they written by Mrs Gale, and secondly, were they written coincidently with the dates on these documents? The deterioration in her health over this period was reflected in her capacity to write and to produce clear, consistent signatures. Reference samples of her known signature from dates over the years 2002 – 2005 were used by Handy in his examination of those on the codicils. Indications of deterioration include tremor and pen-lifts on the ink line due to poor pen control. It was clear, even to the judge, that all the questioned signatures were quite dissimilar to the reference signatures at the start of this time period and bore a greater similarity to those from later on. Handy concluded that these observations provided 'very strong evidence' for the proposition that Gale did not sign the 2002 codicil, or at least not before her writing deteriorated from 2004 onwards.

However, the expert's examination went further. Handy examined the pen lifts and tremor in the ink line under the microscope and made the following observations:

'Within ink lines I noted locations where the pen has been raised and replaced in close proximity. This observation was evidence of good pen control in comparison with the poor pen control suggested by the signatures' overall appearance.
Parts of the tremor in pen lines appear 'unnatural' comprising of relatively small pen movements, particularly on document 2. The 'M' on this document contained a number of very light pen lines.'

[Gale v Gale, 2010, paragraph 113]

On this basis, he concluded that the signatures on all three codicils were not made by Gale and that there was 'conclusive' evidence that they were forgeries.

'The signatures on the three Codicils were not made by a person who lacked pen control due to age/infirmity as suggested by their overall appearance.'

[Gale v Gale, 2010, paragraph 113]

Miss Marsh, also examined the signatures and included a further reference example from 2002, not initially considered by Handy, and that showed greater deterioration in the writing. She focused on this as extending the range of variability in Gale's signature at that time and consequently arrived at the opinion that the evidence was 'inconclusive' as to whether or not Gale was responsible for these signatures. When confronted with this, Handy agreed that, if this example were included, he would need to amend his evaluation to 'very strong evidence' in support of the proposition that the signatures were not written by Gale. He added that direct comparison showed that this additional reference signature from 2002 was nevertheless more fluent than that on the allegedly contemporary codicil.

On the observations on the pen lifts, Marsh disagreed with Handy, observing that they were 'entirely consistent' with a writer possessing poor pen control. He responded by remarking that for an occasional instance that might be true but the number of times these were observed and the accuracy with which the pen was replaced in almost all cases clearly implied the work of someone with good motor control and that this itself was quite inconsistent with the deteriorating writing skills of Gale, had these signatures indeed been genuine. Marsh was asked directly about her evaluation by counsel and whether the signatures were forged:

> "'Are you saying, you can't say yes and you can't say no?" Her answer was: "Yes. You shouldn't come out of "the inconclusive category" unless you're sure".'
>
> [Gale v Gale, 2010, paragraph 127]

In contrast, Handy's final statement was that the signatures were:

> '... "definitely not hers" and that the possibility that she made them is so remote that it can effectively be ignored'
>
> [Gale v Gale, 2010, paragraph 127]

Faced with this conflict of opinion from the experts, the judge ruled that he preferred the evidence of Handy. The crucial evidence related to the outcome that the 2002 codicil was not authentic, as Gale did not have, in any case, the testamentary capacity to have made the two later ones. On this basis, he rejected the claim made by Gale's daughter.

In reaching this verdict, the judge added that he considered the evidence on the signatures to be not as conclusive as he would wish, and commented that he had to rely solely on the testimony conveyed by the experts, as the absence of any enlarged images of the pen lifts precluded him having 'the comfort of exercising my own observations as well'. This is an interesting example of a judge's view on the process of signature examination and the role of the expert.

17.5   The Bridgewater Four (R v Hickey and Others) 1997

The murder of paperboy, Carl Bridgewater, when he apparently came upon an armed robbery at Yew Tree Farm, Stourbridge in 1978, led, not only to one of the most significant miscarriages of justice in the United Kingdom, but also to uncovering corrupt practices by police officers in their investigation of the crime. Another farm burglary in the same area later that year, but one without firearms being discharged, led to the arrest of three suspects, Vincent Hickey, Michael Molloy and Jim Robinson. A fourth man, Vincent's cousin Michael Hickey was later included as a suspect in the Yew Tree Farm incident.

The men were interviewed separately at different police stations. Events took a sudden turn when Molloy was presented with a signed confession to the Yew Tree Farm murder, apparently signed by Vincent Hickey. This led to police obtaining a further confession from him and later to the trial and conviction in 1979, of all four for involvement in the killing of Carl Bridgewater, with Hickey and Robinson being found guilty of the murder itself and receiving life sentences. All four continued to protest their innocence and, despite a failed appeal in 1989, support for their case as a miscarriage of justice increased, endorsed by fresh forensic evidence following examination of the confessions and other documents. Consequently, with the support of the CCRC, a second appeal was agreed and heard in 1997. Molloy had died in prison in 1981. This case involves opinion on writing speed, as well as on signature analysis and ESDA examination.

17.5.1   Molloy's 'Confession'

In his alleged confession, following interrogation at Wobourne police station and being confronted with the alleged confession from Hickey (exhibit 56), Molloy admitted to taking part with the others in the burglary at Yew Tree Farm, which led to the murder of Carl Bridgewater and made a statement to that effect (exhibit 54). Subsequent ESDA analysis of part of the front page of exhibit 54, which had been protected by the evidence label, revealed indented writing produced prior to the writing of the statement itself, and this included a handwritten caution and a signature purporting to be that of Vincent Hickey. The format of that statement corresponded with the statement forms used at Wobourne but not those at Redditch police station where Hickey was held.

Expert analysis, by Dr Hardcastle and Mr Radley, of the handwriting and signature on the ESDA trace was impaired due to its not being the original document, nevertheless it was clear that the signature was not that of Hickey. Request handwriting samples were taken from twelve police officers who had contact with either of the two suspects, including DCs Perkins and Leeke who had taken Molloy's statement, and the document examiners were asked to address the proposition that some or all of the indented writing in exhibit 54 had originated from police personnel. The expert opinion was that there were no significant differences between the indented handwriting and that provided by DC Leeke and significant differences between it and the writing of the eleven other officers.

The signature provided more limited scope for comparison with some characteristics common to the writing of DC Perkins as well as some differences. On this basis, Hardcastle concluded that the signature could have been written by Perkins, whereas Radley said in his oral evidence that:

> 'There is a broad correlation of most detail with the writing of DC Perkins, although there are some points of difference. Of the samples I have examined DC Perkins' writing matches most closely the writing of "Vincent Hickey" and he is the most likely author of the "Vincent Hickey" entry.'
>
> [R v Hickey *et al.*, 1997, part 5 of 15]

Additional testimony, from an expert psychologist, identified that a third of the clauses in police notes of the oral interviews taken by DS Robbins, were identical to the written confession (exhibit 54), a fact that was highly unlikely if the two records were produced independently. Further, evidence relating to the amount of writing it is possible to record within a specified time was also given, both by Hardcastle and by a second handwriting consultant. DC Perkins claimed that it had taken twenty minutes for him to write Molloy's statement at his dictation, and for it to be read through and checked by Molloy. From this

Hardcastle estimated Perkin's writing speed at 170 characters per minute (cpm), a rate of writing that he had not previously encountered. The second expert estimated 214 cpm and both agreed that, in fact, the appearance of the writing did not support it being produced quickly, far less at such impossible speeds. A similar conclusion was reached with regard to the typed version of the police notes taken at the interview. The appeal court judge concluded that:

> '... it is most improbable, if not impossible, that the interview as recounted by DC Perkins at the appellant's trial and the taking of the statement Exhibit 54 occurred as that witness told the jury they did.'

> [R v Hickey *et al.*, 1997, part 5 of 15]

Consequently the appeal court ruled that the police officers involved in questioning Molloy had used deceit to obtain the alleged confession and that this oppressive action made such a confession inadmissible as evidence. It followed that the verdict reached at the trial was a miscarriage of justice and the appeal was upheld. Thus the 'Bridgwater Four' were freed and the murderer of Carl Bridgewater has never been found.

17.6   R v Previte 2005

The conviction of Ian Previte for the murder of English tourist Caroline Stuttle in April 2002, by throwing her from a bridge over the Burnett River in Queensland, Australia, was the subject of an appeal in 2005 where an unusual example of handwriting evidence was debated. At the trial, the prosecution presented a piece of apparent graffiti found on a table in a picnic area near to the bridge, as allegedly written by Previte; it said:

> 'I Throw The girl of The Brige I am sorry'

> [R v Previte, 2005 paragraph 8]

Previte's counsel claimed that the trial judge had erred in admitting the opinion of a handwriting expert who testified that Previte was the likely source of the graffiti.

Two, fully qualified handwriting experts gave evidence at the trial. Both used five pages of specimen writing taken from Previte while in prison. Mr Marheine, an independent expert, believed that the graffiti comprised too few characters of 'very simple, childish handwriting' to enable a comparison, or to say whether all the writing was the work of one person, and so arrived at an inconclusive opinion. He informed the court that he worked with what was essentially a nine-point scale with certainty at the top and three further gradations – highly probable, probable and possible – leading down to a neutral outcome. In contrast, the police QDE, Mr Hettiarachchi, used a five-point scale, with only one scale point between certainty and being unable to reach a conclusion and this was phrased as 'indications ... '. He arrived at the opinion that:

> '... there were indications those words were likely to have been written by the appellant.'

> [R v Previte, 2005 paragraph 8]

Under cross-examination, Hettiarachchi explained that in comparing similarities and dissimilarities between the reference writing and the graffiti, he attributed the latter to either the style of the writer or the use the broad tipped pen. His comment that the writer's tendency to start some words in the graffiti with a capital letter was matched in Previte's writing by his use of capitalisation on his name and the word 'Court', was regarded by the appeal court as less than plausible. On being asked if there could have been more than one author of the graffiti, he replied that he could not answer that without reference writing from potential suspects. This prompted the appeal court judge to comment that Hettiarachchi:

> '... approached his task with a view to demonstrating that whatever was provided to him by way of sample handwriting had points in common with what was on the table; not by starting with the questioned material and first asking what, if anything, could be made of it.'
>
> [R v Previte, 2005 paragraph 52]

Despite the defence counsel summarising this testimony as having so many deficiencies that it should carry little weight with the jury, the trial judge admitted the evidence of Mr Hettiarachchi, declaring that it was for the jury to decide if Previte was the writer of the graffiti on the basis of what they had heard. At appeal, the role of the experts was viewed as providing opinion to assist the jury in reaching their decision even if that opinion was in some way unsatisfactory and this endorsed the view at the original trial. Indeed, as far as handwriting evidence was concerned the appeal court judge went further:

> '... the jury's function was not merely to decide whether it accepted the evidence of one or other of the experts. It was entitled, as the trier of fact in the case, to look at the disputed handwriting against the samples and to form its own conclusions.'
>
> [R v Previte, 2005 paragraph 53]

So as far as this judge was concerned, the task of handwriting analysis was one in which the jury members could take an active part, thereby bypassing the opinion of the expert witness if they so wished.

17.7   Admissibility and Other Issues in Handwriting and Signature Evidence

Although the publication of Questioned Documents by Albert Osborn in 1910 laid the foundations for the forensic examination of documents, particularly in the United States, it was not until that author's testimony in State v Hauptmann (1935) – the Lindbergh Baby Case – proved crucial in identifying Hauptmann as the author of the ransom notes, that handwriting and signature evidence moved into the mainstream of forensic evidence in the eyes of the courts. Despite being an established area of forensic expertise, fifty years further on, forensic document examination in the United States came under scrutiny on several fronts with a view to questioning its admissibility on grounds of reliability, whether it was scientific, and indeed, whether it was an area of expertise outside the common knowledge of the court.

Unlike in the United Kingdom, the pool of expert witnesses called to give evidence in handwriting analysis in the United States, has been quite diverse, including some whose main interest was in deducing personality and psychological traits from an individual's writing (graphologists), as well as many educated and trained in the Osborn tradition, and including everything in between. This diversity proved confusing to a legal profession who were largely unaware of these distinctions, with the result that the appropriate expert was not always assigned to a case, with the obvious consequences for testimony. Even before Daubert, some were questioning whether handwriting and signature analysis was indeed an area of scientific or professional expertise (e.g. see Risinger et al., 1989). Evidence for this was cited as being the absence of an academic base for the subject, little if any published research, no established standards for training and no recognised professional accrediting body. Handwriting expertise was gained thorough apprenticeship or even in some cases self-tuition. The American Board of Forensic Document Examiners, established in 1977, is a certifying body for this discipline.

Indeed, it has been questioned whether the expert should provide the court with opinion that the court itself could acquire through direct inspection of the evidence. Are the similarities or dissimilarities between signatures, for example, not obvious to the layperson without the need for the intervention of an expert? Proficiency tests are often promoted, as a means to establish the expertise of the professional witness and to determine whether the expert provides evidential value, beyond the conclusions of the legal professional or jury member who might directly inspect the evidence. There have been several instances where academic studies of blind trials, intended to evaluate the success rate of QDEs and estimate an error rate, have contributed to the court debate. Indeed, some of these have included comparison with lay people asked to carry out the same tasks. These studies themselves have been debated and criticised in the literature, highlighting the difficulties in designing such experiments, and such research is ongoing.

For those states under the Frye jurisdiction, the testimony of QDEs was routinely admitted, as it was an established area of expert evidence. Indeed, documents analysis was one of the seven founding sections when the American Academy of Forensic Sciences (AAFS) was established in 1949. With the advent of Rule of Evidence 702 in 1975, such evidence continued to be admitted quite readily. Inevitably, the scientific basis of handwriting and signature analysis came under scrutiny under Daubert and later in the NAS Report (2009). Yet, in spite of this ongoing debate, it has continued to be admitted, for example, by being recognised as an area of specialist expertise, rather than one necessarily with a scientific basis.

17.8   Admissibility and Evaluation in the US Courts

In a few notable cases, the judge has limited the expert's testimony; for example, to describing only their observations on the documents thereby precluding an evaluative concluding statement (US v Hines, 1999) or has restricted opinion to a categorical statement on the authorship of the document (US v Starzecpyzel, 1995). Two examples of such instances will be discussed here.

17.8.1   US v Starzecpyzel 1995

Discussion of this, the first challenge to a questioned document examiner's testimony, post-Daubert, is instructive, not because of the details of the case itself – a dispute over the authenticity of signatures – but because it identifies and critically reviews many of the key issues in the forensic process itself. Roberta and Eileen Starzecpyzel were accused of effectively stealing over one hundred works of art from Roberta's elderly aunt, by forging her signature on documents allegedly giving them the authority to sell the paintings and keep the proceeds. The defendants challenged the testimony of the QDE who had concluded that the signatures were not those of the aunt, on the grounds that his expertise was not reliable, since the scientific methodology had never been validated according to the criteria set by Daubert.

When the QDE, Mary Kelly, was cross-examined at appeal on the various stages of the process of handwriting or signature examination her responses were clear, but when pressed on the detailed criteria invoked by the examiner in reaching a conclusion about an aspect of the analysis, her justifications were based on the experience of the examiner rather than on objective criteria. For example, on the required quantity of reference samples of writing:

'Q: How is the notion of sufficient quantity judged? Ms. Kelly: It's based on the training and experience of the particular examiner. Q: So there are no standard measures of sufficient quantity? Ms. Kelly: There is no way to measure that, no.'

[US v Starzecpyzel, 1995]

In a similar fashion, she was unable to provide objective definitions of what comprised minor and major differences in any characteristic in writing. The court regarded these as essential criteria in identifying natural variation in one individual's writing from that of another. Kelly insisted that, when provide with an adequate amount of reference writing, the QDE, 'through unspecified methods', could arrive at a reliable conclusion about the origin of the questioned writing. When pressed on the scientific research underpinning her area of expertise she was unable to provide the court with journal citations.

'Ms. Kelly's inability to cite such studies, given her high standing within the FDE community and the substantial period of time that the government had to prepare both its case and its witness, leads to an inference that there are few useful scientific studies relevant to forensic document examination.'

[US v Starzecpyzel, 1995]

In contrast, academic experts called by the defence focused on the absence of validation studies and error rates for handwriting and signature analysis and that there was no strong statistical evidence for or against either the reliability or the underlying principles of forensic document examination. Indeed, Professor Saks quoted from studies, which, he alleged, revealed that the conclusions of QDEs were little different to those of lay people who had examined the same evidence.

After reviewing this evidence, the ruling from the court on the scientific basis of forensic document examination was quite categorical:

'In sum, the testimony at the Daubert hearing firmly established that forensic document examination, despite the existence of a certification program, professional journals and other trappings of science, cannot, after Daubert, be regarded as "scientific ... knowledge."'

[US v Starzecpyzel, 1995]

However, the court then considered this evidence under Federal Rule of Evidence 702 and concluded that, though it had judged the signature comparison inadmissible as scientific evidence, it could be admitted as non-scientific evidence as long as it 'assists the trier of fact'. Kelly had convinced the court that signature analysis was based on a body of knowledge, and that an experienced examiner could utilise that knowledge to reach a valid opinion on the authenticity of a questioned signature. These were sufficient grounds for the evidence to be admitted without reference to Daubert. In an appendix to the ruling, the judge made the following remark about the QDE:

> '… although forensic document examiners may work in "laboratories," and may rely on textbooks with titles like "The Scientific Examination of Documents," forensic document examiners are not scientists — they are more like artisans, that is, skilled craftsmen.'
>
> [US v Starzecpyzel, 1995]

Nevertheless, although the examiner's conclusion was based on the identification of points of comparison and establishing discrete similarities and dissimilarities, the court believed that this was not necessarily a valid basis for an evaluation on a scale of opinion, such as that based on nine points, and hence the court could decide to exclude such testimony. In other words, the QDE could normally provide only a categorical opinion as to the authenticity or otherwise of a questioned signature. This demotion of non-scientific evidence, as far as admissibility is concerned, was effectively revoked following the Kumho Tire v Carmichael ruling in 1999.

17.8.2   US v Velasquez 1995

In the same year, another US appeal court, appeared to take a different view to that in Starzecpyzel, though once again admitting the evidence of the QDE. Edwin Velasquez was tried and convicted on a series of drug-related offences in 1991. The guilty verdict passed on two of his accomplices at the same trial was based largely on evidence from the QDE, Ms Bonjour, that their handwriting was found on labels used to ship batches of drugs. In 1995, an appeal was considered on the grounds that the trial judge had refused to admit expert evidence from Prof Denbeaux, which sought to challenge the admissibility of the handwriting evidence. It was argued that, despite his academic expertise, Denbeaux had no casework experience, had never been retained as an expert witness and further that, by receiving the evidence of Bonjour, the trial court had indeed accepted the admissibility of her evidence.

In reviewing the Daubert criteria, the appeal court in Velasquez acknowledged the ruling in Starzecpyzel, yet in considering the testimony of Bonjour, it appeared to follow the guidance in Rule 702, 'in an exercise of caution', as to whether handwriting evidence was 'scientific, technical or other specialized knowledge'. In doing so, it first focused on Bonjour's credentials as a QDE and then reviewed her methodology for carrying out the analysis. She described the assessment of the questioned and reference writing as to its quantity and quality in terms of class and individual characteristics, and listed some examples of those characteristics, before adding:

> 'Every single thing in that writing is a characteristic. They, in order to effect an identification, they have to be demonstrated and if they do not match exactly, I have to have a good reason for why they don't…. Once I have made the comparison, I weigh the evidence I have seen and determine whether or not this is a match or probably a match or I don't know or it is not a match.'
>
> [US v Velasquez, 1995]

Finally, she confirmed that this methodology was followed, not only by her in every handwriting examination, but also by those other questioned document examiners with whom she was acquainted. On this basis, the court admitted her evidence, and this was confirmed by the appeal court. In this case, both courts were content with this level of detail in the methodology and did not interrogate her on the extent of subjective or objective criteria in her analysis.

However, in the same way, the appeal court argued that Denbeaux' testimony should also have been admitted at the original trial. He possessed specialized knowledge that enabled him to critically review standards and the methodology of others, even though he was not experienced in casework. In particular, his criticisms had been subjected to peer review, as he had published work as a co-author with Professor Saks. The appeal court proposed that his opinion was relevant and if admitted could have influenced the jury in their evaluation of the handwriting evidence.

> 'His criticisms of the field of handwriting analysis generally, as well as Ms. Bonjour's analysis in this case, would have assisted the jury in determining the proper weight to accord Ms. Bonjour's testimony.'
>
> [US v Velasquez, 1995]

So once again, a court when considering admissibility, decided to allow the opinion while retaining the right to consider any challenges to it when deciding on the weight of the evidence. Thus the appeal was accepted and a re-trial was ordered.

17.9   Conclusions

The admissibility of opinion from the questioned documents' examiner appears to have survived challenges over recent years from both legal and academic critics in the United States while remaining largely unchallenged elsewhere. Nevertheless, difficulties remain in responding to questions where subjective judgements have been made using undefined criteria, and where examiners provide conflicting testimony. Despite attempts to standardise scales of opinion, there is considerable variation in its presentation to the court and how it relates to the observations of the expert examiner.

References

Allen M. (2016). *Foundations of Forensic Document Analysis: Theory and Practice*. Wiley-Blackwell, Chichester, UK.

American Board of Forensic Document Examiners (Online). (2015) http://www.abfde.org/index.html [Accessed 11 November 2015].

Barrett v Benn and others [2012] 2 All ER 920

Ellen D. (2006). *The Scientific Examination of Documents; Methods and Techniques, 3rd Ed.* Taylor and Francis. Boca Raton, Florida.

Gale v Gale [2010] EWHC 1575 (Ch), HC02871

Jarrold v Isajul and others [2013] VSC 461

Jarrold v The Registrar of Titles and T Jarrold [2015] VSCA 45

McAlexander T.V., Beck J. and Dick R. (1991). The standardization of handwriting opinion terminology. *Journal of Forensic Sciences*, 36(2), 311–319.

National Research Council: Strengthening Forensic Science in the United States: A Path Forward, Document 228091 [Online]. (2009). Available at http://www.nap.edu/catalog/12589.html [Accessed 10 October 2015].

R v Hickey and others [1997] Court of Appeal (Crim Div), Official Transcript

R v Maynard and others [2002] EWCA Crim 1942

R v Previte [2005] QCA 95

Risinger D.M., Denbeaux M.P. and Saks M.J. (1989). Exorcism of ignorance as a proxy for rational knowledge: The lessons of handwriting identification "expertise". *University of Pennsylvania Law Review*, 137, 731–792.

SWGDOC: Standard Terminology for Expressing Conclusions of Forensic Document Examiners [Online]. (2015). Available at: http://www.swgdoc.org/index.php/standards/published-standards [Accessed 11 November 2015].

US v Fujii, 152 F Supp 2d 939 (Illinois, ND III, 2000)

US v Hines, 55 F Supp 2d 62 (Massachusetts, 1999)

US v Saelee, 162 F Supp 2d 1097 (Alaska, 2001)

US v Starzecpyzel, 880 F Sup. 1027 (SDNY, 1995)

US v Velasquez, 64 F 3d 844 (US Virgin Islands 3d Cir 1995)

Further Reading

Giannelli P. and Imwinkelried E. (2000). Scientific Evidence: The fallout from Supreme Court's decision in Kumho Tires. *Criminal Justice*, 14, 12–19.

Moenssens A.A. (1996). Handwriting identification evidence in the post-Daubert world. *University of Missouri at Kansas City Law Review*, 66(2), 251–343.

Mnookin J.L. (2001). Scripting Expertise: The history of handwriting identification evidence and the judicial construction of reliability. *Virginia Law Review*, 87, 1723–1845.

Park R.C. (2008). Signature identification in the light of science and experience. *Hastings Law Journal*, 59, 1101–1157.

Risinger D.M. (2007). Cases involving the reliability of handwriting identification expertise since the decision in Daubert. *Tulsa Law Review*, 43(2), 477–595.

Risinger D.M with Saks M.J. (1997). Science and nonscience in the courts: Daubert meets handwriting identification expertise. *Iowa Law Review*, 82, 21–74.

18

Bloodstain Pattern Analysis

Bloodstain evidence is an area of forensic investigation that is subject to particular challenges as to its scientific basis and to the expertise of expert witnesses. The interpretation of bloodstain patterns has been viewed by some as matters of common sense, to the extent that the judge and the jury may be presented with the raw evidence and are expected to arrive at an evaluation, independent of the expert presenting the evidence. Challenges to this view are made harder by the paucity of relevant research underpinning much of this area of work and the unfamiliarity of many legal professionals with such evidence. This leads to bloodstain pattern evidence often being undervalued by the court.

This chapter starts with some introductory remarks about the nature of blood evidence, then the principal issues facing the courts are discussed and illustrated by a number of notable cases. Key issues include how science may inform expert opinion, approaches to the presentation and evaluation of bloodstain evidence, major debates on interpretation and dealing with disagreements between experts.

18.1 The Nature of Bloodstain Pattern Evidence

Bloodstain pattern analysis (BPA) encompasses the examination and interpretation of a wide range of forms of blood deposited at crime scenes, usually following a violent assault on or injury to an individual. It is virtually unique within the forensic subdisciplines as it is based on the combined principles of biology, physics and mathematics and, in most instances, a complex mixture of observations and measurements on the blood evidence is interpreted in terms of activity at the crime scene.

Forensic Evidence in Court: Evaluation and Scientific Opinion, First Edition. Craig Adam.
© 2016 John Wiley & Sons, Ltd. Published 2016 by John Wiley & Sons, Ltd.

The principles of BPA are described in a number of established texts, including those by James, Kish and Sutton (2005), Gardner and Bevel (2009), and Wonder (2014). The International Association of Bloodstain Pattern Analysts (IABPA) and the Special Working Group on Bloodstain Pattern Analysis (SWGSTAIN), both based in the United States, are active in enhancing practice through education, training and encouraging research, with the latter publishing guideline documents intended to set standards and promote best practice across the discipline. In the United Kingdom, the Forensic Science Regulator has recently developed a code of practice and conduct for BPA.

The classification of bloodstains and patterns and the terminology used by scientists to describe and communicate their observations are fundamental aspects of particular relevance to the current discussion. Briefly, bloodstain evidence may be assigned to one of the following broad categories:

- Patterns formed through the impact of blood on a surface where gravity provides the impetus (passive formation of stains)
- Patterns resulting from application of a force, in addition to gravity, and usually directly due to physical assault, such as impact spatter, cast-off patterns or expirated blood (active spatter)
- Patterns where blood is directly transferred on to a surface by contact
- Blood evidence that has been altered, through by some additional factor or factors, such as time, dilution, environment and physiological or physical changes

Classification is important, as debate around the interpretation of bloodstains may often focus on the appropriate classification for a pattern and hence what activity was responsible for generating the evidence.

18.2   Issues for BPA Expert Opinion in the Courts

18.2.1   The Scientific Basis of BPA

Fundamentally, the scientific basis of much of BPA is the physics of complex fluids (fluid dynamics or rheology) applied to blood and sometimes termed blood dynamics; there is also a need for some understanding of the biological and pathological nature of blood. The problem is not that this generic field is not well understood, which it mostly is, or that it is not quantitative, which fluid dynamics most certainly is, but that the scale of the application to blood evidence is so complex. For impact spatter, it is simply not possible to predict the number, size, speed and direction of all blood droplets released following a traumatic injury and the inverse problem of working back from the stains to understand the trauma in all its detail, is also an impossible challenge. Nevertheless, there are clearly many opportunities for fundamental research in this area that could eventually underpin and enhance the analysis and interpretation of blood evidence in forensic casework. Despite these difficulties, there appear to have been no significant cases where BPA has been deemed inadmissible as evidence under Frye or Daubert. Indeed, its admissibility may be attributed to the limited range of fairly straightforward scientific principles used in practice to interpret blood evidence, some of which are founded on fundamental physics but, for the most part, only in a fairly approximate or qualitative way.

These considerations mean that the expert rarely gives substantive technical detail in support of an interpretation, and this may lead to an impression in court that the testimony is based on simply a visual assessment of the pattern. This, of course, may lead the lawyers, judge and jury to ignore the expert and attempt their own interpretation and evaluation. This is dangerous, as most experts would agree that bloodstain pattern analysis is a much more complex and sophisticated process than simply looking to match a crime scene pattern to examples studied during training.

Only by analysing a pattern using fundamental principles can the expert establish possible scenarios, which may be weighed against each other, to arrive at a final opinion on the evidence. Further, where the scientist has carried out experiments, specifically to test the scientific basis of the interpretation of particular blood evidence (reconstruction), this has been viewed by the courts as strengthening that interpretation. The importance of this point is exemplified by the many examples where the courts have been presented with alternative explanations for the blood evidence from competing experts, such as whether fine/mist spatter originated from a gunshot wound, from expirated blood or from a high-pressure artery rupture.

The basis of testimony should be founded on accurate and detailed observations from the crime scene to establish the factual basis, leading to the logical development of an opinion on what the stains mean. Only the expert can satisfy both these requirements; unless the factual information is verified by the expert then no proper evaluation of the significance of this evidence can be provided to the court.

18.2.2   Who is the Expert?

As will be evident through the accounts of cases, testimony on blood evidence may be provided by individuals from a variety of backgrounds and bases of expertise. Across jurisdictions, there appear to be three categories of expert:

1. The law enforcement officer who has developed on the job experience and attended a number of short training courses in bloodstain pattern analysis and does not necessarily have a deep educational background in fundamental science.
2. The scientist, very often from a biology rather than a physics background, who works extensively in this area, both in laboratory and crime scene settings, has the facilities for casework experiments and has maintained an awareness of ongoing developments in the subject.
3. The medical professional, very often a pathologist, whose main expertise is cause of death and who may become involved in the interpretation of blood evidence, even to the extent of carrying out laboratory studies in some cases.

Each of these has a contribution to make but none is an ideal expert witness, in that all may have some limitations to their knowledge and expertise, particularly in their approach to the task of analysis and interpretation, and in the technical terminology they may use in communicating explanations and outcomes to the court. In each case, the balance between experience, training and academic background differs, so the question of whether the court should demand some minimum level of education in biology, physics and mathematics, for example, in order to admit expert testimony is a valid one. Indeed, the NRC Report commented specifically:

> 'This emphasis on experience over scientific foundations seems misguided, given the importance of rigorous and objective hypothesis testing and the complex nature of fluid dynamics.'
>
> [NRC Report, 2009, p. 178]

The report was also critical of the lack of a clear scientific basis in much reporting of BPA evidence to the courts.

'In general, the opinions of bloodstain pattern analysts are more subjective than scientific.'
[NRC Report, 2009, p. 178]

In reviewing examples, it is notable that often there is an absence of scientific precision and polish in the presentation of expert testimony and this may give the court the impression that the analysis and interpretation of BPA lacks a valid scientific basis. For example, compare the testimony of Paul Kirk in the Sheppard case as long ago as 1966 (section 18.3) with some of the other more recent examples to be discussed later.

The status and courtroom experience of the expert may also come into play, particularly when an experienced medical expert moves into providing BPA opinion. Rather than declaring evidence inadmissible, the courts may regard testimony presented by a relatively inexperienced witness as carrying less weight than that from a more established expert. Of course, as with some other forms of evidence, experts in BPA can overreach themselves by drawing more detailed conclusions than are justified by the observations at the scene.

Finally, the independence of the expert in BPA cases has been an issue in some jurisdictions, particularly where that expert is a law enforcement officer, often working alongside those pursuing the investigation for the prosecution.

18.2.3   The Courts' and Lawyers' Knowledge of BPA

BPA is relatively uncommon as evidence in the courts, particularly in the United Kingdom, and most legal professionals, and indeed judges, have limited experience in dealing with it. Consequently, it often appears only in a supporting role. Conceptually and in its contribution to legal debate it is quite unlike most other forms of forensic testimony. Hence, many lawyers may lack confidence in examining expert witnesses on BPA, in asking meaningful questions and in carrying out an in-depth cross-examination. This may happen, in part, because they are unfamiliar with the science and fail to appreciate both the potential and the limitations of the evidence. Sometimes the court may not realise the full potential that BPA could provide as evidence and hence might fail to give it due recognition in the debate. Conversely, the court needs to realise its own limitations and not attempt to interpret BPA without expert assistance, even in the most basic cases. For example, the NRC Report concluded that:

'The uncertainties associated with bloodstain pattern analysis are enormous.'
[NRC Report, 2009, p. 179]

Potentially, an informed defence barrister could educate the jury in the wide range of uncertainties and sources of error in BPA, so undermining the weight of the prosecution's evidence.

18.2.4   The Evaluation and Significance of BPA Evidence

Following observations and measurements at the crime scene, the expert interprets these data using scientific principles, thereby arriving at justifiable conclusions, and finally reviews these conclusions in the light of alternative explanations, uncertainties and experience to reach an evaluative statement on the significance of the evidence. At least this is what we might anticipate is the case. However, this is not always so.

Without a detailed understanding of how the conclusions are reached, a proper evaluation is not possible and unfortunately this is too frequently the case for BPA evidence. Alternative explanations may result in a debate as a duel between experts, rather than seen as an integral part of each expert's own evaluative process. In communicating the testimony, the expert risks the jury assigning a greater weight to it than is justified, particularly if it is presented as a convincing narrative of activity at the crime scene. If explanations are too simple and straightforward, the court's perception may be that the analysis is unsophisticated and lacking a scientific basis thereby reducing its evidential weight. Finally, the presentation of some testimony in categorical terms is not uncommon although this is not in line with current views on evaluation and presentation.

18.3   The Scientific Basis of Bloodstain Pattern Analysis: The Murder of Marilyn Sheppard

Although it is now mainly of historical interest, the murder of Marilyn Sheppard has the distinction of being the first case where bloodstain pattern testimony was systematically explained, and underpinned during cross-examination, by scientific explanations. Indeed, the evidence of the expert witness, Paul Kirk, at the second trial in 1966, has been described by Imwinkelried (2000) as the '… seminal event in the history of this forensic science in the United States …'.

Sam Sheppard discovered the body of his wife, Marilyn Sheppard, in her bedroom when he returned to their home in Bay Village, Ohio, in July 1954. She had been brutally assaulted around the head with a blunt instrument. There was extensive bloodstain evidence at the scene, including wounds to Sam Sheppard, which he said were due to his wrestling with an unknown intruder. Sam was arrested soon afterwards as the police found no evidence of a third person and believed the motive was related to his extramarital affairs; he had no satisfactory alibi and he had a large bloodstain on his trousers as well as small stains on his watch. At the trial in October there was no expert testimony presented on the blood evidence and the defence attorney had not assembled any significant evidence in support of Sheppard's case. Sheppard was found guilty of second-degree murder.

Shortly after the incident, Paul Kirk, Professor of Criminalistics at the University of California, Berkeley was granted access to the crime scene and carried out a detailed examination, resulting in a report that he published in April 1955, four months after the verdict. It is not clear why he was not called to the first trial. Following fresh evidence, including the identification of a potential alternative suspect and the finding of a potential weapon – a dented flashlight – on the nearby shore of Lake Erie, an appeal was successful and a second trial commenced in February 1966. At this trial, Paul Kirk's testimony, based on his clear and effective science-based explanations for the blood spatter evidence, was crucial in the defence achieving an acquittal for Sam Sheppard. At the start of his examination Kirk confirmed that, in all his criminalistics work, he carried out his own experiments to inform and underpin his subsequent court testimony. Here we shall focus on the key points presented by Kirk.

The victim was found lying on her bed and the blood spatter extended over all the surrounding walls, window and radiator. After describing his observations, Kirk proceeded to explain to the court what could be deduced from the shape of a single spatter stain and supported his account with reference to experiments that he himself had undertaken. These explanations detailed the effect of impact velocity and impact angle on the appearance of the stain and included a description of the formation of spine and cast-forward features. He based his interpretation on identifying the impact spatter pattern, arcs of stains corresponding to swing cast-off and patterns of larger stains arising from cessation cast-off. He carried out blood grouping tests on sample stains to confirm they were from the victim; interestingly he thereby identified one solitary stain that could not have originated from either of the Sheppards. He discriminated between spatter and transfer stains when testifying on the blood found on Sheppard's watch and declared that the blood on Sheppard's trousers was deposited after they were wet due to the blood's hemolysed condition.

His principal conclusions, which supported the defence case, related to the position of the killer and the trajectory of the blows:

> 'The killer was positioned at the lower end of the bed on the east side, the northeast corner of that bed, where he was standing, in the region which is delineated by the absence of blood; the head being in the position something like I am indicating, slightly to the west side of the bed and down about halfway. And this, used as a center, would place the person who intercepted all the blood flying in one direction, because there was no blood in this region. This is the only place in the room he could have stood.'
>
> [Trial transcript of Sam Sheppard, 1966, p.1090]

He examined the patterns in more detail to evaluate hypotheses about the handedness of the assailant. The absence of cast-off spatter on the ceiling confirmed that the trajectories of the blows were largely in a horizontal plane. He concluded that the blows had been struck by a left-handed person and, when challenged on whether the alternative of back-handed action by a right-handed person was possible, he countered that the observations could not be explained by the more limited length of swing that implied.

Throughout the ninety-four pages of direct examination and twelve pages of relatively brief cross-examination comprising the transcript, it is clear that the scientific authority and logical explanations in Kirk's testimony, and the absence of any substantive challenge from a second expert witness or indeed from the prosecution attorney in the cross-examination, contributed strong support to the defence case and to Sam Sheppard's acquittal.

Sam Sheppard died less than four years after his acquittal but that was not the end of the story. In 1997, Sheppard's son filed a civil action against the Cuyahoga County for wrongful imprisonment and this resulted in a third, civil trial in 2000. New information about alternative weapons was debated but, interestingly, the outcome was that a majority of the jury decided that Sheppard was indeed guilty of the crime.

18.4 Three Approaches to the Presentation of Blood Evidence

The Sheppard case was distinctive due to the detailed scientific explanations underpinning an authoritative interpretation and evaluation of the evidence, from an eminent expert witness. This is not typical of some more recent cases, however, where a variety of approaches have been taken by the expert witness.

18.4.1   Activity and Propositions: R v Thompson 2013

James Thompson was tried in July 2010 for the murder of Anthony Johnson outside the Early Learning Centre shop in Southport, United Kingdom, by repeatedly kicking him in the head. Thompson was detained at the scene by a passing, off-duty police officer. The incident arose from a drunken argument on a night out and despite the accused claiming self-defence he was convicted of the crime. He appealed on the grounds of provocation by the victim and his consequent loss of self-control. At the appeal the blood-spatter evidence from the trial was reviewed. There was heavy bloodstaining on the ground and around a support pillar outside the shop, Thompson's clothing was stained with the victim's blood and his right shoe was bloodied, particularly around the toe.

Here, the interpretation and evaluation was loosely based on propositions for the evidence, and used similar language and phrases to forensic opinion across other subdisciplines. There was a fairly simple set of bloodstain evidence, which was interpreted in the context of the activity at the scene. An explanation for the spatter pattern on the pillar was that it was:

> '…consistent with force being applied to wet blood at a low level.'
>
> [R v Thompson, 2013, paragraph 21]

Two mechanisms were suggested for this: impact spatter generated at ground level or blood droplets ejected from the airways of the victim. The evaluation of this blood evidence was that it:

> '… supported the conclusion that the victim was injured in the area of the Early Learning Centre and that he was bleeding whilst he was on the ground.'
>
> [R v Thompson, 2013, paragraph 21]

The examination of the distribution of blood on Johnson's footwear, together with a mark found above the victim's eyebrow, led to the expert's conclusion that this provided 'moderate support' to the proposition that this trainer had been responsible for the injury. Overall, she concluded that:

> '… there was strong support for a conclusion that the appellant had been involved in an assault on the victim during which he had kicked the latter to the head.'
>
> [R v Thompson, 2013, paragraph 22]

The judge dismissed his appeal and confirmed Johnson's conviction.

By alluding to propositions and using some probabilistic language, the expert witness, in this case, brought opinion on blood evidence more into line with the evaluative statements the court may receive on many other forms of forensic evidence.

18.4.2   No Expert Testimony: R v White 1998

Jody White was convicted of the attempted murder of his friend, following an argument at a bar in Ontario, but appealed in 1998 on the grounds that the judge had made legal errors in instructing the jury, by not providing a balanced view on how they should consider the evidence. The argument had started on the dance floor but developed into a fight upstairs in an elevated area where the victim became aware that he was bleeding profusely from his neck from a severed jugular vein. The issue was whether the fight was initiated by White slashing his friend on the back of the neck on the dance floor or by the victim chasing White up the stairs and the injury occurring during the fight itself. In the latter scenario, White would have been acting in self-defence. There was contradictory witness evidence about what had occurred, so the bloodstain evidence appeared to be crucial in establishing the facts. However, no expert testimony was presented at the trial to assist the court in interpreting the blood evidence, despite its being photographically recorded and sketched at the scene.

> 'There was no expert evidence to assist the jury in deciding what inferences, if any, could reasonably be drawn from the nature and location of the bloodstains.'
>
> [R v White, 1998, paragraph 14]

The appeal court judge described the positions and nature of the blood evidence from the images, which indicated stains near the foot of the stairs and on the elevated area. The issue was how those stains on the dance floor originated; the defence contended that they were not inconsistent with the stabbing taking place at the top of the stairs.

Expert evidence on the nature of the wounds and aspects of bleeding was received from a vascular surgeon at the trial. However, this did not include questioning specifically on the bloodstains and their formation. The appeal court judge reviewed this evidence through his own interpretation of the images from the scene:

> 'To the untrained eye, at least four of the bloodstains on the dance floor appear to have been produced by blood dropping directly on the floor as opposed to being tracked onto the floor by patrons of the bar. However, absent expert evidence explaining the significance of the location and appearance of the bloodstains and, in light of the possibility that the complainant's blood may have spurted some distance when he started to bleed, I cannot say that the physical evidence renders the appellant's position untenable.'
>
> [R v White, 1998, paragraph 26]

His evaluation was that this evidence 'was more consistent with the Crown's position than with the appellant's position'. Nevertheless, he agreed that, had the jury been presented with that degree of uncertainty about the blood evidence, they may well have given greater weight to the self-defence argument. Accordingly, he quashed the conviction and ordered a new trial.

18.4.3 Reconstructing Activity as a Narrative: R v Hall 2010

The body of Jacqueline McLean was found in a vacant apartment in Hamilton, Ontario in August 2001. She had been sexually assaulted and bludgeoned to death by several blows to the head. DNA evidence from semen swabs from the body identified Carl Hall, who claimed that, though he had had consensual intercourse with Ms McLean, he had not killed her. Despite this, Hall was convicted of her murder in 2006 but appealed on grounds not directly linked to the forensic evidence but related to the actions of the trial judge. The bloodstain pattern testimony provides a good example of the use of narrative evaluation by the expert for the court.

Following examination of the apartment, the expert witness described the sequence of activities, which, he said, were responsible for generating the bloodstain evidence:

> 'the deceased was hit at least once near the apartment door;
> she was probably carried from the door to the middle of the living room floor, where pooled blood was found on the carpet;
> she was dragged by her arms or shoulders, wearing her jeans and underwear (which were both saturated with blood on the rear) to the inner edge of the staircase leading up to the loft, as evidenced by two smaller pools of blood at the base of the loft stairs;

she was dragged feet first up the stairs, which left transfer marks from her head on each step of the stairs;

she was repositioned in the loft and, given the pattern of a pool of blood, it was quite possible that her head had been moved;

she was hit at least once in the loft while already bleeding and lying on the floor; and

she was struck at least once while still wearing her underwear, but after it had been exposed.'

[R v Hall, 2009, paragraph 49]

He further explained that her jeans had been pulled down to mid-thigh and the spatter pattern on her underwear indicated that this was intact during the assault. Further, the presence of spatter above and around the right knee, but absent on the left knee, suggested that her assailant had blocked the latter knee, possibly by sitting on it, while striking the blows to her head. He also observed that there was evidence that the assailant had blood on his body as he moved around the scenes. He stated that transfer stains on the wall at the bottom of and on the way up the stairs were 'likely' to have originated from the action of the assailant. Transfer stains on her socks 'may have been caused' by the body being dragged up the stairs by the ankles. He added that, due to the large size of the suspected weapon, a steel bar, some blockage of spatter would have occurred across parts of the assailant's body. However, the lower legs and feet 'might' have received some blood spatter.

By presenting testimony in this way, the expert assembled a sequence of activities that described to the court one scenario that accounted for the observed blood evidence and that provided a picture, in the minds of the jury, as to how the crime may have been carried out. Each stage in the narration was supported by physical evidence, though the evidential weight varied from one point to another. For example, although she was 'hit at least once', this description was followed by the activity where she was 'probably carried'. At some points, the narration included reference to the supporting blood evidence, elsewhere this was not provided. The narrative strategy was successful in that it provided expert testimony in a direct and readily accessible form for the jury. On the other hand, at many points the expert was open to challenge on the interpretation and its scientific foundation and, in this example, no alternative scenarios appear to have been considered.

Of course, in presenting such a complete scenario, the expert may be in danger of going further in interpretation than is justified by the evidence and may overlook areas where the evaluation is less than conclusive, simply to provide continuity to the whole narration. Similarly, with such an approach it is possible to look to areas of uncertainty in the evidence as providing confirmation of those other parts where the interpretation is more secure, rather than seeking independent evaluation at each stage in the activity.

Following a retrial, Hall was acquitted of the murder of Jacqueline McLean in 2012, but he remained in prison following his confession to the unrelated murders of two other individuals in 2000.

18.5   The Problem of Expirated Blood

In classifying bloodstains, one of the most controversial patterns is that comprising a group of very small stains, often described as fine spatter. However, is such a pattern always spatter, how was it generated and could it, in fact, be due to contact transfer? In the following cases, this was the primary issue; however, these cases also reveal how experts, with different backgrounds and expertise, may be called to provide testimony on blood evidence and the importance of casework experiments in providing scientific support to expert opinion.

18.5.1   R v O'Grady 1995, 1999

In May 1992, the wife of Gerald O'Grady was attacked and brutally murdered in her kitchen as he was watching television in the adjacent room in their apartment in Vancouver, Canada. She had been badly beaten about the head with a sharpening steel from a kitchen drawer and there were extensive bloodstains and spatter at the scene. O'Grady found her and attempted to resuscitate her. When the police arrived, his body and clothes were clearly bloodstained. O'Grady was arrested, tried and convicted for his wife's murder in 1993, despite the defence case that an intruder was responsible. Bloodstain and spatter evidence was central to the prosecution case and when fresh evidence on this became available later, O'Grady appealed against his conviction in 1995.

The activity that had led to the presence of bloodstains on O'Grady's shirt and trousers was the main focus of the appeal hearing. The prosecution asserted these were medium velocity impact spatter generated when O'Grady assaulted his wife around the head with the sharpening steel. On the other hand, based on O'Grady's own evidence, the defence claimed that these stains came from O'Grady's actions while he attempted to give his wife mouth-to-mouth resuscitation. In this case, two mechanisms were debated: the first was that the stains were from expirated blood as the victim attempted to breathe while blood blocked her airways; the second was that blood around her mouth had been projected outwards by the air pressure applied by O'Grady, as he engaged in resuscitation. The latter point received little attention at the original trial.

The prosecution called three expert witnesses to give opinion on the blood-spatter evidence. The first, Staff Sergeant Silvester, was a bloodstain pattern analyst with the RCMP while the other two, Drs Gray and Ferris, were forensic pathologists.

Silvester stated that medium velocity spatter stains could have been generated by an assault such as alleged by the prosecution, but he was unable to confirm that the observed stains were in fact medium velocity impact spatter. To do so he would have had to be able to exclude all other possible mechanisms, which he was unable to do in this case. He added that the evidence could also:

> '... be consistent with aspirated blood drops during mouth to mouth resuscitation.'
>
> [R v O'Grady, 1995, paragraph 7]

Further, he considered that the third mechanism, of blowing air over the victim's bloodied cheek, was also a possible explanation for the observations.

In contrast, Gray discounted the explanation based on expiration as she had found no blood in the victim's airways during the post-mortem examination, although there may have been some in her nostrils. Ferris admitted that his opinion was solely based on reading the notes of others. Despite this, he identified the stains as medium velocity impact spatter resulting from the assault and he also ruled out the mechanism of expiration for the same reason as Gray. Indeed, he added that the source of the blood was between '18 inches to 2 feet' from impact surface. This was in contrast to an estimate from Silvester of 'not more than 6 feet away'. As it was on the basis of these opinions that the trial jury reached a guilty verdict, it appears that they may have regarded the evidence of the pathologists as more significant than the more balanced and cautious view from Silvester.

The new evidence considered by the appeal court related to an undocumented experiment undertaken by Silvester at the time of the original investigation but not reported by him at the trial. In this, he had attempted to produce a spatter pattern through the action of blowing with his mouth up against to his arm where some red liquid had been placed. Although this produced small stains on his shirt, he did not conclude that this activity provided a full explanation for the evidence on O'Grady's shirt. However, he affirmed that:

> 'My experiment produced a pattern similar to the drop stains observed on the Appellant's shirt. I therefore could not exclude the possibility that the resuscitative actions created small projected drop stains observed on Mr. O'Grady's shirt.'
>
> [R v O'Grady, 1995, paragraph 13]

The appeal court regarded this new evidence as significant, not because of what it added to the evaluation, but because it was based on a scientific experiment, albeit of a limited nature:

> 'There appears to be a factual foundation which makes the result of Silvester's test potentially relevant to the source of the blood drops in this case.'
>
> [R v O'Grady, 1995, paragraph 19]

If this evidence had been put before the jury in the original trial and debated alongside the opinion of the other experts, then the appeal court concluded that the jury may have reached a different decision and on this basis the appeal was upheld and a new trial ordered. At the second trial in 1996 the jury was unable to reach a unanimous verdict and a third trial took place in 1999 at which O'Grady was once again found guilty of murder and sentenced to life imprisonment.

O'Grady appealed once again, including the grounds that Ferris should not have been permitted to give opinion on the generation of bloodstain patterns, as he was a pathologist. In response, Ferris commented on his experience in the identification of blood-spatter patterns and stated that the demarcation line was 'mathematical analysis and documentation', which he regarded firmly as within the preserve of the bloodstain pattern analyst.

However, the appeal court ruled that, following R v Mohan (see Chapter 2.3.1) and evidence given by Ferris during a *voir dire*, this appeal should be dismissed. O'Grady died in prison in 2004.

18.5.2   R v Jenkins: The Trial and First Appeal 1999

Amongst the cases which have oscillated between trial and appeal, that of Sion Jenkins for the murder of his thirteen-year-old step-daughter Billie-Jo Jenkins in February 1998, is notable for the debate between experts on the bloodstain evidence which was crucial to the outcome of the case. Billie-Jo had been bludgeoned to death with a metal tent peg while she was painting patio doors at the family home in Hastings, United Kingdom. Her step-father claimed that he found her as she lay dying and that any blood evidence on his clothing was as a result of his attempts to help her. Nevertheless, he was arrested and, at the first trial in 1998, key prosecution evidence was that those bloodstains on his shoes, trousers and jacket were impact spatter resulting from the assault on his victim.

These 158 bloodstains that were not readily visible, had the appearance of quite a fine spray. The prosecution called two expert witnesses. Mr Wain stated that the appearance and distribution of the pattern was 'consistent with' the prosecution's assertion that Jenkins was the attacker. Indeed, the spray was 'typical' of the fine backspatter he would expect on an assailant when a weapon impacted on an already bloodied surface. This view was supported by the second expert witness. For the defence, two further experts gave more cautious testimony. They drew attention to the variation in droplet size that can result from such assaults and that the observed pattern was not what they would describe as typical. However, both conceded that the evidence was 'not inconsistent with' the prosecution's proposition.

Following from the pathologist's report indicating blood obstruction in the victim's airways, the defence experts had carried out experiments that demonstrated that the exhalation of 2.8 litres of air from the lungs in two seconds, under those circumstances, could produce an impact spatter pattern of very fine stains, not unlike those on Jenkins' clothes. Further experiments had been carried out by Dr McAughey, an aerosol scientist, who concluded that, to produce a spatter pattern at a distance of around 0.5 m away, would require a peak airflow rate of around two-thirds of that used in Wain's experiments. However, the pathologist, Dr Hill, suggested that due to her injuries, Billie-Jo would have been incapable of the necessary depth of breath to achieve the conditions required by these experiments that he described as 'wholly unrealistic' and he added that:

> '... the possibility of spraying of droplets by breathing to be so remote that it can be discounted.'
>
> [R v Jenkins, 1999, paragraph 37]

Following the guilty verdict, Sion Jenkins sought to appeal on a number of grounds, including fresh evidence from Prof David Denison who had carried out many further experiments on the exhalation explanation for the blood-spatter evidence. The appeal court attempted to clarify the range of terminology, facts and physiological information that had been provided by the many experts from a variety of scientific and medical perspectives. The key outcome of the discussion was whether it was possible for someone in the victim's condition to generate the necessary pressure in her lungs to deliver the air flow necessary to fragment blood in her lower airways, produce the required dispersion of blood droplets at her nose and then for these to have sufficient energy to travel a further 0.5 m through the air. Although Denison's experiments were considered valuable, he contended that they required a blood blockage at the nasal valve, in contradiction to the testimony of Hill and others, that the blockage was in the lower airways. The judge accepted this latter explanation. The relative positions of Jenkins and the victim, necessary to obtain the observed spatter pattern, were discussed in detail and the judge concluded that:

> '... even if all of that were achieved, blood spattering would not, it seems, reach the height on the appellant's clothing at which spattering was found.'
>
> [R v Jenkins, 1999, paragraph 161]

This fresh evidence was regarded as relevant and valuable but, as it did not explain the facts of the case, it did not contribute sufficient grounds for overturning the original verdict and so the appeal was dismissed.

18.5.3   R v Jenkins: The Second Appeal (2004) and Two More Retrials

The CCRC became interested in this case and, in addition, new histological examination of the victim's lung tissue by Prof Denison revealed evidence of interstitial emphysema. This is a condition whereby gas pressure may build up in the lung tissue, outside of the main airways, and may be a consequence of the blockage of those airways due to injury, for example, in this case by a spasm of the larynx or by a blood clot that had become dislodged prior to the post-mortem examination. The defence also recruited a Canadian bloodstain pattern expert, Joe Slemko, who provided further support to their case:

> 'It's important to look at where the blood is, but also where there is not blood … the telltale blood stain pattern that caught my eye was the pattern that was on the chest area of the jacket. It was a condensed, confused pattern and that could only have been created as a result of an expiration event.'
>
> [Gibson, 2006]

On the basis of this new evidence and their review of the case, the CCRC initiated a second appeal in 2004. The alternative explanation for the blood spatter on Jenkins' clothes put forward at the first appeal was now proposed to have been caused, not by an active pressure from Billie-Jo's lungs, but from the passive pressure, caused by the interstitial emphysema, being released suddenly, possibly when Jenkins first moved the Billie-Jo's body by taking her in his arms. In addition, in interpreting the spread of fine stains on the clothes, the effects of breeze and eddy currents on the patio had not been previously considered.

The appeal court regarded this fresh alternative explanation for the blood spatter as making the conviction unsafe since it may have affected the decision of the jury at the trial to convict Jenkins. The appeal was allowed and a retrial was ordered at which the jury failed to reach a verdict in April 2005. Consequently, a third trial took place resulting in the same outcome. At this point the trial judge conceded that the prosecution's case was unable to achieve a conviction and he declared a formal not guilty verdict in early 2006.

The difficulties faced by the courts when dealing with conflicting experts are not unique to bloodstain pattern evidence but it is worth noting the oft-quoted remark from Prof Graham Zellick, Head of the CCRC, following the final verdict in the Sion Jenkins case:

> ' "The jury may well be the ideal, or at least the best mechanism we have for deciding who's telling the truth," he said. "But to decide detailed technical matters on which some of the world's leading experts are arguing, well that strikes me as being fanciful." '
>
> [Gibson, 2006]

18.6   Experts in Disagreement: R v Perlett 2006

In 1996, James and Carole Perlett were shot and killed in the bedroom of their home in Fort Frances, Ontario. The alarm was raised by their son, also James, who claimed he had been wounded by a gunshot from a masked intruder whom he disturbed at the scene. The weapon, his father's target pistol, was recovered from the scene. Despite his statement, and on the basis of a variety of other evidence, James Perlett was arrested and tried for the murder of his parents in October 1998. However, this process was declared a mistrial after a dispute on allegations of political pressure being put on an expert witness. Although this itself is not relevant to the current discussion, the evidence in question, being blood spatter, is of interest.

At a preliminary hearing the year before, the scientist, Mr Philp, described part of the bedroom wall where he had identified a void – an area of less intense or absent spatter – which he ascribed to blockage of the trajectories of droplets, by the arm of the killer. As no blood-stains had been found on Perlett's clothing, this evidence was deemed to support the defence case. However, as Philp later went on sick leave, the work passed to a colleague, Mr Newman, who, working only from photographs of the scene, re-interpreted this evidence as an 'apparent void' due, he concluded, to:

> '... blood spraying against the wall at different angles from two bullet holes in Jim Perlett's forehead.'
>
> [Young v Toronto Star Newspapers, 2003, paragraph 49]

This explanation favours neither the defence nor the prosecution. Consequently, the two scientists and their colleagues reviewed the evidence and agreed to assign equal weight to both these interpretations of the evidence. This effectively reduced the weight of evidence in favour of the defence, by a significant amount. Not only did these two experts, working in the same institute, disagree in their identification of the nature of this area of blood spatter but their interpretation and evaluation led the court in different directions. Nevertheless, after the second trial, Perlett was convicted of second-degree murder in March 1999.

In 2005, Perlett appealed his conviction on several grounds, including the inclusion of fresh evidence that challenged the testimony on the age of bloodstains given at the trial by the forensic pathologist, Dr Peter Pan.

James Perlett claimed he had called the police a few minutes after the gunshots and that they had arrived only five minutes later. However, statements from officers and paramedics confirmed that, when they arrived, blood from the victims was 'clotted, dried and dark brown' and that there was considerable pooling of blood but that it was no longer flowing from the bodies. This was captured in photographs of the scene, which were the basis of Pan's testimony. He concluded that the victim's wounds had bled for around 15 minutes, followed by a further period of clotting estimated at least 20 minutes, which implied that the police had arrived at least 35 minutes after the shootings and not the 10 minutes or so consistent with Perlett's statement. Under cross-examination, Pan conceded several points that undermined the scientific basis of his opinion. Nevertheless, it was accepted by the courts as evidence for the prosecution's case.

At appeal, Perlett claimed that his defence counsel should have objected to the admissibility of Pan's evidence, as it was unreliable given that the pooling of blood and the ageing of bloodstains lacked any scientific foundation. This was rejected, as the judge ruled that any weaknesses in Pan's testimony would relate to the weight of evidence and not to its admissibility. In reviewing fresh evidence, the appeal court considered testimony from Dr Chiasson, the chief pathologist of Ontario:

> 'In fact, Dr. Pan ventured into areas that are not within the purview of forensic pathology. It is inconceivable to me, as a forensic pathologist, how Dr. Pan could determine the length of time blood loss would have taken in this case as there is no scientific basis for such a calculation. His testimony on this issue is, therefore, not reliable. His testimony regarding the clotting and drying processes is equally unreliable.'
>
> [R v Perlett, 2006, paragraph 146]

Under cross-examination Chiasson took a less critical line, simply stating that his main concern was that the basis of Pan's opinion was not at all clear to him. Additionally, an affidavit from Newman, a forensic biologist, claimed that there was some published scientific support for Pan's interpretation of the clotting and that he believed the time interval stated was conservative. The judge summarised the position as follows:

> 'Therefore, the fresh evidence leaves the court with two experts, Dr. Pan and Dr. Chiasson, who disagree on the issue of blood loss; and two experts, Dr. Pan and Mr. Newman, who largely agree on the issue of blood clotting and drying, and one expert, Dr. Chiasson, who does not agree.'

[R v Perlett, 2006, paragraph 150]

On balance he did not believe that the fresh evidence detracted from the reliability of Pan's testimony and, in any case, the interpretation of this blood evidence was not central to the prosecution's case. He therefore dismissed the entire case for appeal put forward by Perlett.

18.7 Conclusions

These cases have demonstrated some of the difficulties in the presentation and evaluation of blood evidence in the courts. The expert should always be called upon, even for more basic examples, as only then can evaluative opinion be provided. The nature and clarity of scientific explanations and outcomes of relevant casework experiments provide invaluable support to testimony. However, the legal professions must be better educated in the principles and practice of BPA so that they can more effectively interrogate the experts and ensure the full significance of the evidence is revealed to the court. Although there will be many instances of the forensic pathologist and the bloodstain pattern analyst working alongside each other, the two specialisms are distinct. Those giving testimony on BPA should be fully conversant, not only with the fundamental science but also with recent research in the discipline, as only through the rigorous application of sound science can differing interpretations of the evidence be reconciled. Finally, opinion can and should be based on propositions, the assessment of alternative explanations and the use of probabilistic language, which will provide the courts with a balanced view on the evidence.

References

Cuyahoga County Court of Common Pleas, "Volume 04, 1966 Trial Transcript (Retrial of Samuel H. Sheppard): Testimony; State Rests; Motions for Directed Verdict and Time".1966 Trial Transcripts – Sam Sheppard Case, Book 1 [Online]. (1966). Available at http://engagedscholarship.csuohio.edu/sheppard_transcripts_1966/1 [Accessed 7 November 2015].

Forensic Science Regulator: Codes of Practice and Conduct, Bloodstain Pattern Analysis FSR-C-102 [Online]. (2015). Available at https://www.gov.uk/government/uploads/system/uploads/attachment_data/file/484905/C102_Bloodstain_Pattern_Analysis_2015.pdf [Accessed 18 December 2015].

Gardner R.M. and Bevel T. (2009). *Practical Crime Scene Analysis and Reconstruction.* Taylor and Francis. Boca Raton, Florida.

Gibson C. (9 February 2006). Case turned on 158 spots of blood, *BBC News Report.* Available at http://news.bbc.co.uk/1/hi/england/southern_counties/4661302.stm [Accessed 7 November 2015].

Imwinkelried E. (2000). Forensic science: bloodspatter analysis. *Criminal Law Bulletin,* 36, 509.

International Association of Bloodstain Pattern Analysts (IABPA) [Online]. (2015). Available at http://www.iabpa.org/ [Accessed 8 November 2015].

James S.H., Kish P.E. and Sutton T.P. (2005). *Principles of Bloodstain Pattern Analysis: Theory and Practice.* CRC Press. Boca Raton, Florida.

National Research Council: Strengthening Forensic Science in the United States: A Path Forward, Document 228091 [Online]. (2009). Available at http://www.nap.edu/catalog/12589.html [Accessed 10 November 2015].

R v Hall [2010] ONCA 724: C46090 & C45057

R v Jenkins [2004] All ER (D) 295 (Jul)

R v Jenkins [1999] Case No: 98/4720/W3

R v O'Grady [1995] CA017621

R v O'Grady [1999] BCCA 0189CA023203

R v Perlett [2006] 82 OR (3d) 89

R v Thompson [2013] EWCA Crim 1746

R v White [1998] Court of Appeal for Ontario, C24249

Special Working Group on Bloodstain Pattern Analysis (SWGSTAIN) [Online]. (2015). Available at http://www.swgstain.org/ [Accessed 8 November 2015].

Wonder A.Y. with Yezzo G.M. (2015). *Bloodstain Patterns: Identification, Interpretation and Application*. Academic Press. Oxford, UK.

Young v Toronto Star Newspapers [2003] Ontario Superior Court of Justice 99-CV-162162

Further Reading

Giannelli P.C. (2001). Scientific evidence in the Sam Sheppard case. *Cleveland State Law Review*, 49, 487–498.

Gopen A.D. and Imwinkelried E.J. (2009). Bloodstain pattern evidence revisited. *Criminal Law Bulletin*, 45(3), 485.

Murray D.C. (2000). An advocate's approach to bloodstain pattern analysis evidence, parts 1 and 2 [Online]. *IABPA News*, 16(2), 1–10 and 16(3), 1–15. Available at http://www.iabpa.org/uploads/files/iabpa%20publications/June%20Sept%202000%20News.pdf [Accessed 7 November 2015].

19

Conflicting Expert Opinion: SIDS and the Medical Expert Witness

Forensic pathology is a very broad field and virtually all cases involving sudden or suspicious death will require a report from an expert pathologist. However, in the vast majority of these, the opinion is largely factual and not contested, whereas, in a minority, conflicting testimony may arise. This chapter focuses on the short series of cases that came to appeal, principally in the United Kingdom around ten to fifteen years ago, involving multiple infant deaths, allegedly from Sudden Infant Death Syndrome (SIDS), to illustrate some of the important issues that may arise in forensic pathology and cases involving the medical expert witness in court.

19.1   Eminent Experts: Issues and Conflicts

SIDS is the unexpected and sudden death of a young baby where no apparent cause is readily identified by post-mortem examination. Instances of SIDS became of increasing concern in the latter part of the last century, leading to the instigation of studies and surveys intended to determine the actual extent of these incidents and any causal factors that might relate to an increased risk of a SIDS event. In a very few cases, the infant's death was classed as suspicious and subjected to police investigation, with the consequence that the parent, most commonly the mother, was arrested for the murder of the child. Such cases received huge media interest, which contributed to the vilification of the mothers concerned.

In some of these cases, two or more infants had died in circumstances pointing either to SIDS or murder by a parent. The focus at these trials was clearly on cause of death and, in

Forensic Evidence in Court: Evaluation and Scientific Opinion, First Edition. Craig Adam.
© 2016 John Wiley & Sons, Ltd. Published 2016 by John Wiley & Sons, Ltd.

the absence of other substantive evidence, the legal debate centred on the contributions of the medical expert witnesses. In some instances, convictions for murder were later quashed at appeal and these cases have revealed important issues in the presentation and evaluation of medical opinion, especially in relation to competing rare events.

In conveying expert medical opinion, much of which is qualitative in nature and based on personal experience in the field, the pathologist or medical doctor may use their authoritative status to give weight to their testimony, thereby potentially giving it undue significance and excluding alternative explanations from the court's consideration. Such an approach may give the jury unjustified confidence in that opinion, believing the expert to be infallible. Additionally, overconfident delivery may allow the expert witness, without the court being aware, to stray into areas of expertise they do not possess, for example in the interpretation of statistical data, leading to errors and misleading opinion being conveyed to the jury.

Further difficulties may arise where two medical experts provide conflicting opinions, a situation exacerbated if there is little other evidence being presented to the court and the testimony itself relates to rare events, where there is little underpinning scientific basis to support the expert's opinion. How should the court resolve this situation and is the trial able to proceed to a conclusion?

19.2   R v Clark 2000, 2003

When Sally and Stephen Clark's first son, Christopher, died unexpectedly, aged only three months in December 1996, his death was attributed to a respiratory infection. As such, this could be classed as an incidence of Sudden Infant Death Syndrome (SIDS) otherwise known as 'cot death' since the death was sudden and not preceded by any substantive symptoms. The body was cremated but some post-mortem evidence retained. However, just over a year later, the death of their second son, Harry, under similar circumstances, led to a detailed post-mortem, which revealed allegedly non-accidental injuries, such as could have been caused by shaking and smothering the baby. Consequently, Sally Clark was arrested on suspicion of having murdered both her babies. At the trial in 1999, the majority of the evidence was medical and related to the post-mortem examinations. Several expert witnesses gave evidence, including Prof Sir Roy Meadow, who identified features that led him to dismiss the deaths as attributable to SIDS and to regard them instead as due to unnatural causes. The essence of the case against Clark was that unexplained and contentious minor injuries to Christopher and further internal injuries to Harry precluded the deaths being due to SIDS and, together with statements from Meadow as to the rarity, if not impossibility, of two SIDS deaths in one family, this implied that the only logical conclusion was murder by a parent.

This testimony from Meadow, though supported in part by some of the other medical experts, contributed strongly to the jury reaching a majority guilty verdict. Clark appealed unsuccessfully in 2000 on several grounds, including fresh medical evidence relating to the pathological examination of Harry and criticism from the statistical community of Meadow's testimony. This was unsuccessful and it took a second appeal in 2003, based on further medical evidence that revealed that Harry had died from an acute bacteriological infection and further consideration of the statistical issues, for the verdict to be overturned and Clark released from custody. Sally Clark died in 2007.

It is pertinent here to focus on the controversial testimony of Prof Sir Roy Meadow, in particular his use of statistical data and arguments in support of his opinion, and how that was eventually successfully challenged.

19.2.1 The Testimony of Meadow

The prosecution, in expectation that the defence would promote the cause of death as SIDS, had prepared statistical evidence in order to argue that this was highly unlikely based on published research on the occurrence of SIDS cases within the UK population in recent years. This study – Sudden Unexpected Deaths in Infancy, the CESDI Studies 1993–1996 – was intended to provide guidance on causal factors that might reveal a predisposition for SIDS within a family. It was not intended to be a rigorous statistical exercise, though it was extensive, identifying 363 true cases of SIDS in a population of 472,823. Nevertheless, the data, some of which is presented in Table 19.1, was of significance to the evidence, as presented in the Clark case.

Meadow considered the Clark family to be affluent and so took the SIDS frequency, where none of the causal factors were applicable, namely 1 in 8,543. He then presented an estimate for two SIDS death obtained by squaring this value; as he stated at the trial:

'... the risk is 1:8,543 live births ... Thus the chances of two infant deaths within such a family being SIDS is 1:73,000,000.'

[R v Clark, 2000, paragraph 118]

This was then reinforced by adding:

'... there are about, say, 700,000 live births a year, so it is saying by chance that happening will occur once every hundred years.'

[R v Clark, 2000, paragraph 114]

He intended these statements to support the argument that what had happened in the case of Clark was so rare when considered as double SIDS, that the alternative before the court,

Table 19.1 *Factors Affecting Rates of SIDS Occurrence in the UK Population*

Definition of group		Frequency of occurrence of SIDS in the group
Average rate across the population		1 in 1303
Smoker	Smoker in household	1 in 737
	No smoker in household	1 in 5041
Income	No waged income	1 in 486
	At least one waged income	1 in 2088
Mother's age	Age is 26 or less	1 in 567
	Age is 27 or greater	1 in 1882
Number of factors	None of these three factors	1 in 8543
	Any one factor	1 in 1616
	Any two factors	1 in 596
	All factors	1 in 214

Note: These data are taken from paragraph 121 in R v Clark (2000), which were incorporated into Table 3.58 in the CESDI SUDI Study (Fleming *et al.*, 2000).

namely murder, must be the only explanation. After quoting these statistics and the medical evidence in his witness statement, Meadow concluded:

> 'Neither of these two deaths can be classed as SIDS. Each of the deaths was unusual and had the characteristics of a death caused by a parent'
>
> [R v Clark, 2000, paragraph 110]

This was reinforced by the judge in summarising the prosecution case, including their use of the statistics:

> '... which the prosecution suggest make it beyond coincidence that these two deaths were natural deaths.'
>
> [R v Clark, 2000, paragraph 131]

The testimony of Meadow, in particular his use of statistics, formed part of the grounds for the first appeal. First, the method of calculation and the quoted probability for two SIDS deaths in the same family were deemed incorrect. The use of multiplication in combining the two probabilities is valid only if the two quantities are independent, yet it is recognised that the occurrence of one SIDS death in a family leads to an increased chance there may be a second such death, through both genetic and environmental factors. In other words, the probability of the second death is *conditional* on the occurrence of the first death and this would lead to the probability for two SIDS deaths being significantly greater than that quoted by Meadow. Nevertheless, although this mathematical error was accepted by the appeal court, it did not regard the accuracy of the probability itself as being relevant, only that it was numerically very small.

Before moving on, it is pertinent to discuss a probable origin for Meadow's misuse of statistics and for the unfortunate statement that came be to be known as Meadow's Law. In their book Forensic Pathology (1989), DiMaio and DiMaio contended that SIDS incidents were random, implying that occurrences of further SIDS deaths in a family should be regarded in the same way, as independent events. In consequence, they proposed deriving the total probability using the basic multiplication rule and hence, for multiple SIDS, this decreased rapidly, following second and third SIDS deaths. On this basis, they wrote:

> '"... while a second SIDS with one mother is improbable, it is possible..." or "...remotely possible..." [2nd edition] and "A third case, in our opinion is not possible and is a case of homicide"'
>
> [DiMaio and DiMaio, 1989, quoted in Carpenter *et al.*, 2005]

This was later reworked by Meadow into his infamous 'law':

> '... two is suspicious and three murder unless proved otherwise...is a sensible working rule for anyone encountering these tragedies'
>
> [Meadow, quoted in Carpenter *et al.*, 2005]

It was also alleged that statements from Meadow effectively linked the guilt of Sally Clark to this statistical frequency, so falling into the trap of the prosecutor's fallacy (Chapter 7.6.2), and that the judge had erred in not warning the jury of this risk. Once again, the appeal court did not agree with this, arguing that Meadow's opinion was based on his expert view of both the medical and statistical evidence. If Meadow did not explicitly demonstrate the prosecutor's fallacy, there is evidence from contemporary newspaper reports that others in the court did come away with that impression.

In support of their appeal, the defence counsel submitted reports from two eminent statisticians, Dr Evett and Prof Dawid, which were critical of the use of statistical data by Meadow at the original trial. As well as commenting on the mathematical errors, that were directly part of the grounds for the appeal, and the uncertainty inherent in the quality of the original data, they also raised a more fundamental issue in how the statistical data on SIDS occurrence should be evaluated by the court. They questioned the logic of Meadow's opinion in the absence of any statistical data on the occurrence of deaths of infants murdered by a parent, in similar circumstances to the Clarks. In other words, they were arguing for a balanced evaluation of the evidence based on two competing propositions, namely the deaths were due to SIDS or the deaths were due to murder. Although quantifying this was a challenging task, given the rarity of both events in the population, Dawid provided an illustrative calculation, based on reported causes of death, which showed that double SIDS was around thirty times more probable than double murder, albeit using the flawed frequency of occurrence used by Meadow (Dawid, 2000). However, this point was dismissed by the appeal court, citing the D J Adams (1998) case (Chapter 8.3) as precedent for the court's rejection of the logical evaluation of the evidence:

> 'The competing possibility identified is a double infant murder by a mother. That may be capable of being expressed in terms of a statistical probability, but legally speaking the exercise is not realistic... it is not an exercise the courts would perform.'
>
> [R v Clark, 2000, paragraph 160]

19.2.2   The Second Appeal 2003

The second appeal was held in 2003, following referral by the CCRC, based on fresh evidence from microbiological examination of sections taken from Harry's lungs, which suggested that he had suffered from an acute bacteriological infection. This evidence had been recognised at the time of the original trial by the pathologist, but was not disclosed in his report. In addition to reconsidering all the medical evidence, the appeal court also gave some attention to the statistical evidence in the case, specifically to the issue that the jury had been given an exaggerated impression as to the rarity of two SIDS deaths in the same family. In doing so it focused on the testimony of Meadow.

The court criticised Meadow for his consistent highlighting of the statistical rarity, as he saw it, of two SIDS deaths in one family, and his use of numerical data in doing so, despite the inclusion in his report of various statements indicating reservations as to their applicability. The court judged that the presentation of opinion in this way may have had a major effect on the jury's thinking about the case.

> 'Putting the evidence of 1 in 73 million before the jury with its related statistic that it was the equivalent of a single occurrence of two such deaths in the same family once in a century was tantamount to saying that without consideration of the rest of the evidence one could be just about sure that this was a case of murder.'
>
> [R v Clark, 2003, paragraph 175]

In quashing the verdict on Clark, the judge accepted that the fresh medical evidence made her conviction unsafe but he added that full consideration by the appeal court of the statistical evidence and its presentation at the trial would have most likely have resulted in the same outcome.

Interestingly, the Royal Statistical Society was sufficiently concerned about the nature of the statistical testimony and debate at the trial and at the first appeal, for its president to write to the Lord Chancellor of England in 2002 about the inadequacies in the presentation of statistical evidence at criminal trials in general, but with specific reference to the Clark case, particularly by those whose principal expertise was not in statistics (Green, 2002). This was a direct criticism of Meadow's testimony.

19.3   A Bayesian Analysis: Murder or SIDS?

During the Clark appeals and in their aftermath, there was some academic interest in the statistical issues raised by the case. The first of these concerned the need for a balanced approach whereby the two propositions underlying the court's debate could be evaluated in a logical fashion. The second issue related to the actual figures used in such calculations, how they might be derived from published data and their reliability. The contribution from Prof Dawid has already been mentioned and he went on to provide an evaluation based on these propositions using the odds version of Bayes' Theorem. The second development came from Prof Ray Hill who published two papers in which he described how probabilities for double, and indeed triple, occurrences of death from SIDS and by murder may be estimated and applied to this problem. Hill based his discussion on the relative probabilities under each proposition, but it is instructive to use his figures in a Bayesian evaluation calculation.

Following Dawid (2002), the propositions may be stated as:

H_1: Both infants were murdered by the mother
H_2: Both infants died of SIDS

The evidence, E, is simply the deaths of both children. Since this outcome follows from either of the propositions, the likelihood ratio is inevitably unity:

$$LR = \frac{Pr\left(E|H_1\right)}{Pr\left(E|H_2\right)} = \frac{1}{1} = 1$$

To arrive at a view on the posterior odds, the two probabilities contributing to the prior odds need to be calculated, using published data. These will be considered in turn, following the work of Hill (2004).

19.3.1 $Pr(H_2)$ – The Probability of Two SIDS Deaths in the Same Family

The starting point is the CESDI study over a period of years close to that of the Clark case. The shortcomings in these data are evident, but their use, in providing estimates based on some identifiable and relevant information, provides a good example of how a problem in statistical evaluation may be tackled using limited sources of data.

These data were procured primarily to identify causal factors relating to an increased occurrence of SIDS, whereas, for the relatively prosperous Clark family, the opposite is expected to be the case. However, a counter factor is that the condition is twice as common amongst male infants as in females, and both the Clark children were boys; interestingly, this fact was not mentioned during Meadow's testimony. Since there is no complete numerical information on this whole range of social and other class factors, the most reasonable approach is to neglect them completely and work with the average frequency from the survey, namely 1 in 1300 (to two significant figures), which is reliable given the large size of the population on which it is based.

Fortunately, the same survey may be used to estimate the frequency of two SIDS deaths in the same family, as it included data on multiple deaths of infants within families. Hill identified those families with two infant deaths and found there were five instances of two SIDS deaths out of the total of 323 SIDS families and two instances of a SIDS death followed by second death with a known cause out of a control group of 1288. These figures need to be treated with caution as the absolute occurrences are in single figures and the survey is from a period where SIDS deaths were decreasing over time. Nevertheless, they provide an estimate of a dependency factor D_s, or odds, for a second SIDS death of:

$$D_s = \frac{5/323}{2/1288} \approx 10$$

Survey data from earlier years when SIDS rates were higher, provided Hill with an estimate of D_s closer to five but reassuringly in the same range. Further, more detailed, analysis enabled Hill to arrive at his preferred figure of $D_s = 5.7$. This provides the calculation of the required probability as:

$$\Pr(H_2) = \frac{1}{1300} \times \frac{1}{1300} \times 5.7 \approx \frac{1}{296000}$$

19.3.2 Pr(H₁) – The Probability of Two Murdered Infants in the Same Family

National statistics for the United Kingdom provide the starting point for calculation of this probability. These show that over the relevant period there were thirty infants murdered by parents from a total of 650,000 live births. Deriving an estimate for the frequency of double murder was hindered by the fact that, if the first crime is discovered, then the second crime should not take place! Nevertheless, Hill was able to interrogate the data to arrive at the odds for a second infant murder, given the first child was also murdered, of $D_m \sim 176$, a not unexpectedly high dependency. Thus:

$$\Pr(H_1) = \frac{30}{650000} \times \frac{30}{650000} \times 176 \approx \frac{1}{2670000}$$

19.3.3 The Posterior Odds

Using the odds form of Bayes' Theorem (equation 3 from Chapter 7.4.1), the posterior odds P_1 on murder, may be calculated from these figures, using:

$$P_1 = \frac{\Pr(H_1|E)}{\Pr(H_2|E)} = LR \times \frac{\Pr(H_1)}{\Pr(H_2)}$$

Before doing this for the double death scenario relevant to the Clark case, it is instructive to derive the odds for single instances of infant death. Thus:

$$P_1(\text{single death}) = 1 \times \frac{30/650000}{1/1300} = 0.06$$

In other words SIDS is 17 times more probable as the cause of death, than murder. Similarly, for the case of two infant deaths:

$$P_1(\text{double death}) = 1 \times \frac{1/2670000}{1/296000} = 0.11$$

The odds on murder are now higher, but only marginally so, with SIDS as the cause of both deaths being 9 times more probable than murder. Despite the estimations used in arriving at these values, it is significant that, in both scenarios, the SIDS explanation is more probable than that of murder.

To complete his study, Hill attempted to analyse a case of triple infant death (as this was relevant to the Patel case, to be discussed in section 19.5) and, using speculative estimates, he arrived at dependencies of $D_s \sim 26$ and $D_m \sim 2167$. By a similar calculation to the previous cases, this provides an estimate of:

$$P_1(\text{triple death}) \approx 0.55$$

This suggests that the SIDS proposition emerges as around twice as probable as that of murder. Even allowing for uncertainty in his estimates, Hill proposed that this calculation provides a neutral outcome for the posterior odds, which he summarised as:

> 'When three sudden deaths have occurred in the same family, the statistics give no strong indication one way or the other as to whether the deaths are more or less likely to be SIDS than homicides.'
>
> [Hill, 2004]

In summary, this analysis and these calculations reveal that when the evidence is evaluated in a balanced fashion, by explicitly considering competing propositions, the SIDS explanation for two unexplained infant deaths in the same family, such as in the case of Clark, is more probable than the alternative explanation of murder by a parent.

19.4   R v Cannings 2004

The case of Angela Cannings who was convicted of the murder of two of her infant children by smothering, where a third had also died unexpectedly as a baby, had similarities to that of Sally Clark but, in fact, raised different issues. What was distinctive was that statistics, in numerical form, played no part in the legal debate, indeed such evidence may have been avoided given the consequences in the Clark case; rather, the court's attentions were focused on weighing up competing testimonies from the medical experts, including fresh evidence of potential genetic factors within Cannings' family tree.

In giving his expert opinion, Prof Meadow once again emphasised the extreme rarity of multiple SIDS deaths, in this case of the three Cannings babies, though he quoted no statistical data and he concluded:

> 'The fact that a previous child had died in the family is relevant because that combination of circumstances, that sort of story is one that is very typical of a child who has died as a result of smothering. So my medical diagnosis there would be probable smothering.'
>
> [R v Cannings, 2004, paragraph 131]

There was some debate on the purely medical and pathological evidence amongst the many medical expert witnesses, with a view from some that triple SIDS should not be excluded as an explanation. Indeed, Prof Golding regarded the conclusion that more than one unexplained sudden infant death must be attributed to murder by a parent, as becoming a 'fashion' that was not supported by any scientific or other evidence:

> '… there are a few cases where it (smothering) appears to have happened, but it is by no means clear that the claims that so many families where more than one sudden infant death has occurred are due to smothering. The results haven't been subjected to what I would call an appropriate statistical analysis. They are mostly a hunch that the paediatrician….not based on any scientific foundation.'
>
> [R v Cannings, 2004, paragraph 21]

The defence case was strengthened by evidence of examples of sudden infant deaths from within Cannings' extended family, which suggested a possible genetic predisposition for SIDS. Medical research suggests that some types of SIDS incident have a genetic link. Two grandchildren of her grandmother's sister, her second cousins, had died suddenly in infancy and were confirmed as SIDS cases. More significantly, her grandmother herself had had two children who had died suddenly as babies, though detailed medical data was not available as these had taken place seventy years previously. Although the appeal court was sceptical of the reliability of this information, it did recognise the fact that Canning's half-sister had suffered an apparent life-threatening event (ALTE), potentially a SIDS incident, as a baby to be much more significant.

Prof Carpenter, a medical statistician, gave testimony on academic research studies, including one that examined cases of three unexplained infant deaths. He summarised the conclusions from the researcher's notes:

> 'The final case conference concluded that all three deaths were unexplained SIDS. The notes indicate that the possibility of filicide was discussed at this conference, but that the evidence did not support this explanation.'
>
> [R v Cannings, 2004, paragraph 142]

In 2005, Carpenter and his coworkers published the results of detailed medical statistical research into multiple infant death cases where they concluded that second infant deaths are not 'rare' and that the vast majority of these (80 to 90%) are due to natural causes and that other cases of triple deaths have also occurred.

The appeal court rebuffed Meadow's opinion and acknowledged that three infant deaths did not inevitably imply murder by a parent. There was evidence, that in some instances, genetic factors, for example, may suggest that such deaths are attributable to natural causes. The judge emphasised how critical the expert evidence was in this case but added, that even a highly qualified and experienced expert could be wrong, and he was directly critical of the 'over dogmatic' approach taken by Meadow in his testimony. He concluded that the convictions were unsafe and that Cannings should be released from custody.

The Cannings case demonstrates the difficulties for the court and the jury in particular, when two or more expert witnesses present conflicting testimony, especially in relation to the cause of a rare event such as multiple infant deaths. The significance of this case was such that it prompted the Attorney-General for England and Wales, Lord Goldsmith, to make a statement to the House of Lords, following the outcome of Cannings' appeal, where he suggested that it may not be possible to proceed with the trial process under such circumstances:

> 'Yesterday's judgment in the Court of Appeal in the appeal against conviction of Angela Cannings has serious and far-reaching implications. The judgment has demonstrated that, in relation to unexplained infant deaths, where the outcome of the trial depends exclusively, or almost exclusively, on a serious disagreement between distinguished and reputable experts, it will often be unsafe to proceed. I share the unease expressed by the Court of Appeal in relation to such convictions.'
>
> [Attorney-General (Lord Goldsmith), 2004]

He consequently initiated a review of other similar cases by the CCRC with a view to investigating the safeness of convictions.

19.5   Trupti Patel 2003

Unlike the Clark and Cannings cases, that of Trupti Patel who was tried for the murder by suffocation of her three children, all of whom had died suddenly in infancy, never reached the appeal court as she was found not guilty at her trial in June 2003. There were three factors that led to this case being handled differently to the others, by the court. Firstly, the successful appeal by Sally Clark meant that the legal system now regarded multiple SIDS deaths with greater caution than before. Secondly, the relevance of genetic factors within families leading to a predisposition to sudden infant death, albeit still as a rare event, was now becoming better appreciated. Thirdly, the frequency of occurrence of rib fractures in young babies when subject to cardiopulmonary resuscitation (CPR) was also being reassessed.

Profs Hill and Carpenter separately presented expert evidence to support the view that no conclusion with respect to the competing propositions of SIDS or murder as the cause could be drawn from the sudden deaths of three infants in the Patel family. Strong indications of a familial genetic factor were provided when the defendant's elderly grandmother testified that five of her twelve children had died suddenly as young babies. Finally, there was a decisive reversal in the opinion of a pathologist on the significance of the rib fractures observed in one of Patel's babies, an issue which deserves further discussion.

19.5.1   The Rib Fracture Evidence

Rib fractures are believed to occur rarely when cardiopulmonary resuscitation (CPR) is used to attempt to revive an infant, but it was acknowledged that identification of fractures from x-ray images was not necessarily straightforward and, of course, if there is no reason particularly to look for them, fractures may not be noticed. On the other hand, the physical abuse of a baby could clearly result in such injuries and, in such cases, their presence would be looked for at the post-mortem.

An expert paediatric pathologist in the Patel case initially reported that rib fractures, observed in one of the infants, were 'extremely unlikely' to be due to the effects of attempted CPR as he had never come across this in his experience. Once again this type of opinion is based on fallacious reasoning, whereas a statement based on logical evaluation would provide a more robust assessment of the evidence.

For clarity, we define the prosecution and defence propositions as:

H_1: the infant was physically abused
H_2: the infant was subjected to CPR

and also define:

E: the observation of rib fractures

Firstly, in delivering this opinion the expert witness was transposing the conditional by stating that $Pr(H_2 | E)$ was very small, based on his experience of the rarity of observing rib fractures following CPR, which informs the conditional probability $Pr(E | H_2)$. Secondly, he would have been on safer ground by presenting an evaluation by likelihood ratio. Since rib fractures are more commonly found following physical abuse, this implies that $P(E | H_1) >> Pr(E | H_2)$ and hence LR $>> 1$ so favouring the prosecution case.

Two years later, at the trial itself, this expert witness changed his mind following his more recent experience of examining other infants where he had found three cases of rib fractures after CPR, within the space of one month. In agreeing with this revised view, the Home Office pathologist concluded that he could:

> '.. no longer state categorically that the rib fractures were not due to resuscitation.'
> [Vasager and Allison, 2003]

This opinion backtracks substantially on what was stated previously. From the perspective of logical evaluation, this new evidence increases the value of $Pr(E | H_2)$ thereby reducing the likelihood ratio significantly. Consequently, the pathologists' opinion now provided far less support to the prosecution case, to the point where the rib fracture evidence was then effectively withdrawn from the legal debate.

19.5.2   The Judge's Summing Up

The summing up by the trial judge in the Patel case (quoted in the Cannings appeal) provides an excellent summary of the difficulties faced in the evaluation of explanations where these are rare events and where the court relies solely on eminent expert witnesses who present conflicting opinions without any objective scientific evidence to underpin them. The judge emphasised that the key point was that three deaths did not necessarily imply that they were unnatural and he described how the court would deal with the more straightforward example of a single cause, whether common or rare. He then moved on to two competing, rare events – multiple SIDS or murder by parent – as the cause of multiple deaths:

> 'Suppose, however, that the two events are both rare; perhaps very rare. They are nonetheless equally likely as the cause even though they are rare, because they are competing with each other to be the cause.

One has to look at the likelihood of the other possible cause, or other possible causes. That is the danger with what may be happening here in saying that three SIDS deaths in a family would be very unusual, therefore the deaths are unnatural. How rare would three asphyxiations be…. We simply do not know. We have not had any evidence about that. It is hardly common is it? That is obvious. That is the competing cause of the deaths and nobody has evaluated its likelihood.'

[R v Cannings, 2004, paragraph 165]

19.6   Conclusions

Despite the focus on this series of cases from England, the issues raised by the evaluation of medical evidence relating to SIDS deaths have also appeared across other jurisdictions; for example, Wilson v State of Maryland (2002) where the father's insurance policies on the lives of his infant children added another factor to the court's deliberations. Nevertheless the key issues remain largely the same:

The medical expert witness who presents statistical information in support of their opinion needs to ensure they have a full understanding of these data and be confident that their interpretation is valid and robust; otherwise statistics is best left to the statisticians.

Evaluating the evidence on the basis of one explanation, however, unlikely that may turn out to be, does not inevitably imply or support an alternative as the true explanation. Indeed, legal debate on this basis readily leads to the prosecutor's fallacy and the jury being misled as to the significance of the evidence. If the infant's deaths are not proved to be natural then murder by the parent is not the logical implication. Opinion based on detailed consideration of competing propositions provides the appropriate foundation for the interpretation and evaluation of all forensic evidence, including medical evidence.

Nevertheless, such competing explanations from eminent experts, based on their subjective assessment of the evidence and where they are in seriously disagreement, do not necessarily provide a clear path for legal argument. If that is the only evidence before the court then it may not provide a sound basis on which to proceed.

References

Attorney-General (Lord Goldsmith), Lords Hansard, 20 January 2004, column 907 [Online]. Available at http://hansard.millbanksystems.com/commons/2004/jan/20/r-v-angela-cannings [Accessed 14 December 2015].

Carpenter R.G., Waite A., Coombs R.C., Daman-Willems C., McKenzie A., Huber J. and Emery J.L. (2005). Repeat sudden unexpected and unexplained infant deaths: natural or unnatural? *The Lancet*, 365, 25–35.

Dawid A.P. (2000). Sally Clark Appeal: Statement of Professor A P Dawid [Online]. Available at http://www.statslab.cam.ac.uk/~apd/SallyClark_report.doc [Accessed 5 November 2015].

Dawid A.P. (2002). Bayes's theorem and weighing evidence by juries. In R. Swinburne (Ed.). *Bayes's Theorem*. OUP. Oxford, UK.

Di Maio D.J. and Di Maio V.J.M. (2001). *Forensic Pathology*. New York: CRC Press.

Fleming P., Bacon C., Blair P. and Berry P.J. (Eds.) (2000). *Sudden Unexpected Deaths in Infancy, The CESDI (Confidential Enquiry into Stillbirths and Deaths in Infancy) Studies 1993–1996*. London: The Stationery Office.

Green P. (2002). Letter from the President of the RSS to the Lord Chancellor regarding the use of statistical evidence in court cases [Online]. (2002). Available at http://www.rss.org.uk/Images/PDF/influencing-change/rss-use-statistical-evidence-court-cases-2002.pdf [Accessed 5 November 2015].

Hill R. (2004). Multiple sudden infant deaths – coincidence or beyond coincidence? *Paediatric and Perinatal Epidemiology*, 18, 320–326.

R v Cannings [2004] All ER (D) 124 (Jan)

R v Clark [2000] All ER (D) 1219

R v Clark [2003] EWCA Crim 1020

Vasager J. and Allison R. (12 June 2003). How cot deaths shattered mother's dreams. *The Guardian* [Online]. Available at http://www.theguardian.com/society/2003/jun/12/medicineandhealth.lifeandhealth1 [Accessed 15 December 2015].

Wilson v State, 803 A 2d 1034 (Md 2002)

Further Reading

Hill R. (2005). Reflections on the cot death cases. *Significance*, 2, 13–15.

Wilson A. (2005). Expert testimony in the dock. *Journal of Criminal Law*, 69(4), 330–345.

Wilson A. (2005). Court of Appeal: Multiple infant deaths: expert witness testimony. *Journal of Criminal Law*, 69(6), 473–476.

Appendix

Some Legal Terminology

ad hominem: an attack on the character of a witness rather than on the substance of their evidence.

equality of arms: the defence has the same rights to present its case and to question and debate with witnesses as does the prosecution, within an adversarial context.

fact-finder: those whose role is to establish the facts of a case; the judge or jury depending on the nature of the court.

in limine: at the beginning or before the trial starts; often used in relation to pre-trial hearings on admissibility of evidence.

ipse dixit: a statement made only with the authority of the person or group who make it with there being no supporting evidence.

judicial notice: this statement permits a court to find an indisputable fact without hearing any testimony or other evidence, and to instruct a jury that it may do likewise. The aim is to shorten a trial.

mistrial: a trial that is terminated before its natural conclusion, for example, due to a prejudicial error during the proceedings or a deadlocked jury.

obiter dicta: things said in passing by a judge relating to the law and not directly linked to the case under discussion. These do not provide a binding precedent but may be persuasive; may include a dissenting judgment.

plurality: the majority view on an appeal court.

tribunal of fact: those who make the decision in a court, usually a jury, sometimes a judge.

ultimate issue: the issue upon which the court must ultimately decide; this is normally the guilt or innocence of the defendant.

voir dire: an inquiry into some aspect of a case prior to the main hearing; the jury not normally being present.

Forensic Evidence in Court: Evaluation and Scientific Opinion, First Edition. Craig Adam.
© 2016 John Wiley & Sons, Ltd. Published 2016 by John Wiley & Sons, Ltd.

Index of Cases, Individuals and Inquiry Reports

Atkins and another v R, **78–80**, 88, 255, 257

Barrett v Benn and others, 259
Birmingham Six, 7, **15**, 49
Blake, Jacqueline, 14
Bridgewater Four *see* R v Hickey
Bromgard, Jimmy Ray, 13

Caddy Report, 155–156
Cannings, Angela, 49, **300–304**
Chamberlain, Alice, 9

Dasreef v Hawchar, **31–32**, 51
Daubert v Merrell Dow, **24–25**, 39–40, 43, 206, 236, 259, 272
Davie v Edinburgh Magistrates, 59
dingo baby case *see* Chamberlain, Alice
Dotson, Gary, 9
Downing, Stephen, 7
Driskell, James, 8, 44

Fingerprint Inquiry Scotland, 120–121, **200–202**
Forbes v The Queen, 145–146
Frye v US, 22

Gale v Gale, 259, **266–268**
General Electric v Joiner, **25**, 35, 43, 51
Goudge Inquiry, 8, 11, **44–45**
Guildford Four, 7

Hodgson, Sean, 7, **10**

Ikarian Reefer, 60

Jama, Farah, 9
Jarrold v Isajul and others, 263–266

Kaufman Commission Report, 14, 16
Krone, Ray, 15
Kumo Tire Co v Carmichael, **26**, 34, 205–206

Locard, Edmond, 192, 206

Maguire Seven, 7
Makita v Sprowles, **31**, 32, 47–48
Marshall, Donald, 8
Mayfield, Brandon, 16, 120–121, **203–204**
McKie, Shirley, 13, 17, 120–121, **200–201**
Moran Inquiry, 9
Morin, Guy, 8, **14**, 16, 44
Morling Report, 9

Patel, Trupti, 300, **302–303**
People v Collins, **104–105**, 253
People v Marx, 252–253
People v Meganth, 164
People v Nelson, 134–135
People v Smith, 216–217
Pitchfork, Colin, 5

Queen v Hoey, 16, **154–155**
Queen v Murdoch, 165–167

R v Abadom, **214–215**, 217–218
R v Abbey, **29**, 44–45
R v Adams, D.J., 95, 98, 104, **108–115**, 297
R v Adams, Gary, 140–143
R v Bates, 156–157
R v Bonython, **30–31**, 34
R v Bowden, **84–88**, 101
R v Broughton, 159–160
R v Buckley, 194–196
R v Cannings, 300–302
R v Chattoo and others, 232

Forensic Evidence in Court: Evaluation and Scientific Opinion, First Edition. Craig Adam.
© 2016 John Wiley & Sons, Ltd. Published 2016 by John Wiley & Sons, Ltd.

R v Clark, 12, 49–50, **294–298**, 300, 302
R v Cooper, 59
R v Dallagher, **81–83**, 100, 244–245, 247
R v Deen, 135–138
R v Dlugosz, R v Pickering and R v MDS, 162
R v Dobson, 218–222
R v Doheny, **138–140**, 142–143
R v George, 7, **226**
R v Gilfoyle, **33**, 34
R v Gjikokaj, 224–225
R v Grant, 146–147
R v Hall, Carl, 284–285
R v Hall, D.S., 170–172
R v Hickey and others, 268–270
R v Hookway, S. (1999), 255–256
R v Hookway, S. and another (2011), 162–163
R v J, 115
R v Jenkins, 287–289
R v Kempster, 244–247
R v L and others, 216
R v Lewis-Barnes, 215–216
R v Luttrell, 33–34
R v Maynard and others, 259
R v Mohan, **27–28**, 44–45, 287
R v Norris, 218–222
R v Ogden, 146–147
R v O'Grady, 286–287
R v Otway, 256–257
R v Perlett, 289–291
R v Previte, 260, **270–271**
R v Reed and Reed, 157–160
R v Roden and another, 232
R v S, 144, **148**
R v Shirley, 7, **105–108**
R v Smith, 198–200
R v South, 184–185
R v T., 169, **175–187**, 210, 224
R v Thomas, 160–162
R v Thompson, 283
R v Trochym, 29

R v Turner, 33
R v Ward, 7, **12**
R v White, 283–284
R v Wooton and others, 222–224

Scott, Adam, 144–145, **147–148**
Shannon Inquiry, 9
Sheppard, Sam, 281–282
Sophonow, Thomas, 8, 44
Splatt, Edward, 9
State v Garrison, 253–254
State v Hauptmann, 271
State v Kunze, 247–249
State v Stinson, 254–255

Truscott, Stephen, 8

US v Davis, 164
US v Fujii, 260
US v Glynn, 240–241
US v Green, 237–239
US v Hicks, 236–237
US v Hines, 272
US v Llera Plaza, 205–206
US v Mitchell, Byron, 190, **204–205**
US v Mooney, 26
US v Morgan, 164, **165**
US v Saelee, 260
US v Shea, 141–142
US v Starzecpyzel, 263, **272–274**
US v Stifel, 23
US v Velasquez, 274–275

Wilson v State of Maryland, 304
Woodall, Glen Dale, 14

Young v Toronto Star Newspapers, 290

Zain, Fred, 14

General Index

accreditation of forensic science, 17, 43, 58, **61–63**
ACE-V
  bias, 119, 121–122
  fingerprint, **190–191**, 193, 198, 200, 202, 204, 206
adversarial system, **56–58**, 74
alternative explanations for evidence
  bias, 119–120
  bloodstain pattern, 279–280, 285, 289, 291
  DNA, 149
  ear-mark, 250
  facial comparison, 256
  fibres, 221
  firearm, 233, 238
  footwear, 172–173
  general use, 72–73, 80, 83, 93, 100–101, 106
  gunshot residue, 223–226
  handwriting, 263
  LTDNA, 158
  trace evidence, 212–214
  SIDS, 294, 304
American Academy of Forensic Sciences (AAFS), 272
American Board of Forensic Document Examiners, 272
American Board of Forensic Odontology (ABFO), **250–251**, 254
Association of Firearm and Toolmark Examiners (AFTE), **230–231**, 233, 237–238, 240
atomic absorption analysis, 23
Australian Supreme Court, 31
Australian Uniform Rules of Evidence, 30, **46–47**
automatic fingerprint identification system (AFIS), 120, **202–203**, 206

basal principle, 31
base rates, **98**, 119, 123
Bayes' factor, 96

Bayes' theorem
  court, 104–105, 109, 113–115
  definition, **95–96**
  DNA, 135, 140, 143
  footwear marks, 175, 180–181
  general use, 90, 91, 94–97, 99
  odds version, 97
  SIDS, 298
Bayesian double impact, 118
Bayesian inference
  ear-mark, 244
  court, 108, 141
  firearm, 241
  footwear, 180, 183
  general use, 45, **68–69**, 74, 83, 90–91, 97
  gunshot residue, 226
  handwriting, 261
  tool-mark, 235–236
  trace evidence, 213
bias
  anchoring, 119–121
  circular reasoning, 118, 121, 123, 204
  cognitive, 117–118, 123–124, 235, 238
  confirmation, 119, 121, 123
  contextual, 118–122, 191
  domain irrelevant information, 118, 121, 123
  expectation, 119
  mitigation of, 122–124
  motivational, 119–121
  procedural, 123
  reconstructive effects, 120
  reliability, 117–118
  role effect, 120
  sequential unmasking, 123
biometric, 6, 81, 189, 243, 250, 255, 257
bite-mark evidence
  admissibility, 252–255
  cases, 14, 251–255
  class characteristics, 251, 254
  evidential weight, 252–253

Forensic Evidence in Court: Evaluation and Scientific Opinion, First Edition. Craig Adam.
© 2016 John Wiley & Sons, Ltd. Published 2016 by John Wiley & Sons, Ltd.

bite-mark evidence (*cont'd*)
  general, 243, 250–251
  individual characteristics, 251, 254
  methods of comparison, 250, 252–254
  reliability, 250, 253, 255
  statistics, 253–255
  uniqueness, 250
blood group evidence *see* Serology
bloodstain pattern analysis (BPA)
  age of stain, 290–291
  competing experts, 279, 281, 286–291
  court's knowledge of, 277, 280
  experts' expertise, 279–280
  expirated blood, 278–279, 285–289
  general, 277–281
  pathologist, 279, 286–288, 290–291
  scientific basis, 277–281, 290
  terminology, 278–279, 282, 288, 290
bloodstain pattern evidence
  activity, 277–278, 281, 283–286
  admissibility, 278, 290
  cases, 7, 281–291
  classification of, 278
  evidential weight, 280–281, 284–285, 290
  narrative, 281, 284–285
  reconstruction, 279, 287–288
  reliability, 290–291
bomb fragment evidence, 16, 154
British Footwear Association (SATRA), 107,
  178, 185
bullet-lead analysis, 16

capillary electrophoresis, 14, 152
case (pre-)assessment and interpretation, **69**,
  122, 124, 152, 214, 226
CCTV evidence, 34, 78–80, 171, 243, 255–257
chain of custody, 15, 61–62, 118, 149, 151,
  154–155, 166, 217
Chartered Society of Forensic Sciences, 63
civil law, 20, 57
class characteristics, 71, 76
combined probability of exclusion (CPE),
  132, 153
combined probability of inclusion (CPI), 132
common law, 20–22, 28, 30, 32, 46–47, 49, 56
continuity of evidence *see* chain of custody
cot death *see* sudden infant death syndrome

database
  allele frequencies, 130–131, 142, 182
  DNA profile identification, 130–131, 133–135
  ear-marks, 81–83, 245, 247
  facial comparison, 79–80, 256
  fibres, 211–213
  fingerprints, 202–203, 206–207

firearms and tool-marks, 233–236
footwear marks, 173, 177–183, 186
gait, 256
general, 101, 210, 257
glass, 211–213, 215, 217–218
gunshot residue, 212–214, 224
Daubert hearing, 26, 33, 164–165, 190, 204,
  238, 273
Daubert ruling/criteria, **23–26**, 29–30, 35, 37–41,
  43, 46–51, 164, 205, 237, 273–274, 278
Daubert trilogy, **25**, 40–41, 204
Defendant's fallacy, 104, **115**, 215
DNA
  cellular material, 15, **151–152**, 156, 157–159,
    162, 164–165
  CODIS system, 130–131
  degradation, 152–153, 158, 165
  DNA-17 system, 130–131, 144
  Hardy-Weinberg equilibrium, 142
  Identifiler method, 159
  laboratory error rates, 142, 148
  low copy number (LCN DNA), 15–16, 129,
    151–167
  low template (LTDNA)
    admissibility, 156–157, 159–167
    definition, 129, **151–152**
    evidential weight, 154–155, 161–162,
      164–165, 166
    outside the UK, 163
    reliability, 151, 154–155, 157–158,
      160–161, 163–164, 166–167
  mixed profile, 101, 119, 129, 152–153, 156,
    160, 162–163, 165–167
  multi-locus probe (MLP) technique, **130**,
    135, 138–139
  national DNA database (NDNAD), **130–131**,
    147–148, 154
  national DNA index (NDIS), 131
  partial profile, 129, **153–154**, 156–157, 165,
    167, 219
  polymerase chain reaction (PCR), **130**, 142,
    151, 153, 155, 165
  secondary transfer, 152, 155, 157–159
  SGMPlus system, **130**, 153, 157, 159–160, 207
  short tandem repeat (STR) profile, 111, **130**,
    152, 159, 163
  single locus probe (SLP) technique, 111,
    130, 138–139, 140
  single tandem repeat (STR) profile, 111, **130**,
    152, 159, 163
  sole evidence, 108, **146–147**, 149
  stochastic effects, **153–154**, 160, 165
  stochastic threshold, **153**, 155, 157, 160, 164
  stutter effects, **153**, 159
  touch, 152

DNA profile analysis
  errors and mistakes, 142–143, 146, 147–149, 154
  methodology, 41, 105, **129–130**, 135, 138–140, 142, 147–149
DNA profile evidence
  admissibility, 135, **141–142**, 146
  evidential weight, 94, **101**, 108, 133, 135, 139, 142, 144–145, 148, 153, 157, 161–163,180, 219
  cases, 114–116, **135–149**, 154–167, 219–220, 222, 284
  general, 58, 100, 134, 208
  miscarriage of justice, 5–9, 12, 14, 15, 83, 106, 108, 255
  reliability, 148
drugs evidence, 17, 67, 98, 205, 274

ear-mark evidence
  admissibility, 81, 83, 243, 245–249
  cases, 81–83, 243–250
  class characteristics, 249
  evidential weight, 83, 244–245
  FearID project, 244–245
  individual characteristics, 82, 249
  pressure effects, 82, 246, 248
  reliability, 245–246
  uniqueness, 82, 244, 247–248
electrostatic detection apparatus (ESDA), 267, 269
energy dispersive x-ray analysis (EDX) *see* SEM-EDX analysis
ENFSI guidelines
  footwear/tool marks, 174–175, 181, 183, 185, **186–187**, 232
  general, 94, 186
  glass, 214, 218
  gunshot residue, 214
England and Wales
  Criminal Cases Review Commission (CCRC), **7**, 33, 105–107, 226, 245, 269, 289, 297, 302
  Criminal Procedure Rules, 52, 60
  Crown Prosecution Service, 146, 175, 183
  Forensic Science Service, 49, 52, 69, 151, 177, 182–183, 212
  Law Commission Report, 49–52
  Supreme Court, 7
equality of arms, 58
error rate, 25–26, 29, 36, 43, 46, 50, 198, 206, 233, 237–240, 272, 273
ethics, 42, 61
evaluative forensic science, 69
expert witness role, 21, **59–61**
explosives, 12, 14–15, 16

facial comparison evidence
  admissibility, 255–256
  cases, 78–80, 88, 255–256
  CCTV image, 78–79, 243
  evidential weight, 256
  methodology, 79, 256
facial mapping *see* facial comparison evidence
fallacy of the transposed conditional *see* prosecutor's fallacy
Federal Bureau of Investigation (FBI), 13, 14, 16, 120, 203–204, 206, 212, 222, 234, 238, 248
fibre analysis, 210–211
fibre evidence
  activity level, 75–76, 210–211
  cases, 14, 16, 218–222
  evidential weight, 214, 219–222
finger mark, latent, 189–190, 200, 203, 205
fingerprint
  Balthazard model, 192
  first level detail, 190
  points standard (*see* empirical standard approach (ESA))
  ridgeology, 193
  second level detail, 190–195, 200, 202–203, 205–207
  third level detail, 190, 199, 204
  uniqueness, 189, 191–192, 196, 198, 205–206
fingerprint evidence
  admissibility, 26, 192, 195–196, 204–205
  cases, 13, 16, 120–122, 194–197, 198–206
  empirical standard approach (ESA), 121, 192–195, 200–201, 204, 206
  evidential weight, 195–196, 198, 206–207
  holistic approach, 193–194, 198–199, 201, 204
  methodology, 190–198
  reliability, 198, 205–206
firearm evidence *see also* tool-marks
  admissibility, 236–240
  bullet, 122, 222, 229, 231–232, 234–236
  cartridge case, 222, 224, 229, 232, 234–240
  cases, 222, 236–241
  class characteristics, 230–232, 234–236, 238–239
  evidential weight, 240
  individual characteristics, 230, 234–237, 239
  methodology, 229–236
  reliability, 237, 239–240
  rifling, 230, 232, 234, 238
  subclass characteristics, 234–235, 239
footwear mark evidence
  admissibility, 169, 171, 183–184
  cases, 105–108, 115, 170–172, 175–187, 224

footwear mark evidence (*cont'd*)
  class characteristics, 106, 169–171, 174, 177,
    184, 186
  evidential weight, 171, 176–177, 179–180,
    183–184
  individual characteristics, 169–171, 174, 177,
    184, 186
  reliability, 176, 183
  uniqueness, 170
forensic identification science, 5, 189, 204,
  232–233, 243
forensic science paradigm, 70
Fourier transform infra-red (FTIR)
  spectroscopy, 211
frequency of occurrence
  bite-mark, 254
  DNA, 112, 132, 135, 138–139, 143
  fibres, 212, 221
  firearm evidence, 235
  footwear mark, 172, 175, 177, 179, 185
  glass, 86, 211–213, 217–218
  SIDS, 295, 297, 302
  use of, 91, 98, 101, 105
frequentist interpretation, **90–91**, 102, 104,
  105–106, 115, 133, 170, 173
Frye hearing, 164, 247–249
Frye ruling/criterion, **22–25**, 27, 40, 46, 252,
  272, 278

gait evidence
  admissibility, 255–257
  cases, 255–257
  CCTV image, 255–257
gate-keeper role, 21, 23, **24**, 26, 37, 44–46,
  49–50
glass analysis, 84, 210–211
glass evidence
  admissibility, 214
  cases, 84–88, 214–218
  evidential weight, 71, 86, 214–218
Griess test, 15
gunshot residue analysis, 85, 210–212
gunshot residue evidence (GSR)
  admissibility, 225
  cases, 7, 84–88, 222–226
  evidential weight, 87, 214, 222, 226
  reliability, 225
  type, 211–212, 222–224

hair evidence, 6, 14, 16
handwriting analysis, scientific basis, 260–261,
  272–273
handwriting evidence
  admissibility, 26–27, 30, 270–275
  class characteristics, 260, 274

cases, 26–27, 30, 259, 263–275
  effect of age and health, 259, 267
  evidential weight, 260, 262–267, 271, 275
  expert witness diversity, 271–272
  graffiti, 260, 270–271
  individual characteristics, 274
  methods of comparison, 259–261, 273–274
  natural variation, 259–261, 264, 273
  order of writing, 267
  proficiency test, 272
  reference writing, 30, 259–261, 264–265,
    267–268, 270–271, 273–274
  reliability, 26–27, 259, 266, 271, 273
  speed of writing, 269–270
  uniqueness, 259, 261
hot-tubbing *see* pre-trial meeting

individual characteristics, 71, 76, 191
inductively coupled plasma (ICP) techniques, 211
Innocence Project, 8, 10, 255
inquisitorial system, 56–58, 94
International Association for Identification
  (IAI), 194, 196
International Association of Bloodstain Pattern
  Analysts (IABPA), 278
International Society of Forensic Genetics
  (ISFG), 151, 153
investigative forensic science, 68
ISO standards, 42, 61, 63

likelihood ratio
  combination of, **97**, 107–109, 112, 114–115,
    177–178, 183, 185
  definition, **90–102**
  DNA profile analysis, 108, 111–115,
    133–135, 140–141, 143–146, 153–154
  ear-mark evidence, 245
  fibres evidence, 221
  fingerprint evidence, 206–207
  footwear mark evidence, 92, 106, 170, 172,
    175–183, 185–187
  general, 68, 104, 106, 122
  glass evidence, 217–218
  GSR evidence, 223–224, 226
  SIDS or murder, 298–299, 303
  tool-mark evidence, 235–236
  type B evidence, 210
  witness evidence, 110–115
lip reading evidence, 34

match probability *see* random match probability
medical expert witness *see also* sudden infant
  death syndrome (SIDS)
  cases, 11–12, 108, 266, 279–280, 286–289,
    290–291, 294–304

conflicting opinion, 290–291, 293–294,
    302–303
evidential weight, 294
multiple SIDS, 293–304
rare events, 294–295, 301–304
statistics, 294–298, 301, 304
microscopy, 23, 211, 219, 230
microspectrophotometry, 211, 219
miscarriage of justice, 5, **6–10**, 12, 14, 15–17,
    39, 44, 62, 254–255, 268–270, 282

National Registry of Exonerations, 8, 10
neutron activation analysis (NAA), 23
NJI Science Manual for Canadian Judges,
    44–46

office of chief medical examiner (OCME),
    164–165
Odontology *see* bite-mark evidence
opinion
    biased, 42, 43, 44–46, 58, 69, 82, **117–124**,
        264
    categorical
        bite-mark evidence, 251–252, 255–256
        bloodstain pattern evidence, 281
        definition, **70–72**
        ear-mark evidence, 83, 244–245
        fingerprint evidence, 190–191, 193–194,
          196, 198, 201, 206
        footwear evidence, 170, 173–175
        glass analysis, 87, 211
        gunshot residue, 87
        questioned documents evidence, 261–262,
          267, 272, 274
        tool-mark evidence, 229, 231–233,
          236–237, 241
        witness identification, 105
    categorisation of, 70
    evaluative
        bite-mark evidence, 251
        bloodstain pattern evidence, 291
        definition, **68–69**
        DNA evidence, 133, 143–145
        ear-mark evidence, 246
        examples of, 86, 93–94, 99
        fibre evidence, 219–222
        footwear evidence, 170, 174, 177, 180,
          183, 185
        glass, 88, 214–216
        gunshot residue, 88, 225
        propositions, 76, 78
        questioned documents, 259
    exclusion/elimination
        bite-mark evidence, 251, 253
        definition, **72–73**

ear-mark evidence, 82, 245, 249
    fingerprint evidence, 190–191, 196–197,
        200, 202, 206
    footwear evidence, 170, 173–175
    hair evidence, 14
    handwriting evidence, 262
    tool-mark evidence, 231
  explanatory, **73**, 144–145, 158, 225, 283
  factual, **69–71**, 225
  identification
    bite-mark evidence, 250–251
    definition, **70–71**
    ear-mark evidence, 81–83, 244
    facial comparison, 80
    fingerprint evidence, 122, 190–191, 193,
        196–197, 200, 202–203, 206
    footwear evidence, 170, 173–175
    tool-mark evidence, 231, 233, 236, 241
  inconclusive
    bite-mark evidence, 251
    fingerprint evidence, 122, 191, 204, 206
    footwear evidence, 170, 173–174
    handwriting evidence, 260, 261–262, 265,
        270
    tool-mark evidence, 231
  investigative, **69–70**, 76, 78, 83, 86, 88, 99, 224
  posterior probabilistic, 99
    bite-mark evidence, 250
    definition, **72**
    DNA evidence, 140, 144
    ear-mark evidence, 83
    examples of, 99
    firearm evidence, 232
    footwear evidence, 173–175, 179, 181,
        185, 187
    glass, 217–218
  scale of
    bite-mark evidence, 251, 255
    ear-mark evidence, 249
    evaluative opinion, 90, 94–95, 107
    facial comparison evidence, 78–81
    footwear evidence, 107, 169, 173–175,
        180–181, 183
    glass, 217–218
    gun-shot residue, 87
    questioned documents, 261–263, 274–275
    tool-mark evidence, 232–233, 241

persistence, of trace evidence *see* transfer
posterior odds, 90, 91, **95–97**, 105, 109–110,
    112–115, 135, 140–141, 180, 298–300
pre-trial meeting/motion, 45, 48, 49, 50, 60, 238
prior odds, **94–99**, 105, 109–110, 112,
    114–115, 140–141, 143, 175, 185,
    298–299

Procurator Fiscal, 57
propositions
  activity level, **75–76**, 85, 101–102, 124,
    144–145, 167, 210, 212–218, 220–221,
    227, 283, 288
  competing
    definition and use, 68, 74, **76**, 90–92, 116,
     122, 124
    DNA evidence, 144–145, 156, 161
    ear-mark evidence, 81, 245
    fibre evidence, 221
    fingerprint evidence, 207
    footwear evidence, 169, 173, 175, 176,
     181, 186
    glass evidence, 83–88
    gunshot residue evidence, 83–88, 223,
     226–227
    questioned documents, 263
    tool-mark evidence, 232, 235–236, 241
    SIDS, 297–298, 300, 302, 304
  hierarchy of, 74
  offence level, 74
  source level, **75–76**, 85, 100–102, 129,
    138, 144–145, 210–212, 217–219,
    221, 227, 235
prosecutor's fallacy, 91, **99–100**, 115, 130, 135,
  137–138, 139, 141–143, 181, 253, 296,
  303–304

quality assurance, 41–42, 43, 56, **61–62**, 144,
  147–148
questioned documents evidence *see* handwriting

random man not excluded (RMNE) *see*
  combined probability of inclusion
random match probability (RMP), 101,
  111–113, **131–136**, 138, 140–144,
  147–149, 153, 156–157, 162, 220
random occurrence ratio, 140, 143
refractive index measurement, 71, 84–86, 91,
  211–212, 214–217
relevance of evidence, 4, **20–21**, 24–25, 28, 40,
  83, 104, 226, 275, 288
reliability of evidence, **4**, 15, 16, 20–22,
  24–37, 41–53, 58, 60–61, 83,
  104, 257

scanning electron microscope (SEM), 211
Scottish Criminal Records Office (SCRO), 200
SEM-EDX analysis, 85, 211
serology, 6, 9, 10, 14, 104–106, 115
signature evidence, 259–269, 271–274
source probability error, 100
sudden infant death syndrome (SIDS)

cases, 12, 293–304
CESDI studies, 295, 298
genetic factors, 259–269, 271–274
rib fractures, 302–303
SWGDOC (documents), 262
SWGFAST (fingerprints), 197
SWGSTAIN (bloodstains), 278
SWGTREAD (marks/impressions), **173–175**,
  180–181, 183

thin layer chromatography (TLC), 211
tool-mark evidence
  admissibility, 233, 236
  cases, 232, 236–241
  class characteristics, 230–231
  consecutive matching striations (CMS),
    234–235, 239
  individual characteristics, 230–231, 233
  laser scanning techniques, 230, 236
  mechanical damage characteristics, 230
  reliability, 233
  sub-class characteristics, 230, 233
  three dimensionality, 230, 234, 236, 239
  uniqueness, 229–230, 232–233, 237–239
transfer, and persistence of trace evidence, 85,
  101–102, 152, 157–159, 210, **212–214**,
  218–222
t-test, statistical, 91, 211
tunnel vision, 11, 119
type B evidence, 210

UK
  Association of Forensic Science
    Providers, 94
  Forensic Science Regulator, 49, 52, **61**,
    122–123, 144, 147, 154–155, 197, 278
  Home Office, 62, 193, 303
  House of Commons STSC reports, **48–49**, 52
  National Ballistics Intelligence Service
    (NABIS) database, 234
  Royal Statistical Society (RSS), 12, 51, 69,
    144, 298
US
  Federal Rules of Evidence, 23–24, 26–27,
    40–41, 43, 61, 240, 272–274
  Federal Supreme Court, 22
  National Commission on Forensic
    Science, 42
  National Integrated Ballistic Information
    Network (NIBIN), 234
  National Research Council Ballistic Imaging
    Report (2008), **232–233**, 235
  National Research Council Forensic DNA
    Report (1996), 134

National Research Council Report (2009),
15, **40–43**, 44, 118, 170, 191, 194,
232–233, 250–251, 272, 279–280
Reference Manual on Scientific Evidence,
40, **43**, 134

verbal equivalent statements, 68, 87, **94–95**,
107, 112, 133, 144–146, 169, 174,
178–179, 185–186, 236

weight of evidence, 4, 6, 10, 21, 22, 30–37,
47–48, 68, 70, 72–76, 90, **94**, 105, 109,
124, 141
witness evidence, 5, 8, 10, 13, 104–105,
108–114, 118, 146, 216, 255, 284
wrongful conviction *see* miscarriage of justice